# FORGING THE ATOMIC SHIELD

# FORGING THE ATOMIC SHIELD

*Excerpts from the
Office Diary of
Gordon E. Dean*

Edited by
Roger M. Anders

The University of
North Carolina Press
Chapel Hill, London

©1987 The University of North Carolina Press
All rights reserved
Manufactured in the United States of America

Library of Congress Cataloging-in-Publication Data

Dean, Gordon E., 1905–1958.
  Forging the atomic shield.

  Includes index.
  1. Nuclear energy—Government policy—United States.
2. Dean, Gordon E., 1905–1958—Diaries. 3. U.S.
Atomic Energy Commission—History. I. Anders, Roger M.
II. Title.
QC773.3.U5D43  1978    333.79'24'0973    86-11385

ISBN 0-8078-1714-7

Designed by Naomi P. Slifkin

Gordon Dean in May 1949. Dean posed for this official photograph just after he joined
the Atomic Energy Commission. (Department of Energy)

To the Memory of Bernard T. Weaklen

# CONTENTS

# ILLUSTRATIONS AND TABLES

## Illustrations

## Tables

# PREFACE

In the early 1950s the chairman of the Atomic Energy Commission was one of Washington's most powerful policymakers. Although he worked with four other commissioners to formulate atomic energy policy, he presided over an organization vested with authority more sweeping than had ever been given to a peacetime agency. So broad, in fact, was the congressional mandate of the Atomic Energy Commission that it exercised a government monopoly of atomic energy. The chairman's domain was thus aptly described as "an island of socialism in the midst of a free enterprise economy."[1] Indeed, with the consent of his fellow commissioners, he could do virtually anything to put atomic energy to work in promoting public safety and welfare.

Congress, however, gave the commission such sweeping authority in order to expedite the production of nuclear weapons—then a novel, experimental, complex, esoteric, and very mysterious activity both to the layman and to the lay member of Congress. Also a highly secret activity, nuclear weapons production required some of the largest factories ever built, absorbed the creative genius of some of America's best scientists and engineers, required testing grounds hundreds of square miles in area, and necessitated the development of some of the most delicate and sensitive scientific instruments ever devised. In 1950 such activities demanded the efforts of five thousand government employees and sixty-eight thousand contractor employees working on programs greater in scope and complexity than those of any individual private corporation. Although the atom promised one day to deliver its share of peaceful technological marvels, the primary task of the chairman and the commission was to build, improve, and increase the atomic arsenal. The atomic bomb, an experimental product of hastily built facilities, had suddenly brought the largest and most devastating war in history to an end; now the commission was required to forge it into a weapon that would help to guarantee America's freedom from Communist aggression.

The aura and power invested in the commission and its chairman were even reflected in some of the more routine provisions of the agency's legislative mandate, the Atomic Energy Act of 1946. To attract the best talent to the commission, the chairman was not bound by Civil Service regulations or pay scales. Because the commission and its activities were regarded as an experiment, the chairman could shift appropriated funds among programs. He had powers to issue subpoenas, conduct investigations, and hold formal hearings similar to those of congressional committees.

How, we might wonder, did a person act when occupying such a powerful but potentially daunting position? How did events and personalities look from the chairman's perspective? How did he solve the brand-new problems of atomic energy while having to grapple with the more enduring problems of human nature? Fortunately we do not have to base answers to such questions upon speculation or inferences from bland official texts. While he was chairman of the commission during the Korean War, Gordon E. Dean kept an office diary composed largely of notes of his telephone calls. His contemporaneous record of his world provides a unique view of the early days of atomic energy.

The diary allows us to relive events as they unfolded over Dean's telephone. To open the diary is to enter the world of atomic energy during the second Truman administration, a world largely hidden from contemporary America. Through the diary we can follow Dean as he mobilized atomic energy for the Korean War, oversaw the development of the hydrogen bomb, fought political battles, prosecuted atom spies, dealt with the powerful personalities of the day, and, at one point, believed the world had come to the verge of World War III. Few documents give us a similar opportunity for developing empathy with the past.

Dean's diary captures atomic energy at a crucial time. The world was in transition from nuclear warfare to thermonuclear warfare. The Atomic Energy Commission was building a vast complex of plants to produce fissionable materials that would soon bring the stockpile from atomic scarcity to atomic plenty. The deployment of nuclear weapons was becoming global in scope. America's leaders saw themselves as locked in a bitter, endless struggle with godless Communists—both at home and abroad. Their fervor as well as Dean's was fueled by a moral certainty about the righteousness of their cause.

A glimpse of history as it was being made, an inside look at the Atomic Energy Commission when the military atom was paramount, a view of atomic energy at a transitional period, an intimate portrait of a staunch anti-Communist during the McCarthy era—these are the images that we get from Dean's diary.

I have been editing the Dean diary in my spare time for the last six years. A largely classified document when I began the task, now virtually the entire diary has been declassified. Because it was a highly classified document pertaining solely to the official business of the Atomic Energy Commission, Dean left the diary with the Atomic Energy Commission when he left the chairmanship. Now it is preserved by the History Division of the Department of Energy. Most of the diary, including portions not included here, is now available to the public. Access to unedited portions of the diary, as well as to portions used for this work, may be obtained by writing to the History Division, Department of Energy, Washington, D.C.

I owe thanks to many for aid during the preparation of this edition of Gordon Dean's office diary. William V. Vitale, director of the Executive Secretariat of the department, of whose organization the History Division is a part, approved the nonofficial publication of the diary. Jack M. Holl, the chief historian of the department, encouraged me to edit the diary and advised me on how to obtain departmental review and approval for a nonofficial project. Alice L. Buck, Philip L. Cantelon, Francis Duncan, Jack Holl, George T. Mazuzan, and J. Samuel Walker read drafts of the manuscript and gave valuable suggestions for improving it. Good friends as well as colleagues, Mazuzan and Walker also gave constant encouragement and advice during the department's review of the project. David F. Trask gave essential advice at a crucial point during the departmental review. Richard G. Hewlett shared with me his knowledge of former Atomic Energy Commission employees and his evaluations of former chairmen. Susan R. Falb, now historian with the Federal Bureau of Investigation, smoothed access to Dean records at the National Archives. Benedict K. Zobrist, Dennis Bilger, and the staff of the Harry S. Truman Presidential Library in Independence, Missouri, cheerfully fielded inquiries and directed me to pertinent materials in various collections. Annette Barnes quickly and accurately typed portions of the draft manuscript.

I owe my deepest and most devoted thanks, however, to my wife Mitsuko and my daughter Ginger whose spontaneity and creativity have inspired my work and are a continuing source of insight and challenge.

Needless to say, all the opinions and conclusions expressed in the Editor's Note, the introductory essays, and the Epilogue are my own and not those of the Department of Energy. The responsibility for any errors in this book is mine alone.

# EDITOR'S NOTE

Gordon Dean's unfortunate early death and the subsequent passing of his close associates on the Atomic Energy Commission have insured that the origins of his diary will be shrouded in mystery. The diary itself contains no hint of Dean's motives in keeping an office diary. Perhaps Dean simply expanded a habit of keeping a personal diary. He may have merely followed the practice of General Manager Carroll Wilson and Deputy General Manager Carleton Shugg, who both kept somewhat similar office diaries. He surely wanted his own record to defend him from hostile critics and members of Congress. Most likely a mixture of motives led to his keeping a diary.

Gordon Dean's diary is not, of course, the traditional record of the diarist's innermost thoughts, beliefs, and prejudices. Rather it is a record primarily of telephone conversations and of Dean's actions as he conducted the business of the Atomic Energy Commission. Interspersed throughout the diary are memoranda; letters; summaries of meetings, events, and actions taken; draft speeches; copies of press releases; and notes from Dean's secretary and his administrative assistants. The original consists of 1,394 single-spaced typewritten pages. Dean probably intended to create a record of all official calls, but his staff fell short of this ideal.

Like the origins of the diary, the comprehensiveness of the diary must be left to speculation. There is ample evidence in the diary that Dean excluded all personal calls and matters. A comparison with Marion Boyer's office diary reveals calls not recorded in Dean's diary. There are surprisingly few calls to President Truman in the diary. Perhaps some calls simply escaped a busy staff. Perhaps there are other reasons, now lost to the historian, for absences from the diary.

Dean's secretary, Jean MacFetridge, recorded most of the conversations by listening to his calls on her desk phone, making notes during the conversations, and later typing her notes as diary entries. A few entries were typed from Dean's own notes. There is some evidence that occasionally other secretaries recorded and typed diary entries. Dean usually reviewed each day's calls and used the diary as a management tool as well as a record of conversations. He did not tell callers that his secretary made a re-

cord of conversations. Making notes of calls, however, is a common practice in Washington and few officials would have been surprised that Dean
kept such a diary. They may have been surprised, though, by the completeness of his record. Those commission officials who kept diaries or were
close to Dean probably were aware of his practice. Brien McMahon and a
few other close friends outside of the commission very likely knew Dean
kept the diary.

When he became chairman in July 1953 Lewis L. Strauss discovered a
tape recorder hidden in the chairman's office, self-righteously ripped it
out, and implied that Dean had used the machine to capture telephone conversations. Actually Dean had installed the machine to record conferences
held in his office, not telephone calls, and to defend the commission from a
powerful congressman who insisted that a particular company get a lucra-
tive contract before the congressman would vote for the commission's
budget. Dean wanted to record his threat and play it back to him rather
than knuckle under to unethical behavior. Dean got the budget passed
without having to resort to the tape recorder and never used the machine.[1]

There is evidence in the diary that it was compiled without the use of a
tape recorder. A conversation between Dean and Congressman Melvin
Price on July 26, 1951, ends abruptly with the note from Jean MacFetridge
that "GD then asked me to get a chart showing percentages of personnel in
various divisions, so I did not hear the rest of the conversation." Mac-
Fetridge could not get an accurate transcript of a September 19, 1951, call
from Ernest Lawrence because Dean took the call at her desk. An April 8,
1952, conversation concluded sharply with the note that MacFetridge "did
not hear rest of call; had to take another phone." She could not record a
May 21, 1952, call to the secretary of commerce because Dean took the
call in another office. A March 10, 1953, conversation with Gordon Arneson ended with the note that MacFetridge "didn't hear the rest of call; had
to go off the phone."[2] Only a person listening in on calls in order to record
them could have left such notes.

Initially Gordon Dean made his own short notes of calls, simply listing
the main point or points of conversations. Soon afterward Jean Mac-
Fetridge started making notes of his calls. In May 1950 notes of calls became longer and conversations more complete, gradually approaching a
near verbatim account of both sides of the conversation. After Dean became chairman his phone calls captured the most pressing issues before the
commission such as the Korean War, the hydrogen bomb, and the expansion programs. A few verbatim transcripts of calls and notes from Dean's
office staff started to appear in the diary. MacFetridge also began to note
important dates, events, anniversaries, and appointments before typing
each day's quota of calls. She consistently used the following abbreviations

in the diary: GAC (General Advisory Committee); GD (Gordon Dean); JCC (Joint Committee on Atomic Energy); MLC (Military Liaison Committee).

After Dean left the commission in 1953, he spent the next few months going through his office files, removing key documents, and forwarding them to the commission's secretary for integration into official files. Then his subject files were destroyed. All that remains today are the diary and a few chronological or "reader" files. Of the extant Dean materials only the diary truly captures his activities as chairman.

Because the diary is so extensive and filled with so much that is routine, editing has been mandatory. Many entries revolve around personnel decisions, fights for budgets, selection of contractors, and congressional pressures that are an overwhelming part of the post–World War II American government. One part of the diary—the first six months of 1950—contains entries that throw some light on Dean's career but little else. Some conversations are so obscure as to defy interpretation. Some important issues enter the diary only briefly. I have omitted the routine and the obscure conversations, only including in this volume entries that focus on events of major historical importance. Those events are the same as those described in detail in Richard Hewlett and Francis Duncan's *Atomic Shield* for the Dean period.

Every part of the diary directly related to these major historical themes has been included in this volume. In addition I have included all references to Dean's conversations or meetings with President Truman, even the bare notes that indicate that Dean had an appointment with the president. The comprehensiveness of my editorial selection may be checked by comparing these excerpts with the original.

As the notes indicate, the entire Dean diary is not all found in one place. Approximately 97 percent of the diary is preserved in eight large manila envelopes in the History Division, Department of Energy. Fifteen items, primarily Dean's notes of meetings or the excerpts pertaining to the 1951 Korean crisis, were removed from the diary and placed in official Atomic Energy Commission files. Four other items are in a file of former Dean top secret materials. Unless otherwise noted, published excerpts come from the eight large manila envelopes of diary.

I have deleted both classified data and extraneous material from these excerpts. Classified deletions, marked by asterisks, are few and rarely are longer than two consecutive sentences. Most consist of technical words or phrases. In no instance do classified deletions obscure the meaning of the entries included here.

Far more extensive are deletions of extraneous material, which, unless otherwise noted, are marked by ellipses that I have added. Dean's telephone conversations, like anyone else's, at times tended to wander. Some conversations have entire paragraphs of such material edited out. Most extraneous deletions, however, amount to a paragraph or less. My judgment about extraneous material may be checked against conversations in the original diary.

Jean MacFetridge occasionally placed ellipses in the body of telephone conversations, particularly in long conversations appearing in the diary after the spring of 1951. Those ellipses probably marked pauses, interruptions, or other natural breaks in conversations and are an indication of the completeness with which MacFetridge captured conversations. Most likely the ellipses did not mark the deletion of words, phrases, or sentences from conversations. MacFetridge also used dashes to set off parts of conversations. Probably the dashes did not indicate the deletion of material from the diary.

Save for some profanity Dean was usually temperate in his telephone conversations. In one excerpt, however, Dean makes an unfair remark about a scientist who is still alive. I deleted the remark and inserted more temperate language in brackets. Less than ten words have been removed from this excerpt on grounds of fairness.

Some of the telephone conversations reproduced in this volume appear in convoluted or confusing language. Into such conversations, where I believed that I could make a reasonably accurate interpretation, I have inserted clarifying language. I have kept these editorial intrusions to a minimum, but I believe them necessary to avoid needless confusion about the interpretation of diary entries.

Misspellings and typographical errors inevitably crept into Dean's diary. For example, his staff often misspelled the names of Frederic De-Hoffmann, Ernest O. Lawrence, Matthew Connelly, Sidney W. Souers, and Frederick Seitz. Jean MacFetridge often incorrectly placed periods or commas outside of quotation marks. Occasionally errors were struck over with capital Xs. I have silently corrected proper names, other misspellings, obvious typographical errors, misplaced quotation marks, and the X strikeovers. Errors of the original that will not confuse the reader, such as the use of "alright" instead of "all right," have not been corrected.

Dean made handwritten corrections to many of the memoranda in the diary and occasionally to telephone conversations. Frequently MacFetridge and other secretaries added clarifying phrases or other notes in parentheses when they typed up their notes of telephone calls. MacFetridge also used parentheses to indicate that she did not hear some calls. I have explained how I treated such additions to the diary in the list of editorial symbols.

Two final comments are necessary. First, to reduce the number of document notes, I have not identified minor officials who are mentioned only once or twice in excerpts or who are sufficiently identified by the context of conversations or by MacFetridge's parenthetical notes. Second, Dean did not divide the original diary into subdivisions—he merely kept it in chronological order. To make this volume more useful I have arranged diary excerpts into chapters preceded by short introductory essays.

Without the declassification of virtually the entire Dean diary this work would not have been possible. A gratifying by-product of editing the diary has been the declassification of the documents from the secretary of the Atomic Energy Commission's files, which are cited AEC in the notes. A little more than half of them were declassified at my specific request for work on the diary. These declassified source documents, like the Dean diary (including excerpts not in this volume), are available to the public from the History Division, Department of Energy.

With minor exceptions the source documents used for the short chapter introductions are the same as those used for similar discussions in the longer introductory essay. The few occasions in which additional documentation was used in chapter introductions have been noted. All these documents are also unclassified and available to the public.

# CHRONOLOGY

### 1905
*December 28*    Gordon Dean was born in Seattle.

### 1930
*August 9*    Dean married Adelaide Williamson.
*September*    Dean became a member of the Duke University faculty.

### 1934
Dean joined the Department of Justice.

### 1937
*March 18*    Dean became special executive assistant to Attorney General Homer Cummings.

### 1940
*April*    Dean became a law partner of Brien McMahon and Walter E. Gallagher.

### 1941
*December 7*    Japanese attacked Pearl Harbor.

### 1943
Dean joined the United States Navy.

### 1945
*April 12*    Franklin D. Roosevelt died. Harry S. Truman became president.
*May 7*    Germany surrendered.
*May 16*    Dean was named to staff of Robert H. Jackson, United States chief counsel for prosecution of major Nazi war criminals.
*June 26*    United Nations charter signed in San Francisco.
*August 6*    Atomic bomb dropped on Hiroshima.
*August 9*    Atomic bomb dropped on Nagasaki.

| | |
|---|---|
| *August 15* | Japan surrendered. |
| *September* | Dean resigned his Navy commission. |

### 1946
| | |
|---|---|
| *February* | Dean returned to the United States and settled in Vista, California. |
| *June 14* | Bernard Baruch presented his plan for the international control of atomic energy to the United Nations. |
| *August 1* | President Truman signed the Atomic Energy Act. |
| *November 1* | David E. Lilienthal was named chairman of the Atomic Energy Commission. |

### 1947
| | |
|---|---|
| *January 1* | The Atomic Energy Commission assumed control of atomic energy programs. |
| *January 4* | Baruch submitted his resignation to President Truman. |
| *February 2* | The British government informed the Truman administration that it could no longer give financial aid to the Greek government. |
| *March 12* | President Truman announced the Truman Doctrine. |
| *March 21* | President Truman promulgated a loyalty program for federal employees. |
| *April 3* | The Atomic Energy Commission told the president that the atomic bomb stockpile was insufficient to protect American security interests. |
| *June 5* | Secretary of State George C. Marshall announced that the United States would help finance European reconstruction. |

### 1948
| | |
|---|---|
| *February 25* | Coup d'état gave Communists control of Czechoslovak government. |
| *March 5* | General Lucius D. Clay cabled Washington that war could come with dramatic quickness. |
| *April 14–May 14* | Atomic Energy Commission conducted *Sandstone* weapons test series in the Pacific. |
| *June 23* | Soviet forces cut off land access to Berlin. |

| | |
|---|---|
| *June 28* | President Truman ordered B-29s to Europe. |
| *July 21* | At a White House meeting President Truman decided that the Atomic Energy Commission should retain custody of the atomic bomb stockpile. |
| *November 2* | Harry S. Truman was elected president of the United States. |

1949

| | |
|---|---|
| *January 20* | President Truman was inaugurated. |
| *April 4* | The North Atlantic Treaty Organization formed. |
| *May 8* | Nationalist Chinese forces under Chiang Kai-shek retreated to Formosa. |
| *May 12* | The Soviets lifted the Berlin blockade. |
| *May 22* | Senator Bourke B. Hickenlooper charged that he had found evidence of "incredible mismanagement" of atomic energy programs. |
| *May 24* | Dean took his seat on the Atomic Energy Commission. |
| *May 26–August 25* | Senator Hickenlooper grilled Lilienthal and his aides in "incredible mismanagement" hearings. |
| *June 16* | Dean began his office diary. |
| *August 29* | The Russians detonated their first atomic explosion. |
| *September 23* | President Truman announced the Soviet detonation. |
| *October 1* | Mao Tse-tung proclaimed the People's Republic of China. |
| *October 5* | Commissioner Lewis L. Strauss proposed a crash program to develop the hydrogen bomb. |
| *October 10* | The National Security Council approved the K-31 gaseous diffusion plant and the DR waterworks. |
| *October 28–30* | The General Advisory Committee met to consider Strauss's hydrogen bomb proposal. |
| *November 9* | The Atomic Energy Commission sent a divided recommendation to President Truman on the hydrogen bomb. |
| *November 23* | Lilienthal announced his resignation from the commission. |

| *November 28–29* | Lilienthal, Dean, and others discussed management philosophy for commission programs. |

1950

| *January 18* | The Joint Committee on Atomic Energy questioned the Joint Chiefs of Staff about the hydrogen bomb. |
| *January 21* | A second trial jury convicted Alger Hiss for perjury. |
| *January 27* | The Joint Committee questioned the commission about the hydrogen bomb. |
| *January 31* | President Truman ordered the commission to develop the hydrogen bomb and also ordered a major review of American strategic programs, which led to NSC 68, the administration's plan for rearming the United States. |
| *February 2* | Klaus Fuchs confessed to passing atomic data to the Soviet Union. |
| *February 9* | Senator Joseph R. McCarthy asserted in a speech at Wheeling, West Virginia, that there were Communist spies in the Department of State. |
| *February 14* | The Soviet Union and the People's Republic of China signed a treaty of friendship and alliance. |
| *February 15* | Lilienthal left the Atomic Energy Commission. |
| *March 10* | President Truman ordered the commission to prepare to produce the hydrogen bomb and to test thermonuclear principles. |
| *June 8* | President Truman approved the Savannah River plant. |
| *June 17* | David Greenglass was arrested. |
| *June 25* | North Korea attacked South Korea. |
| *June 28* | North Koreans captured Seoul, the capital of South Korea. |
| *July 5* | First American units entered combat in Korea. |
| *July 8* | General Douglas MacArthur was named to command forces in Korea. |
| *July 11* | Dean was named chairman of the Atomic Energy Commission. President Truman ordered nonnuclear atomic bomb components to Great Britain. |

| | |
|---|---|
| *July 17* | Julius Rosenberg was arrested. |
| *July 30* | President Truman ordered nonnuclear components to the Pacific. |
| *Early August* | American and South Korean units finally held the Pusan perimeter. |
| *August 7* | President Truman ordered the commission and the Department of Defense to study a production increase. |
| *August 8* | General Manager Carroll L. Wilson announced his resignation from the commission, effective August 15. |
| *August 11* | Ethel Rosenberg was arrested. |
| *September 15* | MacArthur conducted the Inchon landings. |
| *September 22* | American and South Korean forces broke out of the Pusan perimeter. |
| *September 29* | President Truman authorized MacArthur to cross the 38th parallel into North Korea. |
| *September 30* | President Truman approved NSC 68 as a policy statement to guide American actions for the next few years. |
| *October 2* | The commission and the Department of Defense recommended a $1.4 billion expansion of production facilities. |
| *October 9* | President Truman approved the first Korean War expansion program. |
| *October 19* | American and South Korean forces entered Pyongyang, the North Korean capital. |
| *October 25* | President Truman suggested that the commission could select a continental proving ground. Communist Chinese forces clashed with South Korean units, then withdrew from combat. |
| *October 26* | The sixth South Korean infantry division advanced to the Yalu River, the boundary between North Korea and Communist China. |
| *November 1* | Puerto Rican extremists tried to assassinate President Truman. Marion W. Boyer became general manager of the commission. |
| *November 24* | MacArthur ordered a "final" offensive to the Yalu River. |
| *November 25* | Communist Chinese armies entered the Korean War. |

|                        |                                                                                                                     |
| ---------------------: | ------------------------------------------------------------------------------------------------------------------- |
| *November 30*          | In a press conference President Truman hinted that the United States might use the atomic bomb in Korea.             |
| *December 5*           | American and South Korean forces evacuated Pyongyang.                                                                |
| *December 14*          | The commission decided that continental testing could be conducted at the Las Vegas Bombing and Gunnery Range.       |
| *December 15*          | American and South Korean units withdrew from North Korea.                                                           |
| *December 16*          | President Truman declared a state of national emergency.                                                             |
| *December 18*          | President Truman approved the use of the Las Vegas Bombing and Gunnery Range for continental testing.                |
| *December 31*          | The Chinese launched their New Year's offensive into South Korea.                                                    |
|                        |                                                                                                                     |
| 1951                   |                                                                                                                     |
| *January 4*            | American and South Korean units evacuated Seoul.                                                                     |
| *January 11*           | The National Security Council approved the *Ranger* weapons test series.                                             |
| *January 25*           | American and South Korean forces began a series of limited counteroffensives against Chinese forces in South Korea.  |
| *January 27–February 6* | The *Ranger* tests were conducted in Nevada.                                                                        |
| *February 6*           | Dean reported to President Truman on the *Ranger* tests.                                                             |
| *March 6–28*           | The trial of Julius and Ethel Rosenberg began in New York.                                                           |
| *March 9*              | David Greenglass took the witness stand in the Rosenberg trial. Edward Teller and Stanislaw Ulam signed a report which charted the first half of the path to the hydrogen bomb. |
| *March 10*             | In a Saturday meeting Dean decided which questions prosecutors would ask Walter Koski at the Rosenberg trial.        |
| *March 12*             | Koski testified at the Rosenberg trial.                                                                              |
| *March 14*             | American and South Korean forces recaptured Seoul.                                                                   |
| *March 21*             | John A. Derry testified at the Rosenberg trial.                                                                      |

| | |
|---|---|
| *March 26* | Dean learned that the Russians might enter the Korean War. |
| *April 4* | Teller visited Dean to argue for a second weapons laboratory. That same day Teller signed a report which charted the second half of the path to the hydrogen bomb. |
| *April 5* | The Rosenbergs were sentenced to death for conspiracy to commit espionage. |
| *April 6* | President Truman began a series of meetings over what to do about MacArthur. Later he ordered nine complete atomic bombs transferred to the Air Force. |
| *April 7–May 24* | The *Greenhouse* weapons test series was conducted in the Pacific. |
| *April 11* | President Truman relieved MacArthur. |
| *April 22* | The Chinese launched their first spring offensive. |
| *April 27* | Dean left Washington for the *Greenhouse* tests. |
| *May 14* | Dean returned to Washington. |
| *May 16* | The Chinese launched their second spring offensive. |
| *May 25* | British diplomats Guy Burgess and Donald MacLean defected to the Soviet Union. |
| *June 7* | McMahon asked the commission for cost estimates of increasing production by 50, 100, and 150 percent. |
| *June 16–18* | Dean presided over the hydrogen bomb conference at Princeton University. |
| *July 9* | Dean and Karl R. Bendetsen discussed the use of tactical weapons in Korea. |
| *July 10* | Armistice negotiations began in Korea at Kaesong. |
| *August 15–September 15* | American soldiers fought for Bloody Ridge. |
| *August 22* | Communists broke off armistice negotiations at Kaesong. |
| *August 31* | Dean told Truman that the commission had not yet produced atomic artillery shells. |
| *September 4* | Truman told Democratic party leaders that the country had "fantastic" new weapons under construction. |

| | |
|---|---|
| *September 13–23* | American soldiers struggled for Heartbreak Ridge. |
| *September 28* | Teller met with Dean to discuss his resignation from Los Alamos. |
| *October 3* | Truman announced the second Soviet detonation. |
| *October 5* | Dean delivered his speech, "The Responsibilities of Atomic World Leadership." |
| *October 5–13* | Fighting was renewed on Heartbreak Ridge. |
| *October 22–November 29* | The *Buster-Jangle* weapons test series was held in Nevada. |
| *October 22* | Truman announced the third Soviet detonation. |
| *October 25* | Korean armistice negotiations resumed at Panmunjom. |
| *December 13* | Teller asked the General Advisory Committee to support a second weapons laboratory. |

### 1952

| | |
|---|---|
| *January 16* | The National Security Council approved the second Korean War expansion program. |
| *March 29* | Truman announced that he would not run for reelection. |
| *April 1* | At a meeting of the special subcommittee of the National Security Council, Dean listened to Teller's arguments for a second weapons laboratory. |
| *April 1–May 5* | The *Tumbler-Snapper* weapons test series was conducted in Nevada. |
| *June 6* | The commission decided to establish a second weapons laboratory at Livermore, California. |
| *June 30* | Dean and Norris E. Bradbury briefed Truman on *Mike*, to be the first shot of the *Ivy* weapons test series. |
| *July 28* | Brien McMahon died. |
| *September 10* | Truman approved the *Mike* shot. |
| *October 3* | The British conducted their first atomic test. |

| | |
|---|---|
| *October 31* | *Mike* became the world's first thermonuclear explosion. |
| *November 4* | Dwight D. Eisenhower was elected president. |
| *November 15* | *King*, the second and final shot of the *Ivy* series, was fired. |
| *November 19* | Dean and the commission briefed Eisenhower at the Commodore Hotel in New York. |

## 1953

| | |
|---|---|
| *January 14* | Dean submitted his resignation to Eisenhower. |
| *January 15* | Dean said farewell to Truman. |
| *January 20* | President Eisenhower was inaugurated. |
| *March 5* | Joseph Stalin died. |
| *March 7* | Eisenhower asked Strauss to be his special assistant for atomic energy. |
| *March 17–June 4* | The *Upshot-Knothole* weapons test series was conducted in Nevada. |
| *March 18* | Dean told National Security Council that the commission and Department of Defense budgets must be reviewed simultaneously. |
| *June 19* | Julius and Ethel Rosenberg were executed. |
| *June 29* | Dean's office diary concluded with "Finis" after last entry. |
| *June 30* | Dean left the Atomic Energy Commission. |
| *July 2* | Strauss became chairman of the commission. |
| *July 27* | The Eisenhower administration signed the armistice ending the Korean War. |
| *August 19* | Dean filed for divorce from Adelaide Williamson in Las Vegas, Nevada. |
| *October 19* | Dean published *Report on the Atom*. |
| *November 8* | The *New York Times* carried the announcement that Dean would marry Mary Benton Gore. |

## 1954

| | |
|---|---|
| *April 19* | Dean testified at J. Robert Oppenheimer's security hearing. |
| *August 16* | Dean formed the Nuclear Science and Engineering Corporation. |

## 1958

| | |
|---|---|
| *August 15* | Dean was killed in a plane crash at Nantucket, Massachusetts. |

# ABBREVIATIONS
# AND EDITORIAL SYMBOLS

ABBREVIATIONS

## Abbreviations Used in the Diary

| | |
|---|---|
| AEC | Atomic Energy Commission |
| AFSWP | Armed Forces Special Weapons Project |
| DOD | Department of Defense |
| GAC | General Advisory Committee |
| GD | Gordon Dean |
| JCC | Joint Committee on Atomic Energy |
| JCS | Joint Chiefs of Staff |
| MLC | Military Liaison Committee |
| NSC | National Security Council |

## Abbreviations Used in the Notes

AEC  Official files of the United States Atomic Energy Commission, compiled and maintained, until 1975, by the secretary to the commission. The files, save for portions pertaining to regulatory matters, are now in custody of the History Division, Department of Energy. Copies of documents cited AEC in the notes may be obtained from the History Division. Some may have minor deletions of classified information.

DDE  Dwight D. Eisenhower Presidential Library, Abilene, Kansas.

FRUS  *Foreign Relations of the United States*, cited by volume and year. The *Foreign Relations* series is published by the Department of State and printed by the Government Printing Office.

HST  Harry S. Truman Presidential Library, Independence, Missouri.

EDITORIAL SYMBOLS

[  ]          Temperate or clarifying language inserted by the editor.

⟨  ⟩          Handwritten additions or revisions made by Dean, usually to memoranda.

(  )          Explanatory words or phrases added by MacFetridge or other secretaries to telephone conversations. Also admissions that the secretary did not hear a call and thus could not record it. Parentheses in memoranda appear in the final typed original and do not mark revisions or the addition of explanatory notes.

# FORGING THE ATOMIC SHIELD

# INTRODUCTION

Gordon Dean served as chairman of the Atomic Energy Commission from July 11, 1950, to June 30, 1953. He kept an office diary consisting largely of notes of his telephone calls, and his diary presents a personal look at policymaking in Washington during the period of the Korean War and the rise of Senator Joseph R. McCarthy. Hardly a comprehensive view of Korean War Washington, the diary gives an inside account of the development of the hydrogen bomb, the mobilization of atomic energy for war, the erection of huge plants for the production of plutonium and enriched uranium for nuclear weapons, and the battle to establish a second nuclear weapons research laboratory. The diary captures nuclear weapons in transition from laboratory products to the mainstay of America's defenses, for during Dean's tenure the commission erected a significant portion of what President Dwight D. Eisenhower later characterized as the military-industrial complex.

Dean became chairman just as the Korean War broke out in the summer of 1950. Six months earlier President Harry S. Truman's decision to develop the hydrogen bomb marked the first overt step in an emerging nuclear arms race with the Soviet Union. If the armed clash in Korea and incipient arms race did not provide sufficiently vivid material for Dean's diary, there was the intense domestic concern about communism, spies, and subversives. A Washington of crisis and tension emerges from his diary as it throws new light on one of the more controversial periods in recent American history.

Dean was not a Truman intimate or a key adviser on the Korean War; nevertheless, his diary forms an important historical record of the wartime administration. The diary illuminates informal channels of policymaking during the Truman years and gives insight into how the administration made decisions and formulated policy. Often it is our only source of private presidential conversations about atomic energy.[1] The diary captures in vivid detail the impact of the war upon a key federal agency. It lays forth details about historical events and issues, heretofore only available through official histories or public announcements. In preserving part of policy formulation conducted over the telephone, the diary captures details and insights into people and events too often lost forever.

Dean's diary is not a memoir that reveals the diarist's innermost thoughts about a broad range of contemporary issues or administration programs. It is a working document created as events happened and, of course, is most concerned with the official business of the Atomic Energy Commission. As the footnotes of the official history of the commission attest, the diary is a key supplement to the official files of the commission. Although the official commission files are among the most complete ever compiled by a federal agency, the diary contains details and actions that did not find their way into official records.[2] So crucial is the diary in capturing certain decisions that the commission's secretary later incorporated parts of it into official commission files.

Although the diary is devoted to official business, Dean's personality emerges forcefully from its pages. Inevitably Dean's views of issues, problems, and personalities found their way into his telephone conversations. The diary reveals Dean's victories, his defeats, his wisdom, and, at times, his errors or lack of vision. Gordon Dean accepted the Cold War perception of the Soviet Union as an expansionist, revolutionary power striving for world domination according to a master plan. Often, for example, he credited the Soviets with capabilities they lacked. His diary forms a rich portrait of such a personality and gives insight into Dean and his times.

In the post-Watergate era Gordon Dean stands out as a tribute to the democratic political process. His primary qualification for chairing the commission was the political support of Senator Brien McMahon of Connecticut, who was then chairman of the Joint Committee on Atomic Energy. Yet Dean, a lawyer with no background in atomic energy, became one of the commission's most effective chairmen. He worked hard to gain a good layman's grasp of nuclear technology, generally maintained good relations with Congress, successfully managed large-scale technological projects, and won the respect and admiration of commission employees, of his colleagues, and of President Truman.[3] If Dean's career is a valid indication, technical background is only a minor ingredient for successfully managing a modern federal agency.

Dean was one of the major architects of the military-industrial complex, managing an enterprise larger than General Motors or United States Steel. Between 1950 and 1953 the commission began the construction of two huge gaseous diffusion plant complexes, a tritium-plutonium production plant, and a second weapons research laboratory. Existing facilities at Oak Ridge, Tennessee, and Hanford, Washington, were doubled in size. Capital investment in atomic energy jumped from $1.4 billion in 1947 to nearly $9 billion in the mid-1950s, exceeding the combined capital investment of General Motors, United States Steel, duPont, Bethlehem Steel, Alcoa, and Goodyear. One of the gaseous diffusion plants had more floor space than the Pentagon, and all three diffusion plant complexes consumed more power daily than could be produced by the Hoover, Grand Coulee, and Bonneville dams and the entire Tennessee Valley Authority (TVA) system. The materials that went into the tritium-plutonium factory could have filled a line of railway cars stretching from New York to St. Louis.[4]

The hydrogen bomb program was of the same magnitude. One of the key hydrogen bomb test series, Operation *Greenhouse*, required the efforts of over nine thousand United States Army, Navy, Air Force, and commission personnel. The commission personnel conducted weapons performance tests with sensitive equipment that could measure phenomena occurring one millionth of a second after a nuclear explosion, devised nine hundred civil effects tests on twenty-seven structures erected on Pacific atolls, and raised mice, dogs, and pigs on the atolls for biomedical tests. To support *Greenhouse* the Navy had to move 250,000 tons of cargo from the West Coast to the commission's Pacific proving grounds.[5]

Gordon Evans Dean was born in Seattle on December 28, 1905, the son of a Baptist minister. His family moved frequently and he lived in Seattle, San Jose, Chicago, New York, and Pasadena before his college years. Dean entered the University of Redlands in Pasadena as a prelaw student in 1923, receiving a bachelor's degree in 1927 and later joining the Los Angeles firm of Meserve, Mumper, Hughes, and Robertson as a law clerk. In June 1930 he received a doctor of jurisprudence degree from the University of Southern California and, on August 9, married Adelaide Williamson, who had been a fellow student at Redlands. In a few years the Deans would be proud parents of a son and a daughter.[6]

Soon after their marriage Dean and his bride left for the East Coast so that Dean could help Justin Miller, dean of the University of Southern California Law School, reorganize the Duke University Law School in Durham, North Carolina. In 1934 Miller and Dean left Duke for the Department of Justice where Dean assumed the post of attorney in the Criminal Division, drawing an annual salary of $5,200. He concentrated on legal questions involving the National Firearms Act and the Fugitive Felon Law, and argued cases before the Supreme Court. In two years he rose to head the Appellate and Research Section of the Criminal Division, supervising all appeal, legislative, and prison matters as well as the Firearms Act and interstate compacts to control crime. For his able job in managing the First National Conference on Crime, Dean was made special executive assistant to the attorney general on March 18, 1937. In this position he handled public relations and assembled materials for a book on the New Deal Department of Justice. He also drafted political speeches for the attorney general and in 1939 prepared information on the Justice Department for the San Francisco Golden Gate Exposition and the New York World's Fair.

In 1940 Gordon Dean left the Department of Justice for law practice with two former Justice associates, Brien McMahon and Walter E. Gallagher. Later the Supreme Court asked him to help draft rules governing criminal procedure for United States district courts. He was commissioned a lieutenant, senior grade, in the Navy in 1943 and served in Naval Intelligence during the war.

On May 16, 1945, Robert H. Jackson, chief United States counsel for prosecuting major Nazi war criminals, named Dean to his staff, just as Dean had been preparing to leave the West Coast for the Okinawa campaign. Initially Dean helped Jackson compile evidence against the Nazis. Later he gained firsthand knowledge of Russian negotiating tactics when he helped draft the Allied charter for prosecuting the Nazis. It was in London, after eight strenuous weeks of bargaining over the charter, that he learned of the atomic attacks on Hiroshima and Nagasaki.[7] In Nuremberg he handled public relations for the trials. He finally returned to the United States in the spring of 1946 and settled in southern California. Until appointed to the Atomic Energy Commission in 1949, Dean divided his time between a ranch at Vista, which produced avocados, lemons, and other citrus fruits, and a post as professor of law at the University of Southern California.

Gordon Dean found a "new world" when he returned to southern California. Not only had the world entered the atomic age but the Grand Alliance of the United States, Great Britain, and the Soviet Union against Germany and her allies had also collapsed. President Franklin D. Roosevelt, in whose administrations Dean had served at the Department of Justice, was dead and a former senator from Missouri, Harry S. Truman, now occupied the White House. Although President Truman had to grapple with many postwar problems—demobilization, industrial reconversion, inflation, shortages of consumer goods, and a multitude of strikes—the emerging Cold War with the Soviet Union was the most unprecedented and difficult the president and his advisers faced.[8]

This emerging new world would have a profound impact on Dean's life. He would eventually serve in President Truman's second administration. The worsening relations with the Soviet Union and the effect of the Cold War upon atomic energy would set the stage for Dean's service on the Atomic Energy Commission. The hopes in 1946 for a new world created by the benefits of the peaceful atom would fade and be replaced by faith in the military atom to protect America and the free world from Communist attack. The need to build up the military atom meant that Dean's job as atom chief would be devoted to enlarging and diversifying the nation's atomic arsenal.

Harry S. Truman had been Franklin D. Roosevelt's running mate in 1944 and had succeeded to the presidency in April 1945. Truman "was a gregarious, popular, highly experienced, methodical politician, who had been well established in the Senate, was familiar with government operations, conscientious about detail, accustomed to needs for compromise, and schooled in domestic issues." He was "candid within the limits of a devious profession" but had "a formidable capacity for indignation and anger" and "strong likes and dislikes."[9] He came to the presidency ill informed about foreign affairs, unaware of the strains that rent the alliance with the Soviet Union, and cut off by wartime security from knowledge about the top secret effort of the Army's Manhattan Engineer District to create an atomic bomb of immense power.

President Truman realized that the United States could not withdraw from Europe after the war, but he could not assume Roosevelt's role as mediator among the Allies. He knew nothing of the Yalta agreements and was shocked by Joseph Stalin's insistence on dominating eastern Europe and installing a friendly government in Poland. His abrupt cancellation of lend-lease, Stalin's installation of Communist governments in Poland, then in Bulgaria and Romania, and Churchill's Iron Curtain speech were all symptoms of the increasing rift between East and West. Within nine months after assuming office, President Truman had decided that the Soviets were an expansionistic, revolutionary power out to dominate the world.[10]

President Truman and his advisers were genuinely concerned that Stalin might be the world's next Hitler. Correctly or not, they concluded that Stalin was spreading Communist power at the expense of the United States and its allies. Would Stalin stop with eastern Europe or would it only whet his appetite for conquest? The Truman administration decided that America must stand up to Stalin as Soviet ambitions seemed to spread beyond eastern Europe. By August 1946, a few months after Gordon Dean returned home, President Truman concluded that he must use whatever military or economic weapons were available to contain what he interpreted as Stalin's aggressive designs.[11]

As tensions with the Soviet Union increased, President Truman signed the Atomic Energy Act of 1946. Passage of the act had followed an extensive debate in Congress over how to manage and control the atom. Brien McMahon, Dean's former law partner who was now a senator from Connecticut, successfully led the battle to entrust atomic energy to a civilian agency. So prominent was his role that the Atomic Energy Act was often referred to as the McMahon Act.[12] McMahon's victory meant that custody of the atomic bomb was vested in a civilian Atomic Energy Commission. Pressures for returning the bomb to the military, however, would soon arise.

The Atomic Energy Act created a five-member commission and gave it responsibility for all atomic energy facilities and programs. The act directed the commission to manage the atom "subject at all times to the paramount objective of assuring the common defense and security." It also created a special congressional committee, the Joint Committee on Atomic Energy, composed of nine senators and nine representatives mandated to insure congressional checks and balances on the atom. President Truman named David Lilienthal, a former chairman of the Tennessee Valley Authority, as the commission's first chairman. Joining Lilienthal on the commission were Sumner T. Pike, a former member of the Securities and Exchange Commission, Lewis L. Strauss, a wealthy investment banker, physicist Robert F. Bacher, who led the experimental physics division at Los Alamos during the war, and William W. Waymack, a former newspaper editor.[13]

Lilienthal and his associates inherited an immense but dilapidated empire from the Army. The Army transferred to the commission 254 officers, 1,688 enlisted men, 3,950 government workers, 37,800 contractor employees, and plants costing $1.4 billion. To produce the fissionable uranium 235 for the gun bomb dropped on Hiroshima the Army built huge plants at Oak Ridge to separate uranium 235 from the more common uranium 238 isotope. After the Japanese surrender, inefficient plants were shut down and the gaseous diffusion plants called K-25 and K-27 were linked into a continuous efficient operation.[14]

The Army built three reactors called B, D, and F at Hanford to produce the plutonium used in the implosion bomb dropped on Nagasaki. Operating problems had recently closed down B and reduced plutonium production in D and F to a fraction of the wartime rate. Even worse, the uranium which fueled the reactors, instead of being refabricated into bombs, wound up in waste dumps because it could not be separated from the waste fission products formed during reactor operation.[15]

To design uranium and plutonium bombs the Army created a laboratory, directed by J. Robert Oppenheimer, on a remote mesa at Los Alamos, New Mexico. Led by a galaxy of Nobel Prize winners during the war, the laboratory lost most of its senior scientists, including Oppenheimer, to academia after the war. Morale dropped and only with great difficulty did Oppenheimer's successor Norris Bradbury hold the laboratory together. So badly had laboratory ranks been depleted that Bradbury struggled to retain the scientific and engineering expertise required to keep implosion bombs ready for immediate use in a war.[16] Consequently the commission could not use the plutonium being produced at Hanford and had to rely on the gun bomb which was terribly wasteful of precious supplies of uranium.

The only small part of the fledgling atomic empire was its stockpile of bombs. The commission took custody of a stockpile consisting of between nine and thirteen bombs. Commissioner Bacher was "very deeply shocked" when he discovered the stockpile "did not have anything like as many weapons" as he thought it should have.[17] The commission would have to solve

Hanford operating problems, create more efficient bomb designs, and build the stockpile. The vaunted postwar atomic superiority upon which America relied was in reality only a myth.

Providing scientific foundation for the work of Oak Ridge, Hanford, and Los Alamos were several research institutions scattered across the country. The dynamic physicist Ernest O. Lawrence led scientists at the radiation laboratory on the University of California's Berkeley campus in fundamental nuclear research and in applied research, such as the separation of uranium from waste fission products. Frank Spedding at Iowa State College at Ames conducted valuable studies in metallurgy. National laboratories, with research equipment and facilities no university could afford, were emerging at commission sites at Oak Ridge, at Argonne outside Chicago, and at Brookhaven on Long Island.

As the new commission assumed command, prospects for developing the peaceful atom under United Nations auspices dimmed. A few months earlier financier Bernard Baruch had led a special delegation to the United Nations to present an American proposal for placing the atom under international control. The Baruch plan provided for a United Nations organization to manage and control atomic energy worldwide. The world atomic authority would function under the general direction of the Security Council, but its authority would be supranational. Not even members of the Security Council could veto punishment of nations covertly creating their own atomic energy plants or bomb stockpiles. As the world atomic authority assumed control of atomic energy facilities and uranium mines throughout the world, the United States would gradually relinquish control of its own atomic energy plants and minuscule stockpile of bombs. The Soviet Union, however, steadfastly refused to surrender its Security Council veto power. Soviet diplomats stalled negotiations in the United Nations while Soviet scientists launched their own intensive atomic bomb project. In January 1947 Baruch resigned as prospects for international control grew increasingly remote.[18]

With prospects of diplomatic accommodation with the Soviet Union diminishing, the Truman administration watched as Stalin consolidated his empire, presenting, at times, what seemed to be bold challenges to the free world. As the lines between East and West hardened, relations between the United States and the Soviet Union grew increasingly tense. The experiences of the next two years locked the administration in its perception of the Soviets and the nature of the threat America faced. Wartime allies became peacetime antagonists.

Stalin's first move seemed to come in Asia. General George C. Marshall, sent to China by the president to reconcile Mao Tse-tung and Chiang Kai-shek, returned to the United States in January 1947, his mission a failure. Full-scale civil war broke out and Mao's Communists gradually gained the upper hand. The Truman administration equated Mao's successes with Stalin's subjugation of eastern Europe, searching for the means to halt the rising tide.[19] In a little more than a year Mao would be master of China.

Just a month later Great Britain decided it could no longer provide financial aid to Greece, then in the throes of a civil war against Communist-led insurgents. Without aid it seemed that Greece, too, and the whole eastern Mediterranean might fall to the Communists. Responding to Greek appeals President Truman asked Congress for aid to Greece and Turkey on March 12. Announcing what was later called the Truman Doctrine, the president declared that "it must be the policy of the United States to support free peoples who are resisting attempted subjugation by armed minorities or by outside pressures." He soon signed a bill providing the requisite funds, so successful had been his appeal and so ominous appeared the situation.[20]

At the same time the president took a tough stand against communism at home. He established a loyalty program for federal employees which subjected the beliefs and associations of every worker to the scrutiny of loyalty boards.[21] At the same time the attorney general published a list of subversive organizations, warning Americans that membership in certain groups might be equated with disloyalty. The loyalty program and an accompanying drive to deport subversive aliens resembled internal security measures the government had hitherto only taken during "hot" wars.

In his global contest with Stalin the president might eventually have to rely upon armed might, but America's military forces were hardly in a position to counter a Soviet attack. Postwar demobilization dropped the Army from a peak strength of 8.3 million men to a little over 1 million. The 3.5 million-man Navy and the 500,000-man Marine Corps now struggled to reach a combined total of 571,000. The United States even had difficulty in finding sufficient troops for occupation duties in Germany and Japan. At the same time the president's drive to reduce military expenditures made extensive rearmament impossible. Stalin, meanwhile, kept an estimated 3 to 4 million men under arms.[22]

The meager atomic arsenal was no compensation for the lack of conventional forces. Although it struggled manfully to revitalize weapon production, the commission had to tell the president that "the present supply of atomic weapons is not adequate to meet the security requirements of the United States." Not only was the stockpile minuscule, but the country also lacked teams completely trained in the ponderous process of assembling atomic bombs. The nuclear components being produced for the bombs had never been tested. The president was shocked and ordered the commission to improve the situation without delay.[23]

Lacking sufficient military force the administration had to rely on economic or political weapons. Fortunately economic help was what wartorn Europe needed. The European economy, beset by damaged and outdated capital equipment, a reduced and undernourished labor force, severe drought, and a Siberian-like winter, had all but collapsed. Runaway inflation and the loss of prewar markets and sources of food in eastern Europe hastened the decline. Fearing economic disaster would deliver western Europe to the Soviets, George C. Marshall, now secretary of state, announced in June 1947 that America was willing to finance the reconstruction of the continent. Stalin refused to participate in the Marshall Plan, tightening his grip on eastern Europe as western Europe began to rebuild its shattered economy.[24]

The Atomic Energy Commission, meanwhile, went to work. Commission engineers streamlined the production of uranium 235 and the Oak Ridge gaseous diffusion plants began to exceed production goals. Los Alamos scientists designed an implosion bomb which would use uranium 235 and would replace the inefficient gun model. Engineers at Hanford discovered how to increase plutonium production from the D and F reactors. The commission decided to build two new reactors—dubbed DR and H—at Hanford and approved a new process for separating uranium from waste fission products. No longer would valuable uranium be dumped into waste storage tanks. Working with the Joint Chiefs of Staff, the commission mapped out weapons production goals for the years 1948 through 1953.[25] Gradually the commission took the manufacture of atomic bombs out of the laboratory and put it on an assembly-line basis.

From the administration's perspective the commission's efforts were timely, for in 1948 Stalin issued another menacing challenge to the West. After five days of arrests and political intimidation, all non-Communists were removed from the Czechoslovak government in February. General Lucius D. Clay, the American commander in Germany, cabled Washington on March 5 that he sensed a "subtle change" in Soviet attitudes, warning that war could come with "dramatic suddenness."[26] Clay's warning, arriving on top of the Czech coup, touched off a full-scale war scare in Washington. The mysterious death of Foreign Minister Jan Masaryk, symbol of Czech democracy, five days later sharpened the atmosphere of crisis. The Department of Defense, preparing for the worst, revived its interest in taking control of the stockpile of atomic bombs.

During the crisis the commission completed a series of weapons tests at its Pacific atomic testing grounds which demonstrated that uranium as well as plutonium could be used in implosion bombs and that composite bombs of uranium and plutonium worked quite well. The commission now had efficient weapons systems which utilized the uranium 235 produced by Oak Ridge. Developing more efficient weapons systems doubled the stockpile. Commission production could now exceed the goals worked out with the Joint Chiefs of Staff.[27]

Germany provided the next crisis. In yet another move to unify their occupation zones, the Allies reformed German currency and extended the reforms to the western sectors of Berlin. Stalin interpreted the actions as an attempt to revive Germany, and he cut off all overland traffic to Berlin on June 23, 1948. President Truman, determined neither to back down nor to start a war, ordered the famous Berlin airlift which supplied the city and eventually broke the blockade. The Department of Defense renewed demands for the stockpile during the crisis, but the president refused to give the military custody of the atomic bomb. In a carefully calculated move, however, he sent two groups of B-29s, popularly known as atomic bombers, to bases in Europe. Whether the planes carried atomic bombs was left to the Soviet imagination.[28] But fear and tension gripped Washington as the country again seemed to teeter on the brink of war.

The Berlin crisis spurred the Atomic Energy Commission to greater efforts. The commission increased weapons production, restarted the B reactor, devised new ways to increase plutonium production, and again stepped up the production of uranium 235. The commission also began to study the expansion of the Hanford and Oak Ridge complexes. Yet the two manufacturing centers already consumed all the uranium ore produced by the Belgian Congo and Canada, then the only sources of ore outside the Communist world. A dramatic expansion of facilities, and thus greater production of bombs, would require discoveries of new supplies of uranium ore.[29]

The fall of China, the Czech coup, and the Berlin blockade reinforced the Truman administration's perception of a bitter global rivalry between the United States and the Soviet Union in which there seemed to be little opportunity for compromise through diplomacy. The president and his advisers perceived Soviet moves, which Stalin may have visualized as purely defensive, as fresh challenges that required a response. By 1949 Congress shared the administration's view of the Soviets. The administration and Congress also viewed an enlarged atomic energy program as one means of answering Soviet threats. The next few years saw little change in this outlook.

During the Cold War struggle with the Soviet Union Harry Truman faced a presidential election. He decided to run for reelection in 1948, and the Democratic convention chose Senator Alben Barkley of Paducah, Kentucky, as his running mate. The Republicans meanwhile tapped Governors Thomas E. Dewey of New York and Earl Warren of California as their standard bearers. Most observers predicted an easy Dewey victory, but

Truman, waging a shoestring, whistle-stop, come-from-behind campaign, won a narrow victory. With many strong candidates in House and Senate races, the Democrats took control of Congress as well. Harry Truman's second administration would bring many new faces to Washington, among them Gordon Dean.

Truman's victory was not without its costs. Harry Truman had waged his campaign against the "do-nothing" Republican-controlled Eightieth Congress rather than against Thomas Dewey. Congressional Republicans were bitter at Truman: they had been the butt of his campaign; they had lost when they expected to win; and they were now confronted with four more years of a Democrat in the White House. Their search for winning issues for the 1952 campaign led to ever sharper attacks on President Truman and his administration. Eventually they would charge the administration with corruption, with the "loss" of China, with harboring Communist spies, and with lacking the will to win the Korean War. The supercharged political environment spawned Senator McCarthy who received the tacit and, at times, open support of Republican leaders. Anticommunism dominated partisan political debate and rendered diplomatic accommodation with the Russians even more remote.[30]

Fresh from his victory President Truman proposed an ambitious domestic program called the Fair Deal. The Fair Deal included federal aid to education, federal health insurance, construction of public housing, and civil rights reforms such as antilynching legislation, an antipoll tax law, and a fair employment practices commission. The Fair Deal, however, quickly fell victim to the international situation. Foreign affairs, and after June 1950, the Korean War, dominated Truman's second presidency. Reform at home had to await while the administration, spurred by congressional feeling against communism, waged the global contest with the Soviet Union.[31]

The Atomic Energy Commission held a special place in the administration. Atomic energy was a government monopoly, a highly complex, technical subject, and virtually all commission activities were tightly held secrets. With a legislative mandate that gave priority to the military atom and a grim international situation, the commission, of necessity, concentrated on weapons development rather than the peaceful applications of atomic energy. Secrecy combined with the complexity of nuclear technology tended to separate and isolate the commission from the administration, Congress, and the American people.

Well versed in the atom and possessing the requisite security clearances, the Joint Committee on Atomic Energy exercised an extensive, and at times decisive, influence over atomic energy policy. Most other members of Congress understood little about atomic affairs and left the initiative in atomic energy matters to the Joint Committee.[32] President Truman himself under-

stood little about nuclear technology and left executive branch direction of
atomic energy affairs almost entirely in the hands of the chairman of the
commission. By default the formulation of atomic energy policy then fell to
the Joint Committee and the commission. New policies could be implemented rapidly, but few voices outside the Joint Committee or the commission could influence them.

The commission remained untouched by most of the controversies swirl-
ing about the second Truman administration. Huge sums were spent on
atomic energy, and the commission faced some charges of wasting tax dollars. But actual waste was rarely proved and the one or two commission
employees found trying to profit from inside knowledge of atomic energy
programs were quickly fired. The commission generally had little trouble
with Congress over the communism issue after Lilienthal's departure and,
with one or two minor exceptions, McCarthy steered clear of atomic energy. Security and atom spies were major issues for the commission, but
neither the agency nor its leaders came under fire as did the Department of
State or Dean Acheson.[33] The controversies that divided the commission
were particular to atomic energy and most sprang from the hydrogen
bomb program.

Foreign events had a dramatic impact on the U.S. development of atomic
energy, just as they had during the first Truman administration. The first
Soviet atomic explosion in 1949 led to the hydrogen bomb program. The
Korean War led to two vast expansions of atomic energy production facilities, the initiation of atomic testing in the United States, and the global deployment of bomb components. By the end of the Korean War, the United
States was well on the way to relying on a massive atomic arsenal as its primary strategic deterrent to Soviet aggression. The stage would be set for
the Eisenhower administration, the New Look, and massive retaliation.

Commissioners Robert F. Bacher and William Waymack resigned after
the 1948 elections. Senator Brien McMahon, becoming chairman of the
Joint Committee on Atomic Energy when the Democrats assumed control
of Congress, urged the president to appoint his former law partner Gordon
Dean to one of the vacancies. The president acquiesced, and Professor Gordon Dean's appointment shared the headlines with the lifting of the Berlin
blockade. A few days earlier Chiang Kai-shek had to retreat from the main-
land to Formosa. A little over a month earlier the treaty establishing the
North Atlantic Treaty Organization (NATO) alliance had been signed.
Dean was confirmed on May 20, 1949, and assumed his new post four
days later.[34] Although Europe enjoyed a respite from potential conflict, the
outlook was grim in Asia.

Dean began his new job vigorously, wasting little time before plunging
into the esoteric subject of atomic energy. Unassuming in appearance and

*Table 1. The Atomic Energy Commission, 1946–1953*

| Original Commission (Two-Year Terms) | Terms Extended to June 30, 1950 | Staggered Terms Established |
|---|---|---|
| Robert F. Bacher November 1, 1946– | Robert F. Bacher July 3, 1948– May 10, 1949 | Henry D. Smyth July 1, 1950– June 30, 1951 July 1, 1951– September 30, 1954* |
| | Henry D. Smyth May 30, 1949– June 30, 1950 | |
| David E. Lilienthal (Chairman) November 1, 1946– | David E. Lilienthal (Chairman) July 3, 1948– February 15, 1950* | Thomas E. Murray July 1, 1950– June 30, 1952 July 1, 1952– June 30, 1957 |
| | Thomas E. Murray May 9, 1950– June 30, 1950 | |
| William W. Waymack November 5, 1946– | William W. Waymack July 3, 1948– December 21, 1948 | Gordon E. Dean (Chairman) July 1, 1950– June 30, 1953 |
| | Gordon E. Dean May 24, 1949– June 30, 1950 | |
| Sumner T. Pike October 31, 1946– | Sumner T. Pike July 3, 1948– June 30, 1950 | Sumner T. Pike July 19, 1950– December 15, 1951* |
| | | Eugene M. Zuckert February 25, 1952– June 30, 1954 |
| Lewis L. Strauss November 12, 1946– | Lewis L. Strauss July 3, 1948– April 15, 1950 | T. Keith Glennan October 2, 1950– November 1, 1952 |

Note: Joseph Campbell later filled part of the remaining three years of Glennan's term.

The initial appointments listed in the third column were for one-, two-, three-, four-, and five-year terms respectively. After these initial appointments, all commissioners were appointed to five-year terms.

* Effective date of resignation.

labeled a professor by the press, he was shrewd, pragmatic, and "wise in the folkways of Washington." He resembled a highly capable, middle-aged business executive and displayed little emotion as he blended co-workers and subordinates into a smoothly functioning team. Never a colorful, quotable figure, Dean used compromise and conciliation behind the scenes to achieve his goals. He smoked a pack of cigarettes a day but relaxed with a highball before dinner, a game of golf, or an occasional hunting trip.[35]

Although a serious worker he had a lively sense of humor. Dean referred to the commission as a "radioactive squirrel cage" and described his "pleasant feeling of release" upon finding, after signing stacks of top secret documents, an unclassified document announcing a Christmas discount for commission employees at a local bakery. When a reporter expressed interest in doing an article on him if he could "find any color," Dean shot back: "How about my entering the Miss America contest with a Red White and Blue bathing suit?" He silently suffered his daughter's complaint that his speeches said little other than "we are doing well."[36] Dean would need a strong sense of humor to see himself through the grim trials that awaited him.

Gordon Dean joined Lilienthal, Pike, Strauss, and Henry D. Smyth on the commission. The simultaneous appointment of Dean and Smyth brought the commission once again to its statutory complement of five members. Dean filled the remainder of Waymack's term and Henry Smyth, a Princeton physicist and author of the famous Smyth report about the wartime atomic energy project, took Bacher's place. Lilienthal made broad policy formulation the commission's function and left the details of program management to the general manager. He had worked hard to make the commission a harmonious group, but Lewis Strauss's one-man opposition to decisions often wrecked Lilienthal's attempts at unanimity. By 1949 Lilienthal had ironed out most of the organizational problems that had initially plagued the agency and had built a talented organization. Much of the commission's staff had scientific or engineering backgrounds and had gained valuable experience in managing complex technical programs.

The general manager was the chief executive officer of the commission and in 1949 Carroll L. Wilson, an assistant to Vannevar Bush during World War II, filled the post. Along with Carleton Shugg, the deputy general manager, he directed programs for devising better nuclear weapons, producing enriched uranium and plutonium, guiding peaceful nuclear research, studying the biomedical problems posed by the atom, building nuclear reactors, and finding new supplies of uranium ore. He also supervised administrative units that handled the routine functions of budget, finance, personnel, and public affairs, and the less routine functions of security and intelligence. Providing on-the-spot supervision of the commission's plants and laboratories for the general manager were seven regional operations offices.

The commission's plants and laboratories were run by contractor personnel, not by government employees. The practice of using industrial or academic contractors to operate plants or laboratories was begun by the Manhattan Engineer District and continued by Lilienthal and his associates. Because, at Los Alamos, for example, University of California employees staffed the laboratory, the commission only needed a small complement of government employees in a regional operations office to insure that the University of California properly executed the Los Alamos contract. Similarly Union Carbide ran Oak Ridge and General Electric operated Hanford. In 1949 the commission employed 4,777 government personnel who oversaw the activities of 51,833 contractor personnel.[37] All the new plants built over the next few years would likewise be government-owned but contractor-operated.

Two powerful statutory advisory committees, the General Advisory Committee and the Military Liaison Committee, circumscribed the commission's freedom of action. The General Advisory Committee, chaired by J. Robert Oppenheimer, the wartime director of Los Alamos, operated under a mandate to provide scientific and technical opinion on any or all programs. The committee included such prominent figures as James B. Conant, Enrico Fermi, and Glenn T. Seaborg. Because of its immense prestige and intimate knowledge of atomic energy, the committee sometimes made decisions that were the commission's prerogative. It had even reversed a few decisions made by the Lilienthal commission. The Military Liaison Committee played a major role in formulating weapons research and development programs. The committee had never reversed a commission decision, but its views usually carried the support of the secretary of defense and the Joint Chiefs of Staff.

When Dean joined the commission it was grappling with the erection of more bomb production plants. Since August 1948 the commission had decided to build a third gaseous diffusion plant, K-29, at Oak Ridge, had almost completed the DR and H reactors, and had further improved the process for separating uranium from reactor waste products. Nevertheless, the Joint Chiefs of Staff wanted the commission to increase production. Senator McMahon, arguing that atomic bombs should be "the keystone of our military policy and a foundation pillar of our foreign policy as well," also urged the commission to step up production. To meet the Joint Chiefs' goals the commission decided to add a $30 million waterworks to the DR reactor and a fourth gaseous diffusion plant, K-31, to the Oak Ridge facility. In July 1949, however, President Truman asked the National Security Council to review the proposed production goals.[38]

David Lilienthal was then in the midst of defending himself from charges of "incredible mismanagement" of commission programs by Republican Senator Bourke B. Hickenlooper of the Joint Committee on Atomic Energy.

Lilienthal fought Hickenlooper in a series of hearings during the summer of 1949, emerged victorious in the public eye, but was exhausted and battered in spirit.[39] Dean observed both the expansion debate and the Hickenlooper hearings but played no role in either because he spent the summer absorbing the technology of the atom.

One of his first decisions as a commissioner, though, was to keep an office diary of his activities. It would be the working diary of a busy executive, consisting of notes of phone calls supplemented by memoranda and letters. Intended as a management tool, the diary would not be a forum for philosophical reverie. Dean's diary entries for the summer of 1949 were brief and routine but events would soon lift them to the historical. As Dean's responsibilities grew, diary entries would grow in length and detail from brief notes about calls to almost verbatim accounts of them. The comprehensiveness of his diary would add to its value as a historical document.

The Soviet detonation of August 1949 sparked the hydrogen bomb debate and provided Dean with the first important issue for his diary. President Truman announced the Soviet feat on September 23, 1949, and a few days later Mao Tse-tung proclaimed the formation of the People's Democratic Republic of China. Once again the administration confronted a Communist challenge, and a sense of crisis spurred those who sought a dramatic response to the Soviet detonation. Dean realized that the commission had to increase weapons production once more and warned that Congress and the American people expected action. Then the National Security Council approved the construction of the DR waterworks and the K-31 gaseous diffusion plant. Lewis Strauss, meanwhile, arguing for a "quantum jump" in defense planning, proposed that America develop a hydrogen bomb.[40]

Commissioner Strauss quickly found support from Senator McMahon, physicists Edward Teller and Ernest Lawrence, and the Military Liaison Committee. They believed that a crash program to develop the Super, a thermonuclear device that promised explosions in the range of millions of tons of TNT, would preserve American security in the face of Soviet atomic progress. But Lilienthal, who was morally repelled by the hydrogen bomb, Pike, Smyth, Wilson, and much of the commission staff opposed the Super. The commission's General Advisory Committee in its most famous meeting on October 28 and 29, 1949, joined the opponents of a crash thermonuclear bomb program. The prestigious committee's opposition was partially based on moral considerations.[41] After initial doubts, Dean cast his lot with McMahon and Strauss. Dean was never as staunch a proponent of the hydrogen bomb as was McMahon, Strauss, or Teller, although his decision was consistent with the political realities of 1949. But in supporting the Super, Dean helped propel the United States into a nuclear arms race with the Soviet Union.

Gordon Dean had concluded that America had little choice but to develop a thermonuclear weapon. Dean's decision forced Lilienthal to present the president with majority (against) and minority (for) opinions on the hydrogen bomb. The divided report probably had little effect on the president, who had already expressed interest in the Super. After receiving the commission's report, President Truman ordered the National Security Council to study the issue.[42]

While the National Security Council considered the hydrogen bomb, David Lilienthal announced his resignation from the Atomic Energy Commission. From that moment, Gordon Dean was a candidate for his job. Senator McMahon had wanted Dean named to the original commission in 1946, but the opposition of Lilienthal and presidential aide Clark Clifford blocked the appointment.[43] McMahon now launched another campaign for Dean, but the president was not to be easily swayed.

Despite Lilienthal's opposition, the National Security Council approved a crash program to develop a hydrogen bomb. The chief proponents of the Super, Strauss, McMahon, and Teller, had won their battle. On January 31, 1950, President Truman formally directed the commission to develop a thermonuclear bomb. Together the commission and the Department of Defense were to determine the rate and scale of the effort.[44] The quest for a thermonuclear weapon would be the commission's most vexing and controversial program for the next four years.

Nuclear arms competition with the Soviet Union would be expensive, difficult to restrain, and could result in a war from which neither country could emerge victorious in the traditional sense. Like the president and Senator McMahon, Dean judged the immediate Soviet threat a greater danger than the potential long-range costs of a nuclear arms race. He found a transitory military superiority more congenial than attempts to negotiate long-range security. Dean never seems to have considered whether an unrestrained arms race posed far more danger to America than negotiating with Stalin.

Three days after the hydrogen bomb decision, the nation learned that British nuclear physicist Klaus Fuchs was a Soviet spy. A member of the British team that worked at Los Alamos during the war, Fuchs betrayed the principles and structure of the plutonium and uranium bombs, plans for the improvement of both bombs, and tentative postwar discussions of the Super.[45] Of all the atom spies of the early 1950s, Fuchs struck the gravest blow to American atomic superiority and the commission spent hours assessing the damage. Gordon Dean says little about Fuchs in his diary; rather, he concentrates on McMahon's campaign to have Dean made chairman of the commission.

President Truman wanted a man of high public repute to chair the commission. Moreover, he wanted the new chairman to keep McMahon and the Joint Committee from taking control of the atom. Not only was Dean relatively unknown compared with other candidates, but his chief qualification was McMahon's support. So close was he to McMahon that Dean asked reporter James Reston not to refer to him as "Senator McMahon's candidate." Although Don Dawson, the president's personnel assistant, joined the Dean camp in February 1950, President Truman tried to draft Gordon Gray, who had resigned as secretary of the Army. Dean, who badly wanted the job, at times found the uncertainty excruciating.[46]

Finally McMahon found an opportunity to end the struggle. Because the terms of the entire commission—that is, the appointments of Pike, Dean, Smyth, and Thomas E. Murray, who filled the vacancy created by Lilienthal's departure—expired on June 30, 1950, President Truman had to renominate them formally to their posts or watch commission business come to a standstill. The recent outbreak of fighting in Korea made the commission's tasks even more vital and the appointment of a new chairman urgent. Pike's renomination, however, encountered opposition from Senator Hickenlooper and others who believed that Pike should not be appointed because he had opposed the hydrogen bomb. McMahon successfully pushed Pike's renomination through the Senate, and on July 11, 1950, President Truman named Gordon Dean chairman of the Atomic Energy Commission. McMahon may not have bargained Dean's appointment as chairman in return for Pike's renomination but events suggested that a deal had been struck.[47]

Dean had the job at last. In little over a year he had traveled from novice commissioner to chairman of one of Washington's most important civilian agencies. He had obtained the post through McMahon's political support and was a political appointee in the best sense of the phrase. His skillful leadership would impress skeptical observers, and he made the commission, with the exception of Murray, an independent operator, a smoothly functioning team. Aware that Lilienthal had built a talented organization, he turned a deaf ear to suggestions that he purge the commission of Lilienthal appointees.[48] The twin crises of the hydrogen bomb and the Korean War dominated the commission during the Dean years. Neither Gordon Dean nor his diary can be understood outside of the context of the Super and the war.

As chairman, Gordon Dean treated his fellow commissioners as co-equals to whom he was the *primus inter pares*. Dean thrust the commissioners into a more vigorous role of program management, making the commissioners rather than the general manager responsible for flushing out key issues during policy debates. Dean was usually successful in guiding policy discussions among the five commissioners to a consensus and in using the hydra-headed commission, a type of organization usually reserved for regulatory agencies, to manage complex scientific and technical projects. He succeeded in the difficult task of giving his fellow commissioners equal responsibility in managing commission programs while maintaining the degree of leadership expected from the chairman, who acted as the agency's principal spokesman. He worked hard to keep differences among the commissioners on an intellectual level. Indeed few were as successful as Dean in using a commission to manage large-scale projects.[49]

Dean's associates brought a variety of backgrounds and views to their jobs. The last of the original commissioners, Sumner T. Pike had made a fortune on Wall Street and had held government positions that included duty in the Department of Commerce and in the Office of Price Administration. His infectious sense of humor once led someone to remark that it was virtually impossible to hold a serious meeting with Pike. The iron-willed Thomas E. Murray was an engineer, who held more than two hundred patents and performed with pride his duties as a prominent Catholic layman. Murray constantly prodded the commission to find new ore supplies and consistently supported measures to increase weapons production. Physicist Henry D. Smyth performed the essential function of lucidly explaining atomic technology to his fellow commissioners and to the Joint Committee on Atomic Energy. Selected by Dean to fill the vacancy resulting from Strauss's resignation, T. Keith Glennan had extensive business experience in the motion picture industry and had left the presidency of the Case Institute of Technology for the commission. Joining the commission after Pike departed, Eugene M. Zuckert had served as an attorney in the Securities and Exchange Commission and as assistant secretary of the Air Force for management operations.[50] Melding them into a body that spoke with one voice was a constant challenge for Dean.

Because he was not Truman's choice for the chairmanship and lacked the rapport that Lilienthal had developed with the chief executive, Dean had to build a relationship with President Truman. Gradually Dean gained the president's confidence and trust, and within a few months of his appointment Dean was visiting the White House regularly to keep the president apprised of atomic energy matters. Because the subjects Dean and Truman discussed were so sensitive, Dean usually kept his reports verbal and often they were only recorded as they appear in the diary.[51]

One of Dean's chief accomplishments was his repair of the commission's sagging relations with Congress. Lilienthal often took idealistic positions on issues, and relations with the Joint Committee had become severely strained during his tenure. Although he would not be a pushover to influential members of Congress, Dean knew that the commission had to consider the views of powerful Joint Committee members when formulating policy. He healed the breach with the Joint Committee and used both his pragmatic approach to issues and his ties with McMahon in smoothing ruffled congressional feathers. His practice of often informing the Joint Committee in advance of commission actions contributed greatly to better relations with the Committee.[52]

Dean and the commission worked closely with the Department of Defense but remained remote from other cabinet departments. Dean worked well with secretaries Louis Johnson and Robert Lovett, but, like most others, managed only a formal, official relationship with George Marshall. It is surprising to note that not one call to Marshall appears in the diary. Daily contact with the department, however, was provided by the Military Liaison Committee. Dean maintained good relations with its individual members, especially Admiral Frederic Withington, but his relations with Robert LeBaron, the chairman of the committee, had badly deteriorated by mid-1952. Generally speaking, Dean's practical approach to problems focused attention on issues rather than on personalities.[53]

A good manager and a skillful politician, Dean was also a shrewd leader who manipulated an existing environment without questioning its basic premises. He worked vigorously to build America's military strength but never seemed to consider whether it would be either practical or desirable to use that strength in a world war. He never seems to have questioned whether the strident anticommunism of his day was healthy for the democratic process or actually enhanced national security. Not once in the diary does he wince over the implications of thermonuclear warfare, the arms race, or the growing arsenal of atomic weapons.

Yet Dean was not completely blind to the implications of his actions, and he had a strong sense of morality. Like so many of his contemporaries, he saw a moral America locked in a bitter struggle with an immoral Soviet Union. For Dean the primary moral imperative was winning that struggle. His unrealistic appraisal of Soviet capabilities and his naiveté about foreign relations reinforced his tendency to give more thought to the struggle than to its consequences. Dean's views propelled the country into an expensive and dangerous arms race while leaving little hope for long-range world peace. To many, including President Dwight D. Eisenhower, the fearsome destructiveness of thermonuclear warfare made world war unthinkable, and thus accommodation with the Soviet Union took on a greater moral imperative.[54]

The Korean War had broken out two weeks before Dean's appointment. The North Korean attack presented the administration with an act of unprovoked communist military aggression. Expressing the same sense of moral outrage shared by the president, Omar Bradley, chairman of the Joint Chiefs of Staff, declared that America "must draw the line somewhere" and meet communist aggression in Korea with force. Within a few days President Truman had committed the United States to aid South Korea under the aegis of the United Nations, had committed air, naval, and ground forces to combat in Korea, and had named General Douglas MacArthur to command American and United Nations forces in Korea. The war spurred the administration to the rapid and sustained military buildup envisioned in NSC 68, the administration's yet unadopted blueprint for an expansion of military power.[55] Dean strengthened conventional rearmament by mobilizing atomic energy.

Dean's first contribution to the war effort was to deploy a portion of the atomic stockpile outside of the United States. President Truman believed that the Soviet Union was the real aggressor in Korea and that America must not reduce political or military commitments to western Europe despite the fighting in Korea. Consistent with this strategy the president ordered the transfer of nonnuclear components of atomic bombs to bases in Great Britain. On the very day he became chairman, Dean met with the president, Secretary of Defense Louis Johnson, and Secretary of the Air Force Thomas K. Finletter to arrange the transfer. A few weeks later, when the North Korean advance threatened American supply bases in Korea, President Truman ordered nonnuclear components to the Pacific. Even though nuclear cores remained in the country, the deployment of nonnuclear components substantially reduced the amount of time required to launch a nuclear attack.[56]

Deploying the nonnuclear components breached the principle of civilian control of the atomic bomb because bomb parts were transferred to the custody of the military. Lilienthal had battled the Department of Defense over the principle of civilian custody and President Truman had consistently supported him.[57] Engaged in a shooting war, neither the president nor Dean allowed civilian control to impede the nation's ability to respond to aggression. Dean's pragmatic approach to problems enabled the commission to avoid a confrontation with the Department of Defense over civilian custody in July 1950.

One obvious step in preparing the atom for war was to increase the production of uranium 235 and plutonium and thereby to increase the number of bombs going into the stockpile. With Dean, Johnson, and McMahon supporting a production increase, in August President Truman ordered a study of how best to step up production, and after the study was completed in October, the president approved a $1.4 billion expansion program. The first Korean War expansion program added three more reactors to the Savannah River plant (the commission had initially decided to build a two-reactor plant to produce tritium for the hydrogen bomb program) and an entire new gaseous diffusion plant complex at Paducah, Kentucky. Altogether the new plants would increase uranium 235 production by 125 percent and plutonium production by 50 percent over existing programs. Although not specifically a part of the recently approved NSC 68, the expansion program was consistent with its tone and general goals.[58]

If the commission were going to multiply the atomic arsenal, it would have to test designs and ideas for new bombs at a faster rate than the peacetime pace of the late 1940s. But the commission's only testing ground for atomic bombs was the Eniwetok atoll in the Pacific Ocean. Eniwetok had been selected because it contained islands large enough for shot towers and the complex instrumentation that accompanied atomic tests yet was far enough from inhabited areas to reduce hazards from radioactive fallout. Testing in the Pacific, however, was relatively expensive and time-consuming. Indeed the three *Sandstone* weapons tests in 1948 were the only atomic tests that the commission held at Eniwetok between January 1947 and the beginning of the Korean War.[59]

The Korean War made the Pacific proving grounds less secure and even more expensive. Dean was convinced that the administration had to find a proving grounds within the continental United States to increase the pace and security of atomic testing. Given the green light by the president in late October, Dean set the machinery in motion, and, on December 18, 1950, two days after he had declared a national emergency in response to the Chinese entry into the Korean War, President Truman approved the commission's recommendation to use the Las Vegas Bombing and Gunnery Range for testing atomic bombs.[60] Now atomic testing would take place in Nevada as well as the Pacific. With the selection of a continental test site the initial mobilization of atomic energy was completed. Perhaps no other period in the commission's history was as hectic as Dean's first six months as chairman.

In those months the Truman administration took the initial steps toward today's nuclear arsenal. The overseas deployment of bomb components would eventually become the global deployment of complete bombs and missiles. Military custody of a few bomb components foreshadowed military custody of the greater part of the stockpile. The first Korean War expansion program was a quantum jump in production capacity over the smaller expansions of the late 1940s and led Dean to remark that the stockpile would be "infinitely greater" in "two or three years."[61] Gradually atomic bombs were being transformed from carefully hoarded blockbusters into a common and versatile part of America's defenses. Dean's tenure as chairman marked a break from a scarcity of atomic weapons and movement toward the atomic plenty of the 1960s and later.

Just as significant was the establishment of a continental proving grounds. As much as any other single factor, the continental proving grounds made weapons testing a routine commission activity. More frequent testing reduced the time required to explore new design ideas and to transform them into new weapons. It took more frequent testing as well as greater production to transform nuclear weapons into the backbone of America's defenses.

Continental testing also meant that some Americans would inevitably be exposed to some radiation from the radioactive fallout created by the tests. Because of the proximity of the continental proving grounds and the wind direction, fallout was carried eastward across the United States. In the 1950s testing in Nevada contributed to public unease about radiation hazards and effects expressed in the fallout controversy. Thirty years later Americans living in the immediate vicinity of the proving grounds argued that fallout had also caused excess cancer and leukemia in their communities.[62] Inadvertently the decision to establish a continental proving grounds may have brought home to a number of Americans some of the costs of waging the Korean War and the Cold War.

Dean's next six months in office were perhaps his most difficult. Apparent failure in the hydrogen bomb program, the trial of the Rosenbergs, and renewed crisis in Korea filled the months with tension and uncertainty. No other period during his chairmanship was as dark for Dean. In May he was glad to escape Washington for the *Greenhouse* tests in the Pacific, which offered a welcome respite from the pressures of the commission.

Dean's problems with the hydrogen bomb started when Los Alamos scientists realized they had taken the wrong technical approach to igniting a fusion reaction. Much of the research done on the Super now seemed futile and perhaps a waste of time and resources. Because Edward Teller had been the chief proponent of this approach, he was placed in an especially difficult position. Tempers flared, and Dean soon heard the charge that "Oppenheimer has discouraged, and very effectively, people from getting too enthusiastic about the program." Los Alamos was divided between scientists like Teller and John Von Neumann who urged the development of the hydrogen bomb no matter what the cost and scientist-administrators like Norris Bradbury who wanted to give fission weapons programs relatively more priority when allocating scarce resources. Dean had to retain the confidence of both groups, but, as an administrator, eventually found himself with more sympathy for Bradbury than Teller. Teller probably saved the hydrogen bomb program when he later devised a different approach, which was called the New Super, to igniting a fusion explosion. Ironically, Teller's idea was not too dissimilar from ideas then emerging from fission weapons programs.[63] The dispute over resource allocation between fusion and fission weapons programs would continue to vex Dean, however.

The Rosenberg case came to Dean just as the future of the hydrogen bomb program seemed darkest. Before Dean resolved disputes at Los Alamos and before Teller grasped the key to igniting a fusion explosion, commission security chief John A. Waters told Dean that federal attorneys were ready to bring the Rosenbergs to trial. As Waters explained, Julius and Ethel Rosenberg were accused of passing atomic bomb secrets to the Soviet Union during World War II. With the trial date approaching, prosecutors wanted to know whether previously classified details about the atomic bomb could be introduced into evidence against them. Because they believed Julius Rosenberg was the chief of a large spy ring, prosecutors wanted the death sentence for Rosenberg and a thirty-year prison sentence for his wife. Such severe punishment, the government hoped, would force Julius Rosenberg to name his confederates to reduce his own and his wife's sentences.[64]

To present a case against the Rosenbergs that would justify such severe sentences, federal attorneys had to prove that the Rosenbergs had betrayed vital secrets of the atomic bomb. But unrestricted use of atomic bomb data risked yet uncompromised details about the atomic bomb. Appalled that American citizens might have spied for the Soviets, Dean wanted to be certain that prosecutors would press for the death penalty for Rosenberg if he risked atomic bomb data in court. With the Joint Committee interested in the case, Dean had to be able to satisfy conservative committee members that nothing new would reach the Soviets. When he was uncertain that federal prosecutors would exercise sufficient care with bomb data, Dean took the extraordinary step of appealing directly to the attorney general and dictating the precise questions prosecutors would ask key witnesses.[65]

From a security standpoint Dean successfully solved a problem that vexes spy trials today, that is, using compromised data in court while simultaneously protecting related secrets. From a humanitarian perspective his actions are less praiseworthy. The bomb details compromised by the Rosenberg ring were less valuable than the secrets betrayed by Fuchs, although the Rosenberg data confirmed the general accuracy of Fuchs's information.[66] Yet there is no indication that Dean conveyed the relative value of the Rosenberg data to prosecutors. In other words Dean failed to put the crime in perspective. Like so many of his contemporaries Dean had little mercy for those presumed to have helped the Soviets through espionage or internal subversion.

As the jury heard the last testimony against the Rosenbergs, the Truman administration learned the Soviets might enter the Korean War and, together with the Chinese, drive the Americans from the peninsula and perhaps Japan as well. At the same time General MacArthur, the commander of the United Nations forces in Korea, threatened to reverse America's "tolerant effort to contain the war to the area of Korea." MacArthur had made unauthorized public statements about the conduct of the war before but this one undercut an effort by the administration to put out peace feelers to Red China and "deeply shocked" President Truman. The president decided to relieve the illustrious general but, for the moment, did nothing. Perhaps the Joint Chiefs' opinion that Soviet entry into the Korean War would touch off World War III made the president hesitate.[67] As Dean's diary reveals, the MacArthur crisis coincided with concern about Soviet expansion of the Korean War and the decision to transfer complete atomic bombs to the Pacific.

So concerned about Korea were the Joint Chiefs that they asked Dean to transfer nine complete atomic bombs to the Air Force. Dean had to worry about both a final breach of civilian control and the proximity of world war. Undoubtedly the first few days of April 1951 were his most tense as chairman. On April 5 House minority leader Joseph Martin made public another unauthorized statement by MacArthur, this one urging the use of Nationalist Chinese soldiers in the Korean War. On April 6, the same day he convoked his advisers to discuss firing General MacArthur, President Truman ordered Dean to make the transfer.[68]

Although the results were anticlimactic, several weeks of uncertainty followed. The president relieved General MacArthur on April 11, touching off an angry wave of sentiment against the administration. The Chinese launched an offensive on April 22, then a second on May 16. Both attacks failed and it became apparent that the Chinese could not use their numerical superiority to push the Americans out of Korea nor would the Soviets enter the war.[69] The war settled down to trench fighting accompanied by bitter, frustrating armistice negotiations.

The transfer of complete weapons was a logical step in the global deployment of the atomic arsenal. Although a crisis had been required to wrench complete bombs from the commission, the move followed the precedent established when nonnuclear components were deployed overseas. Now complete weapons under military custody were ready at an advanced base for use in responding to an emergency. Although that anticipated emergency never developed, the deployment would later help justify the Eisenhower administration's transfer of the bulk of the stockpile to the Department of Defense.

Debates over whether to create a second weapons research laboratory and whether to embark upon a second multibillion-dollar expansion of production facilities dominated Dean's second year as chairman. Edward Teller paced the second laboratory debate, eventually garnering support from Ernest Lawrence, Senator McMahon, and the Department of Defense for a new laboratory. The commission's first weapons research laboratory, Los Alamos, had been created during World War II and thus far had made all weapons discoveries. But Teller argued that more resources should be devoted to the hydrogen bomb program and to other promising new avenues of weapons design. In addition he believed that a second laboratory would give Los Alamos badly needed competition. Teller was ready to leave Los Alamos over the issue in April 1951 during the Korean crisis, but Dean talked him into remaining. In September, however, he left Los Alamos, in order, among other reasons, to lobby for a second laboratory. Dean found many reasons for not creating a second laboratory and fought a fairly good holding action against the proposal. Even someone as dedicated as Dean to strengthening the atomic arsenal found it hard to justify a second weapons research laboratory.[70] But the tide was flowing against him on this issue.

Another expansion debate began in May 1951 when Secretary of Defense George C. Marshall (he took over from Louis Johnson in September 1950) asked the commission to reexamine its production program. Again Senator McMahon lobbied for greater production, asking the commission for cost estimates of increasing the production of uranium 235 and plutonium by at least 50 percent. The commission, however, estimated such a program would cost at least $2 billion and consume a significant amount of the nation's supply of nickel, stainless steel tubing, hydrofluoric acid, and sulfur. Dean questioned the wisdom of such a large production increase and argued that the National Security Council should fully explore the issue. Under pressure from the Department of Defense and McMahon, the commission had to devise an interim expansion program before Dean could force the issue up to the National Security Council.[71]

Before either the second laboratory or the expansion debates were resolved, Dean became an advocate of tactical nuclear weapons. Since the spring of 1950, or about the same time a review committee led by Under Secretary of the Army Tracy Voorhees argued that the Soviets could overrun western Europe unless the Air Force could use tactical nuclear weapons, the press had speculated about the advent of tactical weapons. This speculation had been fueled by the Korean War and by statements by Army Chief of Staff J. Lawton Collins that the United States would soon have atomic artillery. Unlike those who sought to relate tactical atomic weapons to the defense of western Europe or to military doctrine, Dean saw them in purely practical terms as a solution to the problem of Chinese numerical superiority in Korea. He believed that the public must accept tactical atomic weapons as just another weapon in America's arsenal before they could be employed in Korea and delivered his most controversial speech as chairman to tackle what he saw as a public relations problem.[72]

On October 5, 1951, Dean spoke to the students of the University of Southern California ostensibly about "The Responsibilities of Atomic World Leadership." In reality he seized the occasion to inform Americans that they were entering an era of atomic plenty with sufficient weapons for tactical as well as strategic uses. He urged Americans to regard the atomic bomb as any other conventional weapon and not attach undue significance to its use in tactical situations. Tactical weapons, Dean declared, could halt "these endless nibbling aggressions" and make the world more secure. Tactical atomic firepower would "cancel out any numerical advantage [an invader] might enjoy," would help stop future aggression, and would give "a real hope for peace."[73]

Newsmen and others interpreted the speech as a hint that America would use tactical weapons in Korea. The speech created a minor flap within the administration because it had not been cleared through routine White House channels. It marked Dean as a proponent of tactical weapons at the same time Senator McMahon was recognizing the value of tactical weapons in justifying the second expansion program. It aligned Dean with J. Robert Oppenheimer and others who saw tactical atomic weapons as an alternative to the terror bombing of cities with large strategic thermonuclear weapons. The speech was a milestone on the road to the incorporation of nuclear weapons into military policies and plans, and it foreshadowed the New Look and massive retaliation. One cannot read the speech today without being struck by how quickly the Eisenhower administration grasped the atomic shield forged by the Truman administration. One cannot also read the speech without being struck by the depth of Dean's acceptance of Cold War assumptions about the moral righteousness of the United States and the immorality of the Soviet Union.[74]

President Truman resolved the second expansion debate, ordering a 50 percent expansion of plutonium production and a 150 percent expansion of uranium 235 production on January 16, 1952. With McMahon, the Department of Defense, and Secretary of State Acheson supporting a production increase, there was little real consideration of whether the new facilities should be built. The major issue for the president and his senior advisers was assigning the commission top priority for materials needed to complete the program within the administration's ambitious deadline. The second Korean War expansion program enlarged the Oak Ridge and Paducah gaseous diffusion facilities, erected a new gaseous diffusion plant complex at Portsmouth, Ohio, and added two large reactors to the Hanford plant.[75] Dean would build a significant portion of the military-industrial complex about which President Eisenhower would warn the country nine years later. The decision meant that the commission could manufacture an ever larger quantity of strategic and tactical weapons in just a few years.

A little more than two months later the second laboratory debate reached a climax when Teller lined up sufficient support to force the issue up to the National Security Council. Dean, still fighting a second laboratory, examined the issue as a member of a special subcommittee of the National Security Council on April 1, 1952. With the two other members of the subcommittee, Acheson and Deputy Secretary of Defense William C. Foster, supporting a second laboratory, Dean could only keep the issue from going to President Truman. When the Air Force threatened to establish its own nuclear weapons research laboratory, Dean and the commission finally bowed to the inevitable.[76]

Although Gordon Dean questioned the wisdom of a second expansion and opposed the second laboratory, he did not lose his effectiveness as the head of the commission. He adjusted to political support for both programs and implemented them vigorously. Although he had disagreed with Senator McMahon, his relations with the Joint Committee remained good. His relations with Teller, however, were not the same after the second laboratory debate.[77] The flexibility and pragmatism Dean demonstrated were essential to any successful agency leader then as now.

Dean's future became uncertain when President Truman announced that he would not seek reelection in 1952. Dean responded with a warm letter thanking the president for his support of atomic energy programs. The president's decision, however, meant that Dean would face a new administration after the election. Senator McMahon's death from cancer on July 28, 1952, rendered Dean's tenure on the commission even more uncertain for he then lost a close friend and his chief political ally.[78] If he had any thoughts about remaining on the commission in a new administration, McMahon's death probably dispelled them.

Dean saw the hydrogen bomb program assured of success before he departed. The "first full-scale thermonuclear device," code-named *Mike*, had been created to test Teller's idea and was scheduled for detonation on October 31, 1952, just a few days before the presidential election. Because the scheduled shot was so close to the election, physicists J. Robert Oppenheimer, Hans Bethe, and Dean's fellow commissioners all argued that *Mike* should be postponed so that irresponsible elements could not use it in a last-minute attempt to influence the election. With even President Truman hoping that technical problems would delay the shot, Dean examined the possibility of postponing *Mike* but concluded the costs of postponement outweighed the benefits of meeting the schedule. *Mike* was fired on schedule, becoming the world's first thermonuclear explosion. Its 10.4 megatons was the largest nuclear explosion to that date, and its complete obliteration of the shot island was the most spectacular effect of the blast. Although not a weapon, *Mike* was a major achievement and assured Los Alamos scientists that they had taken the correct approach to igniting a fusion explosion.[79]

*Mike* pushed the world to the edge of the thermonuclear age. With the development of a specific scientific and engineering concept ready to be translated into a weapon, Dean had moved the program proposed by

Strauss in the fall of 1949 from general idea to concrete design. If he felt any regret about the implications of the accomplishment, Dean did not confide it to his diary. Neither did he argue that the public should be warned about the dangers of thermonuclear warfare. A new administration would have the grim duty of explaining the quantum jump in destructiveness to the American public.

Dwight D. Eisenhower's victory at the polls on November 4, 1952, meant that Dean had to carry the awesome news of the hydrogen bomb to a new president. Because news of the *Mike* detonation had leaked to the press and because he feared that open contact between the commission and Eisenhower would alert the Soviets that *Mike* had been a hydrogen explosion, Dean arranged a secret briefing for the president-elect at his suite in the Commodore Hotel in New York. Like characters in a spy thriller, Dean and his fellow commissioners traveled separately to New York, rendezvoused in Commissioner Murray's apartment, then snuck in and out of Eisenhower's rooms. So successful was Dean in concealing the visit that few outside of the commission were aware of it thirty years later.[80]

For Dean there remained little but housekeeping chores. On January 15, 1953, Gordon Dean and his fellow commissioners presented several atomic energy memorabilia to President Truman. At the White House Dean told the president of his desire to leave the commission. A few days later President Truman thanked Dean (see his letter in the Appendix) for the commission's accomplishments under his leadership and for maintaining a "close and cordial relationship" with the White House. The president was also impressed by the public confidence Dean had inspired in the commission and the spirit of teamwork that Dean had promoted within the commission.[81] Senator McMahon's candidate had become President Truman's chairman.

Dean submitted his formal resignation to president-elect Eisenhower. Because he had little time to study the needs of the commission, Eisenhower asked Dean to stay on until his term expired on June 30, 1953. Dean was a lame duck during his last six months in office, and to confirm Dean's distance from policymaking Eisenhower picked Lewis Strauss as his special assistant for atomic energy matters in early March 1953. Strauss formulated atomic energy policy from the White House until he succeeded Dean as chairman in July.[82]

During these months as a Truman holdover in a Republican administration, Dean had no voice in policy formulation. He played no role in Eisenhower's moves to end the Korean War, including National Security Council discussions concerning the use of atomic weapons in Korea and secret diplomatic threats to employ the atomic bomb unless armistice negotiations were satisfactorily concluded. Without consulting Dean the administration decided to abolish a commission labor panel that had kept prolonged strikes from slowing construction on expansion program facilities. From the newspapers he learned that the president planned to reconstitute the National Security Council without a representative from the commission.[83] In matters large and small, Dean was now an outsider.

Yet Dean was still able to exert some influence on atomic energy policy. Completely silent about the administration's search for an end to the Korean War, Dean's diary most consistently reflects his influence in the review of the commission's budget for fiscal year 1954. The Eisenhower administration was determined to reduce federal expenditures and ordered a comprehensive review of the entire 1954 budget which had been initially formulated by the Truman administration. In the midst of multibillion-dollar expansion programs, the commission was an obvious target for reductions. Because much of the commission's budget was based on military requirements, Dean argued that the commission and the Department of Defense budgets should be reviewed simultaneously. Accordingly President Eisenhower appointed Lewis Strauss to the task, but with Strauss unwilling to cut much from military atomic energy programs, the commission escaped relatively unscathed. A sixth reactor for the Savannah River facility, a program for designing a reactor for powering aircraft, and a nuclear-powered aircraft carrier were the only military programs completely eliminated.[84]

Civilian programs were slashed as well consistent with the administration's policy to leave power reactor development to private industry. The sodium graphite reactor program, upon which the commission pinned hopes for a civilian power program, was canceled as were other civilian reactor projects. Only through the sustained efforts of Dean and Commissioner Murray were the funds from the carrier reactor devoted to a central station nuclear reactor project. Eventually this project built the nation's first civilian power reactor at Shippingport, Pennsylvania. The Shippingport project, however, was all that remained of the commission's civilian power program.[85]

In the midst of budget battles, Dean had to confront the problems of the 1953 nuclear weapons test series. Called *Upshot-Knothole*, the series produced more fallout than its predecessors and, at one point, test officials had to ask residents to remain indoors for three hours while a fallout cloud passed over St. George, Utah. Just as news about the St. George and other fallout problems reached the commission, Los Alamos scientists wanted to add an extra shot to the series. Convinced that the commission must have scientific data from the shot, Dean guided a request for the additional shot through the administration with Strauss's support. The extra shot was fired, producing little fallout, but the 1953 series sent relatively more fallout into local Utah and Nevada communities than did most other atmospheric test series. Thirty years later *Upshot-Knothole* fallout figured prominently in lawsuits alleging that fallout from atmospheric tests caused cancer or leukemia among local residents.[86]

Of these issues the diary concentrates largely on the budget fights. It captures the philosophical differences between the commission and Eisenhower's advisers over civilian-power policy but few of the moves of Dean and Murray to preserve the Shippingport project. It also shows Dean's attitudes about fallout and the 1953 test series. But for this period the diary is far richer in routine details of commission operations than in policymaking at the top levels of the administration.

After *Upshot-Knothole* Dean faced no further major problems. He thanked the appropriate members of Congress for their help on the budget, made a valedictory appearance on the television program "Meet the Press," and gave a farewell press conference. His final week included many farewell parties but few matters of substance. The White House had announced that Strauss would succeed Dean and Strauss had already assumed the reins of power. The diary notes Dean's departure with a "Finis" after the last entry.[87]

Gordon Dean's diary then is a key document for atomic energy matters from the fall of 1949 through the fall of 1952. It captures most of the major issues that came before Dean and his associates during that period. It reveals Dean in action as he dealt with those issues and provides a key supplement to official commission records. It paints a vivid picture of the Truman administration and the problems associated with atomic energy during the Korean War years. Few diaries are as revealing or as fascinating.

# ONE

## THE HYDROGEN BOMB

*September 20, 1949, to January 30, 1950*

The decision to develop a hydrogen bomb was one of the most fateful made by an American president. Eventually it propelled the world into the thermonuclear age in which warfare could be waged with weapons of such destructive power that thermonuclear war seemed to threaten the very existence of civilization. The decision also opened a period of unrestricted nuclear arms competition between the United States and the Soviet Union which lasted until the limited test ban agreement of 1963. It committed the Atomic Energy Commission to a costly and uncertain weapons program just as promising developments were occurring in fission weapons programs. Its potential demand for expensive nuclear materials helped to stimulate the multibillion-dollar expansions of commission production facilities. Differences about the moral implications of the hydrogen bomb created breaches among scientists that took years to heal.

Gordon Dean did not chair the commission during the hydrogen bomb debate, and thus his diary does not capture events from the perspective it did when Dean led the commission. As a commissioner, though, Dean was a key participant in the debate and the diary presents an intimate picture of his reasons for becoming a proponent of the hydrogen bomb. Likewise, Dean's hostile and moralistic view of the Soviet Union and the bitter political struggles of the fall of 1949 are a constant in his diary.

The hydrogen bomb debate was one of the key events in Dean's life because his support for the hydrogen bomb was crucial to his selection as chairman. Senator McMahon never would have backed a candidate for chairman who had opposed the hydrogen bomb. Yet the search for the hydrogen bomb promised to be one of the major tasks of Lilienthal's successor. Only a proponent of the hydrogen bomb could have retained sufficient support from the pro-hydrogen bomb Joint Committee to manage commission programs without a series of incredible mismanagement hearings.

The hydrogen bomb debate focused Dean's views on how the commission should manage atomic energy programs. His ideas on program management and his record of achievement made him one of the most effective practitioners of the commission form of agency organization. Dean's management ideas foreshadowed how he would work with fellow commissioners to run commission programs and how he would operate as one of the most successful agency leaders in the second Truman administration. In no other area could he claim to have created new policy or programs.

Dean began his office diary on June 16, 1949. He observed the controversies engulfing the commission during the summer of 1949 but did not confide them to his diary. Dean worried about the powers of the general manager and Carroll Wilson's directive that the general counsel, the controller, and the secretary report to the general manager rather than to the commission, but he did not criticize the general manager in his diary during the summer. His dissatisfaction with the respective roles of the commission and the general manager would soon surface, however.

The Soviet detonation had surprised the Truman administration, had shocked the nation, and had moved Commissioner Strauss to propose a hydrogen bomb program on October 5, 1949. Strauss thought of the hydrogen bomb as a quantum jump in terms of national security because it based its explosive power on the fusion of atoms and was a substantially more destructive weapon than the atomic bomb. Such a superbomb had been under spasmodic study at Los Alamos since 1943. Los Alamos scientists had managed to map out a particular technical approach to igniting a thermonuclear reaction dubbed the Super, but much remained to be learned about making a workable bomb. Strauss's proposal soon sparked a secret debate within the government about whether to initiate a crash program to develop the hydrogen bomb.

As Strauss sought support for the hydrogen bomb, Dean toyed with a highly impractical plan to create an "iron curtain" around Russia, isolating her from the rest of the world. Inherent in Dean's thinking was a moral, innocent United States contending with an evil, immoral, expansionistic empire. Dean's plan was naive at best, and it soon occurred to him that quarantining the Soviet Union would be virtually impossible and might easily lead to war. But the hope for diplomatic advantage was never far from his thoughts that fall.

When he had proposed the quantum jump, Lewis Strauss had also suggested that the commission seek the advice of the General Advisory Committee. Although Strauss found little support within the commission, Sidney Souers, the executive director of the National Security Council, alerted him to the president's interest in the hydrogen bomb. Finally Lilienthal asked the General Advisory Committee to consider the issue at a special meeting scheduled for the end of October. The historic meeting ruined Dean's plans for a weekend of golf.

The General Advisory Committee began its deliberations on the afternoon of Friday, October 28, 1949. The committee discussed the Super until Sunday noon and spent the afternoon composing its report on the hydrogen bomb. In the report committee chairman J. Robert Oppenheimer stated that the entire committee found the technical problems of igniting a fusion reaction so enormous as to preclude a crash program. In an appendix signed by the majority of the committee, Oppenheimer urged, primarily for moral reasons, that America renounce forever the Super and announce the decision to the world.

The General Advisory Committee was too impractical for Dean and he responded with "The Alternatives," arguing that to renounce the Super would be a mistake. Hoping to reap diplomatic advantage from the Super, Dean advocated a secret approach that would present Stalin with a choice of arms race or United Nations' control of the atom. He hoped that the United States could use the Super to revive negotiations for international control which had stalled in the United Nations in 1946. If no bargain could be struck, the United States could then develop the Super. Dean's views allied him with Strauss and split the commission three to two. But before Lilienthal sent a divided recommendation to the White House, he attempted to use the General Advisory Committee to pressure Dean into changing his mind. The ploy failed and the commission sent majority and minority reports to the president on November 9, 1949. Because he wanted an evaluation of the political and military, as well as technical, factors, President Truman sent the thermonuclear issue to the National Security Council.

The hydrogen bomb debate sparked a sharp dispute over the role of the commissioners in managing atomic energy programs. Lilienthal had tried to delegate consideration of the Super to the staff, but Dean and Smyth successfully argued that the commissioners themselves had to deal with the issue. Dean and Smyth also won Lilienthal's consent to a broad-ranging discussion of commission management. Acrimonious sessions were held on November 28 and 29, 1949, and were more effective in venting Lilienthal's frustrations than in setting new policies. At one point, Lilienthal, exasperated by the commission form of organization, exclaimed that the commission ought to be abolished. His outburst sparked a retort from Dean and moved him to place arguments for the commission form of organization in the diary. The frank exchanges are completely omitted from official commission records, and Dean's diary is virtually the only source for the dispute.

Dean, Smyth, and Strauss also argued that the commission had to take more direct responsibility for program management. Lilienthal had granted relatively broad authority to the general manager, division directors, and field office managers, leaving relatively few areas for initiative from the commissioners. Dean, Smyth, and Strauss wanted to enlarge the commission's area for authority and initiative at the expense of the general manager and his staff. Lilienthal's management of commission programs closely resembled the wartime management of atomic energy when a relatively powerful General Leslie Groves made broad decisions under the loose guidance of a military policy committee. Dean's arguments for a more activist commission looked to the future: Dean and his successors all gradually enlarged the role of the commissioners and slowly diminished the role of the general manager. Dean's activist commission was also more typical of a peacetime agency whose leaders were immediately accountable to Congress, a problem Groves and the Military Policy Committee did not have to face during the war.

Lilienthal had hoped to leave the commission at the end of the year, but he stayed on when President Truman asked him to remain in the government until the hydrogen bomb debate was resolved. The president had ordered a special subcommittee of the National Security Council composed of Lilienthal, Secretary of State Dean Acheson, and Secretary of Defense Louis Johnson to formulate the administration's position on the Super. The subcommittee met infrequently, but with Acheson and Johnson for the hydrogen bomb, there was little doubt about the outcome. As January began and Congress reconvened after a long fall recess, the subcommittee neared a decision.

Senator McMahon lost little time in applying pressure once Congress reconvened. On January 18 he assembled the Joint Committee to hear testimony on the hydrogen bomb from the Joint Chiefs of Staff and on January 27 McMahon and the committee quizzed the commission about the Super. Probably the reluctance of his associates to admit that the commission was less than unanimous about the hydrogen bomb inspired Dean to write the "Sequence of Events" paper. But McMahon's pressure was not really needed, for on January 31, 1950, with Lilienthal dissenting, the special National Security Council subcommittee advised the president to approve a crash program to develop the hydrogen bomb. Within hours President Truman announced the decision and ordered the commission to proceed with the Super. The decision concluded the hydrogen bomb debate and ends the chapter.

For the dispute over the role of the commissioners, see also Lilienthal, *Atomic Energy Years*, p. 603; and Minutes, Commission Meetings 335 and 336, November 28, 29, 1949, AEC.

## ≡ *September 20, 1949*

Carroll Wilson called to say that Pike had talked with the Admiral ⟨Hillenkoetter[1](?) CIA⟩ and indicated that probably we would hear by noon whether a conference would take place. He had heard from Volpe[2] that Acheson is putting the brakes on the conference—somebody is going to New York to talk with him. Further discussion to be held on question of disclosure ⟨of A-bomb explosion in Russia⟩.

1. Rear Admiral Roscoe H. Hillenkoetter, director of the Central Intelligence Agency.
2. Joseph A. Volpe, Jr., the commission's general counsel.

≡ *September 22, 1949*

Senator McMahon called. No date has been set yet. Is calling a meeting for tomorrow morning. All the Commissioners in town except Lilienthal

≡ *September 23, 1949*

Senator McMahon called about conversation with President.[1] Would like to have a stenographer present at the JCC[2] meeting—a historical occasion

1. McMahon was preparing to announce the Soviet detonation to the Joint Committee.
2. The Joint Committee on Atomic Energy.

Pauline Frederick called about President's report of A-bomb explosion in Russia. GD not ready to be interviewed—three Executive Departments involved, State, NME[1] and AEC. GD suggested that she get in touch with McMahon and Vandenberg

1. National Military Establishment, better known as the Department of Defense.

Wrote memo to Commissioners and General Manager stating what probably will be asked for in the way of itemized statement of what we have done and we propose to do in the light of the "Vermont" matter ⟨explosion in Russia⟩.

≡ MEMORANDUM TO THOSE LISTED BELOW:                     September 23, 1949

We will shortly be asked by the Joint Committee for an itemized statement of what we have done and what we propose to do in the immediate future within the AEC establishment in light of the Vermont matter.

While I think it highly important that in our dealings with the general public and with the Joint Committee we give emphasis to the fact that the

AEC has been in an unusual state of readiness and that no major upheaval in our program is indicated or wise; nevertheless, I think we must be prepared to demonstrate that we have in the light of this knowledge taken or considered taking certain definite steps. I have discussed this matter with Dr. Smyth prior to his departure today, and some of the steps which occur to us are indicated below:

1. *The DR Water Works* should be constructed as soon as possible and the General Manager should be instructed to take the necessary steps looking to its construction. We are due for a good roasting if, in the light of our present knowledge, we do not speed the construction of this installation.

2. *Vulnerability studies*: Security has made several vulnerability studies of such plants as Hanford and Oak Ridge. It occurs to me that these should be reviewed, brought up to date and the worthwhile recommendations therein contained acted upon. These deal primarily with vulnerability to (a) air attack and (b) sabotage, and suggest further study of dispersal at certain points.

3. *Boosting the power level and the G/T at the Hanford piles*—a review of the problems presented.

4. *Civilian defense*: In this category there are several items, only some of which are listed below. They include the studies by Biology and Medicine and the plans developed by them for the stockpiling of instruments and the training of personnel. They include the Weapons Effect Handbook which I think should have high priority. They include a review of AEC's mission in the broad civil defense picture, and more specifically firming up plans for civil defense at our own installations.

5. *Getting unfabricated material into gadgets.*[1] This, I assume, falls into three categories: (1) getting stockpile of source material into the pipeline, (2) fabrication of any accumulated Pu or U-235 and (3) the refabrication of obsolete parts by using Los Alamos as well as the facilities at Hanford and Oak Ridge.

6. Reexamination by Reactor Development to ascertain the effect of Dr. Oppenheimer's suggestions concerning neutron needs on the entire reactor program.

7. Consideration of bringing DuPont back into the picture, possibly at Hanford, possibly in connection with Item 6 above.

8. *Selling the Joint Committee on not killing our so-called "non-weapons" program*: In anticipation of the suggestions ⟨such as those made by Senator Connally[2] this morning in the Joint Committee meeting when he said, "I hope this means you are going to cut out this silly stuff about power reactors,"⟩ which will be made to cut down (1) basic physical research, (2) biology and medicine, (3) reactors and possibly other parts of the program which seem to some persons as being unrelated to the weap-

ons program, it occurs to me that if we are not fortified with arguments, some of the programs will be severely cut in the budgets and we may even be ordered to abandon some of them. I would seriously suggest, therefore, that papers directed toward this end be prepared by the respective Divisions demonstrating the essential character of their work, and that these be so written that they can readily be used by us when necessary before the Joint Committee and the Appropriations Committees.

I fear very much that if at our next appearance before the Joint Committee we do not indicate that we have given attention to all of the above and acted at least on some of them, we will lose the confidence of the Committee at the very time when they, like all people, will instinctively look for a scapegoat.

I, therefore, suggest early consideration of these possible steps by the Commission.

Gordon Dean

| Mr. Lilienthal | Mr. Smyth |
|---|---|
| Mr. Pike | Mr. Wilson |
| Mr. Strauss | Mr. Volpe |

1. Gadgets are atomic bombs.
2. Senator Tom Connally, a member of the Joint Committee.


ASSUMPTIONS

1. That Russia has one bomb now, has producing piles,[1] a seven-year supply of uranium and in two years could make 50 atomic bombs.

2. That the United States and the other democratic countries cannot afford to permit Russia to build such a stockpile. If in two years Russia's stockpile is * * * * she still has more than the world can tolerate. This is particularly true since the person who uses the weapon first has at least a 25% advantage in surprise and in disruption of the enemy's power to retaliate.

3. That before the United States uses armed forces it must, for the sake of the long pull, have the support of the other countries of the world. That support must be quickly built up and expressed.

PLAN

With the above assumptions in mind the following plan is suggested:

1. The UN establish a new committee with new faces to study proposals for international control. If there is any hope that the US and Russia can agree through the UN on a plan of international control, it lies in changing the people who have been doing the negotiating and the labels on the respective plans of the two countries. The present negotiators have obviously reached an impasse.

2. After the new committee or group is established, the US through some other sponsoring committee places before the group a new plan. It would not be called the Baruch plan for the reason that new labels are needed if for no other reason than face-saving. However, it would be in substance the Baruch plan with inspection and control provisions.

3. The plan would be reported out and secure world blessing by its adoption in the Assembly.

4. If and when the plan is turned down by Russia, the countries through the Assembly would deliver an ultimatum that Russia disarm. This ultimatum should be prefaced with a recital of Russia's determination to stall international control while developing the weapon. It would list all of the acts of aggression since the close of the war, her noncooperation in all of the organizations set up in the UN, her abuse of the veto power, etc.

5. In the meantime, an evaluation would have been made as to Russia's economic sufficiency and the exact extent to which she depends upon imports of strategic materials and ideas. If that evaluation demonstrated that Russia would lose if she were completely isolated from the rest of the world, and I think it would so demonstrate in spite of her vast resources, the countries of the world would then establish a world "iron curtain," all Russian embassies would be closed, all missions, civil or military, would be returned to their country, all ships would be denied access to the Panama Canal or the Suez and all trade with Russia would cease, whether by land or sea. She would, in short, be quarantined.

6. This would be followed by the establishment of a Joint Western Power Military Command whose first duty would be the establishment west of the iron curtain of strategic air bases, * * * * The plan has the advantage of using sanctions rather than bombs during the intermediate stage. It has the advantage of speedily securing by a series of steps complete unanimity on the part of the democracies of the world. ⟨9/30/49⟩

1. Pile was an early name for a reactor.

≡ *October 11, 1949*

Martha Jane Brown called to say that Mr. Lilienthal had talked with Mr. Pace[1] about the "report."[2] Mr. Pace said he had looked over the report and was going to see the President Thursday. He wondered if that would be soon enough. Mr. Lilienthal said he did not think it would be so Mr. Pace is going to see the President tomorrow and then see Mr. Lilienthal at 2:00 P.M.

1. Frank Pace, director of the Bureau of the Budget.

2. The "report" was probably the National Security Council memorandum approving K-31 and the DR waterworks.

## ≡ *October 12, 1949*

Senator McMahon called to say report[1] has not been released; just approved by the Committee; must be approved by the Senate tomorrow; going to the printer tonight. Will give it to the press tomorrow morning with release set for 4:00 P.M.

1. The majority report of the Joint Committee which found no evidence of "incredible mismanagement" of atomic energy programs. The report generally supported Lilienthal's record as chairman.

## ≡ *October 13, 1949*

GD talked to General McCormack[1] about possible GAC meeting on October 29th and 30th. The suggestion was made by Mr. Strauss that high priority be given to the "super" and the civil defense picture. GD says twice the Joint Committee has asked about this particular development and he made the statement that AEC is quite aware of the situation, is planning a GAC meeting in the near future.[2] McCormack made statement a few weeks ago about the possible threat of a super bomb—theory tells us that it is a possibility but it might be a very large item—delivery by boat, submarine, etc.

1. Brigadier General James McCormack, Jr., director of the division of military application.
2. At Commission Meeting 316 on October 12, 1949, Dean had asked Lilienthal to act on Strauss's "quantum jump" proposal.

## ≡ *October 18, 1949*

GD wrote Ed Burroughs, Cummings and Stanley firm, to regret the invitation to go to Pinehurst [to play golf] on October 29th and 30th. GAC meeting—can't possibly miss it.

## ≡ *October 19, 1949*

Bill Borden[1] called about putting over discussion of civil defense measures with the JCC until later. Hopeful that it can be put over until January for fear of the "capital" that could be made by bringing it out now. Nothing to be done by way of a meeting. Statement will issue from McMahon about next Monday explaining why it is to be put over—will give an interim period in which the committee can get themselves together on the question.

1. William L. Borden, executive director of the Joint Committee.

Senator McMahon called. The President is mad because McMahon gave out news on the expanded program.[1] HT did not want the Russians to think we are afraid of them. McMahon said it was a natural development of plans begun last year. . . .

1. McMahon had leaked the decision to build the DR waterworks and the K-31 plant.

≡ MEMORANDUM FOR THOSE LISTED BELOW:                    October 26, 1949

In an Executive Session of the Commission last week we discussed briefly the question of what type of problems should be referred to the Commission and what types of problems should be delegated to staff. No conclusions were reached but it was left that the individual Commissioners would attempt to clarify their desires—possibly listing items that they would like to review which they do not now review and listing as well items now reviewed which they do not wish to review.

When I attempted to formulate such lists I encountered considerable difficulty and I soon discovered that the difficulty arose from the fact that our role as Commissioners is nowhere clearly set forth. The matter is further complicated by a very sweeping delegation of authority to the General Manager. What then is left to the Commissioners? In short, what are we supposed to do?

The McMahon Act does not quite supply the answer to the question; nor was it intended that it should do so. I think that the answer can only be supplied by the Commissioners themselves. I fully appreciate that in the extremely busy early days of the Commission and particularly with the numerous distractions which it faced it was inevitable that the type of work which would be handled by the General Manager and the type of work which would be handled by the Commissioners could only be determined after considerable experience with individual problems.

While I am certainly not prepared to do it, I think that the Commissioners must somehow determine what their role is to be. I do know that there are certain subjects which I feel it my responsibility as a Commissioner to review and I have listed some of these below. The list is not complete but I fear that we will have to go through the process of listing before we can spell out precisely what our role should be. I also appreciate that any list will never be a fixed one; that the Commission will be greatly interested in a given subject for a period of time and later decide to delegate it; also that in some cases it will decide to take unto itself matters which it has previously delegated.

1. *Budget*: I think we should be prepared to spend considerable time on the preparation of budget assumptions as well as considerable time on the budget before it is presented to the Bureau of the Budget. The budget itself furnishes an excellent view not only of the dollars spent, and they are considerable, but of the purposes for which the dollars are to be spent. I have the feeling that flash as well as firm estimates from the field are based on assumptions of policies which have never been fixed. If we are to review the budget we must have more time in which to review it. Yesterday's presentation of the 3000 Program[1] was not adequate. Perhaps we should have asked more questions at the Commission meeting, but the fact still remains that we did not receive the budget for the 3000 Program until an hour and a half before going into the Commission meeting and the day before it had to be presented to the Bureau of the Budget. Whatever occasioned this, I hope that it need not happen again either with reference to the regular budget presentation or in the case of supplementals. I think we must realize that with the Congress at least the budget is one of the most sensitive of our exposed nerves.

2. *Legislation*: Any proposals to amend our basic Act and any legislation which affects our program should receive the careful study of the Commission. In fact, I think there is some duty on the part of the Commissioners to originate suggestions concerning legislation. Certainly the time is ripe now for a healthy review of the Act and perhaps rather sweeping amendments. In preparing legislative suggestions I think we must anticipate our needs and see to it that sufficient discretion is accorded us in those fields where we need it.

3. *Joint Committee*: Everything concerning our relations with the Joint Committee should be made a matter for Commission decision. Specifically, with reference to the appearances which we make before the Committee I think there should be more participation by the Commissioners. During the past year it seems to me that there has been almost negligible participation by the Commissioners themselves. The result is that the Commissioners sit rather stiffly in the back of the room while members of the staff carry the ball. This gives an impression, correct or incorrect, that the Commissioners are not sufficiently familiar with the subject matter to discuss it with the lay members of the Joint Committee. Since we are not talking to experts in these appearances, it should not be necessary for us to summon

experts if we are thoroughly briefed. If during the course of a Commissioner's presentation he finds himself forced to turn to a member of the staff for information he should, of course, do so, but the Commissioners should carry the ball.

4. *State Department*: The importance of most subjects as to which there is liaison between the Commission and the State Department is such that there should be a more active participation by the Commissioners in dealings with the State Department. In looking back over the Tri-Partite talks[2]—and nothing more important has taken place during the last six months—I think it would have been wise to have had Dr. Smyth from our Commission appear with Dr. Bacher and Dr. Oppenheimer in all of the major discussions. Policy is made in the so-called "ad hoc" committees and I think we should recognize it. If there should be a division of opinion in the Commission on a subject touching the State Department it would be healthy to have the State Department made aware of that fact.

5. *Communists*: I am the last person in the world to hold to the nation that there is a "Red" under every bed; nevertheless, I think we must recognize that if there is one place where Communists will attempt to infiltrate it is the atomic energy program. That fact we cannot overlook. Consequently, any danger of infiltration should be a matter of concern to the Commissioners. Anything touching the subject should come to us. This may have some bearing on the question of whether there should be a more or less decentralized organization of our Security Branch.

6. *The Defense Establishment*: There should be frequent and frank explorations with the MLC of all subjects with which we are jointly concerned. I cannot think of any items touching upon our relations with the military which are not appropriate for Commission consideration, and I think we should be extremely careful lest our relations with the MLC drift to a level where we are simply dealing in routine fashion with the secretariat of the MLC.

7. *The White House*: I assume that there are no relations with the White House which are not conducted through the Chairman of the Commission. I think, however, we have a responsibility to keep the President more fully advised of developments within the Commission. The necessity of this was recognized I think when in June we referred to the President the recommendation of the Joint Chiefs.[3] I think in connection with the new emphasis[4] which Dr. Bradbury[5] advocated for Los Alamos that the President should be made fully aware of the possibilities and the implications, after full Commission deliberation.

8. *The General Advisory Committee*: At the last meeting of the GAC the agenda was prepared by the staff after no Commission consideration and initialed by the Commissioners the day before the GAC meeting. The Com-

missioners were never furnished with the documents which the GAC considered and upon which they acted. This would indicate that no sufficient Commission consideration was being given to extracting from the GAC its best judgment on troublesome, fundamental problems facing the Commission. If the GAC is agreeable, I think we should encourage them to permit us to sit in at greater length during their deliberations.

9. *CPC and CDA:*[6] In this field—our whole raw materials lifeline—I think the Commission should be kept more currently informed. Personally, I feel quite out of touch with the matters to which these two groups devote their time and attention.

10. *Key Personnel:* The Commission should examine carefully the qualifications of all the key personnel. For example, the Commission was recently informed that a new Deputy Director of Intelligence had been selected. I would have thought that this matter was one which properly should have been brought to the attention of the Commission before the fact. Particularly would this be true if there is any thought that he would be the successor to the Director of Intelligence. Admittedly, it is difficult to establish a precise level at which Commission consideration commences. We have already determined that all excepted positions falling under the category "Scientific and Technical Personnel" should be brought before the Commission.

11. *Key Contracts:* While it is obviously not the function of the Commission to negotiate contracts, nor to draft provisions thereof, there are most important policy considerations which arise in this field which should have Commission consideration. One example would be the suggested division of the GE contract.[7]

12. *New Major Construction:* The establishment of the new technical area at Los Alamos involving the expenditure of $121,000,000 is an example. While the presentation by Dr. Bradbury and Mr. Tyler[8] was very helpful, and while the documentation which they supplied was reasonably good, I had the feeling that the Commissioners have not supplied Los Alamos or the Washington staff with a clear-cut determination of just what we want, when we want it and what we are willing to spend for it. On a project as large as this I think the Commissioners might well have taken a joint junket to Los Alamos and gone over the proposition on the site and in considerable detail.

13. *Relations with Foreign Governments:* While many of the papers dealing with our relations with the Belgians, the Indians, the South Africans, etc. are lengthy and occasionally seemingly unimportant, I think nevertheless that all such items should come to the attention of the Commissioners since in dealing with them we are framing a policy which may have exceedingly important implications. The Raw Materials Division has,

I think, done an exceptionally good job in keeping us posted on these foreign negotiations.

14. *Production Figures*: It would be helpful to me if some device could be worked out so that I could spend a little more time on the monthly reports on the stockpile and the production reports. Oral briefing requires one to hold too much in his head.

15. *Personnel*: It would be helpful to me to have a monthly personnel report indicating such items as turnover and broken down in terms of functions (for example, the number of personnel devoted to security) and in terms of the locations of employment.

One other item on which we have had little information is the operation of the emergency clearance program. If there are emergencies existing I think we should be given that information at least by an Information Paper so that we might determine whether there is a criticizable number taken into the program by this route. The emphasis of this subject by certain members of the Joint Committee would seem to indicate that documentation is necessary and that the Commissioners should be kept informed.

The above items represent some, certainly not all, of the subjects which should receive, in my opinion, close scrutiny and handling by the Commissioners themselves.

I commend the manner in which the Secretary to the Commission prepares and presents staff papers for our consideration. There is little left to be desired in this operation, with the exception that there are possibly subjects coming now to us in which the Commissioners are not interested. These items will necessarily change from time to time. For example, I am particularly interested in the establishment of Arco.[9] It is a new project and one which the Commission can follow from the ground up. I am confident that the time will come when many small items concerning Arco will no longer hold any interest for me. At the present time, however, I would be quite happy to omit from the matters coming before the Commission the following:

1. *Foreign Isotope Distribution*: These take considerable time and so long as they are within the export program already approved I see no occasion to bring them to the attention of the Commissioners, if we can be sure that items such as the Norwegian shipment to a military establishment are recognized as presenting a policy problem.

2. *Visits Under the Technical Cooperation Program*:[10] So long as there is a careful staff judgment that these visits are within the Modus Vivendi I see no reason for them to come to the Commissioners. If there is any doubt in the mind on the part of any member of the staff, that doubt should be resolved by the Commission.

I should like to emphasize again that these are random observations; that they are submitted to the other Commissioners simply as a device for commencement of serious discussions concerning our role; and that no list can remain entirely fixed. I should also like to make it clear that we already receive certain information in the above fields. The above list is not entirely a list of information which we do not now receive. I have tried, however, to indicate those general fields in which I as a Commissioner want more information and participation—and precisely why.[11]

Mr. Lilienthal       Mr. Strauss
Mr. Pike             Mr. Wilson
Dr. Smyth                                                    Gordon Dean

1. The 3000 program was the weapons program.

2. Negotiations had begun in September with the British and Canadians for greater atomic cooperation among the three countries. Many members of the Joint Committee thought the proposals for increased cooperation violated the Atomic Energy Act—an opinion which Dean shared.

3. The June recommendations of the Joint Chiefs were the increased weapons requirements which led the commission to build the waterworks for the DR reactor and the K-31 plant.

4. The new emphasis for Los Alamos may refer either to the wide range of technical improvements then foreseen for fission weapons or to putting more resources into thermonuclear research.

5. Norris E. Bradbury, director of the Los Alamos laboratory.

6. The CPC was the Combined Policy Committee and the CDA was the Combined Development Agency. Both institutions had been established to coordinate atomic energy policies and allocate supplies of uranium ore among the Americans, the British, and the Canadians.

7. General Electric ran the Hanford reactors and the Knolls Atomic Power Laboratory for the commission.

8. Carroll L. Tyler, manager of the Santa Fe Operations Office.

9. The commission had recently decided to build a reactor proving grounds near Arco, Idaho.

10. The Technical Cooperation Program was the limited exchange of atomic energy information with Great Britain and Canada established after World War II.

11. Dean put many of these into practice when he became chairman.

≡ *October 31, 1949*

Mr. Lilienthal called. He had talked with Senator McMahon[1] who said he would be happy to see the Commissioners. Is coming here about 5:00 this evening.

1. McMahon discussed the General Advisory Committee report on the Super with the commission. McMahon was hardly pleased with the committee's position.

⟨1. Agreement—Use. Must go higher.⟩
⟨2. Must have a policy.⟩
G. Dean 11/3/49

THE ALTERNATIVES[1]

1. *Renounce and Announce.* This is the course suggested by the GAC. I think it would be a mistake for the following reasons:

(a) It would have a bad effect upon the American people.

(b) It would probably cause us to lose the confidence of the peoples of Western Europe.

(c) It won't impress the Kremlin: ~~except with the fact that~~ we ~~are~~[2] ⟨they would probably regard us as rather idealistic fools.⟩

⟨(d) It says we know enough to make the decision that its military value. We don't⟩

⟨(e) It doesn't make the best capital of situation. ~~Just~~ onetime field⟩

2. *Renounce but not say anything.* This is probably not advisable because, first of all, you can't keep such things secret and ⟨the bad effects noted under 1 above would appear;⟩ secondly, I think it takes away from us an opportunity to use the possibility in the international scene. ⟨Furthermore at this point it is a blind refusal to explore further.⟩

3. Let the President use the possibility to give international cooperation a shot in the arm, and with the possibility exhausted ⟨so most re world opinion to resist ~~the~~ quarantine the aggressor⟩ make a military decision as to its value as a weapon and its general feasibility. I prefer this third approach.

THE PLAN

Under the third alternative above I visualize the following course of action:

That the President would advise ⟨the Kremlin⟩ through secret orthodox diplomatic channels ~~the Kremlin~~ that in our atomic energy program we have come to a dividing point in the road whether to engage in full time development of a "super" bomb;

That we do not wish to take this course if there is any hope of real world control and the elimination of weapons of mass destruction;

That we are ready to reopen negotiations on whatever ⟨concrete⟩ basis the President thinks wise.

This would be a better course than a public announcement since it permits Stalin to save face and could be so presented as to carry a minimum of threat. The overtures and replies would be well documented so that in event of failure, which would be likely, America would have a "white paper" with which to rally world opinion.

The President would then make a decision based on the purely military ⟨and psychological⟩ value of such a weapon. If one or more of these weapons would help to win a war or stave off a war then we should make them. If having one or more of them would serve as a deterrent to Russia then we should have them. The best use of fissionable material ⟨in terms of area damage⟩ would not be determinative in deciding this question since to make from one to five would not be a serious drain on our fissionable materials stockpile.

### ASSUMPTIONS

The above plan is based on the following assumptions, among others:

In making any recommendation to the President we should consider the psychological, political, and military imponderables and should not limit ourselves to the simple question of the feasibility or most economic use of fissionables.

The military has not made a sound and final judgment. It may conclude that the weapon does have a military advantage either to deter or thus prevent war or to deliver a knock-out blow in the event of war.

That international talks have reached an impasse and that this possibility may serve as a spring-board for fresh discussions.

That while all possibilities of international controls should be exhausted, the prospect of agreement is not good and that an aggressive war by the USSR is a good possibility.

That in peace and war we must have the peoples of the world in our corner.

1. "The Alternatives" are now a part of official commission files. There is evidence, however, that the paper was originally a part of the diary. Because it is a key part of the hydrogen bomb story, I have included it here.

2. Dean left "The Alternatives" in draft with handwritten revisions. I have rendered Dean's handwriting as faithfully as I could.

## ≡ *November 8, 1949*

GD talked to Strauss in Los Angeles re memo to the President re super

## ≡ *November 10, 1949*

GD discussed with Volpe question of giving to the JCC the GAC papers.[1] What use is going to be made of them? If Senator McMahon is going to have them at Sandia[2] and Los Alamos on trip, should not Bradbury and a few others have copies also? GD thinks we should not give out any copies at this time.

1. McMahon had requested a copy of the General Advisory Committee report on the Super.

2. The commission's laboratory at Sandia base near Albuquerque, New Mexico, performed certain production and engineering work on atomic bombs.

## ≡ *November 23, 1949*

Mr. Lilienthal's resignation made public today—effective 12/31/49[1]

1. Lilienthal later postponed the effective date of his resignation to February 15, 1950, at the request of President Truman.

## ≡ *November 25, 1949*

Joe Miller (UP) called to ask about other resignations besides Lilienthal's. GD said he will serve out his term. Would he be willing to be reappointed? GD preferred not to answer. Any guess as to Lilienthal's successor? GD doesn't know. Bernard and Buckley suggested, also Conant and DuBridge, but GD doesn't really know. Pike and Strauss hope to leave at the end of their terms? GD thinks that is right. After 3 years they should be ready to leave.

Don Dawson's office called. Arranged a 3:00 P.M. appointment today with GD.

≡ ⟨Original to Don Dawson 1/20⟩                         G. Dean 11/30/49

### THE ROLE OF THE COMMISSION

On several occasions since August, 1949 I have raised at Commission meetings the subject of the role of the Commissioners and the respective roles of the General Manager and the staff and field offices, but particularly the role of the Commissioners. I had raised it because it seemed to me that nowhere was the role defined and that the broadest possible delegation of responsibility had been given to the General Manager in GM Bulletin 20.[1] Commissioner Strauss on several occasions has raised the subject and asked for discussion of various phases of it. This has been deferred time and again in view of the other matters which were allegedly more pressing.

On October 26, 1949 I sent a memorandum to the Commissioners and the General Manager setting forth those matters which I felt should come to me as a Commissioner. I did this largely to stimulate discussion of the subject and clarify our role.

Dr. Smyth likewise has requested on numerous occasions a discussion of the subject pointing out particularly our relations with the CDA, the CPC and the State Department as being a realm in which the Commissioners should have a more active participation.

When the matter on the "super" came up Commissioner Smyth and myself insisted that this was the one subject of all which must be handled by the Commissioners themselves and not delegated to the staff. We prevailed in this point of view only after several attempts by the Chairman to delegate the matter and the preparation of views and assumptions, etc. to the staff. This unwillingness to take on the really heavy problems which it seemed to me the Commissioners should personally handle troubled me considerably and I was quite vocal about saying so.

Finally, it was agreed by the Commission that we should set aside a few days [in] the latter part of November and have this discussion in the so-called "soul-searching" sessions. Actually we did not get down to the subject until November 28. During this meeting Mr. Lilienthal and Mr. Pike stressed the importance in a shop of this size of delegating authority and I inquired what after the delegation was made was reserved to the Commissioners. About the only subject that Mr. Lilienthal could suggest was public relations.

The Commissioners met again on Tuesday, November 29th, to continue the session. This time the Division Directors were present. Most of the meeting was devoted to those things which are handicaps to our program; notably, the MLC, the GAC, the other advisory groups and the Joint Committee and it was stressed that with all these people breathing down our necks and with the necessity of satisfying so many it is hard to get a job done. Mr. Lilienthal particularly stressed this point. I pointed out that I saw no possibility of abolishing the MLC. In fact, I thought it would be highly unwise. I pointed out that it was created at the time when Congress decided on civilian control; that we were making weapons for the MLC and without a very close cooperation with them the program would be handicapped far more than it is by having their cooperation. I pointed out that there had never been any serious disagreements between the MLC and the AEC and at no time did they ever refer a dispute to the President for which the AEC Act provides when the MLC and the AEC cannot agree.

Turning to the General Advisory Committee I stated that I thought it was good insurance for the Commission to have them; that they were prominent men; that we are perfectly free to disagree with them; but to dispense with the privilege of having their judgment seemed to me quite wrong.

As for the Joint Committee I said that I saw no prospect of its being abolished. In fact, we should learn to live with it. That no undertaking, private or governmental, spends as much money and operates in such secrecy as surrounds our program; that in these circumstances the public was entitled to have a stockholders' committee and that that, in essence, is what the Joint Committee is.

I said I was disturbed at the fact that we were not talking to the subject, namely, the role of the Commissioners and that I would like to get some indication of what that role was. Mr. Strauss made several suggestions; Dr. Smyth made one or two stressing State Department liaison, CPC and CDA and said that he had felt that since he had been in the Commission there had been few subjects discussed by the Commissioners of the type which should have been discussed and far too many of the type which should not be referred to the Commissioners discussed.

Mr. Lilienthal then said that when he resigned he wanted to be free to, and he planned to, speak freely and openly concerning the whole program, the necessity for amending the AEC Act radically, the hindrances which the other committees furnished, notably the MLC and the Joint Committee, and so far as the role of the Commission was concerned he would abolish the Commission because he did not think it had a role other than possibly public relations; that he would supplant it with a single administrator.

I then quite frankly told him that the American people would never take it; it was too much power for one man and the balanced point of view which five people from different walks of life give to the program was the only insurance which the country could have that the program itself was balanced; that the Congress would never stand for it; that, in fact, no single man was good enough for it.

1. GM Bulletin 20 was the official statement of the authority and duties of the general manager.

---

G. Dean 12/1/49

Some considerations in comparing the AEC as a government agency with other government agencies with the view to determining whether there is a uniqueness in the program which makes its administration by a single administrator unwise.

1. The amount of money expended by the Commission both in terms of capital investment and operating expenses.

2. The compartmentalization of other departments of the government such as the Department of Interior which while having a single administrator has numerous autonomous departments with a single bureau head. Also illustrations from Agriculture and other departments, the units of which are easily separable from the department and which in fact have in

the past been transferred in toto from one department to another. For example, Rural Electrification, Animal Husbandry, Plant Conservation, Commodity Credit, Bureau of Forestry, Bureau of Fisheries, etc.

3. The extent to which the budget of the agency is frozen, having in mind that AEC has the power to divert funds from authorized projects to other projects, whereas in the average department of the government any substantial change, even in the number of personnel in a division, beyond that authorized by the budget is impossible.

4. The routine character of most of the government operations such as Post Office as compared with the highly unique experimental character of the projects operated by the AEC.

5. The external vs. internal determination of the character of the program. By this is meant that the budget for the Post Office Department, for example, is determined almost entirely by events beyond the control of the Postmaster General such as the estimated workload in terms of mail which will be carried. Another illustration is the Veterans Administration where the budget and pretty much the policy is determined externally by the number of GIs that are now taking training in college, the number of insurance policies handled by the Veterans Administration, in fact, the number of veterans is a factor over which the Veterans Administration has no control. In short, its budget is externally made. This in comparison with the AEC where virtually every determination is internally made and the result of discretion and judgment of the persons inside the program.

6. The integrated nature of the AEC as distinguished from the unintegrated compartments of the average government department.

7. The range of problems even in an integrated program (running from the conducting of fellowship programs to the manufacture of atomic weapons).

≡ *Matters which should be reviewed by the Commission*            ⟨12/2/49⟩
1. Selection of major operating contractors.
2. Major site selections.
3. Employment of key personnel.
4. Major programs (to be handled primarily in annual review of budget assumptions in the Spring).
5. Decisions involving other agencies such as State Department and the Congress.
6. Major changes in the AEC organization and structure.
7. Amendments to the basic Act.
8. Determination of export control policy (indicated that this needs review).

9. Foreign interchange of information.

10. Payments in lieu of taxes—school assistance, funds.

11. Procedures and policy regarding disposal of AEC property, real and personal.

12. Establishment of security policy.

13. Establishment of fiscal officers separate from that of the Controller.

14. Over-all policies concerning the operation and eventual disposition of the Commission.

## ≡ *December 2, 1949*

Wrote letter to Don Dawson suggesting some names

## ≡ *December 19, 1949*

GD talked to General McCormack about National Security Council working group.[1] We have had some correspondence from McMahon on this. We sent him an interim letter on it—we have sent no real reply yet. Hollis[2] is beginning to feel a little anxious about sending a real reply before January anyway. Another reply now would just repeat the words of other one—nothing new. GD does not think another reply is necessary now.

1. The National Security Council working group advised the president about whether to develop the hydrogen bomb.
2. Everett L. Hollis, deputy general counsel.

## ≡ *December 23, 1949*

Wrote to Charles Murphy, White House, congratulating him on new appointment to succeed Clark Clifford the end of February

## ≡ *January 3, 1950*

Talked to McMahon about selection. How is it coming? The Senator talked to Dawson in Florida. He (Dawson) is coming to lunch and will bring a list for the Senator to see. . . .

## ≡ *January 10, 1950*

Bill Borden called to give GD a fill-in on what happened at the last JCC meeting. The Chairman started out with a review of events. They talked out what the Advisory Committee had to say and he read their opinions verbatim. This took some time—frequent interruptions from members of the Committee such as "have we considered that others are involved?" The Chairman read his own letter to the President on the subject.[1] Senator Knowland[2] congratulated the Chairman on the letter. What should be done next? There should be a Committee recommendation on it. Everyone seemed to think that it was a good idea. Suggestion that the Commissioners be invited in, as well as Rabi[3] and Conant.[4] Jackson[5] expressed concern over amount of time that had already elapsed. The Committee will send its communication only after hearings. GD is disturbed about the publication of false reports about the *billions* of dollars estimated. He is afraid something might be said on this point.

1. McMahon had written a long letter to Truman on November 21, 1949, advocating a crash effort to develop the Super and refuting the General Advisory Committee's recommendations.
2. Senator William F. Knowland, a member of the Joint Committee.
3. Physicist Isidor I. Rabi, a member of the General Advisory Committee.
4. James B. Conant, president of Harvard University and a member of the General Advisory Committee.
5. Representative Henry M. Jackson, a member of the Joint Committee.

## ≡ *January 16, 1950*

Bill Borden called about schedule of future hearings. A meeting scheduled with General Bradley[1] and LeBaron[2] for Friday morning. At that time the Committee will try to get action by way of recommendation. Whether there will be insistence on hearing from the Commissioners is not known at the moment. Subcommittee meetings scheduled on Reactor Development. Will give Dr. Hafstad[3] a chance to speak—he has been anxious to get a chance. It depends on whether he is available. He is interested in getting the Committee interested in the problem.[4]

1. General Omar Bradley, chairman of the Joint Chiefs of Staff.
2. Robert LeBaron, chairman of the Military Liaison Committee.
3. Dr. Lawrence Hafstad, director of the Division of Reactor Development. The problem was probably the dilemma of whether to use production reactors to produce plutonium for fission weapons or tritium for the Super program.
4. The Joint Committee planned to submit its own views on the hydrogen bomb to President Truman after holding a series of hearings.

≡ *January 27, 1950*

GD wrote sequence of events leading to the "decision"

GD called Chet Holifield[1] for an appointment at his convenience. Lunch tomorrow at noon in the New House Office Building Room 1006. GD would like to discuss this morning's Joint Committee meeting and give him some background on it. There seemed to be an attempt to put Smyth and Pike under the guns—in a worse position than they are in already[2]

1. Representative Holifield was a member of the Joint Committee.
2. The Joint Committee had discussed the Super. It had pressed the commissioners, especially Smyth and Pike, for their views on the hydrogen bomb.

≡ *Sequence of events leading to the decision on the "super" bomb:*[1]
1. For some time it has been unclassified information that when two nuclei of deuterium get together a proton may be released plus a nucleus of hydrogen-3 or a neutron plus a nucleus of helium-3. In either event a sizable quantity of nuclear energy is released. At the conclusion of World War II there were even public references to the fact that some exploration had been made into the theory by United States scientists and that the energy released from such a weapon could be as much or more than 1,000 times the energy release of a fission bomb. (See McCloy statement of 1945)[2]
2. In 1945 a special study was made by a panel of which J. Robert Oppenheimer was the chairman entitled "Proposal for Research and Development in the Field of Atomic Energy." The report is Top Secret and dated September 28, 1945. At pages 12 to 16 thereof there appears a discussion of the thermonuclear bomb possibilities. It was suggested what a program looking toward perfection of such a weapon would entail and the report indicated the emphasis would have to be placed on nuclear physics, general physics and theory as well as indicating some of the technical matters which would have to be studied.
3. During the course of the last five years considerable theoretical work has been done in Los Alamos on the project. The exact extent of that is indicated in a paper AEC _____.[3]
4. With the President's announcement of September 27, 1949[4] of the explosion in Russia all of the Commissioners commenced thinking about what steps should be taken in our program to best promote the common defense and security. In this connection Commissioner Strauss prepared a paper, dated October 5, 1949, recommending to the Commission that high priority be given to the "super" project. This paper was referred to at a Commission meeting when the Commission had before it the question of

the agenda for the next meeting of the General Advisory Committee. It was decided by the Commission to ask the GAC to go into with us the broad questions of whether the Commission is doing all that it should do. A letter was prepared dated October 31, 1949 for Mr. J. Robert Oppenheimer, Chairman of the GAC, in which we state:

> Another course proposed is the development of the "super," which would conflict with the above in terms of demand for neutrons. Questions such as the following have arisen in this connection: Is it clear that the United States would use a "super" if it had one available? What would be the military worth of such a weapon, if delivered? Would it be worth 2, 5, 50 existing weapons? What would such values be when modified by deliverability factors? What is the best informed guess as to the cost of the "super" in terms of scientific effort, production facilities, dollars, and time?

> In the field of weapon development, the principal alternative to the "super" appears to be improvements in size, weight, and manageability of present types of weapons. How should these possibilities be evaluated in relation to the "super"?

5. The GAC met in Washington on October 29th and 30th during which time they devoted most of their discussions and thinking toward the question of what should be done concerning the "super." They concluded that "no member of the Committee was willing to endorse this proposal" to pursue with high priority the development of the "super" bomb. They gave as their reasons

> (1) that grave contamination problems were involved;
> (2) that the use of the weapons would bring about the destruction of innumerable human lives; that in fact it is not a weapon which can be used exclusively for the destruction of material installations of military or semi-military purposes;
> (3) that sufficient data is not available to determine whether the "super" will be cheaper or more expensive than the fission bomb;
> (4) that there is no foreseeable non-military application.

Two members of the GAC, Rabi and Fermi, while in agreement with the majority that the "super" should not be developed, nevertheless, suggested that this should be the occasion for attempting to secure from the Russians a promise that they would not develop it, but whether the Russians promised or didn't promise we would not.

In the discussions leading to the GAC's conclusion, many things were said, arguments advanced, which do not appear in their written report. They were, I think it is fair to say, visceral reactions. The moral implications were discussed at great length. It was pointed out that this development produced something different in kind rather than in degree and that the general tenor of the discussion was that it is just too big and must not therefore be built.

6. Immediately after the GAC returned home the Commissioners set up a series of discussions of the subject. Mr. Lilienthal stated at the outset that he was against it and this regardless of any international arrangement. He would just have no part of it. This was at a time prior to our having heard any more from the military than the benefit of a brief discussion, jointly with the GAC, with General Norstadt[5] and General Bradley. We all agreed rather early in the discussions that this was a matter which could not be determined and should not be determined by the Commission alone. The foreword to our report and recommendations to the President which later were formulated indicates our attitude, namely, that in determining whether to go ahead with this weapon or not go ahead there were implications far beyond those of the most efficient use of fissionable material; that there were factors of a military and diplomatic nature which required that any decision on this issue should be preceded by securing studies from the military and the Department of State. It was recognized by all of us that a study of all pertinent factors would be a healthy thing for many reasons. It would encourage a reevaluation of our whole military policy. It would require that military and diplomatic considerations be combined in any judgment and that the matter offers, in any event, an opening for further explorations into the subject of ~~mass~~ control of weapons ⟨of mass destruction.⟩

We all agreed, as did the GAC, that we would keep quiet on this subject until the President had made a determination.

On November 3, 1949 the Commissioners gave a rough statement of their views.

About ten days after the GAC meeting I indicated in the Commission meeting that I did not feel that I could go along with the GAC recommendation, namely, the recommendation to forego the development of the weapon and to announce that fact publicly. Mr. Lilienthal and Mr. Wilson, not at my request, arranged for as many members of the GAC as could be gathered together to appear at our Commission meeting to further explore the subject with us. It was quite apparent that this was not to be an attempt to really further explore the question but it was an attempt to answer the doubts that were in my mind. Mr. Strauss was not in the city. At this meeting were Carroll Wilson, Volpe, Lilienthal, Smyth, Pike(?), Oppenheimer,

Conant, Fermi and Rabi. I was rather put on the spot because Mr. Lilienthal opened the meeting saying that "we have gathered here because Mr. Dean has some serious doubts about the validity of the GAC conclusion" and being put on the spot, I then turned to Oppenheimer and Conant and said I would really like the answers to three questions:

> (1) What good effect could such a decision have upon the people of the United States who have a right to assume that in times of international strife we have the best weapons in our armor?
>
> (2) What effect would such a decision have on our friends in Western Europe and the other democracies of the world who look to us as a strong military power and their only salvation in the event of Russian aggression?
>
> (3) What possible good effect could such a conclusion have on the militarists of the USSR?

Oppenheimer talked to these points and said that he thought it was not clear what effect it would have on the American people and the peoples of Western Europe and admitted it probably would have no effect on Russia. Conant said he thought that the answers to my questions had to be considered from the other point of view. What effect would a decision to go ahead have on these people? To that point I talked and suggested that one of the most important effects it would have would be in the form of a deterrent to Russia to use it (everybody assuming that Russia can make one if we can). The meeting led to no definite results. The discussion was useful and did throw some light on one point, namely, the meaning of "at this time" in the recommendation of the GAC—since we had all agreed that we could not ⟨re-do⟩ make the conclusion as Commissioners "at this time" and that we would refer it to the President and that his decision would necessarily have to be at a later time, I was interested in finding out what the GAC had in mind when they said "at this time." Conant said, "Well, one administration cannot bind another." I readily agreed. Dr. Smyth, as I recall, stated that some events would have to come along of considerable significance which would change the present picture before he would be willing to develop the weapon. At that meeting Mr. Lilienthal was not particularly concerned with the expression "at this time." He was just against it.

Finally the Commission came to the place where it was to frame its views. We agreed that we would attempt to find as much unanimity as possible inside the Commission and where unanimity was impossible we would express our opinions to the President in individual brief presentations.

The views of the majority, Lilienthal, Pike and Smyth, are summarized as follows:

(Page 5 of the Memorandum to the President)
Commissioners Lilienthal, Pike, and Smyth recommend that your decision be against the development of a "super" bomb at this time.

Commissioners Dean and Strauss had a different recommendation which may be summarized as follows:

(Page 6 of the Memorandum to the President)
Utilize this possibility to reopen with the Soviet via secret diplomatic channels the consideration of satisfactory international controls of weapons of mass destruction. If this fails, or if it is felt that the possibility cannot thus be soon exploited, then proceed, if the Defense Establishment concurs, with the development, and announce this fact publicly.

It is significant to note that these were recommendations to the President and that they contemplated that by the time the President made his decision he would have before him the views of the military and the views of the State Department. Consequently, the recommendation of the majority that the President's decision be against the development of the "super" at this time was a recommendation against the building of the "super" even though the military and the State Department might think it wise to do. Both Commissioners Strauss and Dean stated specifically that the Departments of State and Defense should be contacted. The words "if the Defense Establishment concurs" in their recommendation assumes that the military have presented a convincing case that such a development is in the interest of our military program. Their recommendation that this development be utilized to reopen with the Soviet consideration of satisfactory international controls implies quite clearly that the State Department was to be consulted.

All of the Commissioners were present when the general conclusions were agreed upon but Commissioners Pike and Strauss were out of town when it came to the formulation of the individual views. They have submitted theirs separately. I think it is helpful to summarize the individual views.

*Mr. Lilienthal*: "The President should state openly that it does not appear at this time that the development of this weapon is consistent with this Country's program for world peace or our own long-term security. . . . I am in substantial agreement with the six members of the Advisory Committee." (Note that these six members had recommended "the majority feel that this should be an unqualified commitment." See page 4 of the GAC recommendations.) There is no room in his recommendation for a reconsideration depending upon the views of the military or the State Department. From the very outset and without, so far as I can ascertain, too close study of the really tough problems involved in this development such as the pollution problem, the most efficient use of fissionable material, the nature of the destruction, the extent of the energy release and the extent of the damage, Mr. Lilienthal has been unqualifiedly opposed to the project. No if, ands or buts.

*Mr. Pike*: On November 28th Mr. Pike submitted his personal views in a memorandum to the Commission in which he stated "I agree completely with the opinion that the Commission should not at this time devote a major portion of its energies to the development of this type of weapon." He also states in that memorandum that his position in general agrees with that of Chairman Lilienthal and Commissioner Smyth. His chief doubt is whether a statement can be devised which can add to the common defense and security. The reasons for his stand are stated in his letter as being two-fold—that there is no foreseeable peacetime use and that there is a doubtful military use so far as targets against which it could be directed and the uncertain factors of delivery.

*Dr. Smyth*: Dr. Smyth takes a slightly different position than Mr. Lilienthal or Mr. Pike. Roughly it is, to use his own words: "I have concluded that the military advantage of the Super to us is doubtful even if the Russians do develop it" but that in any event the occasion should be used to find a new approach to the problem of world peace and, further, he concludes that since events change speedily we should make an early review of our decision, that the negative decision should be publicly stated.

*Commissioner Strauss'* views and *Commissioner Dean's* views are pretty clearly stated.

7. The President, upon receipt of the report from the AEC, established a committee of Johnson, Acheson and Lilienthal to make a report to him. These principals did not get together quickly and Admiral Souers was asked to head up a working group with representation from the three agencies. Dr. Smyth, Mr. Dean, Dr. Fine and General McCormack served as a working group from the AEC.[6] Several meetings took place in Admiral Souers' office during the course of which a paper prepared by the AEC as to the characteristics of the weapon was discussed as well as a paper prepared by the military as to targets and deliverability problems. State Department never did come up with a paper.

Johnson, Acheson and Lilienthal had one meeting, extremely brief and quite inconclusive, and as of January 27th still had only this one brief meeting. The meetings have been difficult to hold because of the absence from the city of one or the other of the three parties for practically the entire time.

8. The GAC at its November 30th meeting reaffirmed its previous position and separate and more elaborate views were added to the GAC report by Buckley, Rowe and DuBridge.

9. The President placed upon the working groups as well as the principals an injunction of secrecy until the matter was settled. However, stories commenced to appear in the press. The first person to actually get a good roundup of the whole picture and obviously from the inside was Alfred Friendly who came to see Mr. Lilienthal about January 11th and explained that he had the whole story and asked Lilienthal's comments. Mr. Lilienthal did not comment. Friendly did not publish the piece but about a week later Joe Alsop commenced a series of three articles in the Washington Post dealing with this subject. Prior to the Friendly piece Senator Johnson made a reference to a "super" bomb in a television broadcast. Then came the deluge of stories on the hydrogen bomb which have filled the papers from the period of January 1st to the present, some of them obviously inspired by persons who are against the project.

10. During most of this period since the original GAC meeting on October 30th the Congress has not been in session. The only items supplied to the Joint Committee were the GAC recommendations and enclosures. A Subcommittee on the "super" was formed by the Joint Committee and during December traveled to various of the installations and talked to Lawrence at Berkeley and Bradbury and Teller at Los Alamos. They came away impressed with the importance of our proceeding rapidly.

With the return of Congress Senator McMahon called a meeting of the Joint Committee on about the 18th of January at which Mr. LeBaron of the Military Liaison Committee and General Bradley testified giving the Joint Chiefs of Staff's point of view that the development should proceed.

About January 24th the Weapons Sources Evaluation Group concluded a paper which was prepared for the use of the Military Establishment and which was shown for eyes only to members of the Commission.

On January 27th the Joint Committee invited the Commissioners to be present to discuss the project. Dr. Smyth carried the ball during most of the session in answering the technical questions concerning the difficulties in the project, the costs, etc. Near the tail-end of the meeting questions were put to ascertain how the individual Commissioners felt on the subject and, while up to this point in the meeting it had been indicated that we were fairly unanimous, I was forced to interrupt to indicate that this was not the truth in any sense, that there had been sharp disagreements among the Commissioners, precisely what those disagreements were and what my position was, namely, that it was folly to go along with the GAC recommendation. Commissioner Strauss then gave his views in more detail. Commissioner Smyth when asked what his views were stated that when he used the expression "at this time" that that was back in November and that his views might be different today. Commissioner Pike said he still did not know what his views were. Mr. Lilienthal, having a White House appointment, had been forced to leave the meeting early and his individual views were not secured.

1. The "Sequence of Events" paper is now a part of the official commission files. There is evidence that it, too, was originally a part of the diary. Therefore, I have included it here.

2. The McCloy statement of 1945 probably refers to a Department of War press statement about the atomic bomb project.

3. I have found no AEC paper which indicated all of the theoretical work done at Los Alamos on the hydrogen bomb.

4. President Truman actually announced the Soviet atomic explosion on September 23, 1949.

5. Lt. General Lauris A. Norstad, vice-chief of staff of the Air Force.

6. Little about the interagency thermonuclear working group appears in the diary.

≡ *January 30, 1950*[1]

Senator McMahon called. He made a press statement: Met and discussed the matter of weapons; took no votes on the question; meeting tomorrow afternoon for further deliberation. Sent to the President certain of his personal views on the bearing that the questions have not only on national security but also on war and peace which all our efforts are designed to promote, etc. There is a note on the ticker that the civil defense problem is coming up next week. The 15th is the date

1. The next day President Truman ordered the commission to develop the hydrogen bomb.

# TWO

## THE IMPACT OF KOREA

*July 11, 1950, to January 12, 1951*

The excerpts in this chapter are drawn from Gordon Dean's first six months as chairman of the Atomic Energy Commission. Dean's diary entries in the five months immediately following the hydrogen bomb decision are brief, disjointed, and illuminate little other than his interest in succeeding Lilienthal. His diary is even surprisingly void of much about the Fuchs case. With the chairmanship, however, Dean became a member of the administration as well as an official of the commission. His diary reflects his new responsibilities and becomes a pivotal document for understanding the actions of the second Truman administration. The major problem confronting Dean and the administration in July 1950 was the emergency of the Korean War, and Dean's diary captures the impact of the war upon the commission.

Gordon Dean's first war-related task was the transfer of nonnuclear components to the United Kingdom, an action not mentioned in the diary. His first major problem of the war cited in the diary was his struggle to prevent the military from canceling the spring Pacific test series, Operation *Greenhouse*. Robert LeBaron, chairman of the Military Liaison Committee, told Dean on July 12 that the Joint Chiefs of Staff wanted to postpone *Greenhouse* in order to free vessels to blockade North Korea. Dean fought for *Greenhouse* because the tests were vital to the thermonuclear program, and he quickly won Deputy Secretary of Defense Stephen Early to his cause. He eventually triumphed, for in mid-September the Joint Chiefs of Staff decided they could spare the resources for the test series.

During the battle for *Greenhouse* Dean decided that the commission should select a continental proving grounds and test atomic bombs within the country. Although a national emergency had not been declared, the war created a crisis that seemed to justify continental testing. In addition a continental test site might enable the commission to conduct part of the *Greenhouse* series should the Department of Defense withdraw support for the Pacific tests. So important was a continental test site that Dean also convinced Steve Early to support continental testing when he won him over to *Greenhouse*.

The outbreak of the war led to calls for greater production of uranium 235 and plutonium from Senator McMahon and Robert LeBaron. With Dean supporting a production increase, Secretary of Defense Louis Johnson took the issue to President Truman on August 7, 1950. After discussing the expansion of production facilities and a continental proving grounds with Secretary Johnson, President Truman ordered the commission and the Department of Defense to study the resources needed to increase production, but postponed a decision on the continental test site. Perhaps because he was in the midst of a crisis within the commission and perhaps because he was unsure of his relations with the chief executive, Dean did not accompany Johnson to the White House and his diary is silent about the president's decision.

Dean was preoccupied with the resignation of General Manager Carroll L. Wilson. Wilson differed with Dean about how to manage commission programs and was uneasy about Dean's ties with McMahon. Dean's support of a bill to make the general manager a commission, rather than a presidential, appointee undermined his standing with Wilson even further. Finally, concluding he lacked confidence in Dean and his ideas, Wilson handed in his resignation.

Wilson explained his reasons for resigning to President Truman privately but later fired a public blast at Dean. His lack of confidence in Dean made front-page news but, as the diary shows, Dean garnered support from the administration and commission staff. Senator McMahon needed just a half hour to get all eighteen Joint Committee members to sign a statement of confidence in Dean, who met the crisis with the masterful talk to the commission staff which he included in the diary. Dean criticized Lilienthal and Wilson indirectly for their management of commission activities without descending to ad hominem arguments and without offending the staff built by Lilienthal and Wilson. He expressed his confidence in the commission staff while making it clear that a new philosophy would guide commission activities.

Wilson posed a serious threat to Dean, for the perception that he was McMahon's tool could have seriously reduced Dean's effectiveness as chairman. Not only would it have undermined the morale of the commission staff but it also might have kept Dean from building an effective relationship with President Truman. It may have been the Wilson crisis that persuaded Dean to let the Secretary of Defense take two key atomic energy issues—the production increase and the continental test site—to the president. Ordinarily the chairman of the commission would have been present when issues of such importance to his agency were discussed with the president. It is interesting to note that Dean did not meet with the president between July 11 and October 25, 1950. Those months were hectic for both the chairman and the chief executive, but few intervals of such length passed during the Korean War without a meeting between Dean and the president.

Dean picked Marion W. Boyer, a vice-president of Esso Standard Oil and a chemical engineer, to replace Wilson. In one of his few attacks on the commission, Senator Joseph McCarthy had recently accused the commission of ignoring the alleged Communist sympathies of some American scientists. Because of the McCarthy attack Dean had to investigate Boyer carefully before he brought him on board. His choice was a wise one; Boyer blended well into Dean's collegial style of management. Leaving policy decisions to the commission, Boyer concentrated on building an efficient staff. For the next three years they worked together closely in managing the commission's business.

The diary picks up the issue of increasing uranium 235 and plutonium production on September 18, 1950, as the joint working group created by the commission and the Department of Defense completed its deliberations on how best to expand production. Anticipating presidential approval of greater production, the commission had already stepped up the production of uranium 235. On October 2, 1950, the commission and the Department of Defense decided on a production increase that would require a new gaseous diffusion plant complex (later erected at Paducah, Kentucky) and three more reactors for the Savannah River plant. Once these new plants were in operation the commission would consume all the uranium ore the free world could produce. Ore supplies—not military need, potential weapon uses, or cost—limited the number of plants the commission could build.

The costs of the new plants were huge. Total capital expenditures came to $1.4 billion, equaling the cost of all facilities erected by the Manhattan Engineer District during World War II. Of the sum, $465 million went for the diffusion plants, $130 million for an electric power plant, $365 million for the reactors, and $440 million for ancillary facilities. Despite the price tag President Truman approved the facilities on October 9. The global contest with the Soviet Union and the war in Korea had now doubled the World War II capital investment in atomic energy facilities.

After the expansion decision Dean led his fellow commissioners to the White House to report on commission activities. President Truman indicated his approval of Dean's leadership during the meeting. Thereafter, Dean's relations with the president were marked by mutual confidence and trust. Dean's diary is one of the best sources for tracing the relationship between the chairman and the chief executive.

Meanwhile, in Korea General MacArthur had conducted the famous In-chon landings, had all but destroyed the North Korean army, and had advanced into North Korea. MacArthur's advance, however, increased the possibility that the Chinese Communists might enter the war to aid North Korea. Perhaps with the Chinese in mind, President Truman now told Dean and his associates that the commission should select a site within the United States for testing atomic bombs. The president was now willing to take a step he had rejected in August—continental atomic testing. Dean's diary contains the only account of this key White House meeting.

The administration's concern about Red China was well founded. On October 25, the same day the president told the commission to find a continental test site, Chinese forces clashed with a South Korean unit. As reports of the fight came in, National Security Council executive secretary James Lay, Souers's successor, urged Dean to move quickly. Lay wanted decision papers prepared for the council, and he put continental testing on the council's agenda. As the diary shows, the president was disposed to favor continental testing before the National Security Council formally considered the issue.

In the midst of preparing for continental testing, Gordon Dean learned that two Puerto Rican extremists, Griselio Tarresola and Oscar Callazo, had tried to assassinate President Truman. White House guards had foiled the attempt but not until after a brief gun battle on Pennsylvania Avenue. Dean's reaction, upon learning of the attempt, was to break open the arsenal and double the guard. Dean feared that other gunmen who might have targets on the commission were involved. The diary is perhaps no more revealing of the tension that gripped Dean and Washington than in the entries that concern this brief episode.

The Chinese finally struck in force in Korea in late November and President Truman, in a well-known press conference, implied that the United States might use the atomic bomb in Korea and left the impression that a decision to use the bomb was General MacArthur's alone. Dean's diary unfortunately is silent about both statements. If Dean corrected the White House and reminded presidential aides that under the Atomic Energy Act only the president could authorize the use of the atomic bomb, the action is not captured in his diary or in commission files. The diary does confirm, though, that the administration was quietly devising procedures for using the bomb in combat when the president made the statement. What discussions Dean and his associates may have held about either the Chinese attack or the president's remark were not conducted over Dean's telephone.

President Truman did respond to the Chinese intervention by declaring a national emergency. Save for being asked to speak to Senator McMahon about the declaration, Gordon Dean had little to do directly in preparing for it. Indirectly he had a larger role—preparing atomic energy for war. As

General Manager Boyer observed in a phone conversation on December 14, 1950, the declaration would have little effect on the commission.

Although a national emergency had been declared, Dean had not yet obtained approval for continental testing. The commission had recently recommended that the National Security Council approve the selection of the Las Vegas Bombing and Gunnery Range as a continental proving ground. Los Alamos scientists were designing missile warheads, atomic land mines, and atomic howitzer shells for tactical as well as strategic uses and had to test frequently to pursue new design ideas. At the same time the Korean War made the Pacific proving grounds far less secure and far more expensive in terms of military personnel and equipment. The commission needed a site whose accessibility could not be threatened by enemy action. Dean and his fellow commissioners knew radiological safety was most crucial in site selection but doubted that very small explosions posed much of a fallout hazard. Besides, they planned to weigh specific radiological safety problems carefully before each test shot. The National Security Council agreed with the commission and on December 18, 1950, President Truman approved the selection of the Las Vegas site.

Almost immediately the commission put the test site to use. The first continental test series, called Operation *Ranger*, was conducted at the Las Vegas site in January and February 1951. Preparing for *Ranger*, however, was not without its problems as the diary shows. First, Secretary of Defense George C. Marshall, who had replaced Johnson in September, feared that revealing the United States had small atomic bombs would complicate an already tense international situation. He asked the commission not to disclose that the explosions would be relatively small. Dean knew that the commission had to reveal the relative size of test shots in order not to create undue public alarm and won the issue when President Truman overruled Marshall.

Next the Joint Chiefs of Staff asked the commission to drop the fifth and final shot. The fifth shot promised to produce a relatively larger explosion than the first four shots and the chiefs opposed it because they had assured the president that no large shots would be fired. Dean retorted that the test was essential and could be conducted safely. He took his battle to the president and the National Security Council and won this one as well.

The National Security Council approved *Ranger* on January 11, 1951. Reflecting the emergency of the Korean War, Dean told the council that the basic reason for *Ranger* was to accelerate the pace of the commission weapons programs. Dean and the council were aware of the radiological hazards the tests posed but judged the war as a far greater threat to the nation. With the green light for *Ranger* Dean quickly set out to inform the Nevada congressional delegation and local politicians—actions richly documented in the diary. Dean had now fully prepared the commission for war.

For the Wilson resignation, see also Lilienthal, *Venturesome Years*, pp. 27–28, 31–32; *New York Times*, August 9, 1950; and *Washington Evening Star*, August 10, 11, 1950. For the attempt to assassinate Truman, see also Donovan, *Tumultuous Years*, pp. 291–94; and *New York Times*, November 2, 1950. For weapons advances, the need for a continental test site, and reasons for *Ranger*, see also Minutes, 23rd General Advisory Committee Meeting, October 30–November 1, 1950, AEC; and Gordon Dean, Background Statement for *Ranger*, January 9, 1951, AEC.

ORDER[1]

I hereby designate Gordon Dean as Chairman of the Atomic Energy Commission.

/s/ Harry S. Truman

≡ THE WHITE HOUSE
July 11, 1950

1. The order is part of official Atomic Energy Commission files. It is not included in the diary. A one-sentence order was the usual manner in which the president designated one of the commissioners as chairman.

≡ *July 11, 1950*

GD's name announced as Chairman of the AEC today.

≡ *July 12, 1950*

LeBaron called. There has been a recommendation that we postpone Greenhouse. Thinks the question should go to Sec. Johnson as soon as possible. Thinks it would be a practical thing to have a joint AEC-MLC meeting this afternoon. GD doesn't see any situation that will run us into an impasse now. Quesada[1] could go over to the White House with GD and discuss it with the President. GD thinks the test *must go now*—at this point we should not say we will cancel it. LeBaron has wire from CINPAC[2] saying that the military is about to push him down. LeBaron would like to have just a discussion with AEC this afternoon—not a decision right now.

1. General Elwood R. Quesada, commander of Joint Task Force 3, the Department of Defense–Atomic Energy Commission organization created to conduct the *Greenhouse* tests.
2. Commander-in-Chief, Pacific Fleet.

## ≡ *July 21, 1950*

LeBaron called about status on JTF-3 test. Wrote memo to Secretary of Defense. Got over to White House. Talked to President. He favored going ahead but thought perhaps we should not reach a final decision [at] the moment. Talked with Quesada later. We may have to make some shifts pretty fast. GD asked if the memo mentioned by Hill[1] on "slow withdrawal" is being prepared. LeBaron doesn't know how far along they are on it. McMahon going to see Secretary of Defense and JCS on Friday. Trying to postpone it. Would like to be able to tell them a little bit about variable consideration of what an expanded program will cost in materials, men and critical facilities, etc.

1. Rear Admiral Tom B. Hill, a member of the Military Liaison Committee.

## ≡ *July 27, 1950*

LeBaron called to talk about JTF-3 test. Discussed letter to President. GD thinks test is essential and we should plug that one. If the place where we are now thinking of should prove impossible, wonders about a continental site.[1] GD thinks we should mention that. We need make no decision right this moment. LeBaron says a mention of a domestic site at this time would get everyone at the Pentagon upset. LeBaron thinks it would be alright. GD suggested we say something like: From our present indications the sites mentioned would seem feasible. However, we would want to make a very careful survey of this and could do so in the immediate future. We suggest that it be done in any event. GD will discuss this with General McCormack. LeBaron said anything GD wants to do is o.k. with the Secretary of Defense.

1. As recently as March 1949 the commission had decided that a continental test site would only be needed in the event of a national emergency.

*Table 2. Key Officials in Gordon Dean's Washington*

| Official | Position | Dates | Relations with Dean |
|---|---|---|---|
| Harry S. Truman | President | *to January 20, 1953 | Dean's boss. He left most atomic policy matters to Dean. |
| Matthew J. Connelly | Secretary to the President | *to January 20, 1953 | Dean scheduled meetings with the president through Connelly. |
| Charles G. Ross | Secretary to the President (Press) | *to December 5, 1950[†] | Dean worked with the press secretaries on those rare occasions when atomic energy was the subject of a public controversy. |
| Joseph Short | Secretary to the President (Press) | December 6, 1950, to September 18, 1952[†] | |
| Roger W. Tubby | Secretary to the President (Press) | September 19, 1952, to January 20, 1953 | |
| Donald S. Dawson | Administrative Assistant to the President | *to January 20, 1953 | Dean worked with Dawson in filling positions in the commission which were allotted to political appointees. Usually these positions were on the commission itself. |
| James S. Lay | Executive Director, National Security Council | *to January 1961 | Virtually all policy issues concerning atomic energy went to the president through Lay. |

*Table 2. Key Officials in Gordon Dean's Washington (cont.)*

| Official | Position | Dates | Relations with Dean |
|---|---|---|---|
| Dean G. Acheson | Secretary of State | *to January 20, 1953 | Dean rarely dealt directly with Acheson. Usually he went through Arneson, who was Acheson's assistant for atomic energy matters. |
| R. Gordon Arneson | Special Assistant | *to April, 1954 | |
| Louis A. Johnson | Secretary of Defense | *to September 19, 1950 | Dean occasionally worked directly with the secretaries and deputy secretaries of defense. Usually Dean worked with them through LeBaron. |
| George C. Marshall | Secretary of Defense | September 21, 1950, to September 12, 1951 | |
| Robert A. Lovett | Secretary of Defense | September 17, 1951, to January 20, 1953 | |
| Stephen T. Early | Deputy Secretary of Defense | *to September 30, 1950 | |
| Robert A. Lovett | Deputy Secretary of Defense | October 4, 1950, to September 16, 1951 | |
| William C. Foster | Deputy Secretary of Defense | September 24, 1951, to January 20, 1953 | |
| Robert F. LeBaron | Chairman, Military Liaison Committee | *to August 1, 1954 | LeBaron handled atomic energy matters which involved the Joint Chiefs of Staff and any other Department of Defense officials. |
| Omar N. Bradley | Chairman, Joint Chiefs of Staff | *to August 14, 1953 | |

*Table 2. Key Officials in Gordon Dean's Washington (cont.)*

| Official | Position | Dates | Relations with Dean |
|---|---|---|---|
| J. Lawton Collins | Chief of Staff U.S. Army | *to August 14, 1953 | |
| Forrest P. Sherman | Chief of Naval Operations | *to July 22, 1951† | |
| William M. Fechteler | Chief of Naval Operations | August 16, 1951, to August 17, 1953 | |
| Hoyt S. Vandenberg | Chief of Staff U.S. Air Force | *to June 30, 1953 | |
| Karl R. Bendetsen | Assistant Secretary of the Army (General Management) | *to May 6, 1952 | Dean worked closely with Bendetsen on the tactical weapons issue. |
| Elwood R. Quesada | Commander, Joint Task Force 3 (*Greenhouse* weapons test series) | *to August 1951 | |
| Percy W. Clarkson | Commander, Joint Task Force 132 (*Ivy* weapons test series) | July 9, 1951, to July, 1954 | |
| Brien McMahon | Chairman, Joint Committee on Atomic Energy | *to July 28, 1952† | Dean's chief political ally. Dean usually dealt directly with McMahon on matters involving the Joint Committee. |
| William L. Borden | Executive Director, Joint Committee on Atomic Energy | *to May 1953 | |

* In position when Dean became chairman.
† Date of death.

## ≡ *July 28, 1950*

Borden called. McMahon is considering making a speech on the floor of the Senate advocating a fundamental increase in the scope and scale of the atomic energy program. Wanted GD to know about it so that he might want to give a thought or so to it. Before any such speech they will get together. The Senator is in Connecticut until Tuesday morning. . . .

GD talked to Shugg about always being on the defensive in appearing before the JCC and the appropriations committees. GD wondered if we couldn't capture the ball once in a while and give them some dope on what we have been doing in our shop. During the last few weeks we have done a lot of things that we might tell them about instead of waiting until they call us up there and ask a lot of questions. GD thinks it would be a good idea if we could start our next meeting with the JCC with a report of our work. Shugg thinks we need a promotion department. All of our relations cannot be through lawyers. He thinks the idea might pay off—particularly if the heat is being put on us. If we can't produce a list of "plus items" every few months then we really should start to worry.

GD called Steve Early and said he thought it would be useful if they could get together and talk about some of the headaches of joint problems regarding the test. GD has a suggested approach that he would like to talk about before he presents it to Johnson. GD made appointment to see Early Monday morning at 9:30.

## ≡ *July 31, 1950*

GD called Shugg to tell him he had had a very profitable talk with Steve Early this morning. He understands we need the test now and agrees that the survey should be made soon for additional sites. Will send letter to Johnson on the test question. GD will let Shugg see it before it goes over.

## ≡ *August 4, 1950*

Carroll Wilson submitted his resignation today to the Commission— because he has no confidence in GD.

GD talked to Don Dawson about Wilson's resignation. Dawson going to speak to the President about it.

GD talked to Senator McMahon about Wilson's resignation. Senator wondered if the resignation letter will be handed out. He doesn't see how it can be stopped. The Senator thinks perhaps Pike should get to work and try to quiet him.

Carroll Wilson called to say that the President had accepted his resignation and is preparing a reply and will release both letters together.

## ≡ *August 7, 1950*

McMahon called. He has been giving some thought to this Wilson resignation. Thinks perhaps the Commission should call a meeting and call him in and ask for a bill of particulars—and have a verbatim record made. Thinks GD should announce Shugg's appointment as General Manager or Acting General Manager, whichever it is to be. Is afraid there is going to be a leak—planted or otherwise—so it should be done this afternoon. Thinks Wilson should be called in immediately and put on record. The Senator wants to find out if he thinks GD and the Senator are working a political deal. GD has a Commission meeting scheduled for 11:30. Will read the Senator the proposed release. Neither Pike nor any one else has been able to get to first base with Wilson. He said nothing very satisfactory to anyone. He doesn't like the fact that GD and the Senator were law partners but he can't put his finger on anything specific. GD will give some thought to the idea and will present it to the other Commissioners.

GD talked to Charles Ross[1] who had talked with McMahon. McMahon suggested that at the time the resignation of Wilson is made public the announcement should be made of Shugg's appointment. Ross said the President just signed the acceptance of Wilson's resignation. He will make it public in a little while.

1. President Truman's press secretary until his death from a heart attack on December 5, 1950.

Trapnell[1] came down and worked out a statement to be issued by AEC this afternoon in connection with Wilson's resignation.

1. Edward R. Trapnell, associate director of the Division of Public and Technical Information.

Volpe called from Rehobeth Beach. Just heard the news. Thinks it is the most fantastic thing he has ever heard of. Offers to do anything he can for

GD but GD tells him there is nothing to do. GD is not going to say anything beyond the prepared official statement being put out by the AEC.

Frank Carey, AP, called about statement from Wilson as to his reasons for resigning. GD has no comment. GD doesn't think the program can stand much more controversy and GD doesn't want to be a party to any.

Dr. Smyth called. Wilson has released a statement substantially the same as his memorandum to the Commissioners. Smyth thinks it is most unfortunate but there is nothing to do now but sit tight.

GD prepared his "Remarks to the Washington Staff"

LeBaron is coming over. Would like to talk to GD about the events of the day.

Senator McMahon called to say that he has 18 signatures on his one-line statement: "Senator McMahon announced today that the Joint Congressional Committee on Atomic Energy had expressed its confidence in Gordon Dean, Chairman of the Atomic Energy Commission." The vote was unanimous—each member of the House and each member of the Senate.

≡ [The diary is silent about Wilson on Tuesday, August 8.]

≡ *August 9, 1950*

McMahon called about articles in this morning's N.Y. Times and N.Y. Herald-Tribune.[1] The Times article very long and over on the inside page it has one line about the JCC and then it mentions that GD and the Senator used to be law partners. The Senator thinks the whole thing will be a "one day story"—with the possible exceptions of people such as the Alsops.[2]

1. Both newspapers had printed articles about Wilson's resignation.
2. Columnists Joseph and Stewart Alsop.

Senator Hickenlooper called about Wilson controversy. Thinks the result is a fine thing. Wanted GD to know he has his backing.

Vice President Barkley called about Wilson controversy. Told GD not to worry.

GD talked to Ben McKelway, Editor of the Evening Star, about Wilson resignation. GD doesn't want to make any statement. McKelway asked GD if he would mind giving him a little guidance on the thing. GD explained about the closeness between Wilson and Lilienthal and that Wilson did most of the work when Lilienthal was here. GD feels that the Commissioners have a heavier responsibility than to just delegate the running of the program to a General Manager. Thinks five heads are important. There has been no intention on GD's part to break down the line between the Commission and Management—that would be a mistake—but there is going to be an effort made to see that the Commissioners know the problems of the Commission. Thinks Wilson has been unhappy generally and doesn't know just what it is about and GD has become the symbol. Each Commissioner has talked with Wilson and could get nothing concrete from him. GD doesn't think we have sold our program to the JCC or anything like that. As a matter of fact, we must sell it to him. We need understanding of our program. The JCC today knows much more about our program than they ever knew before. The same is true of the Military Establishment. GD suggested that the AEC program has suffered from too much controversy already. From the beginning has been bedeviled by it. GD thinks the Commissioners get along very nicely together and the staff works very well with the Commission. McKelway asked about Wilson being away for the past month. GD said this is true. He hasn't been here since GD has been Chairman.

Dr. Pitzer[1] called from Berkeley to ask GD if there was anything he could do in connection with Wilson's resignation. GD promised to send him a copy of his "Remarks to the Washington Staff." Dr. Lawrence[2] was amazed but not too excited about the affair. Doesn't see how it can help Wilson much.

1. Dr. Kenneth S. Pitzer, director of the Division of Research.
2. Dr. Ernest O. Lawrence, director of the Radiation Laboratory at the University of California's Berkeley campus.

Tris Coffin called about Wilson resignation.

Doris Fleeson[1] called about Wilson resignation. GD sent her a copy of Remarks to Washington Staff.[2]

1. A reporter for the *Washington Evening-Star*.
2. As a result of Dean's chats with McKelway and Fleeson, the *Evening-Star* wrote an editorial in Dean's favor.

*August 11, 1950*

ATOMIC ENERGY COMMISSION
*Memorandum for Information*

TRANSCRIPT OF REMARKS OF CHAIRMAN GORDON DEAN TO
COMMISSION AND WASHINGTON STAFF OF THE AEC,
AUGUST 9, 1950[1]

*Note by the Secretary*
The attached is for the information of
Atomic Energy Commission personnel at all operations offices.
ROY B. SNAPP
Secretary

TRANSCRIPT OF REMARKS OF CHAIRMAN GORDON DEAN
TO COMMISSION AND WASHINGTON STAFF OF
AEC AUGUST 9, 1950

Ever since I was named to the Chairmanship of the Commission I have wanted to get all of the staff together, along with the Commissioners, and talk with you. The resignation yesterday of Carroll Wilson, our General Manager, suggests that this is the time.

There have been no clashes between Carroll Wilson and myself. As a matter of fact, he hasn't been here since I have been Chairman. His going is not my idea—it is entirely his own—and I had no control over his resignation. Nor was the President permitted any alternative but to accept it. I like frankness and Carroll has been frank. I think it is unfortunate for the program that he chose this *manner* of leaving; but only time can tell whether I am right or wrong about this. I am most anxious to minimize any harm that may be done.

I do want to say that the statement which I prepared yesterday, and in which the other Commissioners joined, is a sincere statement.[2] I doubt if there is any person who has been associated with the atomic energy program who has given more time and energy and intelligence to the task. This I have said and this I believe. I have seen fit not to say more than this directly or indirectly to the press for the reason that I think that if this be a controversy, I do not think the program can stand to have it prolonged. I think any further comment on Mr. Wilson's resignation on my part would prolong it.

Now I would like to take up some other matters. I have had a conviction ever since joining the Commission fourteen months ago that if we have suffered from any one thing it has been controversy. We have been bedeviled by it from the outset. I am not suggesting that this is anyone's fault, but I do think it is an unfortunate situation—and to be avoided whenever possible. Controversy is good at times, particularly when there is a real issue to fight over. Too much of it is obviously bad. Sometimes I think we have encouraged it by insisting we are always right. This irritates people. I think that we have been too reluctant to admit that we are only human beings; that we have occasionally made mistakes—measured at least by the hindsight of Monday-morning quarterbacks. I think also that perhaps we have carried too many chips on our shoulders. On this I may be quite wrong, but I do believe there is such a thing as becoming punchdrunk from minor league fights only to lose out in championship battles.

What does this mean? Does it mean that we should become subservient to our critics? Of course not. Does it mean that we should succumb to every pressure, whether it is Congressional pressure or from labor unions, or universities, or industry? Of course not. It means simply that this is an hour in the life of the Commission when we will have to do some selling—not by asserting our perfection, but by demonstrating our skill and our sincerity. There is a big educational job to do with many groups, including the Congress, the military, scientists, industrial concerns, labor and the public.

Dr. Smyth once told me—and I hope he won't mind my repeating it—that what the Atomic Energy Commission needs is love—needs it from the outside and needs it internally. He meant "understanding." If we are not understood we will always be suspected. And it will be one of my policies to make this program of ours understood in all quarters. We need supporters, not opponents.

The five-man Commission and the General Manager, together with the Operations Offices, is a rather anomalous setup in government. It has been difficult, and it is going to be difficult, to make it work perfectly. Nevertheless, at this time I think there is much to be said for it. I think it is important on the Commission level that it not be a one-man show. I do not think one man is big enough to run this program. I think in determining policy matters it is well that we have five people from different walks of life, with different experiences, who can, in the give and take of frank discussion, formulate policy. I think this is healthy. It may be time-consuming—but it is worth the time. I think, furthermore, that the Commissioners have been working as a pretty smooth team. We have tried to pool our brains and not simply count our votes. I have come to know each of the Commissioners well. I have a deep respect for each one of them. If I didn't have, I would have said "no" to serving as the Chairman.

Now when it comes to preserving the line between the Commission and the General Manager further difficulties are presented. As you all know, this is not an easy tightrope to walk. We attempt to do it, and we will continue our efforts to see that we do not become enmeshed in the problems of management. However, if we do, let us have it out across the table and resolve the difficulties. I do not think there is any room for personal feelings or peeve if we should occasionally cross the line, and there should be no feeling of peeve if the General Manager crosses the line—wavy and uncertain as that line must sometimes be. When people understand each other these things can be worked out. So far as I am aware Carl Shugg and I have had no difficulties in this respect during the month that I have served as Chairman.

We, as Commissioners, can't know all the details of this program, and we should not attempt to know all the details, but I will say this: I think the Commissioners should know as much as they humanly can about this program, and if they don't I think they are derelict in their duties. This does not mean that you are going to have management by Commissioners. This, admittedly, would be quite unfortunate. But it does mean that the Commissioners should know enough about the program so that when the larger policy questions do come before them they will have the requisite knowledge to understand the effect of the policies they work out.

One difficult thing about our organizational setup is the fact that so many critics and advisers have been provided for. We have the Military Liaison Committee, the Joint Congressional Committee, the Appropriations Committees, the General Advisory Committee, etc. But I think this is the nature of the beast. I think the people of the country would not like it otherwise; although it is difficult for us. We expend a huge sum of money. So much is dependent upon how we decide the important issues that come up in our program that I think we must always have these organized appraisers of our deeds. But this is not altogether bad. If these Committees understand our program and our problems, they can be most helpful. Most of them really want to be just that. It is only when they speak without understanding that they are dangerous. So again it comes back to the question of building understanding.

I have said it before, and I will say it now, and I mean it—that I think that we have an unusual staff in the Atomic Energy Commission. To know the men who do the work is to respect them and to have confidence in them—and I have that. I do not think there is a team—not certainly in any government department that I am familiar with, and so far as I know in no private industrial concern—that works on more varied problems with more intelligence and devotion.

With the state of the world such as it is, those of us who have looked forward to a long period of peace and the development of peacetime uses have naturally had our hopes rather dimmed by events over which we have no control. World conditions are compelling. Whether the weapon is ever used or not, our weapons program becomes one of the strongest influences, perhaps the strongest, for discouraging war and thereby maintaining peace or winning a war. Let's not apologize for being strong.

Another great responsibility that we have is in keeping a sensible balance between the weapons program on the one hand and the long-range program which, if neglected, we may pay for dearly. The one thing which stands out about Americans is that we have never been ready for war when war came in peacetime, and we have never been ready in wartime for the peace that inevitably followed. I hope that the Atomic Energy Commission program will always be kept in such a healthy state of readiness that we will be ready for any eventuality, whether it calls for the peacetime or wartime applications.

And in this connection the potential strength of science rests in a large part upon the Commission. Our intelligent utilization of scientific talent raises many questions which can affect the whole scientific progress of the country. We have an obligation to plan in broad long-range terms not only in the field of scientific research, but in other fields as well. What we initiate today in the way of new plant facilities, for example, may bear no results for two or three years. That is one reason why our program must not be constantly juggled by the crisis of the moment. We must be ahead of the crises and prepared for them when they come. This program is more important and much bigger certainly by far than any of us as individuals. I am confident that none of you will ever regret that you came with it and that you made your contribution to it. And I hope you stay with it. We are engaged in one of the most exciting and one of the most challenging programs ever established. We must continue our work in good spirits convinced that our program is going to roll right along. I am confident that we will always be proud of our participation in it. And if we have this attitude we simply cannot lose.

1. Dean's "Remarks" were printed in the format of an Atomic Energy Commission staff paper. He put them in the diary after the August 9 entries.

2. The commission had issued a statement on August 8 announcing Wilson's resignation and praising him for his contributions to atomic energy programs.

## ≡ September 18, 1950

LeBaron called to say that the production study had been signed and sealed. The three secretaries signed it and Howard of Munitions Board recommended going ahead. Joint letter Johnson has already signed which gets it going forward and is a transmittal. Will read new chief (Marshall)[1] into the background. LeBaron sending Johnson letter over this morning.

1. General George C. Marshall, the World War II chief of staff of the Army and Truman's secretary of state from 1947 to 1949. He came out of retirement to serve as secretary of defense from September 21, 1950, until September 12, 1951.

Called Peterson,[1] in Production, to say that Dr. Smyth feels that we can compress some of the tabs into the text of the production report. It would mean another doing. Peterson will try it. Might have an overlay of figures, etc., to take care of any leaks. The production figures and stockpile figures should definitely be left blank to be filled in later. GD wants to get something over to the White House very soon. Can't get Acheson until after Wednesday but should be ready to go in a couple of days. GD thinks the Defense Establishment will take our formulation of the report; it won't have to be checked with them.

1. Arthur V. Peterson, chief of the fissionable materials branch in the Division of Production.

## ≡ September 21, 1950

Lay called to say he had received report. Wants to check on a couple of points. Arneson[1] is going to get together with the other State Dept. people and give Lay a call on it tomorrow afternoon. At that time we will try to sit down and draft a report to the special committee (Sec. of State, Sec. of Defense and Chairman, AEC) that is to go to the President. Unless Acheson or Marshall have some different slant on it, it should be a pretty easy job. GD personally quite satisfied with it and the other Commissioners too. Lay thinks we should be able to get up a draft and send it around without a formal meeting of the group. GD is interested in getting it started as quickly as possible because we have to go to Budget with it and then present it to the President. GD thinks that Peterson, Production, might represent the AEC. From the ME they would probably want Nichols[2] and Arneson from State.

1. R. Gordon Arneson, Dean Acheson's adviser for atomic energy matters.
2. General Kenneth D. Nichols, chief of the Armed Forces Special Weapons Project and a member of the Military Liaison Committee.

## ≡ September 25, 1950

LeBaron called. . . . On Wednesday we might get a formal agreement on the letter[1] that AEC Chairman and Secretaries of Defense and State will sign. GD has the language and will discuss it with the other Commissioners before Wednesday meeting (AEC-MLC meeting). LeBaron will get together with General Loper[2] to make sure that the letter is in form. GD would like to see it before the meeting—even in rough draft. Loper will call GD the first thing tomorrow. . . .

1. The letter was a formal report to the president recommending the expansion of Commission production facilities. Dean, Marshall, and Acheson signed the letter which then entered formal National Security Council channels for approval.

2. Brigadier General Herbert B. Loper, a member of the Military Liaison Committee.

## ≡ September 28, 1950

GD talked to Lay about NSC 68:[1] GD asked if the following states Lay's feeling: "and is in constance with NSC 68 and not additional to the programs presented in NSC 68/1." It is really a part of NSC 68. This should not be considered as an isolated program on its own. It is part of the overall program. Lay is trying to get away from singling this one out for a separate approach to it—it is really not a separate approach. It is really carrying out the general line as proposed in NSC 68. Lay thinks the wording is o.k. with the footnote about the cost estimates left in to explain that question.

1. NSC 68, the Truman administration's plan for rearming the United States.

## ≡ October 9, 1950

Williams[1] called to say that the President had approved our program. Asked if GD wanted a press release on it. Or if GD thought he should contact the President's Office to see what he wants to do about it? GD thinks we should wait a few days to announce it. The story may be simply that the AEC will ask the Congress for money to do certain "things." GD will check with the White House about it.[2]

1. Walter J. Williams, director of the Division of Production. On February 1, 1951, he succeeded Shugg as deputy general manager.

2. President Truman decided not to announce the expansion of production facilities until December 18, 1950.

## ≡ October 11, 1950

General McCormack called about meeting with the President that GD had mentioned. The President is going to see MacArthur. McCormack wanted to know if GD's appointment with him would be pre- or post-MacArthur.[1]

1. The meeting with MacArthur was the famous Wake Island conference.

Matt Connelly[1] called. The President would like to have the Commission come over at 3:00 P.M. on October 25th.

1. Matthew J. Connelly, secretary to President Truman.

James Lay called to report back on 25th meeting. The President agreed that he would like a letter sent out on the publicity—not setting any date for publicity, nor giving any figures until he determines that it is the time in connection with the overall "68" picture—expanded production picture.

## ≡ October 25, 1950

Whole commission went over to see the President today—at the President's request—to report on the status of the program.

Admiral Tom Hill called GD to tell him he had heard that GD did a very fine job this afternoon at his meeting with the President on the question of tests. GD said he thought he had helped the other one along too—(the Alaskan one).[1] GD told the President that while we had not made a survey we thought it would be a very good idea. The President agreed with him on it.

1. The commission was planning to fire an underground shot in Alaska. The plans were shelved a few weeks later and the shot was never fired.

Salisbury[1] called about Boyer's swearing-in. GD thought it would be a good idea to get some Judge to come down and give him the oath. Talked about idea of Boyer having some sort of small press conference. Decided against it. Salisbury said question of Boyer's salary will probably come up. GD said it is perfectly ok to announce what it is. GD also mentioned to Salisbury that he had had a very successful meeting with the President today. Salisbury asked if the matter of the ban on the new program had come up.[2] GD said that was the one thing he forgot to mention to the President. GD said he was met by some members of the press when he left the White House. GD told them they were simply talking about the AEC program in general. Almost slipped and told him about the new General Manger.

1. Morse Salisbury, director of the Division of Public and Technical Information.
2. The ban Salisbury mentioned was probably the president's decision to delay public announcement of the expansion program approved on October 9.

≡ *October 26, 1950*

Boyer called to say he had talked with Salisbury and they had come to the conclusion that he really didn't have very much to say to the press at this point. So, decided not to have press conference after swearing-in. GD said he saw Judge Schweinhaut last night and mentioned the swearing-in to him. He would be glad to do it. Thought we might invite just Commissioners and top staff members. GD told him about wonderful visit with the President and told him the President is very interested in our whole program.

Ed Darby (Time Magazine) called. Said they were scheduling story on Boyer appointment. Would like to have some significance to the appointment. GD told him it represented a very intensive search of top men in American industry. We feel very fortunate to be able to get him—he is a very high-priced individual. GD said Boyer's background is unusual—he has been involved in manufacturing, production, development and research in the earlier stages at Shreveport. GD would say he has made a reputation of getting along with staff—getting the most out of people without their being aware of it. Darby asked if AEC planned to keep Shugg. GD said "yes" and added that as a matter of fact there is no one on the staff that he would like to fire. Darby asked if Shugg were more valuable as an assistant than in the top post. GD said it is hard to say—Shugg performed extremely well—has done an awful lot of work during the last 2½ months that he has been Acting General Manager. Darby asked if we were gearing up for the expanded program. GD said "yes." GD said in a period like this one of our biggest jobs is the production job—whether we use the materials for weapons or not. GD mentioned the gaseous diffusion and piles at Hanford and the feed materials processing plants from the time they leave the ground until they get to Hanford or Oak Ridge. It is an industrial operation. GD cautioned that he should not relate the program to the H-bomb project alone. GD said in Boyer we found the exact man we are looking for. It took a great deal of work to persuade him to leave his job with ESSO. GD thinks they have done a patriotic service to give him up and he has done one to give up the salary and take over the "heat" you get in these jobs (not to mention articles in Time Magazine). Darby asked if there was any arrangement made with ESSO to keep his pension going. GD not sure of the details. GD thinks he maintains some of the benefits. There is no side salary. He is not allowed that. He has terminated his connection with the Company. You can have a termination bonus but you have to leave. Can't have any one in the AEC program that might have divided loyalty. The law requires that in the case of the Commissioners but that does not apply to the General Manager. It is just an ethical question as far as the General Manager is concerned.[1]

1. The diary contains other entries about the Boyer appointment that have not been reproduced.

## ≡ *November 1, 1950*

Attempted assassination of the President today. As soon as we got the ticker GD called LaPlante. Figured it was a rather concerted effort since three men were involved (later decided only two involved). Think one of the three got away and might have others on his list. LaPlante will break open the arsenal and double the guards around the building.

GD called Captain Waters[1] and read ticker to him. He had not heard of it yet.

1. Captain John A. Waters, director of the Division of Security.

LeBaron called. Just got back from Arlington—didn't know what had happened until little while ago. GD gave him the names of the two men involved in the attempt. No motive has been definitely established yet—but attempted assassination is pretty obvious. LeBaron said at Arlington no one knew anything about it. Thought perhaps something was up, however, because the place was crawling with Secret Service men. A newspaper man came up while he was at Arlington and told him about it.

James Lay (NSC) called and stated that he understood the question regarding testing ground came up when GD and the other Commissioners had conference with the President. GD stated that while there Matt Connelly brought in a note to the President and that the President stated it was about the tests. GD told the President that AEC thought well of the idea and that it was a necessity to have these more frequently and that he would like to bring up the matter some other time and discuss it. The President said that he could see that the situation was quite different now than it was in the past. Lay stated that he would like to look into the question. GD said a paper was being prepared now. Lay said he would like to follow it up and get it on the agenda, pointing out energy releases, etc. GD said that if Lay has not seen the chart that he might be interested in it. Lay stated that he had not seen it and GD said he would be glad to bring it over and let him see it. . . .

GD called Colonel Coiner[1] to ascertain the progress being made on testing site. GD said Lay had called and stated that he understood the subject came up during the conference the Commission had with the President on October 25th. Coiner said the test activities group was shaping up a paper on site selection on Continent and that he would check into its progress. GD said that probably since it has come up that we should decide how far to go before taking it up with working group committee. Lay agrees that we should go ahead and get it to the working group committee. GD said that the working group may be different but that no doubt Arneson from State would represent AEC. GD is going to talk to LeBaron about it. Coiner will check with Col. Schlatter[2] and see what the progress is on paper and report back to GD.[3]

1. Colonel Richard T. Coiner, deputy director of the Division of Military Application.
2. Colonel George F. Schlatter, chief of the test activities branch in the Division of Military Application.
3. On November 14, 1950, James Lay sent the commission formal orders to select a continental test site.

## ≡ *November 2, 1950*

Mr. LeBaron called. . . . GD mentioned that Lay had called regarding Continental testing ground site having come up during conference with President and that Lay thought we should strike fast. GD said that McCormack and Lay both think working group committee good place to start and stated that enough paper work had been completed for them to get started. LeBaron said they could put Loper and Wortington[1] on committee. LeBaron said that he would have to create a piece of paper saying that they were studying the matter in order to get it started internally but that it would be very easy if Lay would set it up first and then they could just follow along. GD said he would call Lay and tell him that.

1. Wortington may have been Rear Admiral Frederic S. Withington, who joined the Military Liaison Committee on November 7, 1950.

## ≡ *November 9, 1950*

Captain Russell[1] called to say that Lay had just called him saying that he was going to set up a working committee on the continental test site. Suggested that he deal directly with Russell to find out the names of the people we should have on it—said GD had recommended this. Lay will call back some time today and will probably meet some time tomorrow.

1. Captain James S. Russell, deputy director of the Division of Military Application.

≡                                                          November 10, 1950
*Ad Hoc Committee of NSC on Continental Site and Procedure for Authorizing Use of an Atomic Weapon*

At the suggestion of Mr. Lay, Secretary of the NSC, that a working committee be created of the Special Committee of the NSC, I yesterday asked Captain Russell, in General McCormack's absence, to represent the AEC, together with any other persons that he might designate, from our shop. There were to be representatives from State Department and the Defense Establishment as well.

At a meeting held at 11:00 A.M. this morning, the upshot of the discussion was that the NSC would direct this committee to study a site for continental tests.

The other item agendaed and which was discussed this morning was that of the procedure which should be followed in getting together a recommendation to the President to use or not to use the atomic bomb in the event of an emergency. Mr. Arneson had prepared a list of some fifteen questions he thought should be answered by any group that made a recommendation. Captain Russell showed me these in advance of the meeting. Typical of the questions are these:

What would be the effect of the drop on our allies in Western Europe and world opinion in general? Etc.

Several of the questions were obviously questions which would be of primary interest to the State Department or the Defense Establishment. I suggested to Captain Russell that to the meeting he explain that AEC would definitely be interested in two questions. These were:

What would be the effect of its use on public opinion in the United States, in allied countries, in Asia?

Should we obtain UN concurrence before using it?

It was agreed at the meeting that in the event that the Joint Chiefs of Staff should suddenly make a recommendation that an atomic bomb be used at a particular place that the NSC subcommittee (Secretary of Defense, Secretary of State and Chairman of AEC) would meet and address itself to an agreed-upon set of questions such as those in the Arneson memorandum. It would be only after an analysis of the situation and the answering of the questions that the Special Committee would then make a recommendation to the President. This is a significant step because it establishes a procedure whereby AEC will participate in any such decision.

≡ *November 25, 1950*

Went over to see the President this morning. (See attached memorandum) ⟨removed[1]⟩

1. Dean occasionally removed notes, letters, or memoranda that he had initially placed in the diary, and he usually annotated the diary accordingly. Whenever I could, I tracked down such items and included them here. I could not find the November 25 memorandum, so I left Dean's handwritten note about its removal in the diary.

As of September 30, 1950, total from January 1, 1947 was 203,395 cases handled. Cases referred to AEC as containing derogatory information: 2,387 or 1.12%. Of these 2,387, 696 were granted clearance and 385 denied clearance. Of this 1,081 total, there is a balance left of 1,306 which were disposed of by separations, non-hires, resignations, etc. Of all cases received approximately 15% to 20% contain some kind of derogatory information, but only 1.12% contain substantial derogatory information. Of those containing substantial derogatory information, 76% reflected upon the character and habits and only 24% upon the associations and loyalty. Of these, the contractor employees were 92% and AEC employees were 9.2%. The number that finally get to administrative review (board hearing) is approximately .01%. We still don't have a convicted traitor in the AEC.[1]

1. This is one of Dean's notes to the diary and demonstrates his keen interest in security.

## ≡ *December 4, 1950*

GD called James Lay (NSC) and asked how the working group was coming along and stated that he [Dean] had not attended meetings between State, Defense and AEC to set up the procedures for transfer, etc. Mr. Lay said they were going on on that [working on the procedures for transfer]. Arneson of State was talking to military people to get us an outline of points the military would like to have included in any such decision. GD stated he had seen Arneson's list of questions. Lay stated that they have not met on the draft since the military had been asked to include points they want incorporated. GD stated he wondered about the mechanics in the chain of command as far as he was concerned and that the subject had not been taken up with the President and that he did not believe it had been discussed with the President and that he was concerned that there should be no "iffiness" about it. Lay stated that there should be two things in the decision: (1) directive to you (Dean) to turn over and (2) authorization as to time to use it. GD said that was right. Lay stated it should never be telephonic but should be in certain form. GD said he was thinking of the difficulties on non-nuclears and that he did not want to stand in the way.[1] Lay stated that there was a discussion in the staff that theoretically GD ought to have a report to follow a certain outline and that they were trying to draft such an outline. GD said that if things get critical an outline would serve as basis of discussion with the President in attendance in which he would get all views but in any case a written directive to you (Dean) and Defense. Lay said that that would be the minimum that would be necessary. GD said he had just called to see how crystallized this thing had become. Lay said Arneson should be able to come up with his questions and that he would move on it right away, particularly the military, and get out a report. On the assemblies they have asked Defense to come up with inventories on what they have and where. GD said we have those in our shop. Lay said [we] should have on record for the President and that any changes in inventories could be handled on a reasonable basis as they go along. GD said that a current inventory is essential and that for instance if a Captain of a ship decided he did not want them on his ship and unloaded them on dockside at Capetown or Cairo that we ought to know about it.[2] Lay said this would call for current inventories and make it a routine procedure that any changes in disposition would be reported to the President and special committee so that they would know where they all are at any given moment and that they were proceeding on that in Defense. Lay then asked if GD had had a chance to vote on the paper. GD asked if he meant paper on last requested transfer. He had seen it around and that it was in our shop and that he would get on it right away. Lay said that they had an ok from Acheson and Marshall on it.

1. The difficulties Dean had in mind were the problems he faced in transferring nonnuclear components to the military at the end of July. See Hewlett and Duncan, *Atomic Shield*, pp. 524–25.

2. Dean was concerned about storing nonnuclear components aboard naval vessels because the Joint Chiefs of Staff were preparing to request permission to store nonnuclear components on the aircraft carrier *Franklin D. Roosevelt*.

≡ *December 6, 1950*

Senator McMahon called GD. . . . McMahon said, "I know you are fully conscious of living every day in a Pearl Harbor atmosphere, therefore, I would put myself, if I were you, in a pre–Pearl Harbor frame of mind. Where are you going to be if they hit tonight?" GD said AEC has done that very thing—specifically on the stockpile.

≡ *December 13, 1950*

Charles Murphy of the White House called about meeting tomorrow morning at 10:00 A.M. at the White House. Says the purpose is to invite a group of Congressional leaders to consult with the President on the situation in general although mostly interested in economic controls. Particularly trying to get McMahon to come. Also asking Republican House member of the JCC. Wants to talk about controls and atomic energy at the same time. Not inviting Hickenlooper, but getting Elston[1] from the House. GD might be thinking of what he might want to say on the subject. GD will say it "off the cuff" depending on what comes up.

1. Representative Charles H. Elston of Ohio, a member of the Joint Committee on Atomic Energy.

## ≡ December 14, 1950

GD called Boyer about conference this morning.[1] Trying to anticipate what effect a declaration of a national emergency would have on our program—and apparently no direct effect. Boyer agrees except to increase the atmosphere of emergency. We would begin to pick up speed all along the line. For example, the Hanford piles would increase production. We have plans to raise that even greater over the next six months, etc. Would have a psychological effect at Los Alamos. GD says if he is asked this morning whether it is a good thing or a bad thing, he will have to explain why. Boyer says we are probably in more of an emergency over the past six months or ever since the time the Korean situation looked bad when the President came along with increased production—maybe we have anticipated this emergency.

1. Dean was scheduled to testify that morning before the House Appropriations Committee.

GD called Fred Warren about going over to the White House this morning. GD wants to know our mobilization requirements in terms of materials, steel, concrete, etc.—not because of the emergency but because of our program. Warren says he has the figures which we discussed with Symington[1] a month ago. None of the materials are very significant as far as national production is concerned. For example, 12 to 15 thousand tons of steel a month—which is some 150 thousand tons a year—as compared to 80 million tons in national production. For copper and aluminum also I would say our requirements are similar—fractions of 1%. When we get to alloy steel AEC preparations are higher—in short, they may amount to 1% to 5%. At the moment we are discussing with the Munitions Board this general question. It appears that the fields in which we are most likely to have significant requirements are this problem of columbium where our requirements are something like 40% and particularly where our requirements will step up from 1% of national production to about 3%. This has been surveyed by NSRB and we have a preliminary report which indicates this can be handled and will create conditions no worse than conditions right after the last war.

1. W. Stuart Symington, chairman of the National Security Resources Board.

## ≡ *January 5, 1951*

GD called LeBaron and said we are sending over our memorandum to NSC and wanted to be sure we have an understanding with you. We assumed from the last MLC meeting that there is no disagreement on the need for a release (on RANGER). LeBaron said that is correct. He has GD's letter with release and also a memorandum for the Secretary of Defense and he proposes to talk to Lovett about it. There is no disagreement and no need for waiting. GD said if we can get it before the weekend started it would give Lay time. LeBaron said the Defense people are working on a news release—making it official today—"The director of information has been made aware of these possibilities and is familiar with the press release being proposed to NSC. In short, the Defense Department should leave the matter of timing of the release to the judgment of the AEC." Is sending that memorandum to Marshall. LeBaron said, on the other part of it: On actual approval of the paper that goes to NSC to release the test material, we have to wait until the JCS acts. They have agreed to act on Monday—thinks there is a chance at the end of their discussion at 1:00 P.M. today on personnel, we might be able to get this thing in. LeBaron checked with McCormack and Arneson this morning on it. There will be no hold-up at State Department on it. Arneson is all for it, so LeBaron thinks it is all on the beam. . . .

## ≡ *January 8, 1951*

Salisbury called to find out if GD had spoken to LeBaron since this morning. The Secretary of Defense doesn't want to o.k. the release on the new site without a meeting with Secretary of State and GD. That will be tomorrow afternoon after Cabinet as far as we can tell now. Salisbury wants to talk to GD about it.

GD called Harold Brown[1] to ask if the radiation safety group had submitted a formal report in connection with Nevada site. Brown said Dunham would be the one to know about that. GD will call him.

1. Howard C. Brown, Jr., a member of the staff of the Division of Biology and Medicine.

GD called Dr. Dunham[1] and asked him if he had seen any kind of a report of the Radiation Safety Group concerning the tests out West. Dunham
said there was no such report as far as he knew. Didn't know that one was
actually being proposed. The actual radiological setup has not been set yet.
Cooney[2] is still out there trying to button it up. He will be back at the end
of the week. By that time the final plans should be set. The prevailing wind
is from the Southwest and it is planned not to do anything unless the wind
is in the direction. GD asked if there was any danger from a fall-out to the
Colorado River water. Dunham said there couldn't possibly be any damage
to the water downstream there. He just got in this morning; has been out
there last week—looks pretty good. There are no serious problems; the
monitoring is to be done mainly for record purposes. Dunham said the
only ones we are concerned with are the people who live in the first valley—a town called Alamo. It is not the first valley from the test site; it is
about fifty miles as the crow flies from the site to the town. There are several mountain ranges in between. GD said the first shot is pure uranium so
that the fallout would be less dangerous in that case than in some of the
others—the unfissioned particles. Dunham said Dr. Shields Warren[3] will
be in Kelley's[4] office in New York tomorrow should you need him for anything.

1. Dr. Charles L. Dunham, chief of the medical branch in the Division of Biology and
Medicine.
2. Brigadier General James P. Cooney, chief of the radiology branch in the Division of
Military Application.
3. Director of the Division of Biology and Medicine.
4. Wilbur E. Kelley, manager of the commission's New York operations office.

GD talked to General McCormack about the 5th shot. LeBaron told him
the JCS wanted to go along on the 4 [the first four *Ranger* shots] and they
are going to have some very slashing recommendations on the press release.
GD feels that we have a public relations problem here (and feels very
strongly) that the JCS don't appreciate. McCormack said that two members of the group who agree with what is said in that have requested that
their names not be used—Fermi and Kennedy.[1] Norris (Bradbury?) called
Trapnell and told him. Trapnell said he would call Salisbury and tell him
about it. GD said the JCS wants to eliminate all reference to radioactive
dangers and any "intensive" effort. McCormack said he didn't get it so

clear from him (LeBaron?) on the radioactive business—didn't tell Le-Baron about people objecting to having their names used. Just told him there had been some worries about the use of names. GD said in regard to the dropping of the 5th, knows it has *been* uncertain in the program. Is there any way we could document what we would lose if we didn't shoot 5, if we thought it was the thing to do? What does that 5th shot do? Mc-Cormack said it boils down to the stockpile problem. If you feel you are up to it and you bang it then you can work on your stockpile. GD thinks that makes a pretty good argument. It is a matter of $3\frac{1}{2}$ months or so. Mc-Cormack wishes the JCS wouldn't worry so much about this. Doesn't understand why they caution us on this unless they think we will use "dire emergency" to do something that is unsafe. McCormack said Shields Warren feels it would be completely based on completely satisfactory radiological effects of previous shots. McCormack thinks that is a good one to think about. The only worry about it would be if it goes sour and then the Commission had to do it because of the military emergency of the situation. GD said even if it goes sour, don't they want to try it? Can you get decent measurement on the 5th one if you took it out over the water, for example? McCormack said you would get something but Norris is very lukewarm about that. Thinks you might load one in an airplane and bang it somewhere without waiting for the Greenhouse test. GD said the question is how hard to fight this. Not too sure about that, but thinks he can appreciate the stockpile arrangement. McCormack said the primary point in connection with this is stockpiling. Norris said that the other day. GD said you might be thinking about it and perhaps we can get together before the meeting tomorrow. . . .

1. Enrico Fermi and Joseph W. Kennedy were both members of a scientific panel which evaluated the radiological hazards of continental testing.

Admiral Withington called GD and said that the proposed release (on the Nevada site) had run into rough sledding on "that side of the river." GD said it would probably come up at a conference on Tuesday with Marshall, Acheson and himself. Withington said Admiral Sherman was not opposed to the idea and he believes the JCS will support a release but does not know what Marshall will do. GD said he hoped they would not tie our hands as things break so fast. Withington said his boss would not say "no" to any release.

LeBaron called to say he had been down with the JCS talking about Ranger and Mercury;[1] that they did not like the big "F" test[2] but they did like the little ones. He said they claim they will lose face with the President as they had promised no big tests. LeBaron said that right now it would be a question of whether you wanted to take off with the little ones or waste time arguing about the big ones. They suggest that we let things develop on the basis of first four and that they did not want to say "no" to the other right now. GD said they were missing the boat and that he would have Jim McCormack document this as to what would happen if you left out the 5th. LeBaron said he had talked some to Jim about it. GD said Los Alamos did not want to go on with 2 until after 1, or 3 until after 2, etc. LeBaron said they wanted the press release down to a small and somewhat misleading announcement; no reference to intensive tests, eliminate names and radiological on page 2. LeBaron said they said everybody would be calling them and that they would get into trouble. LeBaron then said that it would all come out at the meeting on Tuesday; that Acheson was there now [with LeBaron] and that he had been well primed through Arneson. LeBaron said he was sorry they could not do any better but that maybe it could be stretched back where it was at the meeting.

1. Mercury was a code word for the Las Vegas test site.
2. The fifth or "F" shot was much larger than the other four *Ranger* tests; hence, the concern in the Department of Defense.


≡ *January 9, 1951*

Mr. LeBaron called GD. Said meeting with Marshall at 4:45 today was official and that General Loper was going with LeBaron. He said Loper and Luedecke[1] were developing wording of press release that the JCS would like GD to know before he went over just exactly what they will have in their portfolio. LeBaron said that as soon as the draft is ready they will bring it in to GD. GD asked what will you say on questions of "F." LeBaron said they think it is a separate proposition and test should not be made at this time; however, it should not be called off and that he felt General Marshall believes this does not keep face with the President because the test is too big. GD asked what paper does he refer to regarding statement to President as to size of tests. LeBaron said it was small tests initially in this site. GD said that when he talked to him he thought his only alarm was over bang 6 or 7 times. If representations were made we ought to be clear what they were and they should not oppose on ground that the President would not like it. LeBaron said it was one of the questions which must go to him for resolution. JCS felt it would prejudice the little tests. GD said that if that is the only reason against the big bang because the President would not like it—it should not be asserted in NSC meeting. LeBaron said that is only reason that came up in meeting with JCS and will say they thought better to separate them at this time—it is just a lack of education.

1. General Alvin R. Luedecke, executive secretary of the Military Liaison Committee. He later served as general manager of the commission from 1958 to 1964.

GD called Dr. Dunham. GD said he was going over to meet with Secretary of Defense and Secretary of State and he was wondering do you think of any other difficulties in radioactive hazards other than sheep? Dunham said he could think of nothing, except weather. If there was a pretty good sized burst, there might be trouble in the valley, if it poured right after, that that is a remote possibility. GD asked what would happen to the people. Dunham said, nothing, if they get out and that they would have several hours to evacuate—it would not have to be done in a matter of a few minutes. Dunham said Army Engineers have been approached and will take over if necessary for evacuation. GD asked how much time? Dunham said 24 hours. Dean said it would depend on where the cloud was and Dr. Dunham said rain would have to fall within the first two hours and GD asked that if it did, would it mean minor skin burns. Dunham said he thought that would be the worst thing that could possibly happen to the people. The sheep problem cannot be controlled so the trouble would be with friends in Interior. GD said he would not have any trouble unless a rain storm developed and Dr. Dunham said that was right—even for a large blast—big ones might not carry as high but would not be serious.

≡ *January 10, 1951*

James Lay called about the memorandum to the President on this release on the Nevada site. Going to use the one you originally submitted but thought AEC signals have changed since then. AEC going to release it on Thursday? GD said yes, we would like to. Just the fact that we have acquired the site and what it is for—nothing more. Lay said "which the Commission proposed to make tomorrow to go with the official notifications." GD said that is o.k. The release deals with a program which is described more fully in the attached memorandum etc. Thinks something like that would do. Lay said he is going over to the White House at 10:30 and is going to try to get an o.k. on the press release first. GD asked him if he felt that he had enough feel for the subject if he (the President) puts questions to you in there. GD said he agreed with Marshall that there should be a span of time between the release and the tests—to let things slow down. Lay said he thought he could handle the questions o.k. Said he talked with Joe Short after our meeting and he thought it was o.k. (Short is White

House press secretary).[1] He is planning to take it in two bites since AEC wants to make the release tomorrow in order to make it early as possible prior to the tests. GD said he would like to explain to him who we are going to notify about the release: The governor of Nevada, the Congressional delegation from Nevada, the Mayor of Los Angeles and health and safety officials in three counties involved in this tract of land. Planning on tipping them off two or three hours in advance of the release which is tentatively scheduled for noon tomorrow. We have advised the JCC by memorandum hand carried to each member. The GAC is enthusiastic about approving it—they just met here last week. The MLC is unanimous in approving it. Thought Lay might want to have this background. Lay said as soon as he gets to the material he will try to get that over as soon as he can.

1. Joseph Short became press secretary after the death of Charles Ross.

GD called McCormack to bring him up to date on the call from Lay. GD told him he (Lay) proposed to separate the two ideas—the release and the paper for the tests. Will take the release in to the President today and get his approval as soon as he can. McCormack said he thought that was good. The Los Alamos delegation will have to leave their place by mid-afternoon. If we receive LeBaron's statement of the problem, McCormack would like to have it as soon as possible.

GD called Salisbury and told him about conversation with James Lay about handling things separately—taking the release in first and the other paper in some other time. Salisbury said he would change the letter to say "proposed for release on Thursday." He will call when he comes back from the conference with the President? GD said yes.

GD called Senator Pat McCarran of Nevada and told him he had a matter of mutual interest to discuss with him and would like to come up and see him. GD suggested that he would like to talk to the entire Nevada delegation at the same time, but McCarran said that he and Malone didn't always see eye to eye and thinks it is best if GD comes up to see him alone. GD coming up at 12:15 today in the Senator's office.

GD called General McCormack and asked him if he had a small map that he could take with him when he went to see McCarran. There has been a little bit of advanced leak and he will probably want to know the dimensions, etc. GD also said if you have the names of the officials in the three counties it might be helpful. McCormack said we here in Washington do not have those names, but will check and see if he can dig up a map of something that will do.

LeBaron called to say we are in the clear on the paper that GD sent down (Memo to President from Lay on Nevada tests).[1] It is precisely what the discussion was with the JCS and he is sure that they will be satisfied with it. Will send it back to GD.

1. The Lay memorandum asked the president to approve the *Ranger* tests.

GD called Governor Charles Russell of Nevada and told him that one of our top men at Los Alamos together with the Director of the Laboratory are very anxious to come up and see the Governor tomorrow morning some time to talk over something of mutual interest to both the Governor and our program. GD asked if there was any particular time that will be best for the Governor. They could be there as early as 10:00 AM. Governor Russell said that would be fine. GD told him the name of our man is Carroll Tyler, Chief of AEC Santa Fe Operations—all of our South West activities. The name of the other man is Dr. Norris Bradbury who is the Director of the Los Alamos Laboratory. Russell said that would be fine; he will be expecting them.

GD called McCormack and told him the Governor of Nevada is looking forward to seeing Tyler and Bradbury both at 10:00 A.M. tomorrow. His name is Charles Russell. McCormack said o.k.; thanks a lot.

GD called Bill Borden (JCC) and said he had heard that maybe the Senator would want to tie in with this release on the Nevada site with some kind of a statement. Asked if he had worked up anything like that yet. Borden said he had not; has been working on a mighty speech for the Senator—one he is considering giving on Friday. The Senator will have to comment on the release, but hasn't gotten to it yet and would like to have any suggestions GD might have. GD said if we don't have a few people who know the program make a statement about this—or if they do make it and say it represents real progress, it will help us a lot. Borden said he had been trying to get Durham[1] to do it but he didn't want to do it. He agreed to say he had no objections if anyone asked him, but that is all. GD said we must have something more positive than that. Borden asked GD what he thought about something like this: "The factors and circumstances involved here are known to all the members of the JCC and have been considered by them. I believe it is safe to say that this step is wise and prudent and in the interest of the country and proper precautions, etc. have been taken, etc.,

etc., etc." He also suggested that he might refer to the AEC release in some fashion. GD asked him what the speech on Friday was about. Borden said it is another peace speech calling for Congressional action on that resolution he introduced last year and analyzing our situation especially from the atomic energy standpoint, etc. Borden not sure whether the speech will go or not. Said it is really an attempt to duplicate the speech of February 2nd of last year. GD told him the release would be out tomorrow late. Borden said he didn't think we would experience much difficulty in it. Thinks it was a good omen the good briefing with the Chairman of the Judiciary (McCarran). GD said the meeting was very pleasant. GD asked if Borden thought there were any reservations on the part of any of the members of the JCC on this thing. Borden said some are glad that it isn't where "I live." There is some feeling of concern about the hazards of it. Hickenlooper seemed to be quite pleased about it. Borden said you will probably have an audience of 18 members of the JCC at the tests—they have all indicated a desire to go. Jackson was quite concerned over the wisdom of having a pre-event announcement. He felt that it could only result in security hazards even if you omitted the references to time. Borden mentioned that he thought it was amazing that it has not leaked out yet.

1. Representative Carl T. Durham of North Carolina, a member of the Joint Committee on Atomic Energy.


≡ *January 11, 1951*

Appointment with President. Met Mr. Lay in Matt Connelly's office. An off-the-record meeting Nevada site.

Went up to see Senator Malone of Nevada to tell him about new site.

Went to see Congressman Baring of Nevada to advise him of new site.

General McCormack called and said GD had asked him about the sort of work that was being done in the way of construction at MERCURY. McCormack said he talked to Tyler yesterday evening and he says there are only three major categories which are being worked now:

1. a control point—some instruments, etc.
2. the wiring out to instruments which is being put underground
3. a road maintenance—getting trails ready so that you can get over there, etc.

Said they have had very disappointing water so far; will probably have to haul it; but are going to keep on with that. As to the total figure involved, we are using the figure of $300,000 for the first go. Tyler agreed with that figure—they might get up as high as ½ a million. For the long term, if everything works out, he will want to build a site somewhere more convenient, and perhaps then four or five million dollars will be about what he would recommend. They are now using disused barracks—we will have to put up some new buildings eventually and we would like to put them near the working place, etc. GD said he would like to have some kind of map today (meeting with President). Have to go over to see the President at 10:45 this morning. This is going to be an explanation of what these shots are about, etc. McCormack asked if the map GD had yesterday combined with a smaller one of the immediate area would be satisfactory? McCormack said if "F" is still a problem, it is now set up that it would be reconsidered to make sure about the hazards, etc. The Commission, as a Commission, will make the decision for the Los Alamos crew. If anyone is really worried about this, we will refer it to the NSC. Only as a last resort will we go to the President again with it.

GD called Shugg to bring him up to date on the status of the release for Thursday. Shugg said he had kept up with the progress and knew that the President had approved the release. He offered to be of any assistance, after the release came out, that he could as there will probably be a reaction. GD said that they had had no trouble with anyone and that he had talked to the President about the program—thought he ought to tell a little about what we have been touching base with. GD said the JCS objection was to the "big bang" but that a statement regarding it had been approved by Acheson, Marshall and GD.

Tried again to complete call to Governor Warren of California. No luck.

GD called Shugg and McCormack to report on the meeting with the President this morning. The President approved everything even the "F" shot.

GD called to Mayor Bowron of Los Angeles and told him we have acquired from the Air Force a site in Nevada in the region between the towns of Tonepah and Las Vegas. We are going to perform a few explosions in connection with our program. When it is announced that we have acquired the land, there might be some rumors to the effect that these explosions will contaminate Los Angeles water supply. In fact, they will not be harmful. We have had competent people on the ground who have studied it. We have Dr. Stafford Warren of UCLA. Bowron said Warren had talked to him about it last night. Bowron said he assumed AEC does not want to announce about how long an event this will be. GD said we are very reluctant to give the exact time of the blasts. Bowron asked how long do we have to be on the lookout to see that there are no harmful effects. GD said we will announce only the acquisition of the land today; we will not announce the time of the explosions. We have found that if we tried to keep it, it will leak out anyway. Bowron thanked GD very much and assured GD that he would see from Los Angeles that there is no one who gets the wrong idea. GD said that is important so that we will not get any false rumors started.

Col. Schlatter called and said he had talked to Morgan at Los Alamos and said bad weather did stop them from getting there (to see the Governor of Nevada about the new site—Tyler and Bradbury) but a conference call had been arranged for this morning with the Governor. Not sure whether they will still consider it worthwhile to go up in person on it. GD thinks that sort of thing pays dividends—this going to see people personally—if even late. Schlatter said in any event Shelby Thompson[1] was there waiting for the rest to come (Thompson later got caught at the airport and was late getting to see the governor).

1. Shelby Thompson, chief of the public information branch in the Division of Public and Technical Information.

GD called Salisbury and asked if there had been any leaks yet on the Nevada release. Salisbury said at Las Vegas there was what looked like an Air Force leak in the morning papers—$7\frac{1}{2}$ million for construction; $3\frac{1}{2}$ million for AEC and the rest for Air Force; but it didn't identify the purpose of the construction. GD said he talked with Stafford Warren at UCLA and the Governor of Nevada and the Congressional delegation; had been unable to complete call to Governor Warren of California. Salisbury asked if GD wouldn't want to try to talk to the Lt. Governor, but GD said there is a rivalry there. Salisbury said thin[g]s worked out pretty well in spite of weather troubles in Nevada. GD said he would assume that Shelby Thompson could give the Governor all the dope he needs. Salisbury said that Senator McMahon issued a statement shortly after 3:00 P.M. today. Bergman[1] checked it with Salisbury first—looked at it and it looks o.k. Will send GD a copy of it.

1. Harold E. Bergman, deputy director of the Joint Committee staff.

GD called LeBaron about reaction to release. LeBaron said that they had been deluged with inquiries, particularly the press, and that they had been referred to AEC. LeBaron had told his office, off the record, that AEC would act as executive agency on inquiries of the release. GD said things were going much as normal and that if any reaction came, it would probably come within 24 hours. GD told LeBaron that the President had approved the whole program this morning. LeBaron said that Col. Roper[1] was coming into his office at 10:00 Tuesday and that he would call GD. GD said he would probably be out of the city, but would see him at a later date.

1. Colonel Harry McK. Roper, on the staff of the Military Liaison Committee.

Col. Schlatter called and said he had just learned that Carroll Tyler was having difficulty with his mission as the weather was very bad. He was not clear whether they got there or not. They had planned to go by air, and that train connections might have made him late. GD said he hoped they had talked to the Governor by phone. Col. Schlatter was going to try to get more information on what had been or was being done.

≡ *January 12, 1951*

Joe Myler of the United Press called for some quote he could use on these tests in Nevada. He assumed that this decision reflects the sense of urgency on atomic energy matters. GD said it had been enthusiastically endorsed by our GAC and by the MLC which represents the three services and by the Commission which has been pushing it. The matter was fully explained in advance to the officials involved in Nevada, to the Congressional delegation of Nevada, etc. Myler asked if they had been assured that it would not be in any sense a hazard. GD said we assured them that every precaution was being taken; that there was less danger in it than taking an automobile from here to Richmond. We are very enthusiastic about the thing—it means a great deal to us. Myler asked if he could use any of the above in direct quote. GD suggested that he say that Gordon Dean said . . . and leave out the quotes.[1] Myler mentioned the story in the Washington Post this morning which goes back to the notion that you can have small scale atomic explosions. Myler asked if that were more possible now than it was at the time of the Smyth report. GD said if he started talking to that he might get into intelligence problems that he would rather stay away from. Would say that it had to be a pretty good bang, though.

1. The ellipses appear in the original.

Boyer called GD from Oak Ridge. Boyer said, referring to release of yesterday on Nevada, that there was good reporting down there on it. GD said that because of a snow storm Tyler could not get to the Governor but that he had talked to him on the phone himself, and that Tyler had had a public relations man explain about it over the phone. Also covered the counties by telephone and that a delegation had gone out. GD said that there had been no adverse comments to the present time. GD told Boyer that the program had been approved in full yesterday by the President and Boyer was quite happy about that ("Oh—that's swell"). . . .

# THREE

## THE ROSENBERGS, THE HYDROGEN BOMB, AND KOREA

*January 26, 1951, to June 17, 1951*

The diary excerpts in this chapter take Dean through his most difficult days as chairman. Crises in the hydrogen bomb program, the Rosenberg trial, and Korea produced a period of sustained strain and tension. The excerpts pick up with the *Ranger* tests, which were all successful, including the fifth shot, which had worried the Joint Chiefs of Staff. As the diary shows, the series was not without its problems. A dry run for the first shot was leaked to the press and numerous claims for repair of broken windows were filed with the commission after the test explosions. The *Ranger* tests advanced fission weapons programs, created few fallout hazards, and allowed Dean to give the president on February 6, 1951, a favorable report of the first continental test series.

The hydrogen bomb program, in contrast, had come up against seemingly unyielding natural phenomena when Los Alamos mathematician Stanislaw Ulam demonstrated that it was extremely doubtful that the Super concept would produce a fusion explosion. Whatever chance remained for the Super required relatively large amounts of tritium to ignite a fusion explosion. Because Ulam's analysis revealed that the Super concept had been partially based on incomplete data, some physicists wondered whether Edward Teller had led the laboratory into an adventurous program not completely supported by sound scientific methods. Inevitably tensions rose among the scientists on the remote New Mexico mesa.

At first Teller thought Ulam's calculations were in error but soon recognized their soundness and their meaning. But just as Teller's fundamental ideas had been cast into doubt, the laboratory put more resources into preparing for the *Greenhouse* tests and less into theoretical investigations. For Teller the allocation of resources was especially frustrating: he believed that the General Advisory Committee would convince the commission to abandon the hydrogen bomb program if the Super proved a failure. Because he feared the commission might shelve the hydrogen bomb program, he began to argue for the feasibility of the hydrogen bomb to all who would listen.

The clashes at Los Alamos found their way into the diary on February 8, 1951, when Dean heard of a lack of enthusiasm about the Super among some scientists. He also heard that Teller was in Washington talking to people about his fears and that some of the most basic scientific calculations had not been made. Four days later Lewis Strauss discussed with Dean the lack of enthusiasm about the hydrogen bomb including the allegation that J. Robert Oppenheimer had sabotaged the program. Strauss argued that something radical would have to be done to save the program. Although Dean believed Los Alamos had enthusiastically pursued the program, he was willing to consider several solutions, among them removing the thermonuclear program from Los Alamos and entrusting it to a new weapons research laboratory. For the moment there was little Dean could do, for the Rosenberg case commanded his attention.

The government had arrested Julius and Ethel Rosenberg during the summer of 1950 and formally charged them with conspiracy to commit espionage. The government's principal witness was Ethel Rosenberg's brother David Greenglass, who had admitted to passing atomic bomb secrets to the Soviets but claimed he did so at the behest of his sister and brother-in-law. The government was ready to bring the case to trial in early February 1951 but had not yet decided which technical details about the atomic bomb would be disclosed at the trial. Now the Department of Justice wanted to know what technical data about the bomb could be revealed in court.

Dean and his associates hoped to control the technical data revealed in court by circumscribing the technical testimony of Greenglass and the experts who would have to take the stand to support him. United States attorney Myles Lane was amenable to this strategy and joined Dean in explaining the Rosenberg case to the Joint Committee on Atomic Energy, which is the point at which the diary picks up the case. Lane's willingness to exercise care when revealing bomb data satisfied both Dean and the Joint Committee. For a moment it seemed as if Dean could devote less time to the Rosenberg case.

Before Dean could reassess the hydrogen bomb program, Irving Saypol took over the prosecution of the Rosenbergs. Saypol wanted to get every bit of evidence into the record and refused to let the commission dictate how he would examine his witnesses. Because Saypol was adamant, Dean went over his head to Attorney General J. Howard McGrath. In a weekend meeting at the attorney general's home on March 10, Dean determined the questions Saypol would ask Greenglass and supporting expert Walter Koski. The diary is a major source of details about this crucial meeting in which Dean and commission attorneys determined the exact bomb details that would be revealed in court. In protecting uncompromised data and in determining the technical evidence used in court, Dean played a far more important role in the Rosenberg case than in any other atom spy case of the early 1950s.

Teller, meanwhile, had found the path to the hydrogen bomb. Ulam had suggested an approach to igniting the fusion reaction which gave Teller yet another idea. By early March, Teller and Ulam had penned a report which charted the first part of the path to the fusion reaction. By late March, Teller and physicist Frederic DeHoffmann had solved the remaining difficulties. DeHoffmann's preliminary calculations confirmed that the approach, later called the New Super, showed great promise. For the moment Teller's success did not find its way to Dean or into his diary.

Teller's breakthrough came just as the Korean War seemed on the verge of erupting into a general war between the Soviet Union and the United States. As the diary reveals in a depth not found in other published sources on the Korean War, the Truman administration had just received intelligence that the Soviets might enter the Korean War and together with the Chinese make an all-out attempt to push American forces out of Korea. Such a massive offensive might not be aimed at Korea alone but might be part of a Communist attempt to take Japan. Soviet entry into the war would probably spark a global conflict between the United States and the Soviet Union. For the next few weeks President Truman and his advisers had to consider whether World War III was imminent.

The intelligence was particularly worrisome to the administration because the Chinese were soon expected to launch their spring offensive. After their entry into the war, the Chinese had driven the Americans and their South Korean allies out of North Korea and deep into South Korea. The Americans and South Koreans had recently recovered and had begun a series of counterattacks which brought the front lines back to the 38th parallel, the prewar boundary between North and South Korea. As the advance continued the administration watched carefully for the Communists' next move.

Because Dean kept detailed notes of the crisis, his diary is virtually the only source that reveals another facet of the problems faced by President Truman and his advisers in April 1951. As the diary shows, one of the Joint Chiefs' first reactions to the intelligence was to consider the immediate transfer of nine complete atomic bombs to the Air Force. The proposed transfer raised many thorny issues for Dean and the commission, all of which Dean reported in his diary. Not really knowing how the Joint Chiefs

planned to use the bombs and feeling the weight of his responsibility for
the atomic arsenal, Dean decided that the issue should be thoroughly explored by the National Security Council before the commission released
the bombs to the Air Force. For the next few weeks Korea was uppermost
in his mind. At the same time, the crisis that led to General MacArthur's
relief erupted.

While wrestling with the Korean crisis Dean learned on March 31 that
Teller wanted to fly to Washington to discuss the hydrogen bomb program.
Frustrated by the laboratory's concentration on the *Greenhouse* tests,
Teller wanted Los Alamos to devote an entire division to the thermonuclear
program. Although laboratory director Bradbury considered several pro-
posals for the new division, Teller thought none of them devoted sufficient
resources to the hydrogen bomb. Having little success at Los Alamos,
Teller decided to argue his ideas directly before the chairman.

Teller spent two hours with a rather inattentive Gordon Dean on April
4, 1951. Unfortunately Dean left only fragmentary handwritten notes of
the meeting for the diary. Teller gave Dean a brief history of the Super concept, explained his new ideas for igniting a fusion reaction, and handed
him his resignation from Los Alamos. Teller now wanted to devote an entire second weapons laboratory to the thermonuclear effort and wanted to
staff it with 50 senior scientists, 82 junior scientists, and 228 assistants.
Dean failed to grasp Teller's technical ideas but readily understood the political implications of his departure from Los Alamos. Playing for time, he
got Teller to agree to postpone his decision to resign. It was not the last
time Dean would hear Teller's frustrations with Los Alamos, and his diary
is an excellent source for the clashes among the scientists at Los Alamos
and for Dean's role in trying to mediate among them.

A few hours after talking to Teller, Dean learned that the military wanted
the custody of complete weapons. He and his fellow commissioners readily
agreed that the National Security Council should examine the issue before
the commission made the transfer. So firmly did Dean want the National
Security Council to review the transfer that he put his recommendation in
a letter to the president. If the military took custody of complete weapons
before the matter had been discussed, Dean feared it might be impossible
to have the National Security Council examine whether the transfer should
have been made.

As Dean tried to force the transfer issue up to the National Security
Council, House minority leader Joseph Martin read into the *Congressional
Record* yet another unauthorized statement in which MacArthur advocated the use of Chiang Kai-shek's Nationalist Chinese troops to open a
second front in Asia. Coming close on the heels of the unauthorized threat

to expand the Korean War, President Truman decided that he had to act. Perhaps weighing MacArthur's statements against the imminence of global war strengthened his resolve. On the morning of Friday, April 6, President Truman began a series of meetings with his advisers to discuss what to do about General MacArthur. As the diary shows, Truman summoned Dean to the White House that afternoon and ordered the transfer to the Pacific. The president's action left no time for the National Security Council to consider the issue.

The next few days were tense for Dean. He arranged the transfer and worried about how to inform the Joint Committee of the action. He worked with James Lay to insure that the National Security Council would be part of any decision to use a bomb. While the transfer was being carried out, Dean watched the tremendous controversy that ensued as a result of the president's action in firing MacArthur, but he reported nothing about it in his diary.

As Dean's role in the Korean crisis abated, he could turn to the hydrogen bomb program again. On April 16 he listened to Norris Bradbury rebut Teller's call for a second laboratory but left no detailed notes in the diary. Later Dean left Washington for the Pacific and the *Greenhouse* weapons test series. Dean saw the last two shots and left his impressions of the tests in the diary. It was a *Greenhouse* test which demonstrated that Teller's concept for the New Super would probably function as anticipated.

After the series Dean decided to hold a conference at Princeton, New Jersey, to analyze the *Greenhouse* results. The commission and its top scientists spent two days discussing the data and the hydrogen bomb program. The *Greenhouse* results were so promising for the New Super that everyone agreed that the future of the hydrogen bomb program looked bright. Discussions at the meeting were very technical, quite sensitive, and highly classified. Probably because of the nature of the Princeton discussions, Dean left no account of them in the diary. But at last success seemed assured in the hydrogen bomb program. Dean may have found it a fitting close to his first year as chairman.

For sources that mention the intelligence about the Soviets, see also Bradley and Blair, *A General's Life*, pp. 629–30; Matthew B. Ridgway, *The Korean War* (New York, 1967), pp. 121–22; James F. Schnabel and Robert J. Watson, *The History of the Joint Chiefs of Staff: The Joint Chiefs of Staff and National Policy*, vol. 3, *The Korean War, Part I* (Washington, D.C., n.d.), pp. 485–86; and Walter S. Poole, *The History of the Joint Chiefs of Staff: The Joint Chiefs of Staff and National Policy*, vol. 4, *1950–1952* (Washington, D.C., 1979), pp. 152–53. For accounts of the Dean-Teller meeting, see also Teller, *Legacy of Hiroshima*, p. 51; Hewlett and Duncan, *Atomic Shield*, p. 541; and Blumberg and Owens, *Energy and Conflict*, p. 281. For information on *Greenhouse* and the Princeton meeting, see also Hewlett and Duncan, *Atomic Shield*, pp. 541–45; Teller, *Legacy of Hiroshima*, pp. 51–53; and York, *The Advisors*, pp. 80–81.

≡ *January 26, 1951*

LeBaron called and said International News Service has started talking about a report from the Governor of Nevada quoting full details of the activities last night (dry-run on Nevada tests). Says AEC local official at Carson City made a statement—spills Tyler's name and Governor says that dry-run was made, etc. The newspaper boys are asking Defense Establishment for a statement. GD said he thought there was a dry-run last night. LeBaron said it was his understanding that we were not going to say anything to the press until we got together—other than the release on the 11th. LeBaron said the Defense people need to know what is being said, etc., so that they won't say the wrong thing. GD said he would check on it and call LeBaron back.

GD called Trapnell and asked about the news stories about the dry-run. Trapnell said we have said that UP story is correct; Tyler talked to the Governor. GD asked if this was after the fact of the dry-run. Trapnell said Tyler's call was after the dry-run. GD asked if there was any light in the sky. Trapnell said evidentally not, but UP correspondent heard a report about somebody running into a road block. The correspondent asked the Governor about it and he told him that it was a dry-run. We had to confirm it after the Governor gave it out. GD said the way it reads now it says an AEC official said, etc., etc., and names Tyler. (GD read to him the ticker on it). GD asked what is planned for tomorrow's announcement. Trapnell said we plan to say "one of the periodic tests announced by the Commission on January 11th took place early this morning." In response to anything else we will give the full paragraph of security restrictions, that is, no comment. On hazards, we will say that reports of the field indicate that there is no hazard. GD said he would pass that along to LeBaron so he will feel that he is in on everything. Trapnell said Morse Salisbury thinks everything is under control.

GD called LeBaron and gave him the story as Trapnell gave it to him. Tyler simply told the Governor that we were going to have a dry-run explosion. Didn't indicate whether it was to be nuclear or non-nuclear or the size, etc. Our policy is this: It isn't necessary to announce unless questions come in. The UP man called the Governor and told him about the road block and asked about that. The Governor told him what he had been told by Tyler. LeBaron asked if they couldn't just have said that it was part of our planning; that we are getting ready, etc. GD said we make no comment unless there is a question (read to LeBaron the prepared statements). GD thinks we will get inquiries on it. LeBaron said he already had them by the thousands. His off-hand reaction is that this was not the most skillful way to handle it. Do we have to tell the Governor? Couldn't we tell him simply that tests are going on there. GD thinks for the future there will be no more telling him in advance. He knows that there will be a series. LeBaron asked if GD had seen the release. GD said he hasn't seen the release, just saw the ticker which attributes the story to the Governor who says AEC officials told him. He quotes Tyler that there was going to be a dry-run. LeBaron said he thought we would simply say that we are getting ready for tests. GD said this is the statement he thinks we should use: "one of the period tests announced by the Commission on January 11th was held early this morning." And use this only in response to inquiry. LeBaron asked what about when they inquire when is the next one going to be. GD said we should say nothing more.

## ≡ *January 27, 1951*

GD called Senator McMahon and told him about the success of the first shot.

Trapnell called to say he had had some inquiries for a better description of the shots. GD said it just doesn't make any difference. It is still one of a series. Trapnell said he has been telling them that we have nothing to characterize them at all. We are leaving it completely fuzzed up. We had a question for pictures from Acme, and Trapnell told him that they would be of more interest to a historian than the daily press. We had none available now.

## ≡ *January 29, 1951*

Mr. Boyer called and said that he, Dr. Glennan, Mr. Murray[1] and Bob Bacher[2] had been talking in Keith's office. He asked if GD had been completely briefed on the results of the tests. GD said he had talked to Schlatter and he was interested to know about "F." Boyer suggested that he and General McCormack come in right away.

1. T. Keith Glennan filled Strauss's post on the commission and Thomas E. Murray filled the vacancy created by Lilienthal's departure.
2. Dr. Robert F. Bacher, one of the original commissioners. He left the commission for the faculty of the California Institute of Technology.

Senator McMahon called GD and chided him about suits resulting from tests. GD said probably will have a suit for every window that has been broken for the last 25 years in Nevada. GD asked if McMahon was free for him to come up for a few minutes. McMahon said he was and GD went right up.

GD called Matt Connelly, White House, to ascertain if the President would be interested in a report on the Nevada tests. If so, GD will go over. Connelly said he would let GD know—at present the President was swamped with Frenchmen.[1]

1. French Premier René Pleven was then in Washington for talks with President Truman.

GD called Boyer. . . . GD mentioned that he had talked with Matt Connelly and asked him if the President were interested in the Nevada tests we stood ready to come over and give him a report on these tests any time he wanted. GD said he also saw McMahon and talked to him about the results. Asked him generally about the stockpile letter which involves the question of the way we answer the letter. The Senator thinks the Committee is eventually going to have to ask for stockpile figures.[1] Boyer said he thinks we should give them. . . .

1. The commission eventually gave the stockpile numbers to the Joint Committee in September 1951.

Matt Connelly called and asked GD how long did he think it would take for him to make his report to the President. GD said only a minute or two, but I am going out of town tomorrow and will be back sometime Thursday. Appointment made for 9:45 A.M. Friday morning—off the record.

≡ *January 30, 1951*

GD prepared statement to press on the Nevada tests to be used at Press Conference this afternoon.

≡ *February 5, 1951*

Mr. Hollis and Williams came in to discuss the Greenglass case with GD.

Col. Schlatter called to say that because of mechanical difficulties with the plane nothing is going to happen this morning.[1] It is at least 24 hours postponed. The weather looks problematical for tomorrow. Schlatter has asked the Las Vegas crowd to keep us posted. The party arrived at Las Vegas (Smyth, Glennan, VIPs from the Defense Establishment, etc.) GD said he hoped with all those boys around we could keep things in line and not make any public statement. Schlatter said that Secretary Matthews[2] is standing by to go out as soon as things are all set up for the "big one." It will be tomorrow morning unless the weather prevents it. #3 engine in the plane went out this morning. They had trouble because they couldn't land it with that much gas aboard and yet they couldn't do a good bomb run with only three engines. They finally got back to Kirkland. It was too heavy to pull an emergency landing someplace, repair the engine and take off again—they had to go back to Kirkland.

1. The plane had taken off from Kirkland Air Force Base in Albuquerque, New Mexico, with an atomic bomb which it was supposed to drop for one of the *Ranger* test shots.
2. Secretary of the Navy Francis P. Matthews.

## ≡ *February 6, 1951*

Meeting with President, off the record, on the Nevada tests.

Col. Schlatter called to say that "the thing" went this morning. They haven't had a report yet from Jack Clark at the control point. Will call back as soon as we get that report. Got a confirmation from Tyler who saw the reverberations. It went at 5:47 A.M.

Col. Schlatter called about this morning's shot.[1] Instrumentation generally successful. No damage reported as yet. Shock felt in Las Vegas was particularly less than size 4 shot—believed due to atmospheric conditions. Shot itself was materially larger in magnitude—the cloud was in good shape—top around 43,000 feet. Tyler said to tell Mr. Dean "very successful shot." The party will probably return tonight. Matthews and Vandenberg[2] did get back for it by the skin of their teeth.

1. Schlatter was reporting on the "F" shot.
2. General Hoyt S. Vandenberg, chief of staff of the Air Force.

GD talked to Hollis about the mechanics for paying off claims for broken windows out there (Nevada). Hollis said he doesn't know—some of the cases are under the Federal Tort Claims Act—that might be the first place they would try. The law of negligence is involved and the law of extra hazardous activities might come into it. That is the best Hollis could think of right off the bat. GD asked if there was any appropriation or secret fund from which we can make the payments. Public relationswise, I think it is important that we pay off the claims fast. Hollis mentioned another angle: What are our relations with the insurance companies to be? Whether the Federal Government should immediately start paying off is another problem. GD asked if Hollis had seen any policies. Hollis said he had not. GD said for very large windows they usually make out a separate policy. Hollis said he thinks it is not unusual for large chain stores and large businesses to carry these policies for large windows. GD asked where these claims are being funnelled. Hollis said to Tyler's office. He (Hollis) has not seen a single one yet or heard about a single one coming in to us. We have been giving some thought to it but have not come up with much yet—insurance might be the answer to it. . . .

GD called Dr. Colby[1] and asked if Dr. Colby had any available information showing Russian reaction to the Nevada tests. Colby said "no," but that they were trying to get such information. GD asked if he had heard about the latest one which went off this morning. It was very successful and due to atmospheric conditions blast was not felt too badly in Las Vegas—probably will be some reports of broken windows. Got about what we hoped for.

    1. Dr. Walter F. Colby, director of the Division of Intelligence.

Senator McMahon called. . . . GD then mentioned the Greenglass case—Greenglass has been talking and they hope to get the fellow Rosenberg, the big one. The problem is how much can Greenglass be allowed to say? How important is it to get the death sentence by having Greenglass tell everything (putting on a big case) or putting on a small case and maybe having Greenglass get life?

≡ *February 7, 1951*

GD called Jim McInerney[1] and said we need some top people from Justice tomorrow to go with us to a meeting with the JCC on this question of the Greenglass case. We feel we need someone over there who could explain to the JCC what the odds are in getting some good information out if we let this thing go on the stand—we realize you cannot be specific. Perhaps someone could point out if there has been any indication. McInerney said there is no indication at this point and [he] doesn't think there will be until we get a death sentence. He talked to the judge and he is prepared to impose it if the evidence warrants. GD asked if he could come along tomorrow but McInerney said he had to appear with Johnston and OPS people. Said Whearty[2] would be there and Lane,[3] the prosecutor who is down from New York. McInerney said Peyton Ford is *the* Assistant to the Attorney General and is all informed about it but he couldn't contribute anything—he is so very brittle—won't say anything that isn't exactly necessary.

1. James M. McInerney, chief of the Criminal Division, Department of Justice.

2. Raymond Whearty, first assistant attorney of the Criminal Division, Department of Justice.

3. Assistant U.S. attorney Myles J. Lane had originally been assigned to prosecute the Rosenbergs. Irving H. Saypol, the U.S. attorney for the Southern District of New York, replaced Lane and supervised the prosecution of the Rosenbergs.

Scheduled meeting before JCC meeting tomorrow to go over Greenglass case.

## ≡ *February 8, 1951*

Met with JCC this morning to discuss Greenglass case, etc.

During the course of the past two weeks five nuclear detonations were exploded at the Bombing and Gunnery Range at Las Vegas, Nevada. No residual radioactivity. Much was learned in the way of cloud pattern, monitoring techniques and instrumentation for measure for energy releases—all of which will be useful at Greenhouse.

One of the most significant accomplishments was the proving-in * * * * Team work with the military was perfect.

I reported to the President one-half hour after the last detonation which took place on Tuesday, February 5th,[1] at approximately 6:00 A.M. He was pleased with the results. Said that we were doing a good job in the Commission. Wanted to have a written report on the tests when it could be prepared. Expressed a desire to see an explosion and indicated that possibly he might be able to attend one of the Eniwetok tests. Expressed the hope that we would never have to use atomic weapons and stated that, however, we could never afford to be anything but strong with them.

1. The final *Ranger* shot was actually fired on February 6, 1951. President Truman never did see a test shot.

Reported yesterday to the JCC on tests—several members of the Committee having attended one or more of them. I actually attended only shots three and four. Notified them of . . . our inclination to reveal in the forthcoming espionage trial, in the testimony of Greenglass, certain information concerning * * * * This being necessary in the opinion of the Justice Department to secure the death sentence penalty for Rosenberg, the principal defendant.

Learned yesterday through Dr. DeHoffmann, in a conversation which I promised not to divulge, more of the difficulty within Los Alamos Laboratory resulting from strong view-points on the part of Teller, Wheeler, Von Neumann, etc. to push the super project and the contrary views of Manley, Holloway, Jetty and probably Bradbury,[1] who advocate the more leisurely approach. Teller is in Washington and has talked to several people about his fears; Wheeler is considering going to Princeton; Von Neumann and possibly Teller to do certain calculations on the Princeton machine. They look upon this as at least a year's project. Bradbury would be against this. He would feel under his direction it is hard at this time to support the program at Los Alamos in view of the attitudes of the key people there. Oppenheimer has discouraged, and very effectively, people from getting too enthusiastic about the program and would like to see it follow a rather leisurely course. I do not know the answer to this one, but we will have to find one no matter how unpleasant the results may be. Even some of the most basic fundamental calculations have not been made, including cross-section of U-235 and the data on the T-D$^2$ reaction.

1. The scientists mentioned in the conversation are Edward Teller, John Wheeler, John Von Neumann, John Manley, Marshall Holloway, Eric R. Jette, and Norris Bradbury. Wheeler did go to Princeton to organize a group to work with the Princeton computer. Wheeler's group came to be called Project Matterhorn.

2. T-D is tritium-deuterium.

[I received a] memorandum from Murray the other day inquiring [about] whether we were making a study of what was involved in going all-out in our program. [It] brought a response from me to him to the effect that if one assumes, as we have been, that all the facilities [that] should be built to handle all fissionable ore [have been built, then] this is an all-out program. The only additional step that can be taken, outside of expediting such significant parts of the program as refabrication of pits and cores, [or] expediting TBP and Redox,[1] is [an] expanded program for the discovery and acquisition of additional raw material. I purposely omitted from the memorandum another place where we might well be pushing hard and this is the super project. I did this because Dr. Smyth is now at Los Alamos looking over the situation and will not be back until late today.

1. TBP and Redox were both chemical processes for removing fissionable materials from the waste fission products generated by the Hanford production reactors.

≡ *February 12, 1951*

Boyer called GD. . . . Boyer said that Teller came in to see him on Friday evening and that he found the conversation quite interesting.[1] Boyer thought he and Jim (McCormack) might talk to Harry (Smyth)—to find out from Wheeler about Teller.

1. Teller asked Boyer to devote more resources to the thermonuclear program and suggested that thermonuclear work should perhaps be moved away from Los Alamos.

GD called Dr. Smyth and said he had been thinking about Norris' visit on Wednesday. It is rather important to have "super" future—to know weakness and strength of each one. Suggested informal discussion today. (Meeting was held at 10:30 with Boyer, McCormack, Williams and Commissioners on "super" program, in Chairman's Office)

≡                                                                    G. Dean
                                                          February 12, 1951

MEMORANDUM OF CONVERSATION WITH LEWIS STRAUSS:

Late Friday afternoon Mr. Strauss came in to see me. He had an outline of the remarks that he wanted to make, amounting to several pages, which recalled matters which I was fully familiar with; such as his interest in getting super project pushed, the views of the GAC, the views of the several Commissioners in memorandum to the President in the Fall of 1949, the President's directive of January 30, 1950, etc.

He said that he had been advised from several sources (I assume these to include Teller and DeHoffmann) that the program was not an all-out program; that Oppenheimer's words had been sabotaging the project; that unless something radical was done that those working at Los Alamos would be so discouraged that they would leave and that, in short, we were not living up to the President's directive.

I told him I was inclined to agree except, of course, [for] the assertion that the matters were in the hands of people who did not believe in it. This is hardly true since people at Los Alamos were most enthusiastic about the super at the time the Directive went to the laboratory. I said, assuming most of what he said was true, the real hard problem was the question of what to do about it. That there were several alternatives, such as (1) setting up a new division for thermonuclear work at Los Alamos; (2) setting up a brand new weapons laboratory; (3) removing to a place such as Princeton work on the calculating machines; (4) putting an enthusiastic man in charge at Los Alamos who would in addition farm out certain problems in the field to our laboratories, to universities and to the Princeton calculators if the latter were set up.

Strauss did not suggest any particular solution although [he] seemed not to be unfavorable to a new establishment. We did not talk about the alternative of having one of the services operate a weapons laboratory. Had we done so I would have had to express quite strongly my objection to any such development.

I asked Strauss if he would leave his notes with me and he said he preferred to burn them and he proceeded to the fireplace and burned them.

Today, February 12th, Mr. LeBaron told me in a conversation that when he talked to Strauss a few days ago Strauss said that he was proposing to go to the President with the matter and that LeBaron had dissuaded him. I told LeBaron this amazed me since Strauss made no mention of the fact in his talk with me and seemed to be happy that we understood the problem which faced us in correcting the situation.

≡                                                                    G. Dean
                                                           February 20, 1951
In order to bring the Commissioners a little closer to the daily operations of the Chairman's Office I am incorporating a daily summary of correspondence received, correspondence signed, together with miscellaneous items of importance that come through the telephone or as a result of conferences on matters which would not ordinarily come to the attention of the other Commissioners.

≡ *February 26, 1951*

LeBaron called and said the military are going into this H-bomb business a little bit. He understands that apparently he is going to get a letter later this afternoon which the military would be expected to go along with so that the Commissioners can go over and talk to the President tomorrow. GD said he thought what he referred to is this: For some time GD had felt that we should give the President a report on the status of the thermonuclear.[1] Orally I think I should tell him tomorrow what the status is and tell him a memorandum is coming over. It is not too optimistic a picture the way it is presented but indicates what our policy should be regarding this urgency, etc. LeBaron said he had understood that AEC was to determine feasibility but what we were to do with it was to be a joint responsibility. GD agreed with that and said you don't have enough time to do anything like that by tomorrow. LeBaron said before they (JCS) take a vote on it, we should take a look at it and see what we should do on it. GD said he saw the draft on Friday and said it was o.k. with him—but it has not come to the Commission formally yet. LeBaron said he thought it should be an agenda item some time soon. LeBaron said the figures we have are quite different from those we got at the briefing out at Nevada. The burn-up[2] is a lot faster than they thought and they can't keep the slugs in the pile as long as they thought. Therefore, I think you will have to tie up a little more material than originally planned. GD agreed—said that is expecting too much.

1. Dean and Secretary of Defense George C. Marshall sent President Truman a formal report on the thermonuclear program on April 4, 1951.
2. Burn-up refers to the irradiation of uranium in the Hanford reactors.

≡ *February 27, 1951*

Commissioners went to see President today.

≡ *March 1, 1951*

Today received from the President his approval of the "requirements"[1] letter left with him on February 27th when the Commission went over to see him.

1. The "requirements" letter was a formal directive from President Truman specifying the annual amounts of uranium 235 and plutonium the commission would produce.

≡ *March 2, 1951*

Peyton Ford, Deputy Attorney General, came over to see GD about the Greenglass case. Ford was made fully aware of AEC's position and promised complete backing for that position in the event that it became necessary.

≡ *March 5, 1951*

GD returned General McCormack's call. . . . GD then asked if MLC had had a chance to look at the statement on the thermonuclear. McCormack said they had and that LeBaron said the scale and rate would be read by Dr. Bradbury; also that GD would be asked about Hanford G/T level on basis of future ore and redox capacity and that it is well to say the capacity for separating is such and such and run out of ore eventually. McCormack also said GD might be assaulted as he had been on why not have two Los Alamos, one run by someone else. GD said he would listen.

GD called Snapp[1] and asked whether the Commission had approved (during his absence last week) the draft report to the President on the thermonuclear. Snapp said it had not—but had agreed to talk about it at AEC-MLC meeting, but that no action would be taken this afternoon. When brought up Dr. Smyth will have some direct comments to make. Snapp said LeBaron did not want to be in a position of not being on both sides of the fence in this. Snapp thinks it warrants only casual comment of it being particularly helpful to have their comments early in our thinking.

1. Roy B. Snapp, secretary to the commission. Dean, of course, was concerned about the formal report to the president on the thermonuclear program, which was then being drafted.

GD called Dr. Smyth and said he was going to count on Dr. Smyth for the Hanford pile program this afternoon (MLC meeting). I don't know what their concern will be, but it may be some growing out of McCormack's reservation—what effect will be on weapons. I suppose LeBaron will start from there. Smyth said he thought his reservation was essentially met by any program which meets the directive o.k. GD said he didn't know just [what] was intended and what they expect to say. Smyth said he would be there and he thinks he understands the program—although the papers have not been very good. GD asked him about the thermonuclear paper; had he seen that? Smyth said that seems to be o.k. with me although it is not entirely thermonuclear. Doesn't care much for the last section or two of it. Doesn't believe we want to start talking about a second lab to the President yet. It doesn't say that specifically, but it implies it. GD said he had forgotten that there is any reference to the other labs. There is still that push in the military for that other lab and we don't want to walk into that. That may be in the background of the discussion this afternoon—we should keep our ears open.

≡ *March 7, 1951*

Boyer called about Greenglass trial. Asked if GD would like to get Denson, Rolander and possibly Derry[1] down to give their personal reactions. Derry is worried—is afraid he might get into a box on this thing. (Derry to be one of the expert witnesses for the government in the case). Williams told him to stop worrying about it. GD said he would like to see what they are calling on him to testify to. Boyer said he would get hold of him and tell him to come right down.

1. William Denson, an attorney from the commission's general counsel's office. C. Arthur Rolander, Jr., chief of the violations and visitor control branch in the Division of Security. Denson and Rolander served as the commission's liaison men to Saypol's office. John A. Derry, executive officer of the Division of Biology and Medicine. Derry was worried that he might be asked to disclose yet uncompromised and still-classified details of the atomic bomb.

GD called Peyton Ford at Justice and said our men had had a conference with the men from the District Attorney's office in New York on Monday. We are quite disturbed about the extent to which the cross-examination is going to be opened up judging from the direct examination—the questions that were put to our two key witnesses. The two fellows assigned by Saypol to handle this case are pretty young fellows.[1] Lane who worked with us so well has been relegated to a back position. GD said he understood some of the reasons for this, but it makes things a little difficult for us. Ford said he understood that this fellow Cohn (who is handling the case) is a very bright fellow—one of the smartest to come down the pike in a long time; he has an outstanding mind. GD said he was sure of that. GD just doesn't think he appreciates the danger of opening this thing up completely. GD would like to make this suggestion: that if we could have the list of direct questions that are going to go to Derry and Koski, then I think we can be very helpful. Ford said he could do that—absolutely; and said he thought AEC should keep somebody on the ground up there who has some responsibility. GD asked if the questions could be gotten to him soon. Ford asked if he wanted the questions to be put to Greenglass too. GD said it would be helpful if they had it, but Derry and Koski are the important ones—they are both expert witnesses on the insides of the bomb. Ford said o.k. he would take care of that; also said he would try to get Lane back in the picture a little bit more. GD said that may be difficult; but if Lane could, for example, handle the examination of Derry and Koski we wouldn't have any fears. It is the breadth of questioning that bothers us. Ford said he would take care of it; he will follow up on it and if he doesn't call back, Jim McInerney will. Ford said he has been trying to get a case worked up to present to the Supreme Court on Friday and getting away from the office is the only way to get anything done on it—that is why he has been unavailable for the last day or so. GD said he certainly understood that—the only way to get it done is to hole-up someplace. GD thanked him for his cooperation on this Greenglass case.

1. Saypol's young assistants were Roy Cohn and James B. Kilsheimer.

≡ *March 8, 1951*

James McInerney (Justice Dept.) called and said that Peyton Ford has spoken to him and that Saypol would handle the three witnesses himself (Derry, Koski and Greenglass) and that one would go on today; the one to-day would be Koski. Would not have time to clear the direct examination here, so they will clear it with AEC liaison man up there. McInerney men-tioned possibility of "knife-work" and GD said he did not think so. They had talked to Lane and had formed a very good impression of him; also that he was not suggesting that he be in or be out, but that he (Lane) did understand our problems. GD said that some of the others were fresh and independent and that it was the old story of the New York office. GD said that he was very fearful of Koski and Derry if they open up as they want them to. McInerney said that Saypol would handle the witness this after-noon and the two AEC witnesses. GD then asked about direct examina-tion of Derry, and McInerney said that it would be submitted to him over the weekend and also the direct on Greenglass. . . .

GD called Hollis' secretary and gave her the following message for Mr. Hollis: "In my talk with McInerney of the Justice Dept. this morning he said that Koski in New York would probably be a witness on this afternoon and that it was impossible for them (the New York U.S. Attorney's office) to get the direct questions to us in time. However, the direct examination of Greenglass and Derry will be submitted to me (GD) this weekend."

Senator Hickenlooper called and said for the last month he has been per-sonally quite concerned about the question of this trial (Greenglass et al.) and his fears were revived again today by a man who was briefed in antic-ipation of being called as a witness. His concern was raised on the very ex-tensive revelations—or declassification—that the Justice Department in-sisted it had to have in the case. Asked GD how he felt about it. GD said every day now for the last week I have been in touch with them on this. He said yesterday he finally demanded from Peyton Ford that we have the ques-tions on direct examination that we are going to have submitted to Green-glass and Derry who will be one of our experts. If we don't get the direct questions and know what [they are], then cross examination will never be-gin to be controlled properly. GD said they have got Saypol, the District At-torney up there, to agree. The fellow, named Lane, who appeared before the JCC with us—GD said he was considerably impressed with him. Hick-enlooper asked GD if he remembered that at the time of the JCC meeting he [Hickenlooper] had raised this question of keeping away from declassification. The witness or counsel for the government might [then] well plead in an objection that the question to be answered on cross-examination, if too broad, was a violation of the law for this man to answer. [He also] thought that the defendants might go out and subpoena a lot of fellows and try to bring out a lot of stuff on public record that would enable them to talk about it later within the law. GD said the only way he could figure was to get the questions to be used on direct and we could take Derry, who doesn't want to violate the espionage act, and personally go over it with him and no matter what the District Attorney thinks the answer should be, we will have agreed on that down here. Hickenlooper said the subject raised on the direct governs the cross-examination. GD said that is the point and I think that is the only way we can control it. GD also said he was concerned about Lane having been shelved a little bit; they have brought in a couple of younger fellows who are smart but eager. The show is run by the United States Attorney and they have been a very independent group. Hickenlooper asked if it wasn't the Attorney General's prime responsibility. Hickenlooper said, with all due respect and with no personal animosity, he has a feeling that if McGrath is talked to about this— McGrath is a pretty decent person and a good lawyer and outside of disagreeing on politics McGrath and Hickenlooper have been good friends and Hickenlooper has always found him to be most anxious to try and work such things out. Ford, on the other hand, is strange. Hickenlooper said sometimes he doesn't understand Ford. GD said, as a matter of fact, he would tell the judge that we are concerned about the scope of this thing. There is a national interest in this and if it comes to that, GD thinks he will do that.[1] Hickenlooper said he had thought about that a little but we just have to rely on people who know. GD said the one he is keeping his fingers crossed on is Koski. Apparently we are not going to have any trouble on the others—we will have the questions in advance. Hickenlooper said he was just concerned about the whole thing and this call is not in any aspect of criticism, but it is just an expression of concern in which I join you. GD said he was glad to hear that Hickenlooper feels that way because we have done a lot of work on it this week in one conference or another. GD is afraid the District Attorney will "feel his oats," and not listen to reason up there. GD said if there is any occasion of a rift on this thing growing out of this afternoon's session, I am going up there myself; I have done some criminal cases myself; and I know you can do it and do it right; without doing a lot of things that will hurt us.

1. There is no indication in either the diary or commission records that Dean spoke directly to Judge Kaufman about the problems of protecting uncompromised atomic bomb data.

≡ *March 9, 1951*

GD called Attorney General McGrath and said he hesitated to call him but he had talked to Peyton Ford and that something had come up which disturbed the AEC very much in regard to the Greenglass case. We had an understanding that certain of the Greenglass testimony would be explored and therefore wanted to try to hold the direct examination down as much as possible so that the cross-examination could be held down. GD talked to Jim McInerney yesterday and he had told him the direct of Greenglass would be furnished this weekend, but that according to our people in New York today Saypol refused to submit the questions. McGrath asked why and GD said he thinks Saypol wants to remain independent and since we expect to have called on Monday a scientist [Koski], it must be handled very carefully. The Attorney General suggested that they (GD and Hollis and Rolander, etc.) come out to his house around 10:00 A.M. tomorrow morning (Saturday) and talk about it. GD said it won't take too much of his time, but they would like to give him the picture [and] it is considered very serious.

≡ *March 10, 1951*

Held a conference at ⟨Attorney Gen.⟩ McGrath's home this morning (GD, Hollis, Rolander and Denson went from AEC). This together with numerous telephone calls has resulted in working out what seems to be a highly satisfactory relationship for the handling of information in the Greenglass trial. We were finally able to secure from Saypol the direct questions which are being put to the witnesses Koski and Derry and in the Monday afternoon examination of Koski, Saypol stuck literally to the agreed-upon direct questions. The cross examination by defense counsel was unexpectedly brief (the above was taken from notes dictated by GD).

GD called Peyton Ford at the Sherry-Netherland in New York. Ford said he had talked to Saypol. Denson would probably be the man from AEC here going to New York and would get in touch with Ford tomorrow (Sunday).

Hollis called GD and GD told him that Ford had had a two-hour session with Saypol and AEC will get the questions. Ford said somebody should be up there with the responsibility to act for AEC—someone who can say "no, you can't ask that, etc."

## ≡ *March 12, 1951*

Hollis called to say that at last we have a little good news on this Green-glass et al. trial. The direct examination [was] handled by Saypol himself today and he stuck to them [the agreed-upon questions]. Koski was a brilliant witness. They only asked him three questions on cross examination. The feeling among our fellows up there is very different now. The boys seemed to "light up" over night. Hollis said what they finally did was what we tried to work out originally—interrupt the Greenglass direct and put Koski on and get him off and back to Greenglass again. GD asked if we have the Greenglass questions on direct: is there any reason to send them [the Greenglass questions]? Hollis said there was not; he gets things all balled up anyway. Hollis said before Koski went on Greenglass was talking about the bomb and the defense counsel got up and said in view of the national security involved in the subject he suggested that the Court be cleared and the record impounded. So, the judge cleared the court and the press got mad and got hold of Senator O'Connor.[1] The press got back into the court but the public did not. The judge told the press they didn't know whether the information they were going to hear had gotten to the Russians actually or not, and to act accordingly. GD was worried about this because he thought they had laid the foundation for an error in the appellate court. GD said "that is very foolish." Hollis agreed and said particularly when it was the kind of testimony that it was. GD said he was afraid they have some grounds for a "reversible error" even without the defendant's consent. Hollis said that may be true, but he thought if they tried it on appeal, they would be stretching the whole idea—since the press was left in. Hollis said again for the first time in this whole case our boys are talking with their chins up a bit.

1. Probably Frank O'Connor, a New York State senator.

## ≡ *March 13, 1951*

GD called Hollis and asked him if, after this trial is over in New York, he would prepare a letter to Attorney General McGrath thanking him for bringing about this control. Hollis said he thought we should wait until Derry gets through. Hollis said he thought McGrath did well by us and will make a note to get such a letter prepared after the trial is over.

GD called Captain Waters and told him he had just recalled that Rolander had said that Greenglass had names of the people at Los Alamos. Captain Waters said that was right; that a list of 18 had been sent to the General Manager and were to be shown to GD. GD said that since AEC was now on the spot that additional checking should be done and Captain Waters said that they had the list and that this was going to be done—or was being done now.

## ≡ *March 19, 1951*

Peyton Ford, Deputy Attorney General, called to find out how we were doing and how we were feeling about the Greenglass et al. trial in New York. GD told him the whole complexion had changed since the decision to give us the direct questions to work on and look at before they were presented. GD said he didn't know if John Derry had gone on the stand yet but was sure he would have no trouble when he does. GD thanked Ford for calling and for everything he has done to cooperate with AEC in this case. GD said he was planning to write to the Attorney General and thank him for the cooperation AEC has received from the Dept. of Justice.

## ≡ *March 20, 1951*

GD called Hollis' office to ascertain when John Derry would go on the stand in connection with the Greenglass et al. case in New York. Hollis' office said he would probably go on some time today.

Boyer called. . . . McCormack is going to ask for the report on the TN [thermonuclear]. Boyer said he had the advise on personnel, so we are all clear on that. Boyer asked if there was anything else that required action. GD asked if it was left to him to ask LeBaron on the briefing. Boyer said there is a letter being prepared for GD's signature. GD asked Boyer if he thought this thing on the TN was worthwhile. Boyer said he thought it was very worthwhile—it is going to start things that will be constructive. It was that conflict of manpower situation—those two stories just didn't agree. Boyer said he thought the idea of getting Norris (Bradbury?) in and batting it out with him is very important. Boyer thinks we kind of let our thinking get a little loose with regard to that. Boyer thought it helped a lot. GD said there is a conviction in McCormack's mind that we are not doing enough. Boyer said that is right—it worries him too whether we are doing all we could. Boyer said he was inclined to think that with Froman[1] going in and a little change in the atmosphere, we might make the most progress pursuing the present general direction. Will keep Wheeler et al. quiet and some of the outside people. A lot of the trouble in the temperamentality of Teller—that is the answer to a large part of the thing that Pike was questioning. GD said he thought that was in large part true. Boyer said you know you can get things done if you spend a little time with people.

1. Darol K. Froman, technical assistant to the director of the Los Alamos laboratory.

≡                                                                    G. Dean 4/5/51

On March 26th Mr. LeBaron told me that the situation in Korea looked rather unfavorable; that the Chinese were massing large forces; that they apparently intended to use their air forces for the first time; that this was coming about with definite support from the Russians; that Molotov had been delegated by Stalin to handle matters in Asia; that it might even result in a decision by the Russians and Chinese to launch an offensive against Japan. * * * * It was this situation that accounts for my thinking as represented in [the] attached memorandum.[1]

1. This note is the first of a "mini-diary" Dean kept pertaining to the transfer of complete weapons to the Department of Defense. The remaining parts of the "mini-diary" are Dean's notes of March 27 about the situation, Dean's notes of April 5 of the conversation with Boyer and the conference with the commission, Dean's letter (never sent) of April 5 to President Truman, Dean's memorandum of the April 6 conference with President Truman, Dean's memorandum of April 9 of his conversation with Boyer regarding specific weapons to transfer and of his conversation with Truman regarding informing the Joint Committee, Dean's second memorandum of April 9 concerning his meetings with the Joint Committee, and Dean's April 10 notes of his phone conversation with James Lay. Dean locked up the "mini-diary" separately from his regular diary, doubtless because it was considered too sensitive to handle as part of the regular diary. I have integrated it into the regular diary in chronological order with one exception. The exception is the above note which was attached to the notes of April 5 of the conversation with Boyer and the conference with the commission. I placed this note slightly out of chronological order to show how the "situation" actually unfolded.

≡                                                                         3/27/51

1. *The situation:*[1] The Atomic Energy Commission is asked to express its views on the recommendation of the Joint Chiefs of Staff that 9 nuclear cores be transferred to the Defense Establishment for transshipment * * * *

2. ~~Responsibility of the Commission in such a situation: In the first place, i~~It would seem that the Commission has a responsibility not to permit the problem of custody or of ultimate control of fissionable material or the use thereof to be resolved by any back-door method. In short, if by anything we do now in this situation we are tying our hands or charting a

course from which we cannot turn, we should know what we are doing. It seems to me that we have two responsibilities:

(a) an immediate responsibility to see that the military is in no way hindered in acquiring, once Presidential blessing has been given, both nuclear and non-nuclear parts for immediate and effective use. In all of our procedures we have had this obligation well in mind. We have each year exceeded the requirements set by the Military Establishment for fissionable material and we have never permitted our control or custody in any way to slow up procedures for transfer.

(b) ~~We have a responsibility to the American people to to see that the weapon is not used unwisely. This means in any decision to use it~~ our knowledge concerning the stockpile, the percentage that would be represented by any transfer, and particularly our knowledge of weapons effects should be an important part of the decision. For example, in the present case we should be very careful to determine how the figure "9" is arrived at. Apparently it is arrived at because there are * * * * non-nuclear parts, but perhaps there should be 90 if the international situation justified. Should the non-nuclears * * * * be used at all since they do not contain * * * * This involves a technical judgment, but one on which the Commission's voice should certainly be heard. Would it be better today to send the required number, whatever it might be, * * * * and return the non-nuclears * * * * for refabrication? The time of the shipment measured in terms of apparent nearness of an emergency becomes extremely important because of the short half-life of the initiators. This is a technical consideration. Since those in high places, including the members of the National Security Council, do not appreciate what any given number represents in terms of percentage of stockpile, a decision at the highest level, but only with all possible facts available, involves a determination of what percentage of our stockpile we would be willing to risk in such a venture. The term "risk" includes such problems as method of transport. Should we not, for example, address ourselves to the question of whether more than one nuclear part should be carried in any single plane?

⟨insert⟩
⟨at⟩
⟨p i⟩
We ~~also~~ have a long-range responsibility to the American people to see that this extremely valuable material is not denied to them by an ill-considered commitment to use it up. The American people today assume the AEC controls such decisions. If we don't, the minds of the American people should be disabused. ⟨Having the responsibility to see that it is not used wastefully or unwisely, the AEC must bring to any NSC decision our⟩

~~3. By what device do we get the necessary facts to make the judgment that is necessary if we are to play a part in the decision?~~ It would seem that the Special Committee of the National Security Council is the beginning point. It would give to us the State Department reaction and the military judgment. It also seems clear that this cannot be done by memoranda, but it must be done in meetings with the full information on the table so that it can be discussed. It would also seem that this Special Committee should in turn report to the full National Security Council and that in such a full meeting the AEC, particularly in the event that it was a dissenting party to a decision to transfer or use, should be asked by the President to participate.

4. Is it possible to separate the problems presented by a decision to use the bomb from the problems presented by a decision to transfer a portion or all of the nuclear stockpile to the Military Establishment? It would seem that the problems are somewhat separable, but at the same time they are related and the one merges into the other. It is possible today to make a decision to transfer a given number of nuclears to an advance base to match non-nuclears already there, the same to be held in military custody subject to Presidential order regarding use. In addressing ourselves to ~~this narrow~~ ⟨the⟩ question ⟨whether transfer should take place⟩ it would seem that we should answer the following questions:

(a) Do we run any risk of losing the material in making the trans-shipment?

(b) Is it clear that this is material "on loan," the only significance of the transfer being that the Military Establishment assumes complete responsibility from the date of the transfer for the surveillance, care and return of the material in the event it is not used?

(c) Are we sending it in a direction where it ever could be effectively used?

(d) What are the numerous technical questions, such as which weapons, * * * * initiator supply and replacement, etc.

A decision to use, on the other hand, requires the analysis not only of the questions listed above, which must be examined in the event of transfer, but many additional.

What would be the effect upon the enemy of its use and the effect upon Western Europe and upon Asiatics generally who have felt that the "white man" picks only "yellow men" upon whom to drop bombs—this particular line having been exploited heavily by the Communists.

If the commander in the field determines upon targets where the use would not be fully effective, such as for example in an area with hills on either side, what price would we pay in terms of prestige which we now have because of the popular notion that the atom bomb is an infinite weapon.

Advance decision must be made, again, on what percentage of stockpile we are willing to commit in any given operation, in any theatre of war, having in mind attrition losses, reserves for other areas, etc. Any decision to use now must be made in the light of the fact that we are just beginning to spurt in the production of weapons, that our stockpile a year or two or three years from today will be infinitely greater than it is today. Should we not, therefore, by almost any possible means postpone the occasion where it would have to be used, if it is within our power, to a time when the use of it would *guarantee* victory?

The questions of delivery are not, I think, entirely outside the sphere of AEC knowledge. What is the best plan for delivery? * * * * At what places will it be refueled? What tactics are contemplated for such situations as:

    (a) a fully assembled bomb in a plane which is shot down over enemy territory;

    (b) or over friendly territory;

    (c) what of parachutes * * * * in the event that the insertion has not been made;

    etc., etc., etc.

In any event, I think it is our responsibility to make it clear to the President that any decision to transfer temporarily nuclears to an advance base is in *no sense* a decision to use and that the decision as to use will require a further huddle on the part of the National Security Council. It should in no event be left to the commander in the field who, in the case of Mac-Arthur, has little knowledge concerning effects, in particular.

    1. Dean later incorporated some of these points into an April 5, 1951, memorandum to his fellow commissioners on civilian control of weapons and also into an April 11, 1951, letter to Truman on civilian custody of nuclear weapons.

## ≡ *March 31, 1951*

Dr. DeHoffmann called from Los Alamos to set up an appointment for Dr. Teller to see GD on Tuesday. Wants a long time—an hour or so. Teller has talked to Froman and Bradbury about this and they know he is coming in to see GD. Appointment set for 10:00 A.M. Tuesday but later changed to Wednesday.

## ≡ *April 2, 1951*

Arnold Kramish said that he had just heard that Teller's plane had to turn back and could not make appointment—changed to Wednesday, the 4th, at 10:00 A.M.

## ≡ *April 3, 1951*

Boyer called. . . . Boyer then mentioned that they had had a very nice talk with Budget people at Los Alamos. What delighted Boyer as far as he and General McCormack were concerned was that they could have just kept their mouths shut—Bradbury and Tyler, with a little urging, seemed to view the thinking in a logical sort of way—and we could work out the problems. The compromise came from the Los Alamos people; they made the suggestions. GD mentioned that Teller is coming in tomorrow. Bradbury has written a letter saying he is glad Teller is coming in. GD said he would like Boyer to take a look at the Bradbury letter and a memo from Froman and also a letter from Libby.[1] Boyer said he had talked to Bradbury and he has been much more objective—when he was here he got very tense about the whole thing. GD said he had never really worried about Bradbury's attitude on the "effort," but has worried about Manley's and Oppenheimer's. Boyer said he and Bradbury chatted about the situation. Boyer said our thinking is that since we finished Greenhouse we should be sure we have our program clearly in mind—disappointed with the idea of bringing some people in. He said he could understand that. Mentioned people like Oppenheimer, Bethe and Fermi and by all means Teller and Bradbury himself. Boyer said his whole attitude was so objective, he (Boyer) is sure we can work the whole thing out. . . .

1. Dr. Willard F. Libby, a chemist (and later Nobel Prize winner) named to the General Advisory Committee in August 1950.

## ≡ *April 4, 1951*

Dr. Edward Teller came in for over two hours this morning to discuss situation at Los Alamos and progress on thermonuclear.

GD called Boyer and asked if he saw any objection to GD's circulating to the Commissioners and General Manager for inside consumption only the various papers on the thermonuclear division; that is, (1) Libby's letter to GD; (2) Teller's to Bradbury; (3) Bradbury's letter to GD telling him that Teller is coming in; and (4) memo to Bradbury from Froman.[1] GD said it is all rather basic thinking. Boyer said he thought it important that the Commissions have just about as full knowledge of the problem as possible. Boyer said he would be hesitant to circulate anything that might embarrass any individual, but . . . GD said he didn't think there is anything in this that would embarrass anyone; if Boyer sees no harm, GD will circulate them. Boyer said on the contrary, he thinks it is important that the Commission be fully informed; they have to carry the responsibility, so they should know. GD mentioned that in talking with Teller he had said that we had in mind getting in some of the people who have been very close to this thing for our own guidance. He said he thought it would be a very useful thing to do. Teller urged us to bring in people who have been working on it such as Von Neumann, Wheeler, Bethe, Fred Seitz[2] (a little new, but has been in it), and Bradbury. Boyer said it looked like the boys are working along the same lines now. Boyer thinks we should get Oppenheimer in on it, or he and one other member of the GAC he might select—or we would ruin ourselves with the GAC forever. GD said he thought Fermi would be a good idea—anyway, he thought he would report on this thing. GD doesn't believe it will be as hard as we thought. Teller is going to be away all of May. GD told him our thinking would crystallize by June. Boyer asked if he were taking a vacation. GD said he is going to Eniwetok and what else he doesn't know. Boyer said Bradbury would be happy to have him take a vacation and quiet down—he seems to be under quite a bit of tension. GD agreed but said that for a fellow with as much intensity in this field generally, he has much more objectivity than we give him credit for. Boyer said maybe this cooling-off period is not delaying a sane approach to the problem. Boyer hopes that is the case, anyway. Boyer thinks Bradbury was much more objective in his whole attitude—thinks he appreciates it better. GD said Teller makes his proposal to Bradbury—it is a plan for setting up a separate thermonuclear division. Bradbury says "no" and comes back with the Froman memorandum. GD says Teller will not stay at Los Alamos unless we ordered him to. Boyer asked if he gave any indication that he wouldn't work with Froman. GD said "no" but added that Froman's conception is so small (25 people); Froman accounts for the 25 by saying that a large number of the laboratory divisions would be called upon for their personnel and help and Froman would be going both to the lab divisions— but these same people have no contact with thermonuclear, no history, no knowledge. The only exception is McDougal.[3] All of the rest, including the head of cryogenics, just don't know about it. GD said "well, we will have many a talk on this." Boyer agreed and said both sides will have to be explored; Boyer agreed that it is important that the Commission be kept fully informed on all aspects. . . .[4]

1. The papers were circulated as AEC staff paper 425, dated April 5, 1951.

2. Dr. Frederick Seitz, professor of physics at the University of Illinois.

3. Duncan P. MacDougall, a division director at Los Alamos.

4. The ellipses at the end of the conversation mark the deletion of extraneous material; the other ellipses appear in the original.

Notes:[1] Conference with Teller 4/4/51

Thermo-nuclear History

Spring of 42 Fermi possible temperature from A. Soon apparent it wouldn't go alone.

Summer 42 Berkeley Oppy,[2] Boethe,[3] Teller. Fission talked less than *fusion*. Several weeks discussions. Ex. (gun type assembly with * * * *)

Fall of 42 Oppy went East with a report of *feasibility* (????) Optimism completely wrong. Implosion unthought of at that time. Oppy said it should be looked into and established * * * * at Los Alamos. Purpose— to experiment with thermonuclear. * * * * * * * * Later took over the shop and ???? the plane.

April 43 first group to Los Alamos discussed thermonuclear. All this shows that L.A. has regarded the thermonuclear as its baby to *solve*.

Inverse Compton Effect.[4] If radiation is present it.—not known if in 42 feasibility report of early 42. Consequently all thought in 40s it was very doubtful.

In 1944 assumed as approach to fission ???? Fermi and Oppy urged Teller to look again at the thermonuclear and most of 45 there was a small talented group. Interest in a *D-T* reaction. Tritium was selected. It was hoyle (good) [Dean].

Spring 45 after Trinity.[5] became clear that the thermonuclear should be the project ????.

With VJ day—the small group became slowly dissipated. It should be done Oppy said under an international authority but not unilaterally. i.e., *moral reasons*.

Prior to Norris' heading the list he had worked almost entirely with implosion—not thermonuclear. None of the crew that stayed on at L.A. had really worked with thermonuclear.

Fall of 46 Bradbury asked Teller to take on theoretical division. Spring 46 feasibility report prepared by Ed ???? ???? Could be carried to a successful conclusion but nevertheless put on the shelf.

Summer of 46 Alarm Clock. High density—not high temperature. *Family Committee* (all division leaders. poor structure. unwieldy, things be frozen. ????) The committee working on present cylinder never spent ???? consecutive days working on thermonuclear.

Calculations not here now. Experimental program *essential* Ex. diffraction ???? ???? ???? ???? what happen in turbulence.

Main quarrel with the Froman case is that the main load would be placed upon people who don't have any background or understanding of the thermonuclear needs.

1. These notes are now found in a file of former top secret Dean material but were once a part of the diary. They have been reproduced from handwritten notes Dean made of the meeting. I have interpreted Dean's handwriting as best I could. Each set of question marks, however, marks a word which I could not decipher. Most of Dean's notes appear to list conferences and reports on the thermonuclear [program]. Two pages of drawings, which are attached to the original copy of the notes, remain classified as do some words and phrases in the notes themselves.

2. Oppy is J. Robert Oppenheimer.

3. Boethe is Hans A. Bethe, Nobel Prize-winning physicist who led a division at Los Alamos during World War II.

4. The Compton effect is one mechanism through which gamma rays lose energy.

5. The Trinity shot on July 16, 1945, was the first detonation of an atomic explosion.


≡                                                           G. Dean 4/5/51

I learned from Mr. Boyer last night that General Ludecke of AFSWP had called Col. Coiner to alert him to a possible request which might come from the Joint Chiefs of Staff within a matter of twenty-four hours * * * *

I, therefore, first thing this morning called together the Commissioners who were available (Smyth, Pike, Murray, Col. Coiner and Mr. Boyer) and told them of the situation. I learned that the Joint Chiefs were at that moment discussing whether they should make the request. It seemed to me that the first thing that we should be clear on was the procedure for transfer and specifically whether the subcommittee of the National Security Council would have an opportunity to discuss any recommendation from the Joint Chiefs before the matter was carried to the President. The Commissioners agreed that the NSC was the appropriate body for such a discussion and that the Commission did have a real interest in exploring the factors involved in such a transfer. They also agreed that a decision to transfer was not a decision to use, and that this should be made clear. It was the consensus that I should call Mr. Lay, Executive Secretary of the NSC, and apprise him of the situation and make sure that it was his understanding that this is the way that the decision would be made.

I made an appointment with Mr. Lay, found out that that was his opinion, and told him that I thought if there were any question in the President's mind it should be resolved. He said he had a 12:00 noon appointment with the President and would take the matter up with him then and if there were any doubt about it, he would let me know. I suggested for his consideration the attached letter. He said it seemed to him a proper way to secure a confirmation of our understanding. I told him I would not dispatch the letter, however, until I had heard of the results of his conference with the President.

At 12:10 he called me to say that he had raised the question with the President and the President was very firm that in his determination any decision would go through the subcommittee of the NSC—there was no misunderstanding in the President's mind—and that Lay gathered that the letter to the President under the circumstances was probably unnecessary. It seemed to me that it was both unnecessary and perhaps might be unduly irritating, and I am consequently not sending it. At this writing (12:15) we have not had any word from the JCS concerning their recommendation.

≡

United States
ATOMIC ENERGY COMMISSION
Washington 25, D.C.

The President[1]                                                           April 5, 1951
The White House

My dear Mr. President:

The procedures whereby the Atomic Energy Commission would accomplish the emergency transfer of atomic weapons to the appropriate agencies of the Department of Defense have been fully developed and are subjected to test from time to time. The manner by which you will instruct the Chairman, AEC, to make such a transfer, however, has never been firmly established.

It is our understanding that any recommendation of the Joint Chiefs that complete weapons or nuclear cores be transferred to the Department of Defense, would be discussed by you with the Special Committee of the National Security Council on Atomic Energy, and that you would give appropriate instructions at that time to the Secretary of Defense and to the Chairman, AEC. If the understanding outlined above is correct, your confirmation will be appreciated.

Respectfully,
UNITED STATES ENERGY COMMISSION
/s/ Gordon Dean
Gordon Dean
Chairman

1. Dean never sent this letter to President Truman.

≡ *April 5, 1951*

GD went to see James Lay this morning on transfer.

Continued budget hearings this morning for 3rd supplemental before House Subcommittee of Independent Offices.

Dr. DeHoffmann came in at 12:30 to talk about thermonuclear situation at Los Alamos.

Mr. Boyer called and asked if he and Col. Coiner could come right down to see GD. GD said he had an appointment waiting to come in but this thing was more important and for them to come on down. (re transfers).

GD called Col. Coiner and asked him to come in with stockpile positions as of today and also as of January 1, 1953.

GD talked to Col. Coiner about GD's going over to see James Lay anyway and doesn't think perhaps there is as much reason for him to see the President if the decision [is] not the President's—leaving to Lay to straighten out what the procedures will be. Coiner said Wilhoyt[1] has a draft of a letter from GD to the President. GD asked if they had a copy of it handy. Coiner said he would try to find a copy and bring it up. GD said if we do get any word, please let GD know. Coiner said he would right away.

1. Colonel Ellis E. Wilhoyt, in the production, utilization, and storage branch of the Division of Military Application.

Mr. Lay called GD and said he had checked with the President and that GD's understanding was correct. GD asked if letter would still be in order and Lay said his reaction was that it was all settled and that he (Lay) got the idea that he did not want to put it on the record but that he (Lay) would leave it up to GD's judgment as to sending the letter. Lay said he got a little bit of negative reaction but very strong orally. GD said he will not send it under the circumstances; just so we understand each other; and Lay said he thought it would be safe to let it ride that way and wait and see if that comes out o.k.

GD wrote memo to other Commissions on Civilian vs Military control of weapons.

≡ *April 6, 1951*

Went over to the White House ⟨at the President's request⟩ at 4:00 this afternoon. Re transfers.

Called meeting of Commission, Boyer, Col. Coiner and Captain Jackson upon return from White House. ⟨see TS memo on record of events[1] on transfer⟩

1. The TS—top secret—record of events is the "mini-diary."

*NOTE*: memoranda dealing with transfer presently stored in Emergency Transfer file.

≡                                                                April 6, 1951

At the President's invitation I went over this afternoon at 4:00 P.M. to the White House and was told by him that the situation in the Far East is extremely serious; that there is a heavy concentration of men just above the Yalu River in the part of Manchuria across from the North-western corner of Korea; that there is a very heavy concentration of air forces on several fields and the planes are tip-to-tip and extremely vulnerable; that there is a concentration of some 70 Russian submarines at Vladivostok and a heavy concentration on Southern Sakhalin—all of which indicates that not only are the Reds and the Russians ready to push us out of Korea, but may attempt to take the Japanese Islands and with the submarines cut our supply lines to Japan and Korea.

He told me he had a request from the Joint Chiefs of Staff * * * * that no decision had been made to use these weapons and he hoped very much that there would be no necessity for using them; that before there was any decision to use them the matter would be fully explored by the special committee of the National Security Council; that in no event would the bomb be used in Northern Korea where he appreciated, as I pointed out to him, that they would be completely ineffective and psychological "duds" if used in Northern Korean terrain.

I told him that there were many considerations we would like to bring to the council table when the question was up as to the use. * * * *

He then said if I saw no objection he would sign the order to me directing me to release to the custody of General Vandenberg, Chief of Staff, USAF, nine nuclears * * * * The order stated that General Vandenberg would approach me to arrange the details incident to the transfer.

I reported to the other two commissioners available, Dr. Smyth and Mr. Pike, and to Mr. Boyer, Col. Coiner and Captain Jackson.[1]

I have called General Vandenberg and told him the President had signed the order; that we were prepared to discuss details with him. He designated General Everest[2] as the man to represent him and I told him our Acting head of Military Applications would represent us. I then inquired whether tomorrow was soon enough to arrange the details and he assured me that it was.

~~Gordon Dean~~

1. Captain A. McB. Jackson, chief, research and development branch of the Division of Military Application.

2. Major General Frank F. Everest, United States Air Force, a member of the Military Liaison Committee.

GD called General Vandenberg—as a result of his visit with the President this afternoon. GD told Vandenberg that the memo he (Vandenberg) had left with the President had been signed. GD said on the implimentation of it (the transfer) there are some details—wondered if it might be well for the Acting head of our Division of Military Application to get in touch with you or your people in order that no time will be lost. Vandenberg said it is going to take a little time anyway; would like to have General Frank Everest get in touch with whomever you suggest. GD asked if tomorrow would be satisfactory. Vandenberg said that will be plenty of time. GD said that is fine; we will do it then.

GD called Col. Coiner and told him of the conversation with General Vandenberg. Told him the General says that Frank Everest is his representative on any details and tomorrow is plenty of time. GD said he would leave it to Coiner to get in touch with him on types, etc. GD also asked that Coiner keep Boyer fully informed. Coiner said he would.

GD called Boyer and told him he had talked to Vandenberg and advised him that the memo had been signed by the President—also that there were some details in connection with a thing like this and GD suggested that the head of Military Applications be our man to arrange from our side and that he or his designee be the person on his side—he designated General Frank Everest. GD said he has told Coiner about that and they will meet tomorrow. GD said he has asked Coiner to keep Boyer fully advised. Boyer said he will be in the office tomorrow and will tell Coiner. Boyer suggested that GD advise the telephone operator where he can be reached this weekend—if you go out. GD said he would do that. Boyer said some times these things pick up momentum. Boyer will always be available to Coiner through the operator. GD said that is fine.

≡                                                                     April 9, 1951
On Saturday, April 7th, Col. Coiner, who had sent an alert by code to Tyler, got together with Everest on the details. * * * *

Mr. Boyer called me in the morning to say that Everest actually wants Mark 4s rather than Mark 6s * * * *

I told Mr. Boyer to keep a running diary[1] of all events touching upon this tranfer. Later in the day he called to say that he had heard through Coiner that the military were fearful lest we report this to the Joint Committee and that I might be getting some high-level calls during the day on this point. In the afternoon the President called me to say that he was aware of our obligation to report to the Joint Committee but he thought it highly important that word of this transfer not get to the full Committee at this time; that this was a highly sensitive military move designed to secure readiness and it was not something that should be thrown into debate in the Congress. I told him that the Commission was in the middle on a proposition such as this because of our statutory responsibility to report what we do. He said he appreciated this; that he didn't want to keep us in the middle and he therefore suggested that he rather than I call the Chairman of the Joint Committee and give him all of the background on the decision to transfer the weapons. I thought this to be a good move and told him so.

In another call Mr. Boyer advised me that the transfer had been made; that there were no hitches except that we were well ahead of the Air Force planes which were to pick them up.

Gordon Dean

1. I searched for a diary General Manager Boyer may have kept of the transfer, but was not able to locate such a document.

## ≡ April 9, 1951

Dr. DeHoffmann called from New York to talk to GD about setting up meeting to discuss thermonuclear division, etc.

April 9, 1951

At the meeting with the Joint Committee this morning I was asked by Senator Hickenlooper whether there were now outside of the U.S. any atomic weapons. I answered "no." This was followed by a question from Senator Millikin[1] in which he asked whether there were weapons parts available anywhere abroad so that an atomic bomb might be assembled. I answered this question "no."

After the meeting Senator McMahon told me that the President had gotten in touch with him this morning and explained to him the decision to transfer to the military for * * * * Apparently, the President gave McMahon about the same background statement that he gave to me stating the reasons for concern in Asia, etc. I told McMahon that I was somewhat disturbed at the way the record stood with the Joint Committee. We have an obligation to advise them, but the President had thought it best that they be advised by McMahon through the President rather than through the Commission. This was alright with me, but I didn't like to give the Joint Committee the impression that trans-shipment of fissionable material or weapons was not imminent—when it was.

Incidentally, I learned this morning from Mr. Boyer that the Air Force did not pick up our weapons at Able and probably will not until tomorrow.

McMahon called in Congressman Durham,[2] ranking member on the House side of the Committee, and told him of the President's conversation. They in turn discussed whether the full Committee should be advised. Durham suggested that both Hickenlooper and Millikin certainly should be advised and probably the ranking minority member of the House side, Congressman Cole.[3] I asked McMahon if he wished me to join him in notifying Millikin and Hickenlooper. He said he did.

About 2:00 P.M. this afternoon Millikin, Hickenlooper, McMahon and myself sat down in the D.C. Committee Room in the Senate and went over the proposition. Hickenlooper raised the question of the President's power under the Act to transfer the fissionable material. We sent out for a copy of the Act and both Hickenlooper and Millikin were convinced that the President's authority was clear.

On the issue of whether the entire Joint Committee should be advised, Millikin strongly urged that the entire Committee should be told and that at the same time it should be impressed upon them the sensitiveness of the information. McMahon decided to do this tomorrow morning at 11:00 A.M. and asked that I be present to represent the Commission.

I told the three Senators of the President's assurance to me that before any decision to use there would be a huddle of the Special Committee of the National Security Council.

Gordon Dean

    1. Senator Eugene D. Millikin, a member of the Joint Committee.
    2. Representative Carl T. Durham, a member and vice-chairman of the Joint Committee.
    3. Representative W. Sterling Cole, a member of the Joint Committee.

James Lay called and said Arneson had just told him about a conversation Acheson had had with the President yesterday [at which] this transfer was discussed—said "the boss" agreed to it. Lay asked if GD had a directive to that effect. GD said he had—got it Friday when he went over to see the President. Lay asked if this had happened before he talked to GD. GD said "no" and that there might be some misunderstanding that the procedure applied only to the decision to *use*. GD said he thought this was a possibility because when he was over, he made sure that we were in agreement. Lay asked if GD talked to the President about it. GD said he did; he was the only one there. He had a recommendation from the Joint Chiefs and said he wanted to talk about it. GD said he told the President he hoped this didn't resolve the question and the President said "not at all." The President didn't sign the directive until we explored it for about 15 or 20 minutes. GD said he expressed the importance of the group sitting down and the President said that will take place. GD's own personal opinion is that the National Security Council should not wait until the recommendation to use comes; if it comes that late then things are pretty hot. Lay said he didn't [think] this was to be the procedure at all. GD said there may have been a misunderstanding. Lay said he had raised this specific question—had anticipated getting this recommendation at the time he talked to the President. GD said on the next action: there are several things that I think the Committee should address itself to and they are things they could be discussing profitably now even in the absence of another decision from the Joint Chiefs that it is time to use one. GD said we are going to get up a memorandum to the President tomorrow suggesting that this is the time now to be calling the NSC together to get some of the factors on the table and explored in advance of an emergency. GD asked if Lay didn't agree and Lay said he certainly did and that Arneson has been working on a paper laying out the factors. GD mentioned that Arneson has been working on that paper for three months now and that we hope to get some of the factors from our side over to the President by tomorrow. Lay asked if GD was going to put the question up in that memo. GD said the question he is going to put up is shouldn't they start meeting now and not wait for a recommendation from the Joint Chiefs to use and GD said he would hope that the President would say "yes" because there are so many important factors in this that there is no time to lose. Lay said he certainly agrees with that. Lay then asked if GD was proceeding on the directive to transfer. GD said he has no alternative. Lay asked what GD thought the President meant when he told Lay he wanted the question explored. GD said he thought the President probably was referring to the use; GD said he had understood that the Committee was to act on use. Lay said he understood that it was to apply to this transfer problem also—Lay said he didn't raise the use point. GD said there must be a misunderstanding somewhere. Lay said he wishes now he hadn't discouraged GD in writing that letter, but that might have been too late anyway. GD said he thought the big one is ahead of us and whatever has happened, has happened—perhaps our memorandum over there will start it off. Lay said he thought it was fine. GD said the memo will be over by tomorrow.[1]

1. This conversation appears twice in the diary; once as typed by Jean MacFetridge in the April 9, 1951, entry, once as transcribed from Dean's notes in the April 10, 1951, entry.

≡ *April 10, 1951*

GD went to meeting of Joint Committee this morning to discuss with them this question of transfer.

Boyer and Captain Jackson came in to bring GD up to date on the transfer.

Yesterday, April 9th, at about 4:00 P.M. in the afternoon James Lay called to say that he had just had a call from Arneson who had been told by the Secretary that a transfer had taken place. Lay inquired, "What has happened to our NSC arrangement?" I said that apparently the President's understanding was that the NSC committee would not sit until the question of use arose. I told Lay, however, that I thought the NSC should be sitting now mulling over the factors involved in the decision to use rather than wait until the last moment when we would be faced with a request for speed to use by the Joint Chiefs; that the Commission was getting up a recommendation to this effect that should be in the President's hands some time today (April 10th). Lay said, "I wish now I had urged you to send your letter requesting clarification." He said, "My understanding of the President's position was that there would be huddles both on transfer *and* use."

Mr. Boyer advised me this morning * * * * that the nuclears were not to be picked up until some time today.

## ≡ *April 11, 1951*

Sent letter to President on transfer question. Mr. Murray sent over a separate letter containing his personal views.

James Lay called to say that he had called Arneson to ask expedition of this transfer procedure question; said Arneson had now sent to him, for work by staff group, a State Department version on that which he tells me he has discussed with the Secretary—not putting up formally as State Department views—does apparently represent what is o.k. by Secretary Acheson. GD said we were preparing one that was going over to the President this morning. It suggests an early calling of NSC—that that need not be the principles—early and continuous study [by] NSC of the problem—should not wait—we urge this on the President—not a statement of action, but suggests topics which we should address ourselves to. Lay asked which group GD would like. GD said it was pretty important and should be pretty high up in our shop. Lay agreed it was a major question and that what Arneson sent was a purely procedural paper which would firm up the procedure in definite terms, not making recommendations to the President on this. Arneson mentioned that they have a paper well-advanced in the State Dept. on the considerations and factors which should be considered.

GD said that this was what we have done. Lay said that Arneson is anxious and so is Acheson to see procedure agreed upon—also follow right along with statement of factors, but not wait on the agreement of definite procedure. GD said that as far as procedure is concerned, all we say is the NSC subcommittee. Lay said that Arneson had sent it in to him informally. GD asked that Lay send it to him and that he was reluctant to name any people right now as he had not thought about it—this thing will be in the President's hands by noon anyway. Lay said he would get it out to GD and LeBaron and that GD could let him know.

## ≡ April 16, 1951

General McCormack and Dr. Bradbury came in this morning and had a two-hour conference with Mr. Dean—on thermonuclear situation at Los Alamos among other things.

## ≡ April 20, 1951

Dr. DeHoffmann called from Los Alamos to say that a memorandum was on its way—or would be tonight—to GD giving some detailed thinking on the new thermonuclear group. It is a rather long letter with a covering note. On the whole DeHoffmann thinks it is a reasonable picture—although he doesn't agree with all of it. He is leaving Los Alamos on Thursday by air—and returning by air—so will be back sooner than originally planned.

≡

G. Dean

Re: ENIWETOK                                                     May 17, 1951

I attended the third shot which was the cylinder, leaving the States on May 3rd and returning on Saturday, May 12th. In order that I can recall for future purposes the outstanding impressions I would like to jot down a few headings:

1. The unreclaimed planes, tanks, ships etc. which have been bull-dozed off the Islands into the lagoon and ocean indicating the terrible wastes of most war operations.

2. My conference on roll-up procedures to prevent a similar waste in our operation.

3. The excellent teamwork in JTF-3 under Quesada.

4. The complexity of the air operations designed to secure samples of the cloud, trail the cloud, and make experiments on the resistance of planes to shock and thermal burn.

5. The color of the water, the coral formations, the marine life, etc. Sharks after the test killed the fish. Live shark on the lagoon Manta Ray.

6. The lessening importance of security measures and no signs of Russian subs. The ability of an enemy to make rough measurements of energy release at great distance by observing the light and experiments made by us in this field.

7. The decision by Security, over-ruled by myself and Quesada, to tear down a heavy concrete structure built by the Corps of Engineers on the theory that the Russians could determine the energy release of the second shot on Engibe.

8. Amazingly intricate work done by those engaged in taking measurements of X-ray and the 19 MEV neutrons in the third shot.

9. The impressions upon seeing the third shot—the first daylight shot since Bikini and the amazing destructiveness of the third shot as indicated by the complete disintegration and disappearance of the block house used for the X-ray experiments. The vaporization of the 200-foot steel tower, together with 283 tons of equipment on top of tower. The complete disappearance of the 6 cast iron, 6 feet tall, sample catchers and the crater filled with water.

10. The number of take-offs and landings of island planes and helicopter planes with only one mishap to a liaison plane.

11. The complicated operations orders and procedures for "shot day." Location of the control posts, the sound of the shot through the intercom at Perry before it reached Eniwetok.

12. The story of the Chinese cook and the menus, and the book with the blank pages entitled "Sex Life on Eniwetok."

13. The enthusiasm and anticipation and satisfaction of those interested in thermonuclear work, such as Teller (with his understatements), De-Hoffmann, etc.

14. The trip to the Curtis:[1] description of its labs and the fine bolting-up of the cylinder. Teller's remark that Eniwetok would not be large enough for the next one and the low dip to Bikini on the way back.

15. The snafu in connection with getting away from Travis to Honolulu.

16. The return on Bendetsen's[2] plane.

17. The 85 degree heat, the 85 degree humidity and 20-knot breeze which is Eniwetok in April and May. The change of the season to rain in early May and the general moisture. The impossibility of keeping clothes dry—the heat lockers. The corrosive effects of weather on almost all metal. The snorkle, flippers and goggles for diving.

17. The military history of the island. Notably the gradual capture of the Atoll, island by island, in 1944, as described in the "Operation Greenhouse" pamphlet.

18. The amazing complexity in cost of the total operation.

1. The *Curtis* was one of the Naval vessels used in conducting the *Greenhouse* series.
2. Assistant Secretary of the Army Karl Bendetsen.

## ≡ *May 17, 1951*

Dr. DeHoffmann came in at 2:00 this afternoon to discuss forthcoming meeting on thermonuclear progress—spent two hours.

## ≡ *May 18, 1951*

Dr. DeHoffmann called from Princeton and left the following message for GD: "What is happening is that Edward (Teller) is writing one of 'those letters'—but a very mild one—to Smyth saying that the time is inconvenient because of Wheeler's plans and also suggesting that perhaps Nordheim[1] of Los Alamos and Libby should also be invited." This brings a new name into the picture which wasn't there before. Letter will go out today or tomorrow air mail, special delivery. Should have it over the weekend.

1. Lothar W. Nordheim, a Los Alamos physicist.

## ≡ *May 23, 1951*

Jim Bennett[1] and Irving Saypol, U.S. Attorney in New York, came in this afternoon—to discuss the Rosenbergs and Greenglass.

1. James V. Bennett, director of the Federal Bureau of Prisons.

## ≡ *May 31, 1951*

Dr. Smyth called from Princeton and left this message for GD: "Tell Pat to tell Mr. Dean that we have been having a very profitable meeting up here with Teller, Oppenheimer, Wheeler, and Von Neumann and I am having lunch with Teller and Oppenheimer here in his office and I think things are going pretty well—so far as I can make out. This remains to be discussed with Norris and the others out there, but there seems to be a fairly good meeting of the minds between Oppenheimer and Teller."

≡ *June 1, 1951*

Wrote to Dr. Oppenheimer accepting invitation to attend meeting at Princeton on 16th and 17th on thermonuclear.

≡ *June 4, 1951*

General McCormack called to say he had just had a call from Dr. Oppenheimer who says that Bacher would be delighted to be invited to the meeting at Princeton on the 16th and 17th. In the light of his outspoken previous observations and objections to the plans and in light of the present plans at Los Alamos, Oppenheimer thinks it would be a good idea. McCormack checked with Dr. Smyth, who also thinks it would be a good idea, but said for McCormack to check with GD on it. GD said he didn't see that he had an alternative—although "it was my wish in the beginning to make this a meeting of the people who have been working on the thermonuclear, but at this point I guess it is o.k. for Bacher to come. Oppenheimer has made it so broad with four people from the GAC, etc. Well, anyway, I suppose we should say 'yes, delighted.'" McCormack said o.k.; he would do it.

≡ *June 12, 1951*

Went to see the President today at noon to give him a picture of one of the Ranger shots and also report verbally on the Eniwetok tests.

≡ *June 14, 1951*

Dr. DeHoffmann came in to talk about forthcoming meeting on thermonuclear at Princeton.

≡ *June 16, 1951*

Meeting today at Princeton—Institute for Advanced Study—of thermonuclear group.

≡ *June 17, 1951*

Meeting today at Princeton—Institute for Advanced Study—of thermonuclear group.

The commissioners of the Atomic Energy Commission in 1952 during
Dean's leadership. This photograph was probably taken in the commissioners' conference room in the Washington headquarters building. Left to
right: T. Keith Glennan, Henry D. Smyth, Gordon Dean, Thomas E. Murray, Eugene M. Zuckert, and General Manager Marion W. Boyer. (Department of Energy)

Dean with test officials. This photograph was probably taken at the Nevada Proving Grounds during one of the continental test series. Left to
right: Gordon Dean, Carroll L. Tyler, Alvin C. Graves, and Kenneth E.
Fields. (Department of Energy)

The Portsmouth gaseous diffusion plant. With more gross floor space than the Pentagon, the plant is indicative of the magnitude of the construction projects Dean oversaw. (Department of Energy)

An aerial view of the Livermore laboratory. This photograph was taken about 1960 when the laboratory had become what Dean had fought against—a full-scale weapons research laboratory. (Department of Energy)

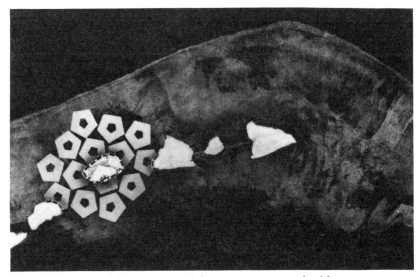

The *Mike* crater. The outlines of fourteen Pentagon buildings are super-imposed over the crater. The heavy dashes indicate islands or parts of islands obliterated by the shot. (Department of Energy)

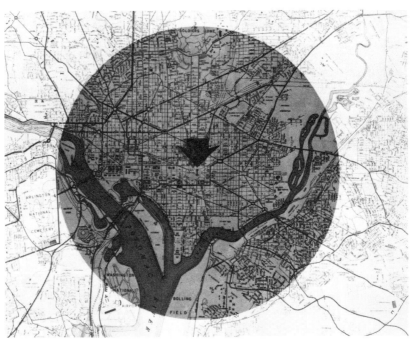

*Mike* blast effects overlayed on Washington, D.C. The shaded circle would have been completely destroyed if the shot were fired in Washington with the Capitol as ground zero. (Department of Energy)

# FOUR

## TACTICAL NUCLEAR WEAPONS
*June 21, 1951, to January 17, 1952*

The summer of 1951 marked Gordon Dean's first anniversary as chairman of the Atomic Energy Commission. Although the year had been grueling, his remaining two years on the commission would not be quite as exacting. In addition to the problems described in this volume, Dean faced the normal pressures of an agency head: fights for budgets, congressional pressures, personnel problems, and innumerable daily management decisions that required attention. Running an agency taxed reserves of patience, tact, and sheer physical endurance.

By July 1951, with the hydrogen bomb program on the road to success and armistice negotiations beginning in Korea, Dean sensed a pause in the rush of events. Concerned that the Communists were not negotiating in good faith, Dean now began to devote time to tactical nuclear weapons. For months Dean had followed press speculation about tactical weapons. Army Chief of Staff J. Lawton Collins's statement that the United States would soon have atomic artillery shells came at the close of the successful *Ranger* series and irked Dean. In a March press conference Commissioner Pike had gone out of his way to warn the armed forces not to reveal new atomic weapons ideas to the Soviets. Despite Pike's admonition Secretary of the Army Frank Pace and atomic energy patriarch Vannevar Bush told reporters that the country could equip its armies with tactical weapons. So popular was the topic that the *New York Times* was quick to speculate that oblique references to atomic weapons in one of George Marshall's reports to Congress meant that atomic artillery shells had actually been tested in Nevada.

Like other administration officials Dean was frustrated by events in Korea and concerned that the Communists were using the negotiations merely as a breather to reinforce their armies for another major offensive. As the diary shows, he saw tactical nuclear weapons as a means to counter Chinese numerical superiority and explored using tactical nuclear weapons in Korea with Assistant Secretary of the Army Karl Bendetsen. The Dean-Bendetsen conversation is a revealing look at Dean's personal views of the

Soviet Union, communism, and world reaction to the use of the atomic bomb as well as his thoughts about tactical weapons. It reveals his one-dimensional view of the Soviets and his naiveté about reaction to the use of the atomic bomb. It also marks one of the few times Dean tried to create administration-wide policy.

Dean and Bendetsen hoped to put their views into a memorandum for Secretary of Defense Marshall and eventually the president. A somewhat garbled version of their conversation, indicating that the commission had atomic artillery shells ready for use in Korea, did get to the president. Advised of presidential misconceptions by Senator Brien McMahon, Dean had to explain to the president that it would take at least a year to create an atomic artillery unit. Tactical weapons, however, had struck a responsive chord.

As Dean nurtured his thoughts about tactical weapons another atom spy case broke. Two British diplomats, Guy Burgess and Donald MacLean, had disappeared in late May, and Dean had recently learned that they had defected to the Soviet Union. MacLean had betrayed information about uranium ore supplies and had perhaps even obtained access to other data about American atomic energy programs. Dean could do little except keep another Soviet penetration of British atomic energy programs from undermining negotiations for greater atomic cooperation with the Canadians. Because references to Burgess and MacLean are scattered and superficial in the diary, I have not reproduced excerpts concerning them.

Pressures, perhaps partially fueled by the April crisis when the administration faced the threat of global war with the Soviet Union and China, now began to build for another massive expansion of facilities for the production of uranium 235 and plutonium. Technical successes at *Ranger* and *Greenhouse*, which suggested new designs for tactical weapons, spurred those calling for an expansion of production facilities. Secretary of Defense Marshall and Commissioner Murray prodded the commission to examine ways to increase production. Senator McMahon added pressure on June 7, 1951, demanding that the commission estimate the costs of increasing production anywhere from 50 to 150 percent.

Dean and his associates could not give McMahon an immediate reply because the issues raised by expansion were complex. What was the best ratio for producing uranium 235 and plutonium? Would new generations of weapons use relatively more uranium 235 or plutonium? Was there sufficient uranium ore to fuel new plants? Should more efficient production reactors be designed for plutonium production? The expansion debate went on throughout the summer and fall of 1951, but the diary does not consistently reflect expansion discussions until just prior to the January 1952 National Security Council meeting.

The second weapons laboratory debate also vexed the commission during the summer of 1951. Commissioner Murray supported the establishment of another weapons research laboratory and insisted that the commission study the issue. Not convinced of a real need for a second laboratory, Dean, Smyth, and Glennan feared that taking work and scientists from Los Alamos would damage laboratory morale and might cause sufficient disruption to delay the hydrogen bomb program. Murray, nevertheless, pressed for a second weapons laboratory, becoming a major advocate for it.

The diary picks up the second laboratory issue in detail on September 11 when Dean learned from Frederic DeHoffmann that Edward Teller, dissatisfied with the pace of the thermonuclear program, had handed in his resignation. This time it seemed as though there might be little Dean could do to keep Teller at Los Alamos.

On September 24, in a reorganization to place more emphasis on the thermonuclear program, Norris Bradbury appointed Marshall Holloway to coordinate Teller's work on the New Super with other laboratory divisions. Holloway was probably the best man for the job, but Teller and Holloway had frequently clashed—most recently over the amount of time needed to prepare the New Super for testing. Teller, naturally, wanted to test the New Super several months before Holloway believed the device and the laboratory could be ready. Teller interpreted Holloway's appointment as an invitation to leave and handed in his resignation for the last time.

Teller later gave several reasons for leaving Los Alamos. His disagreements with Bradbury over laboratory administration and the earliest date for testing the New Super had become a well-known secret. He believed a second laboratory would introduce an element of friendly competition into weapons research and stimulate both laboratories to greater accomplishments. Furthermore, he believed there were now too many promising weapons designs to be investigated by one laboratory. Finally, he could press for a second laboratory far more effectively and openly if he were not an employee of Los Alamos.

Just after Teller left Los Alamos, the Soviets detonated their second atomic explosion. Dean's diary shows that he precipitated a small debate over the explosion when he suggested that the administration not announce the Soviet achievement until after the Americans saw how the Soviets propagandized the event. The diary is our only source for this debate in which Dean was soon overruled. A few weeks later the Soviets fired their third shot.

Speculation about tactical weapons, meanwhile, had been continually fueled by semiofficial pronouncements. With European battlefields in mind, Air Force Chief of Staff Hoyt Vandenberg told members of the Air

Force Association that the Air Force had experimented with atomic projectiles. In San Francisco for ceremonies that marked the signing of a peace treaty with Japan, President Truman startled Democratic party stalwarts when he told them that the country had fantastic new weapons, including new atomic weapons, under construction. Then Senator McMahon announced that atomic weapons were cheaper than conventional weapons and argued that they should form the backbone of the country's armed services. Dean himself favorably compared the cost of atomic bombs with the cost of tanks and told the House Appropriations Committee that the commission was working on atomic artillery shells, torpedoes, and rockets. Hints of these pieces of the tactical weapons debate found their way into the diary.

In this atmosphere Gordon Dean delivered his "Responsibilities of Atomic World Leadership" speech. Both his remarks that atomic bombs could be used tactically and strategically and his association of tactical atomic bombs with conventional weapons aroused criticism. The speech was his most controversial as chairman and increased speculation about tactical weapons, an effect welcomed by McMahon and others building support for another expansion program. As the diary shows, President Truman was not concerned about reaction to the speech, but Dean had to mend some fences with White House Press Secretary Joseph Short.

The commission's second continental weapons test series, called *Buster-Jangle*, started on October 21, 1951, but found its way into the diary only when a test shot failed to explode after a control circuit failed. Dean did not watch succeeding continental tests as closely as *Ranger* because the first series had been such a success and had generally produced little fallout outside the test site. Continental testing increasingly became a routine activity from Dean's perspective.

While the commission conducted *Buster-Jangle*, support for another expansion program grew. Senator McMahon demanded a report on maximizing the role of atomic energy in national defense, and the next day Dean learned that the Joint Chiefs of Staff had decided to support a major expansion of atomic energy facilities. By now Dean realized that another multibillion-dollar expansion program was inevitable, but he believed that expansion was an administration-wide issue involving the Bureau of the Budget and the Office of Defense Mobilization as well as the commission and the Department of Defense. Dean, Smyth, and Glennan argued that only the National Security Council could resolve issues of such magnitude. Commissioner Murray alone wanted to launch a program immediately. To carry out another expansion program successfully, however, the commission would have to have highest priorities for raw materials.

Despite the commission's opposition the second laboratory issue remained very much alive. In early November Teller asked J. Robert Oppenheimer for permission to address the General Advisory Committee on the issue. Oppenheimer consented and, as the diary shows, Teller's request sparked several conferences. Unfortunately Dean placed no notes of the conferences in his diary. Teller spoke to the committee on December 13, 1951, but failed to win support for a second laboratory. Teller would now take his crusade for a second laboratory outside the commission.

A month after Teller's rebuff the National Security Council examined the issue of expansion. Dean hoped the council would fully explore the economic consequences of expansion and the Department of Defense's reasons for pressing for such a large expansion of production facilities. The position paper that he placed in the diary dwelt heavily on its economic impact and indirectly questioned the wisdom of the move. Dean took notes at the National Security Council meeting and placed them in the diary. With so much support for expansion, most of the discussion at the two-hour meeting revolved around priorities. Dean overawed no one with economic consequences, but he did keep Robert Lovett from justifying expansion on the grounds that uranium and plutonium fabricated into weapons could later be retooled and converted into fuel for reactors to produce electric power. After the council approved an expansion program, the commission embarked on another ambitious construction effort.

For additional information on the tactical weapons debate, see also the *New York Times*, February 6, March 2, 13, 22, 25, August 25, September 5, October 8, 1951; the *Washington Evening Star*, September 5, 1951; the *Washington Post*, October 8, 1951. For the Burgess and MacLean case, see also Hewlett and Duncan, *Atomic Shield*, pp. 481–83; and David C. Martin, *Wilderness of Mirrors* (New York, 1980), p. 52. For additional data on the second laboratory debate and Teller's reasons for leaving Los Alamos, see also Thomas E. Murray to Gordon Dean, June 21, 1951; Minutes, Commission Meeting 582, July 26, 1951; Roy B. Snapp to the Commission, with enclosures, AEC 425/3, September 17, 1951; TWX, Norris Bradbury to Gordon Dean, September 26, 1951; Edward Teller, Statement to the General Advisory Committee on Need of Second Weapons Laboratory, December 7, 1951; and Minutes, 28th General Advisory Committee Meeting, December 12–14, 1951, all AEC; and Teller, *Legacy of Hiroshima*, pp. 54–55.

## ≡ June 21, 1951

Dr. DeHoffmann called from Los Alamos and said he believes GD knew there was an agreement made at Princeton for Teller and Bradbury to have a talk; DeHoffmann said they had a very long talk at which no agreement was reached. Teller made an offer to stay if he had administrative responsibility over that part of the program only (thermonuclear) and could actually help it along—that led to a deadlock. Bradbury has written a memorandum to Teller in which he says: following our conversation of yesterday afternoon there appears to be three proposals I would like to make: (1) I strongly believe that it is of the utmost importance to the country that you remain with the program—as Assistant Director for Weapons Development; or (2) would like to suggest your becoming a consultant to the laboratory; will be willing to furnish you with a staff; or (3) we might establish a consultant agreement at Chicago with you so that you could continue the work—and establish a project at Chicago. Would like to have you consider favorably the first suggestion. GD said the first one is certainly preferable to the other two suggestions. Dr. DeHoffmann says from Teller's point of view there is no change in the situation; DeHoffmann thinks the situation is this: Of the three alternatives, he (Teller) leans toward #2 or #3. Of course, there is a 4th alternative: gradually going out of the program entirely—this is a great possibility. GD said he would certainly urge him to take the 1st alternative for the time-being at least. Dr. DeHoffmann said he thought if GD found it possible to discuss the situation with him [emphasizing] the project's importance, rather than [as] a personality problem, he is willing and anxious to see you. He could be there tomorrow. I think you might convince him. GD said let me sleep on it tonight; I wish you would urge him to take #1. DeHoffmann said if GD thought he would do any good by his coming also, he would be glad to come. GD said he would think about it—will you urge him to take #1? GD promised to let DeHoffmann know tomorrow. DeHoffmann gave his phone numbers in case GD wanted them: 2-3037, 2-4140 and 2-3353 (home) and also gave Teller's home: 2-3408.[1]

1. On June 21 Commissioner Murray sent Dean a memo supporting a second laboratory. Thereafter Murray consistently supported a second laboratory.


≡ *June 22, 1951*

General Quesada called to say that he and Graves[1] were going over to see the President and if GD would like to see them before they went, they would be glad to come over. Said there are two points they will try to leave with the President: (1) our progress. We have a very simple chart on yield—indicating how much material was used. (2) we have a chart that shows that the experiment in the thermonuclear was a success—in which there is a rise of certain measurements in 5,000,000,000ths of a second. GD asked if Quesada would so something for him. GD asked if Quesada knew about the meeting at Princeton recently in the thermonuclear. GD said there are a good many problems—thinks one of these days he will probably want to give him a little more on this. Would appreciate it if Quesada would tell the President that GD has been at the meeting at Princeton and that GD will hope to give him a little more information soon on it. GD is afraid he might think that the thermonuclear is just around the corner—GD doesn't want him to do that. Quesada said he planned to be very careful about that. . . .[2] GD said that was his only concern. Quesada said that is why he is carefully separating the two items. Quesada then asked if GD would like to see him before he goes over and GD said that would not be necessary. Quesada said if there is anything significant in the talk, he will call GD and report. GD then told Quesada he had delivered the book to Caldwell[3] and it sobered him a bit on the other tests—thinks maybe we should get the results of Greenhouse first, before we talk about having other tests in Nevada.

1. Dr. Alvin C. Graves, director of the Test Division, Los Alamos, and deputy commander for scientific operations for *Greenhouse*. Quesada and Graves were going to brief President Truman about *Greenhouse*.

2. The ellipses appear in the original.

3. Millard Caldwell, chief of the Federal Civil Defense Administration.

GD asked me to call and give the following message to Dr. DeHoffmann at Los Alamos: "Had to leave for a conference, but wanted to be sure this message got to you: I have decided it would be unwise for me under the circumstances to call Teller, although I am very anxious that he accept the first proposal offered. I think from our conference here that there will be a little more flexibility provided and that there will be considerably more sympathy for Teller's needs, particularly talents such as he had to get from CMR.[1]

1. CMR was the Los Alamos division, led by Eric Jette, which performed chemical and metallurgical research on fissionable materials.

≡ *July 12, 1951*

On Monday Karl Bendetsen, Assistant Secretary of the Army, called to inquire whether I would meet with him and Frank Nash of the Department of Defense that evening to discuss the question of tactical weapons. General McCormack went with me to Bendetsen's home in the evening and there we joined Frank Nash.

The whole problem seems worth exploring and the upshot of our conference was that since Bendetsen was leaving for Paris on Tuesday ⟨the next day⟩ McCormack and Frank Nash would try to work up a memorandum for General Marshall to present to the President. The matter had been explored by Bendetsen and Pace[1] with Marshall and Lovett the morning of Monday, the 9th, and Marshall did not seem unfriendly to the idea and willing to consider it. I told the group I could not speak for the Commission's attitude on the matter but I thought the Commission would look favorably upon a decision by the President to transfer to the military x numbers of nuclears and non-nuclears * * * * to be used by the commander in the field when substantial targets of operation⟨tunity,⟩ notably troop concentrations, developed from intelligence. The decision to use the weapon must be made so rapidly following the development of the target of opportunity that the decision cannot be made in Washington. This requires the establishment of certain minimum target conditions justifying the employment of the weapon.

The memorandum should stress the importance of new terminology; the reference to this use as a tactical use; the findings of the Army Research Committee headed by Rumbaugh and Johnson, and the importance of breaking the stalemate in a fashion which takes the heart out of the Chinese Army effort. The report should conclude with a recommendation to the President that the matter be submitted to the Special NSC Subcommittee composed of the Secretary of State, Secretary of Defense and the Chairman of AEC.

I was asked by Pace to attempt to anticipate the questions which would be raised by State and Defense in such a conference and I listed the following: (1) What would be the affect on the Kremlin of such an effective use— would it, for example, tee-off a third world war? I told him I thought that the answer to this question was "no"; that the Russians do not act except by plan and that our use of it against the Chinese Reds should have no affect on the Russian plan to move across Europe; in fact, that the affect might be the other way, that it might make the Russians think twice in that tactical weapons might be applied to them in Europe should they march. (2) What would be the affect on 400,000 people in the Middle East, ranging from Pakistan and India to Iran, with Nehru the most important to consider? (3) What ⟨would⟩ the affect would be upon the people of Western Europe? (4) What would the people of the United States say? On the last point I volunteered that I thought the people of the United States, after such use of tactical weapons by us, would approve the plan; that people today are tired of the stalemate; they are frustrated by it; that the MacArthur statement that in war there is nothing like victory has popular appeal; and that if the employment were so effective as, for example, to eliminate 40 to 60% of a 250,000 man army, which would inevitably result in complete retirement of the remaining Chinese forces from Korea, that it would be generally applauded. Bendetsen as a result of his visit to Eniwetok has been concerned, and General McCormack and I have shared that concern, that the Russians will so develop their aggressions in various parts of the world without full scale war that over a period of time they could have complete victory without having provoked at any time an incident large enough for the United States to feel it necessary to use atomic bombs. We agreed that one of the real hurdles is the fact that the A-bomb is associated in the minds of the people, and even in the minds of officials such as the President, with strategic targets, meaning specifically cities (Nagasaki and Hiroshima being the outstanding examples) in which civilians rather than military personnel would be the victims.

While the term "tactical weapons" has been frequently used during the past year, notably in rather loose fashion by General Collins,[2] the people still believe pretty much that the A-bomb is a strategic weapon. As a result of the studies made by the Special Research Committee set up by the Army under the leadership of Rumbaugh and Johnson, which went to Korea to study the possibility of tactical applications of the A-bomb, it has become clear that at least on three occasions there were targets, notably the Pyongyang triangle, in which large numbers, in one case some 250,000 Chinese and North Korean troops, were concentrated in a comparatively small area. They also made studies of the terrain and have pretty much killed the notion which has generally prevailed that the Korean terrain, being hilly, would not lend itself to the use of A-bombs. This concept was pretty much put to rest by studies which showed the vulnerability of troops to air bursts at recognized altitudes.

The need for tactical weapons for use by the Army and the need for a new terminology in referring to weapons to be strategically employed was discussed at great length by Bendetsen, McCormack and myself and formulated at Eniwetok. The situation was discussed also by Bendetsen McCormack, Pace and Sibley[3] and Pace is in agreement with our notions. The cease-fire talks now progressing in Korea raised this question: Assuming that the Russians are indulging in this effort simply to gain time to mass large bodies of troops and that they are not undertaking the talks with any real desire for peace; the question then arises as to what the course should be of the United Nations troops in that area. It seems that we cannot forever have a stalemate in Korea nor does it seem wise, as under the MacArthur plan, to enlarge the theatre of war, perhaps risking a Third World War being called. This leaves the alternative of so effectively dealing with the Chinese troops that they can be virtually destroyed in the Korean operation by an intelligently planned atomic attack * * * * The * * * * core produces approximately this bang and we are now in production of * * * * cores. There is no need to wait for the purely tactical weapons

\* \* \* \* and we may not have the time to wait for it. We probably should not use stockpile models with \* \* \* \* cores: first, because we do not want to in the first tactical use employ our "Sunday" punch and second, we want to honestly be able to say that this gadget is a small bang gadget or a tactical gadget for the purpose of securing the support after the attack of people in the Middle East, Western Europe, Asiatics generally and for that matter the people of this country. We discussed at some length the terminology which might be used. I stated should such a weapon be dropped, the term "tactical" was the best yet evolved but it was the feeling that a new term was needed, such as ~~junion~~ "small bang weapons," "Nevada bombs," etc. No very good names were produced.

The memorandum[4] should be ready by the time Bendetsen returns on Monday. It will then be presented to Marshall who will determine whether to take it up with the President.[5]

1. Frank Pace, Jr., secretary of the Army since April 1950.

2. General J. Lawton Collins, chief of staff of the Army.

3. General Alan K. Sibley, secretary of the Army Policy Council and special assistant to the secretary of the Army for politico-military affairs.

4. I have not been able to trace the fate of the memorandum. I doubt that it was ever written. No atomic weapons were turned over to field commanders during the Korean War.

5. Dean's notes of the conversation with Bendetsen are now found in a file of former top secret Dean materials but were originally a part of the diary.

≡ *August 27, 1951*

GD called Bill Borden. . . . Borden found out from DeHoffmann that Teller is going to be in town on Friday and Borden asked them to have dinner with him at the Metropolitan Club on Friday night. Borden suggested to McMahon that he might want to come along—might make the Senator's shoulder available for crying and talk him into staying. The Senator wondered if GD would want to come. GD said he would like to come but the only thing is this whole question of personal relationships is a very tough one out there. Borden said, as you know, I have gotten to know Teller a little bit through past associations. GD said anything that could be done to encourage him to stay on is all to the good. Borden said he could also understand why GD might not want to come along to dinner. GD said he thinks he better not come; it puts him in a bad spot with Bradbury and he has a tough personality problem out there. Borden agreed and said we don't want to make the problem any more difficult. GD said he would like to come, but there is that one fact. . . . GD mentioned that Teller would never be completely happy. Borden agreed; said it is like Dr. Smyth once said that Teller requires a great deal of "crying on the shoulder" time.

## ≡ [*August 31, 1951*]

On Friday, August 31, 1951, at noon, I had a conference with the President, arranged at my request. I asked for the conference because it had come to me, through Senator McMahon, that the President was laboring under the impression that we had available for immediate use, if necessary in Korea, atomic artillery fired projectiles and that this is the type of atomic weapon, if any is used, which would and could be used in the event of a new aggression there and in the event intelligence revealed that an attractive concentration of troops appeared. I first reviewed briefly the purpose of the forthcoming tests in Nevada,[1] explaining that * * * * was the only item in the 7 shot program which would become a stockpile item. The President expressed a desire to see at some time an atomic explosion and asked me to give him the data of * * * * shot so that he could consider whether he could fly out to see it.

I next gave to him a quick summary of our weapon capability as of today, as of January 1, 1952, and as of May 1, 1952; this in terms of available cores and available non-nuclears, laying stress on the fact that the artillery fired pieces would not be available until May 1st and then only in very small number and that because of a bottleneck in the manufacture of the 280 millimeter rifles it would probably not be an operational capability for this particular weapon until the fall of 1952. I emphasized, however, our capacity for the existing weapons to employ these effectively at any moment against troop concentrations. . . .[2]

1. The forthcoming tests were the *Buster-Jangle* series of seven shots fired in Nevada during the fall.

2. Dean also discussed with the president the Joint Committee's request for stockpile data, a British request to use the Nevada test site, recent uranium ore discoveries, and a film of the *Greenhouse* tests. Attached to the notes of the conference with the president were notes of a conference with LeBaron and General Bradley about amending the Atomic Energy Act to permit greater cooperation with the Canadians. The notes of the conversation with the president are now found in a file of former top secret Dean materials but were originally a part of the diary.

## ≡ *September 11, 1951*

Dr. DeHoffmann called from Los Alamos to say that Dr. Teller had this morning handed his resignation—in writing—to Dr. Bradbury. It looks like this may be the real thing, although he has threatened this so many times before. He is sending in a letter to GD on Thursday morning by Dr. DeHoffmann.

GD called Mr. Boyer and said he had just received word that Teller handed in his resignation today and that it may be the real thing. Boyer asked what caused it. GD said it may be because of the meeting today. Boyer asked how the word got to GD, if he doesn't mind telling. GD said [DeHoffmann] telephoned me. Boyer said Bradbury will be here tomorrow. GD said maybe we better wait before we do anything; when do we sit down with him? Boyer said either Thursday or Friday. The time suits our convenience. Boyer said he would think there would be a reaction to this thing in the morning. GD said we better wait until then. Boyer said he sure hopes we can get something worked out. GD agreed; said it will be hard to explain to the JCC, the military and to Lewis Strauss. When he came in and talked to me, I urged him (Teller) not to do anything like that and asked him to let us look over the program. GD thinks that the trouble between the two (Teller and Bradbury) is very basic. If Bradbury says no tests in 1952 or 1953, that may have done it. Boyer said he doesn't want to be too optimistic. Boyer said we will have to put the pressure on Bradbury ourselves, and that will add to "our associates" feelings. GD said one thing is that the talk with Teller had no bearing on this thing—you will get to a test no faster by setting up a new site; it is after, and not before, the test that the new site suggestion is proposed. . . .[1]

1. At an executive session on September 11, the commission decided not to establish a second weapons research laboratory. The commission did direct the general manager to examine workloads at Los Alamos with an eye toward expanding weapons research activities.

## ≡ *September 12, 1951*

GD called LeBaron and told him Bradbury is going to be in town today and tomorrow. It occurred to GD—we mentioned the possibility of discussing at the next MLC meeting on Tuesday something on this thermonuclear—it seems too bad to let him get out of town without at least the MLC having an informal chat with him and get some of the current thinking. GD asked if there was a possibility of setting up a meeting; GD mentioned that he was the only Commissioner in town. LeBaron said he thought such a meeting would be highly desirable. GD said he was wondering if there is any possibility of a substantial number of your people getting here in the afternoon; LeBaron could suit his own convenience as to the hour. LeBaron said he would canvas his fellows tomorrow morning and see what it looks like. We can perhaps set it up for right after lunch. . . .

## ≡ *September 13, 1951*

Dr. DeHoffmann came in this morning at 9:30. Brought with him some thoughts from Dr. Teller. (Teller later decided to wait two weeks before making a firm decision about resigning.)

AEC-MLC meeting this afternoon with Dr. Bradbury on thermonuclear. GD was only Commissioner present.

## ≡ *September 14, 1951*

Dr. Smyth called from Ames Laboratory. . . . Smyth asked about Bradbury. GD said Bradbury has come and gone—there have been some emergencies, but everything has worked out well. GD said he thought it wise for him to give a briefing to the MLC on the thermonuclear which he did; this made quite an impression; he impressed them with the possibilities and with his own enthusiasm. He left last night for Los Alamos. GD said he would tell Smyth in detail some of the other things we talked about with him. . . .

## ≡ *September 20, 1951*

Dr. Oppenheimer called GD and said he wanted to be sure GD knew of the discussions with Teller. He often changes his mind and I think there is a substantial chance that Teller will stay on this time. He would like one of three persons in authority and would stay on for (1) Fermi or (2) Bethe or (3) Oppenheimer. My [Oppenheimer's] reason for not setting it up is not entirely just Teller, but I think that is a bad administrative practice. Bethe's feeling is against it; he said he would not because (1) he wanted to work on purely technical and theoretical work and (2) he believes this thing is going to be an administrative monstrosity and (3) his feeling is that he is willing to work on it, but is not willing to make it his baby. He said he could not change his schedule. I do not believe it is anything to get really hot and bothered about, but we should be in the position, if Teller does quit, to be prepared with information. I realize this is completely unworkable, but not the kind of thing I want to completely throw out of mind. GD said there may be some alternatives. Oppenheimer said Teller is in a bad mental way; one cannot help noticing it and deploring it. If you want, I will call him again. Oppenheimer then mentioned that he received a copy of the Senator's speech.[1] GD said it was almost inevitable. Oppenheimer said he thought the Senator's suggestions are (a) not quite that far and (b) will not save that much money. GD said going back to this Teller thing again, Bradbury wired Teller not to resign until he had talked to me. He agreed to a couple of weeks wait. This has happened four or five times and I have induced him to stay on. Oppenheimer said he thought the job would go quite well with him as a consultant. GD said he thought that was realistic, for we would have great difficulty. . . . Oppenheimer said let me know after you have thought about it; I am not prepared to say yes to anything, but I am willing to think about it. . . .[2]

1. Oppenheimer was probably referring to McMahon's remarks before the Senate on September 18 in which he argued that atomic weapons were cheaper than conventional weapons and that the United States should have an atomic army, navy, and air force.

2. The ellipses at the end of the conversation mark the deletion of extraneous material; the other appears in the original.

## ≡ *September 24, 1951*

Dr. DeHoffmann called this evening to say that Teller wants to come to see GD on Friday, following the request in Bradbury's telegram that Teller not resign until he talks to GD again. What brought on the final decision is that Bradbury has appointed Marshall Holloway into a position between Bradbury and Teller and this is just like waving a red flag before a bull. Teller would never stay under those circumstances. GD will call DeHoffmann next morning early and talk to him about it.

## ≡ *September 25, 1951*

GD called Dr. DeHoffmann at Los Alamos first thing this morning to get more details on Teller resignation. DeHoffmann said I suppose you got some of the background on this from Pat.[1] GD said yes, when did it happen. DeHoffmann said it finally happened yesterday as follows: Last Monday there was a second one of those meetings. The first one of which more or less gave the occasion for this. At this meeting Norris (Bradbury) outlined a different plan by having a Mr. X, Mr. Y and Mr. Z. Mr. X would be an overall man who would report directly to Norris. Mr. Z. would have all the functions you would expect to be carried by Teller. Mr. Y is to be an industrial man from an industrial company. All of this in general appeals to the people at the meeting. Norris asked me to tell Teller which I did; he was at that time in Chicago; he didn't react violently one way or the other. Thereupon I went to Chicago for two days and tried to discuss this with him in more detail. Teller then said he wanted only a really top person on the job for Mr. X. He mentioned somebody like Enrico (Fermi) himself. He would have to know what he was doing. Now, in the meantime, Marshall Holloway (presently at Los Alamos) volunteered to be Mr. X. I don't know if you remember him. . . .[2] GD said I certainly do. . . . DeHoffmann said he was one of the people who both in an indefinite way had been very slow about this (the thermonuclear program) and in a direct way had clashed many times with Teller. He had been one of the real slow points in the business. GD said is that decided definitely? DeHoffmann said it is decided in the following situation: When Teller walked in yesterday and had a talk with Bradbury, Bradbury told Teller Mr. X will be Holloway. Bradbury asked Teller to accept the job of being Mr. Z. Teller said he could not do it. Teller said he would gladly talk to Holloway—which Norris suggested—but there would be no point to it. Teller said he would take Norris up on his original idea of seeing GD as an end-post to this series of talks. Bradbury gave DeHoffmann the feeling in this last week that he considered the thing as pretty final. He told me immediately when Holloway volunteered for the job. He wasn't greatly surprised when he heard that Teller had not found this acceptable. Bradbury made the statement that we now have to make arrangements how we carry on. He did make the private statement to me and again to Teller of worrying how Teller would announce his departure; he suggested Teller just say he is very, very tired. I think Teller told him he thought it was quite clearly not the reason he was leaving—and would be obvious to anyone. I think that is the story—this is an outline of what happened. GD asked if Ken Fields[3] was out there at the time. DeHoffmann said he has not been out yet—he is due Wednesday morning. The kind of thing that has gone on is that after my trip to Chicago, Teller came back to Los Alamos earlier than expected and Bradbury took the attitude of not knowing why he came back earlier. GD said well, I will see what happens Friday when he comes in. DeHoffmann said there is a chance I will be East in any case before or after then. Would you like a chance to discuss any of this first, or before or after Teller's visit maybe—whichever you wish. . . . GD said he thought it would probably be profitable; would like to see you before. GD then asked DeHoffmann if he was interested in the Univac. DeHoffmann said he had been asked this; in general terms, the answer is probably yes. Specifically, we are making a little bit of a problem; we will have to get personnel to use these machines. I think it looks nice and I will make sure today what the theory is on that. GD said I guess you never really know about them, until you put a problem in. . . . De-Hoffmann said it is probably a good bet. If you will turn me over to Pat I will set up a time for my coming in. . . . GD said o.k. fine. (Time set for 4:30 on Thursday and Teller to come in at 3:00 on Friday.)

1. Patricia L. Stewart, Dean's administrative assistant.
2. All ellipses appear in the original.
3. Brigadier General Kenneth E. Fields succeeded General McCormack as director of the Division of Military Application on August 20, 1951.

## ≡ ~~February~~September 27, 1951

Dr. DeHoffmann came in this afternoon to brief GD a little on Teller's resignation before Teller's appointment tomorrow.

Col Coiner called. . . . Coiner said Bradbury said what he is interested in is your discussing relationship between the Commission and the military forces, rather than contractor-owner cooperation. Would you like that? He would like to have you give the lab a pat on the back and in view of the philosophy of McMahon about expansion, how you feel Los Alamos fits into this. I will pass this information on to Townsend.[1] Coiner said, incidentally, did you get a TWX from Bradbury regarding Teller? GD said he had not seen it yet. Coiner said he sent one, so you will probably get it soon. Teller is headed here to talk to you; he said Fields will call you on it. GD said he wanted to talk to Fields about Teller. GD said he had an appointment with Teller at 3:00 P.M. tomorrow. Coiner said tomorrow? GD said yes; maybe there has been some change.

1. Oliver Townsend, Dean's primary assistant and speechwriter.

## ≡ September 28, 1951

Dr. Teller came in this morning at 11:00 to meet with GD and tell him officially of his resignation. GD later called in Dr. Smyth, Mr. Murray and Mr. Boyer, so that they could talk with Teller about his future plans and his ideas on future of Los Alamos lab.

Dr. Colby went up on the Hill this afternoon to tell GD (who was at that time in a Joint Committee meeting) that there was evidence of another Russian atomic explosion.

Col. Fields called from Los Alamos to talk to GD about Teller resignation. Asked if GD had received the TWX from Bradbury. I have checked around and talked to quite a few of the people here. I believe, actually, it would work out best if he (Teller) went back to Chicago and worked as a consultant with the lab here. Fields said he had talked to Teller on the phone. He indicates he would be glad to do that. I told him I hoped his connection with the program would continue to be quite close. In talking to Bradbury and everyone, I think they have all concluded that if Teller could come back here and accept the "ground rules" and the people (Holloway) who have been put into the setup here, it would be alright. But Fields said he doesn't see how, in the present circumstances, you can work it out any differently than it is now. GD said the only thing that surprised him was the selection of Holloway. I would assume it would be better to have someone like Froman. Fields said Froman would have to be told to do it; Holloway is a good man technically for this and he has indicated a willingness to try it. From all angles, except with his relationship with Teller, he would be the best man. Any man from the lab would have difficulties if Teller stayed on. Holloway is a tough character. He is a very good man. I don't think it is reasonable to go outside the lab to get anyone. It has to be from the lab and there are only two or three people who would be in a position to do it. Also, Paul Fine,[1] who is with me here, agrees that Holloway is the best choice.

1. Paul Fine, Fields's technical assistant.

Dr. Teller called to say he had an appointment to see McMahon this evening. Made the appointment after seeing GD this morning, but wanted GD to know about it.

## ≡ October 1, 1951

James Lay called and said he just wanted to check with GD on "this latest news" [the second Soviet atomic explosion]—that the Air Force picked up. Do you recall the procedure that went on the last time we had the same news? GD said he did not; he was on the Commission at the time, but was not Chairman. Lay said that is what he thought. The President wanted to not distribute it outside the family—the Executive branch—until the facts were in and then make an announcement. I don't know that he has made any decision at this time as to a public announcement. It is clear that at the appropriate time, by the law, the JCC has to be advised. GD said he had not done that yet and he was not going to do it until he discussed it with the President. He was sure, however, they would treat this [as] confidential. You would not have to worry about a leak there. I had this idea which I might pass along to you for whatever it is worth: On this one there is not the same rush for making a public announcement. . . . Lay said he was not sure what the President's views are on a public announcement; it depends on what this is; whether it is a new type; if it is more of the same, he may not want to announce it. GD said one thing that appeals to him very much is this: (and I have not discussed this with CIA) I think this offers us a very unusual opportunity to see how the Russians play it. Suppose we just keep quiet for a while. It might lead us into a lot of things—what they say, their propaganda line, etc. See if for any reason they want to make propaganda about it. If we kept quiet for three or four weeks it might be a little study for us. This is a rather intriguing idea to me. Lay said he agreed; we are not under the compulsion this time as we were last time. GD said we will not know for a few days anyway on this. . . . Lay said all he wanted to do was to tell GD about what happened last time . . . if you were wondering. The President did hold it up until the facts were definitely known. I think that is the important thing in all this; and it would seem to me that everybody in the family be together on the President's agreement before anything goes out. GD said he seriously questioned whether anything should go out at this time. Lay said there are two questions: telling the public and telling the JCC. There is a question of when you advise the JCC.[1] If he follows what he did last time, it will be after confirmation and the facts are pretty well known. GD said suppose I just hold up on making them aware until we get all the facts. Lay said everything is so uncertain now that I have not checked his views yet. I gather something more is coming in. GD said it is coming in daily. GD said he wished Lay would tell the President also, for the purposes of our relations with the JCC, it is pretty important that I don't withhold something they are really entitled to know. This is quite different [from] telling it to the other groups. These people will keep it quiet. Lay said he knew that. . . . GD said suppose I wait until I have talked to you again. Lay said the President may want to say "go ahead." GD said the sooner, the better to the JCC. Lay said he would keep GD advised and anything you want to do is o.k. . . . or if you want to check with the President directly. GD said he would do it through Lay in any event. . . .[2]

1. When McMahon learned of the second Soviet explosion, he used it to urge Dean to reconsider the second laboratory. Part of Dean's reasons for wanting to delay announcement of the explosion may have been to ease pressures for the second laboratory and the second expansion, although the diary is silent about this.

2. The ellipses at the end of the conversation mark the deletion of extraneous material; the others appear in the original.

LeBaron called GD and asked if there was anything surprising that "turned up over the weekend that you know of, was there?" GD said Colby brought me up to date on what was known on Saturday. LeBaron said he had just finished talking to Lovett. I carried out the orders of the British Ambassador, so that is all the story I have. I am just going to sort of drop it there; I gather from what they told me, it would be about ten days before they [would] be able to do anything concrete. We are not letting anybody speculate about the size, etc. until we really know. GD said he had talked to Lay about when we should tell the JCC. My own feeling is that I would like to wait as long as possible, consistent with good relations with them, which would mean at least ten days in order to get a good reading. LeBaron said he had talked to Souers[1] on it; I think the President wants to do that himself. GD said it might be well for Lay to talk to the President about it. It might be smart this time not to make a public announcement—at least for a period of time. LeBaron said he had talked to Arneson about it. We have no view on the mechanics of that; the only thing that seemed logical to me is . . .[2] We should not make any speculations; that is what I am doing here. I am trying to follow his instructions which are to keep it close as long as possible. GD said he didn't propose to tell the JCC until I have cleared with Lay and I will do the same with you at the same time. LeBaron said Souers apparently has had a talk with the President "so you might make a little money by checking with him."

1. Admiral Sidney L. Souers had turned over the position of executive director of the National Security Council to James Lay on January 15, 1950. He remained, however, a special consultant to the president on security matters.
2. The ellipses appear in the original.

GD called Gordon Arneson. . . . Arneson then mentioned one other thing: We may have the problem of saying something about "events over the weekend." I would like to suggest that it might be useful to ask Lay to get AEC, State and Defense fellows together fairly soon to determine what should be said, etc. My own feeling is this should be at a lower level than last time—maybe you are the one to announce it. GD said his feeling was that the same reasons for making an announcement last time do not prevail this time. I think it might be a good idea to let this cool off for about thirty days and see what is said by the other fellow. Arneson said he thought we should have to have something ready in the event of a leak, however. Thinks maybe all this should be discussed with the President to get his feelings on it. GD said he would not report to the JCC on it until he had had a chance to talk to the President about it, but I would expect to have to do this in about a week. Arneson said that might be a good time to have something ready. Whom would you like to work on this with us—Trapnell? GD said he didn't think Trapnell knew about it; we have kept it very close here. Arneson said suppose I talk to Lay and he might give you a call on getting together. GD said he was leaving town on Wednesday afternoon for a week. Arneson said maybe we should try to do it before then. GD said if we can do it tomorrow, then that will be grand. Arneson said o.k. fine.

Mr. Boyer called GD. . . . GD said . . . We got a confirmation on this "other matter" by the way (the Russian explosion). We got a confirmation definitely on Saturday. Boyer said he thought he would call Colby up and ask him to brief him on it. GD said it is a very quick story; we will know more next week.

Boyer called back and said he just checked with Colby on "the news." I was interested about our friend McMahon on this thing. Have you made up your mind on that? Would you like us to come by? GD said I think that would be a good idea. Boyer said I will be right down and will bring Colby with me. GD said o.k.

GD called Admiral Souers and said he was going to give a talk at Los Angeles and there are about five pages of this thing that raise some interesting thoughts and I just thought perhaps you should take a look at it and give me your good judgment on it. Souers said I don't know what the judgment will be on it . . .[1] how good it will be . . . but I will be glad to give you the best I possess. GD said perhaps I could bring it over—how about some time tomorrow? Souers said tomorrow will be fine. GD said how about 10:00 A.M. tomorrow; I can come over before then if you like. Souers said 10:00 A.M. would be fine—and then said that is interesting information you folks are getting—were you around in 1949? GD said he was on the Commission but was not Chairman. Souers said there was a terrific battle waged over what, if anything, would be said. They pulled and they hauled on the President. He wants to do it this time the same way. There are some political aspects and domestic political aspects and the JCC and the Defense Establishment to consider too. GD said I have an idea I would like to pass on to you: perhaps some of the reasons which led us to the public announcement are not quite as compelling this time as they were; it might be a very interesting psychological study if we said nothing for a period of about thirty days to see what and how the Russians played it. Souers said that is a good idea if we are sure . . . if between the scientists who must tell everything they know and the military . . . if you have 300 or 400 people who know something, you can hold them for a little while, a very little while, and that is about all. GD said I was thinking on the order of three or four weeks. Souers said I certainly don't think we should say *anything* until we *know* what it is. So you are getting almost to that timing anyway. I don't know how long you can keep from telling the JCC. In 1949 Lilienthal wanted to publish it immediately and tell the JCC immediately. The President talked Lilienthal into not telling until it was time. GD said he thought we notified them just before the Presidential announcement. Souers said that was right and the Cabinet was notified just before and kept in session—so they couldn't leak it. And it all broke at once that way; otherwise it will leak as sure as hell. GD said he certainly didn't want to tell the JCC until we get some kind of an evaluation of what it really is. Souers said that is right. They accepted that from Lilienthal—that he had waited under the direction of the President. Steve Early and Louie Johnson just raring to tell it. GD said two outfits who might have interest in how to do this would be CIA and our Psychological Warfare people. Souers said once the President takes command of the situation . . . the other time it went beautifully. This time we should know pretty well whether it is one or the other thing. O.K. I will see you at 10:00 tomorrow. GD said that will be fine.

1. All ellipses appear in the original.

Dr. Smyth called GD and asked if we were to receive any kind of briefing on the subject we were talking about Saturday. GD said only what you got; I talked to Colby this morning. Smyth said he had told Keith about it and Murray already knows about it. GD said I will run into Murray's office and tell him what Colby told me this morning. It is the same as what you had on Saturday, nothing new on it.

≡ *October 2, 1951*

Dr. Glennan took his oath a year ago today.

10:00 A.M. appointment with Admiral Souers to have Souers look over speech to be delivered on the 5th in California.

2:00 P.M. meeting in James Lay's office (Lay, LeBaron, Arneson, Dulles of CIA, Souers and GD) on the new Russian explosion and what to do about it.

Executive session here at 3:15 P.M. to discuss same as above.

James Lay called and said he had talked to Arneson about this question of how we handle this latest news. In their shop they have been trying to study the international foreign policy implications of it and what might be said, if you are going to say something, how and by whom and when, etc.

He (Arneson) has suggested if we could have a little meeting over here. . . .
GD said I think it would be useful; . . .[1]

1. The ellipses at the end of the conversation mark the deletion of extraneous material;
the other appears in the original.

## ≡ October 3, 1951

Meeting in Lay's office called for 2:00 P.M. today. Same persons present
as at yesterday's meeting and on same subject.

President's secretary, Joseph Short, announced this afternoon to the
public that the Russians had exploded another atomic bomb. (Did not receive as large a headline in the evening paper as the play-off for the world
series games.)

Transmitted by special messenger on October 3rd copies of my speech to
be delivered at the University of Southern California on October 5th to
Pace, Bendetsen and Lovett.

On October 2nd I went over those portions of the USC speech dealing
with the new look at tactical weapons with Admiral Souers at his office.

On the 3rd of October also sat in on a conference in James Lay's office,
attended by Arneson and Chase[1] of State Department, Dulles of CIA, Bim
Wilson of Defense,[2] Admiral Souers, Henry Smyth and myself, to consider
whether an announcement should be made of the Russian explosion, what
its form should be and by whom it should be made. Left the meeting early.
Picked up a paper in Chicago to find that the White House had made the
announcement.

1. Joseph Chase worked in Gordon Arneson's office in the State Department.
2. Bim Wilson may have been E. Bright Wilson, Jr., deputy director of the weapons systems evaluation group in the Department of Defense.

## ≡ October 5, 1951

Dr. Glennan unhappy about speech GD gave at USC this morning.
Didn't think, for some reason, that GD should have said what he did about
the tactical use of weapons and these nibbling aggressions—in other
words, advocating the use of A-bombs today in Korea.

## ≡ *October 8, 1951*

Mark Childs[1] called to find out if GD's speech in California on Friday had been cleared with other government agencies. When told GD was out of town and could not be reached, he talked to Shelby Thompson. Joe Short at the White House said, if he is asked whether the speech was cleared at the White House, he is going to say it was not and should have been—because of the Presidential Directive of December 5, 1950[2] which says that all speeches of that sort must be cleared with Short. It later turned out that the AEC had not been included in the list of agencies to whom this Directive was sent and Short's face was a little red. He knows the speech was cleared with Admiral Souers, but he doesn't think that was sufficient.

1. Marquis Childs, the noted journalist and author.
2. The December 5 presidential directive had been issued to stop General MacArthur's unauthorized statements.

## ≡ *October 10, 1951*

GD, Glennan, Smyth and Boyer went to see Secretary Lovett at 4:30 today. Much speculation in the press whether the meeting was on use of A-bombs in Korea.[1]

1. Dean and his associates actually went to see Lovett to urge that further study be made before the administration decided to expand production facilities.

Admiral Souers called. . . .[1] GD asked him if he thought the reverberations on the speech were serious. Souers said the funny part is that he doesn't know why they should be. . . . GD said it came in a funny setting—different than when it was written. Souers said he couldn't tell whether they were criticizing the Senate and House testimony or the speech.[2] Souers then said this is confidential: There was a directive back in December 1950 that was addressed to a whole group of outfits; Army, Navy, Air Force, etc. When the question was raised at the White House with Short whether you had cleared it over there . . . you were not included in the list, it was discovered. GD said that is true; but it might have been better judgment for me to have done it. Souers said on the Collins' artillery shells stuff[3]—I was in on that—Steve Early told them they could not run it but it was in the afternoon papers—it leaked!! They have all been talking about artillery pieces, etc. GD said he was trying to straighten out our thinking so that we regard these things like any other weapon. If the thing is muddy at all, perhaps I had better see the President. Souers said let me check with Short and see if the President is worked up. GD said they have

asked whether I cleared it. . . . I have not answered that. Souers said Short
has been kidding me about it. . . . I didn't know you were not included in
the Presidential Directive on 1950. GD said on the Coast the speech was
very well received and I think it is going to do some good. Souers said Short
has been sensitive about talking to you about this; doesn't want to add
AEC to the list on the Directive at this point—it looks like a reprimand. I
told Short if he would just call you and ask you to clear such things in the
future, that is all that would be necessary. GD said certainly. Souers said he
would check with Short and see what he thinks about your seeing the President. GD said o.k. thanks.

1. The ellipses at the beginning of the conversation mark the deletion of extraneous material; the others appear in the original.

2. The House Appropriations Committee had recently released testimony in which
Dean had stated the Commission was working on dozens of new atomic weapons including artillery shells, guided missiles, torpedoes, and rockets. Dean stated the United States
could use an atomic bomb in a tactical way against enemy troops in the field without risk
to American soldiers.

3. In February General Collins had told *U.S. News and World Report* newsmen that the
United States would soon have atomic artillery shells. Since Collins's statement there had
been many reports in the press about tactical weapons.

Admiral Souers called and said he had just raised the question with "the
boss" about our conversation and he said to tell you he was not worked up.
Thought he got into a worse mess in California than you did.[1] GD said he
was glad to hear that. Souers said he talked to Short too and told him that
so far you have not indicated anything to the press. First you thought of
saying "no" but then decided to say nothing. GD said that is what he
wants. If I said I did not then it would look like I did not know the rules of
the game, and if I said I did that would be false. Souers said he understands
Lovett had read the speech and cleared it. GD said I sent it to him two days
earlier. Lovett told Short that their analysis of it indicated that the speech
was 100% alright; it is just that the qualifications did not get into the papers. I told Short to get the point over that the President wants them to stop
talking about weapons. GD said he would call Short. Souers said he thinks
GD should do it on his own accord. GD said he would do that. Thanks for
being an intermediary. Souers said just because those fellows play it up differently is not your fault.

1. On September 4, during a visit to San Francisco for the Japanese peace treaty conference, President Truman told Democratic party leaders that the nation had some fantastic
new weapons under construction.

≡ *October 11, 1951*

Mr. Short at the White House returned GD's call. GD said he was sorry about the reverberations and it occurred to me that the President at his press conference might be asked the question as to whether it had been cleared with him. I had it and said that I refused to comment on it because I think who people talk to in preparing a speech is not for publicity. Do you see anything wrong with that? Do not want to imply that it was cleared anywhere because that would not be true, nor do I want to say "no" for that would be false. Short said that is one of the things we have not taken up for the press conference yet, as to what to say. The truth is "no." GD said if the President says it, of course, then I can say it is true. Short said since you have already taken the attitude I think he is going to have to say "no." We will have to go on from there as he will be asked "why"—the answer is that the memorandum sent out 12/5/50 did not include the AEC. GD asked if that was made public. Short said it was made public at the time of the recall of MacArthur. GD said in regard to that directive, we will follow it whether or not we are on it. We will certainly do it in the future, now that we know about it. Short said he thought about after this thing blows over having the President sign a memo including the AEC. GD said that would help him personally. You might consider this: that if the topic said anything about atomic weapons that a copy be cleared with us. Short [said] it now goes to Defense Department, State Department and then comes to the White House. If there is anything we do not like we call State and Defense and say do something about it. We have cut stuff out on atomic weapons on a lot of publications. For example, Vandenberg's Look article.[1] GD said it is that sort of thing that should be sent to the AEC. They frequently get a bigger play than a speech. Short said GD was right; and I think we should go after that. GD said he would be happy to sit in or help in any way. Short said "thanks, Gordon."

1. In the October 9, 1951, issue of *Look* Air Force Chief of Staff Hoyt Vandenberg published an article in which he argued that tactical atomic bombing could be used to offset Russian manpower advantages in a European war. Vandenberg made it clear that the Air Force counted on increasing quantities of atomic bombs.

Senator McMahon called GD. Said he just called to tell him how very excellent the speech was that you delivered. I very much approved of it. GD said a lot of people think I over-stated it. McMahon said "really?" In the Executive Department? GD said the President is not excited. Lovett thinks it is technically correct, but that it creates ideas of present capacity that are not there. If it is read carefully it is not there, but I wanted to get the people thinking. McMahon [said] . . . Between us, I think we have things pretty well stirred up. GD said he thought he would like to pick up the pieces, but the President is satisfied. McMahon asked if GD had seen him personally. GD said actually he called Admiral Souers to see what it was—Souers read the speech in advance but did not tell anyone, did it as a courtesy to me. He said the President would be happy to see me but that he is not worried. I got a very lovely letter from Bendetsen. McMahon asked if GD had heard anything from Lilienthal. GD said no, but I suppose I will.

## ☰ *October 15, 1951*

Dr. Oppenheimer called and said he thought he knew the answer to the question he was about to ask, but he wanted to be sure. Would it be troublesome to GD if his letter[1] to GD were delayed until Wednesday or Thursday. GD said it would not. Oppenheimer said he had been having a combination of secretarial troubles here and he would like to look it over before he sends the letter to GD. As you know, you are facing a lot of very tough issues and we don't want to put anything in writing that will make them any tougher. Libby felt very strongly on the new lab idea and the other members of the GAC felt just as strongly. I am turning in a report on our views and Libby has written a letter on his views—very eloquent and very inflammatory. His letter is an attachment to ours. I had to put in a reference to his dissent, but wanted to have it clear what I was doing. In talking about this new lab we kind of define our terms a little bit (1) across the board development or (2) speciality lab which might develop into something or (3) a special lab at Sandia. I think it is important to define this term. GD said it would not bother him to have Libby's comments in a separate document. Oppenheimer said GD could or could not attach it when you send it to Congress. GD said he would like to feel free to do that; I don't feel any compunction to send a copy of this to the JCC. Oppenheimer then mentioned one final point: this was an extremely instructive meeting and from all the comments I heard, everyone is full of admiration of how you are managing. GD said that is nice to hear; I also felt that the suggestions covered and the way they were tackled made this an unusual meeting. Oppenheimer said if the people on the GAC would spend more time thinking about these things, they would be more helpful, but that is one of the problems of a part-time advisory group. GD agreed.

1. Oppenheimer was discussing the letter report to the commission describing the General Advisory Committee meeting held from October 11 to 13.

## ≡ *October 16, 1951*[1]

Yesterday Mr. Lovett delivered an address at the American Legion Convention in Miami ⟨copy of which is attached⟩.[2] While he said in substance that we can't win today's wars with tomorrow's weapons he left the impression that we could substantially win a battle with today's weapons and to my mind that is quite unfortunate as it undoes the good my USC speech did which was played heavily by the Voice of America as an indication of American strength. No advance copies of the speech were sent here so we had no opportunity to make any suggestion. Nor, I learned this morning, was it cleared with Gordon Gray who heads the Psychological Warfare Board.

1. The excerpt pertaining to the Lovett speech is now found in a file of former top secret Dean material, but it was originally a part of the diary.
2. Lovett's speech is not reproduced.

## ≡ *October 17, 1951*

Bill Borden called. . . .[1] GD then mentioned that he would like to talk to Borden on the chapter in the JCC report on the second lab—that is going into the report. This concerns me. This has been a subject of considerable discussion here and study also during the past four or five months. It gets into some very ticklish situations—what is the role of Los Alamos, for example? There is almost unanimous opinion that a second lab, but not at Los Alamos, has a lot to be said for it, although there are different views on it; it is almost unanimous . . . where would you get the people to run a second lab, etc.? So the thinking has gone into two facilities, building prototypes, making gadgets, reducing waste, etc. Borden said you are sitting right in the middle there. GD said his one big concern . . . the [wording about the] thermonuclear [program] does not bother me because of the terrific strides which have been made . . . it is after the tests. . . . Borden said here is the way we have it in the report and then read ". . . since that time the h-bomb program has gone forward and the Committee renews its urging that no stone be left unturned. . . ." We then suggest early consideration be given to a second laboratory to Los Alamos to furnish a competitive spirit. Concern is felt over the increasing burden on Los Alamos. We congratulate the lab for the past tests. GD said that part where you mention the second lab and the competitive approach is the one that would hurt out there. They are very touchy on it. Borden asked if GD really thought it would hurt. GD said personally he doesn't buy it; theoretically he agrees but as a practical matter I have serious reservations of an across-the-board weapons research lab—and I speak for myself—there have been fifty different views on this. The GAC is unanimous in saying we don't need a second research lab. Borden asked if this feeling of the GAC reflects true unanimity or the domination we have had in the past. GD said well he (Oppenheimer) is a very determined fellow, of course, but I think Whitman, Buckley,[2] etc. have their own ideas. It comes down to people; admittedly, there are some who are not in, but this is not a sufficient number to staff another lab. We have approximately 85% of the physicists of the country now. Borden said he wondered if we should. . . . GD said change the language to refer to the wonderful job Los Alamos has done. Satisfy the concern of the Committee that is that they have gotten too much, in their enthusiasm, into the developmental which should go somewhere else. I think that is a sound point of view. Borden said he was wondering if we might. . . . I would like to think this report is well trimmed. . . . you walk that knife-edge with Hickenlooper and Millikin. I wonder if we shouldn't wait and see what the boys do with it. . . . In the event they do favor it, perhaps we could get together on it. GD said he would be most happy to do this, particularly on the second lab deal. Borden said perhaps he could come down to see GD later today or tomorrow. Borden said in the event they approve it, he will contact our office. . . .

    1. The ellipses at the beginning and the end of the conversation mark the deletion of extraneous material; the others appear in the original.
    2. Walter G. Whitman and Oliver E. Buckley were both members of the General Advisory Committee.


≡ *October 19, 1951*

Commission meeting this morning on expanded program.

Captain Jackson called and said he just received a call from Carroll Tyler. The shot this morning was "a dud."[1] They pushed the button and nothing happened. There was a failure in the control circuit. They are checking everything now before they go near the tower. It will probably be at least a 24-hour delay and probably a 48-hour delay. GD said then the gadget itself was not a dud? Jackson said oh, no. GD asked then are they going to try to shoot it? Jackson said yes. But it will be at least a 24-hour delay and probably 48. GD said there was just a failure. . . .[2] Jackson said in the control circuit—between the control building and the tower. They don't know just what happened yet. GD said it must have been an awfully funny feeling. Jackson said they have prepared an answer to press inquiries which they are sure they will get. . . . the general time of the shot was known—they had to notify CAA.[3] Tyler is saying there was a failure in a control circuit. GD asked why. Jackson said he felt he should be honest with the people. GD asked if the people know what we are doing there. Jackson said people know there was to be a nuclear detonation this morning. GD asked did they? Jackson said it became public knowledge since they had to stop the airlines. GD asked what about saying "the test was postponed due to technical difficulties." I think that is much better than saying there was a failure in the control circuit. Morse Salisbury, who is here with me, feels the same way. Jackson said let me try to get Tyler back on the phone right away and tell him. GD said o.k. (Captain Jackson later called back to say the release had already been put out—could not stop it.)

1. The first *Buster-Jangle* shot was finally fired on October 22, 1951.

2. The ellipses appear in the original.

3. The commission asked the Civil Aeronautics Administration (the Federal Aviation Administration today) to halt commercial traffic around the Nevada test site whenever atomic tests were fired.

Jackson called back to say that they had found a bad connection in the cable; relatively minor, but it will delay the shot 48-hours.

Captain Jackson called back to say he just talked to Tyler again and it was too late; the release had already gone out. He stated the reasoning with Bradbury, Smyth etc. for doing it this way was that the newspaper people out there were already speculating that this was the first time that an atomic bomb had failed and they wanted to make clear to them that it was not a failure of the bomb, but was in the control circuit. They are sorry it happened this way, but they were on the spot—literally on the spot with newspapermen and the judgment—the newspapermen were in their office. [The decision] of the people out there was to give out this release; they are sorry we did not agree with them. GD said he felt it would have been better to say that it was not a bomb failure, but postponement on account of technicality. Now they will speculate on symmetry and other things.

## ≡ October 22, 1951

GD away.

White House announced this afternoon a 3rd Russian explosion.

≡                                                                  October 26, 1951[1]

*Meeting with Mr. Charles E. Wilson[2] on October 25, 1951*
Attending: Chairman Dean, Walter J. Williams, Thomas F. Farrell[3]

1. Mr. Dean gave a general statement on the scope of the expansion under consideration and which the Joint Chiefs of Staff had recommended on an interim basis. He gave Mr. Wilson a summary of data on the attached sheet (Appendix) as indicating the critical requirements in personnel and materials. Mr. Dean indicated a need for higher priorities for the expansion than we now have and stated our difficulties in meeting present schedules.

2. Mr. Wilson reviewed in detail the need for electric power equipment and thought it feasible to meet the need if the units were scheduled in the immediate future so that they be programmed to be finished when required. He expressed a concern for the large amount of copper and other critical materials involved. Mr. Williams suggested that a considerable amount of copper could be salvaged at Y-12[4] and Mr. Wilson urged that it be done soon.

3. On nickel, Mr. Wilson expressed concern because of the large needs and urged that commitments be made promptly. The same applied to stainless steel.

4. Mr. Wilson pointed out that structural steel would be critical all through 1952 and said that an early program of our needs should be submitted if delivery were to be made in the latter part of the year. The total plant capacity for structural steel is just over five million tons per annum and is not expected to increase. There is a large backlog of deferred requests which would make heavy demands in 1952. Wilson urged that wherever possible reinforced concrete be used instead of structural steel.

5. For highest or overriding priorities, Mr. Wilson said those would need Presidential approval, or agreement with the Defense Department. Some discussion was had on the subject of a high band of priorities to be used by AEC and selected Defense projects. Mr. Wilson was somewhat skeptical of such priorities, as in the past too many programs were eventually included in the bands and thus their value was lost. He spoke of the CMP[5] control and it was pointed out to him that a large percentage of the items needed for the expansion are not under CMP. In those fields, there would be an urgent need for high priority.

6. Mr. Wilson said the best results could be obtained if the program were firmed up early and the material scheduled with the agencies of ODM. The needs would then be recognized and approved before materials were allocated to other programs.

7. Mr. Wilson expressed his appreciation to Mr. Dean for the early and accurate presentation, in contrast to the various rumors which were cur-

rent. He would like to have the details given to the ODM agencies as soon as the program is firm.

APPENDIX

*Critical Requirements*

*JCS Interim Program Recommendations*

*Expansion* * * * * Plutonium. Additions to present sites and development of a new site.

* * * * U-235. Additions to present sites and development of new site.

| | |
|---|---|
| *Estimated Cost* - Direct Construction | $ 4,500,000,000 |
| Direct Annual Production | $ 550,000,000 |
| *Schedule* - Assumed Authorization Date | January 1, 1952 |
| Construction Completed | January 1, 1957 |

*Critical Requirements*

| | |
|---|---|
| Peak Manpower (1954) | 112,700 |
| (Technical) | (13,500) |
| Steady State Manpower (1958) | 65,200 |
| (Technical) | (7,500) |
| Electric Power Total - Expansion only | 3,830 MW |
| Increments 1954 | 630 MW |
| 1955 | 1760 MW |
| 1956 | 1010 MW |
| 1957 | 360 MW |
| 1958 | 70 MW |
| Nickel - Maximum (1954) | 11.5% 1951 Production Capacity |
| Stainless Steel Tubing - Maximum (1954) | 34.1% Production Capacity |
| Sulphur Annual Steady State reached 1959 | 17.6% Production Capacity |
| Hydrofluoric Acid Annual Steady State reached 1959 | 33.3% Production Capacity |

(Above requirements are for Production only. Not included are estimates for Biology and Medicine, Reactor Development, and Research. For example, operation of Mark II would require 500 MW additional electric power.)

1. The notes of the Wilson meeting are in a different format from the diary because they had been removed from the diary and issued as a commission staff paper. They are now found in official commission files.

2. Charles E. Wilson led the Office of Defense Mobilization (ODM).

3. Thomas E. Farrell, assistant general manager of the Atomic Energy Commission.

4. The Y-12 plant had been erected at Oak Ridge during World War II to separate uranium isotopes by the electromagnetic method. The plant had been shut down after the war.
    5. I could not determine the meaning of this abbreviation.

≡ *November 21, 1951*

Sent letter to GD from Teller on 2nd lab to Boyer to look at confiden-
tially and return—not to be distributed or duplicated.

GD called James Lay (NSC) and said I have just been thinking a little bit
about whether the President has been kept advised on the possible expansion program and wondered if I have been at all remiss in not sending
something over or if you have kept him informed of the magnitude. Lay
said up until he left for Key West I have kept him informed and that included the last staff meeting. Gave him the general order of magnitude and
very briefly the problems it created and told him we were working it out
and would have something coming up. GD said I just did not want him to
be surprised when he saw the report from NSC. Lay said it might be helpful to him if you have some information and have a chance. . . .[1] GD said I
know Lawton[2] is going to Key West and thought that he might hear in
terms of dollars from him, but that I guess will not be the case. Lay said he
did give him a general impression of dollars. GD asked if there was any
particular reaction from him. Lay said no; he was anxious that Wilson be
brought in at an appropriate stage. GD said he was convinced more and
more that you can talk about this as a possibility only if we have the highest priorities. I do not mean primarily to compete with essential military
needs, but must recognize the extreme importance in order to get it done
in time. Lay said, as you know Wilson has on his mind 114/2 we had at the
Council meeting[3] and Wilson said it was alright to start with bench memorandum approach on 45 basis in the military,[4] but he did not see how you
can make a decision on what you can do until we see this other field. Even
the present program is creating a problem. GD said I had a very nice talk
with him before going to Brazil. Lay said I gather you are talking on the
power problem now. GD said we are. Lay said any direct discussion you
can have would be very helpful. Have you gotten the report from the field
on requirements? GD said it is not quite ready. I am not sure of the exact
day. Lay said he came over on procedure while you were away and agreed
on not going much farther on this until we send requirements to the Munitions Board and they have given the impact on other programs. GD said
we have done that. Lay said you agree we have to have those facts? He said

you are going to work up some questions that might be raised in your field. I have also asked Chase, in Arneson's absence, to do the same, regarding foreign questions. GD said it is a big program and it is going to have a big impact. Lay said the time matter is the problem. GD said something should be done in the meantime on highest priority. Lay said he thought the three agencies should get together the first time and then meet with Wilson. First have a rather detailed security discussion and then bring in Wilson on requirement side. I will wait until I hear your brief summary on feasibility. GD said right; I think we will have everything in good shape by Tuesday. On the first problem, you think he is informed so that he will not feel that we have not kept him posted? Lay said no, I am sure he is. I am going down on the 75h,[5] so if there is anything then I would be happy to give him a little more of a fill-in. GD said he may want to make something of this in the State of the Union address. I have dictated something on the order of that he can say this matter is being given careful consideration in the government and hope they will give favorable consideration to it. Lay said I understand Charlie Murphy came back East and is staying here to work on that. You might want to get in touch with him on that. GD said he would do that; will give him a call. Lay said that would be fine.

1. The ellipses appear in the original.
2. Frederick J. Lawton, director of the Bureau of the Budget.
3. NSC 114/2 was an updated plan for American rearmament.
4. I cannot identify the "bench memorandum approach."
5. I cannot identify "75h."

## ≡ November 26, 1951

Executive session of the Commission (GD not present) at which Dr. Bradbury discussed the thermonuclear program and the 2nd lab, etc. Pike, Smyth, Murray, Hollis, Williams, Snapp, Col. Fields and Paul Fine attended this meeting.

## ≡ November 27, 1951

Executive Session of the Commission this morning to hear Bradbury on the thermonuclear and the 2nd lab problem. Those attended were GD, Glennan, Boyer, Murray, Smyth, Hollis, Williams, Snapp, Col. Fields and Fine.

≡ *November 28, 1951*

Dr. Bethe came in this afternoon to discuss with the Commission in executive session the work on the thermonuclear and the 2nd lab.

Dr. Libby (from University of Chicago) called to say he was in the building and wanted to just say hello. GD asked if he was going to be present at the next GAC meeting. Libby said he was; I see they have "our old subject" on the agenda (the 2nd lab problem). Libby said he was visiting Murray and he showed him a copy of the letter from Oppi to GD asking about bringing Teller in for the meeting. GD said he didn't recall seeing it, how recent a letter is it? Libby didn't remember that, but anyway apparently Teller is going to be in and speak his piece on the matter at Oppi's invitation, if you approve, of course. . . .[1] GD said "of course." Libby said he had a very nice talk with Murray. Going back to Chicago tomorrow. Teller has arrived in Chicago and is pretty well settled down. He has had the flu; that may account for his having been a good boy recently. GD said he saw Hans Bethe and I think for the time-being we can hope to get as much out of Teller as possible; they work pretty well together and as long as we can keep Bethe at Los Alamos, we can keep Teller in I think; I think they have great respect for each other's ability. Libby said if I can do anything for you, don't hesitate to call on me. GD said thanks a lot; he would do that.

1. The ellipses appear in the original.

≡ *November 29, 1951*

Lewis Strauss called. . . . Strauss then asked if anything had happened on the idea of a 2nd lab—is that dead?[1] GD said it is not dead. Libby was in town yesterday and we had a little chat. So was Hans Bethe and we talked to them about this issue. Teller has furnished me with two different possibilities. Neither one of which is an across-the-board competitive lab. . . .

1. On December 19, 1951, the commission reviewed the study initiated in September of the workloads at Los Alamos. During the review the commission once again stated its conclusion that a second laboratory was not needed.

≡ *December 2, 1951*

Today is 9th anniversary of first controlled nuclear experiment led by Dr. Fermi at Stagg Stadium at Chicago.

## ≡ December 13, 1951

GAC meeting today. Teller and Froman in to talk on thermonuclear and 2nd lab possibility.

## ≡ December 21, 1951

Appointment with the President at 3:15 this afternoon.

Dr. Hafstad stopped by and left the following message for GD: Dr. Zinn called and said that the EBR is now operating and delivering 100 KW of power.[1] This has to be kept TS until GD and the other Commissioners decide what to do with it—whether to use it as a bargaining item in dealing with the British, or rather to counteract their bargaining point about a power reactor (Churchill's visit in mind).[2] It will be decided next week how and when to make this announcement.

1. The day before the Experimental Breeder Reactor I, designed by Argonne Laboratory scientists under the leadership of Walter H. Zinn, had become the first nuclear reactor to produce electric power.
2. Winston Churchill, recently reelected British prime minister, visited Washington January 5–10, 1952. Among other things Churchill pressed unsuccessfully for greater atomic cooperation between the two countries.

## ≡ January 7, 1952

Lawton called and asked what is the current status of the expansion program. GD said the way it stands now we are waiting for James Lay to call a meeting of the NSC at which we want to show what they would get for their money and when before they make a decision to do it. Lawton said we have had a question as to what the Bureau of the Budget would do with it; but we will just make some hazy reference to it. GD asked if the President had mentioned it to Lawton. Lawton said he said he might talk to GD about it. GD said the President told him he wanted to explore it in the NSC. Lawton said the President said GD had some reservations and some doubts—along the lines you have expressed now. GD said his feeling was let's know what we are buying and then if you can make an intelligent military decision on it, then go ahead. Lawton said at the various costs. . . .[1] GD said yes; this is certainly the maximum for a good long time. Lawton said one of the problems is the question of priorities. GD said he would think in connection with this that it should not have any priorities but on our present program which I am trying to work out with Wilson; we must have them because we are slipping behind on some of our stuff. Lawton said there has been so much discussion on the fact that McMahon is pushing for it; we will simply state there has been some discussion of the expansion program. GD asked if this was in the budget message. Lawton said yes; no provision is made for it in here. GD said he sent language to that effect to Murphy for the State of Union message. We will probably catch hell for not slipping it in this budget, but it is much more important that we be right, I think. Lawton said the President wants a pretty careful exploration on the thing—wants to know what the alternatives are. GD said it is an awfully big chunk of money. Lawton said "and men and power and some materials that are pretty badly needed in other places." Lawton said certain changes in technology may be in the offing before too long that may mean some reconsideration of part of it—may alter the picture a bit. GD said that is true; it is not that I am against it, but it is time we quit saying "more and more and more" without knowing what we are talking about. Lawton said some of your colleagues have that feeling very strongly. GD said yes and I agree with them. Lawton said he just wanted to be sure nothing was very apt to come up within the next ten days. GD said it is this possibility that Lay will be calling this meeting within a week. Lawton said he couldn't put it in the budget at this time anyway. GD said he thought the language Lawton had is o.k. Lawton said o.k. thanks a lot.

    1. The ellipses appear in the original.

## ≡ *January 8, 1952*

James Lay called and asked if GD had had a chance to read Charles Wilson's memo (on expanded program).[1] GD said it is a very tough document!! That is the stuff that has to be done, in my humble opinion. Lay said he thought it furnished pretty good material for the agenda of the meeting to be scheduled. Lay said the President has suggested some time within the next ten days; what is the urgency of it? He is not as concerned about McMahon as you are. GD said he knew that. It could be one of necessity if we let it go too long. I am sure McMahon himself would go along with us but he is only one of 18. Lay said he had hoped he would be willing to call the meeting the latter part of this week, but my impression was that he would like to hold it up at least ten days. But I am perfectly willing to go back to him if you think the urgency is important enough. GD said why don't we go back and find out what our headaches are on it. Lay asked if GD would then advise him; he is going to pull all these papers together on this and give them to the President in the next day or so, and then I could get more specific about a date. GD said his general reaction is the sooner the better—that suits the President's convenience. Lay said his guess is that he won't get around to it within ten days unless you advise me it is more urgent than that. GD said o.k. . . . GD then said his whole attitude on the expansion question is this: The time has come, and it is coming quicker than we thought, when it is not enough of an answer to say "more and more and more." Some thinking must go into it. The only reason we have taken the position we have in the paper to the NSC is to generate some thinking. Lay said he hoped with these papers we can get a lot of this out on the table. GD asked if he would be carrying the ball on a lot of this. Lay said probably so; maybe we ought to get together before the meeting and arrange some sort of presentation by you and the military and Wilson, to the extent that you can do it. GD said he would give Lay a call within the next few days and suggest what he thinks should be said before the group. Lay said in the meantime he would be working up an agenda. GD said that would be fine.

1. Wilson's memorandum pointed out that the Joint Chiefs of Staff had failed to justify such a large expansion of atomic energy facilities.

## ≡ January 9, 1952

Dr. DeHoffmann came in at 2:00 this afternoon to talk to GD about the latest on the thermonuclear.

## ≡ January 14, 1952

GD called James Lay, NSC, and said we got a letter Friday evening from McMahon expressing disappointment at not having received the report from DOD and us (on expansion program) and asking for it this week-end.[1] Well, we could not get it to them this weekend. I talked to Foster on Saturday and we would like to tell McMahon that we want to take it up with the President today and let him know tomorrow. You see their thinking is from the standpoint that they have not asked the NSC; they have only asked the two agencies. I think it desirable that Defense and AEC thinking be resolved before. How could I take it up with the President? I could come up and give them the paper that we have jointly worked on. Lay asked if GD had a paper which follows the Joint Chiefs of Staff recommendations. GD said it talks to the feasibility of the 50-150% and has Defense answers on maximizing. Lay said he could go up and see if the President wants to get all slants into one meeting. GD said he was afraid that if we wait ten days to two weeks that there will be a storm up there. Lay asked if GD and Foster were going to try to see the President today. GD said he thought they should. Lay said he thought it would be helpful if GD could see him and give him that picture. Asked if GD had called Matt Connelly yet. GD said he had not; I was going to call Foster and thought we could go over together. Lay said he was going over at 11:30. GD said if we could go in together at 11:30 that would be pretty nice. Lay said he would check with Connelly. Would you mind if I got in on that? I would like to be sure that our schedule is all laid out. I am having a meeting this afternoon to get the meeting set up. GD said he was hoping Lay could have the other three Commissioners in that meeting. What with all the Joint Chiefs and others, it will be kind of lonesome for me. Lay said he would check with Connelly and see what he could do for GD and Foster. GD said fine.

1. The commission had failed to provide McMahon with a report on maximizing the role of atomic energy in national security. Dean had withheld it at the president's request until after the National Security Council meeting of January 16, 1952, on expansion.

Lay called back and asked if a 12:45 time was agreeable. GD said o.k. Lay asked if GD wanted to call Foster. GD said he would.

GD called Foster and said he got the letter off to McMahon and told him he had talked to Lay this morning and told him of our problem. He set up an appointment at 12:45 with the President. GD asked if he could make it. Foster said yes, surely I can. GD said he would meet him in Matt Connelly's office.

≡ *January 16, 1952*

NSC meeting on Canadian information question and expansion program at the White House today (see attached statement used by GD and also Memo for the Files for January 17th)

GD called Mr. Boyer. . . . Boyer asked what time GD [is to go] over to the White House today. GD said it is 3:30. It is not quite clear, as Hollis pointed out yesterday, if this meeting would have a definite recommendation at the end, or if it would be a preliminary go-round. It is rather broad and if they are asking our suggestion for a recommendation I think we ought to be prepared, assuming the 50-150%, on what we would and would not want in the way of a directive. The 50-150% has PU [plutonium] and [uranium] 235 at a certain time, also calls for rate at an intermediate point, at a certain time in between the final. The means of accomplishment to be determined by the AEC and the priorities of the present programs in the form of a directive to Wilson; do you agree? Boyer said yes; would like to have something ready. GD asked him to try and see what he can do. Boyer asked if GD wanted him down while Sporn[1] was there. GD said let me see how it goes; I think this other is more important.

1. Philip D. Sporn, an electric utility executive who would organize the electric utility industry to provide power for the new gaseous diffusion plant facility at Portsmouth, Ohio.

Mr. Lawton, Bureau of Budget, called GD and said I understand I have an estimate staring me in the face. GD said is it ready? I am having a meeting now and about ours I don't know. Lawton said what I wanted to know regards questions of how much would be financed from the obligation authority right away. GD said 4 odd; I do not remember exactly. Lawton said he thinks it is 4 something. I suppose your people are alerted and I would like to come over. GD said you mean come over tonight? Lawton said no, tomorrow. What about the question of announcement (on the expanded program); are you going to work that out with them? GD said he had to report next to the Joint Committee. Lawton said timing of that is what I mean. GD said if I could, I would like to have 48 hours and make it Friday. Lawton said here is one of the problems that we are faced with, in part. The President is sending the budget up on Monday; it is already locked up in the printing office; no figure in it. GD said yes. Lawton said he had a report coming up just about the same time. GD asked if it would be Friday that it would be made public. Lawton said no, Monday; but the President will have a press seminar on Saturday morning. GD said, and he gives them a fill-in? Lawton said at the press seminar I would assume that they would raise the question and he will say something. GD said I have not thought it through, but I will call you in the morning.

### Statement to the NSC re: EXPANSION PROGRAM[1]

(1) The position of the Commission concerning an additional expansion program, and more specifically * * * * proposal, was set forth in our letter to Mr. Lay dated November 30, 1951. It would be quite incorrect to assume from that letter opposition to the expansion. We simply felt that some of the underlying assumptions, military and otherwise, were not within our province, as a Commission, to make unilaterally.

(2) In brief, we indicated that while *raw materials* taken alone justify such an expansion, we nevertheless felt that in exercising the role assigned to us by the Atomic Energy Act of 1946, we would be *remiss* if we did not

point out to the NSC that *any recommendation* for additional expansion *must be predicated upon the premise that in the period from 1955 onward,* the *steady increase of weapons production which will be reached by current expansion, is inadequate for the defense of the country.* We felt that this question should be explored by the NSC and that if a determination was then made that that period beyond January 1955 is so critical as to require the incremental numbers furnished by * * * * expansion, the Commission believes this program to be both reasonable and feasible.

(3) The DOD-AEC study on the expansion program reveals the two departments to be in agreement on practically all of the questions except two:

*First,* the agreement to some priorities; and

*Second,* the general conclusion. The DOD says the program is not only feasible but wise. The AEC says the program is feasible, but as to the wisdom, we do not know. We do not think the answer can be found in any assertion that "you simply can't get enough of this material," although we have enthusiastically been breaking our backs on three expansion programs[2] in the past three years.

(4) Now what do we get with * * * * expansion? I have here a set of charts which show our present rate of production of plutonium (Chart #1) and present rate of production of U-235 (Chart #2) and the steady state reached in 1955. These reveal the effect of present and past expansions. (Charts #3 and #4 show cumulative plutonium and U-235 under current and expanded programs.) I also have a chart which shows the number of bombs which can be had at any given time in the next fifteen years or so, if we have no expansion beyond those on which we are now engaged; also, a line of this chart indicates the number of bombs that would be available at any particular time if such an expansion goes through.

If we do not go to a large percentage of small bombs (maintaining the same percentage between large and small that appears in our current stockpile) we will have

    *with no expansion*, in October 1957 _____ bombs;

    *with such an expansion*, we get them somewhat sooner, namely, in September 1956.

If we set as a goal _____ bombs, we would get these

    *with no expansion*, in mid-1963;

    *with an expansion*, however, we would shorten the period to mid-1959.

If we set as a goal _____ bombs, these would arrive

    *with no expansion*, in July 1974;

    *with an expansion*, in mid-1964.

If we went to a heavy percentage of small bombs * * * * we meet our goals much sooner. (Illustrate by weapons curve showing Distribution I and V.)

(5) I have indicated both what an expansion buys us and in what years. The big unknown to us in the AEC is *how important those years are* and *whether we can pay the price* for the incremental numbers that we will get during those years.

(6) We are talking about a program which will, if full authorization is given by the Congress by the 1st of July, call for the expenditure in a period of over four years of $5,600,000,000 for plant and equipment over and above our regular program. This does not include operating costs for the expanded facilities during and after that period. The dollars, in fact, are perhaps not the most significant cost.

(7) There are some economic impacts. These are primarily in the field of *electric power* and the *generating equipment* necessary to produce that power. (See power chart) (1957 - 6.4% of total power.)

Another impact (substantial, but nevertheless one we can probably hurdle) is in the field of *manpower*. (Scientific and technical) (Use manpower chart.)

In the field of strategic materials the greatest impact will be in *copper*, *nickel* and *sulphur*. And there are others which perhaps Mr. Wilson should talk to.

(8) Where would we be spending this money? It would go almost entirely to the building of additional stages in our gaseous diffusion plant at Oak Ridge; additional stages at the gaseous diffusion plant at Paducah; and an entirely new gaseous diffusion site which might when completed be comparable to Oak Ridge or Paducah. In the field of plutonium production, it would mean approximately six additional reactors, three might be planned at Hanford, three additional at Savannah River. We might put some at a new site with a little loss of time. In any event, we would hope that the directive from the NSC would not freeze the method by which we seek to get plutonium because new designs for reactors are coming along. This, and other factors argue for flexibility.

(9) I should, in all frankness, make one other observation. It must be appreciated that while none of the material processed into plutonium or U-235 is wasted, in the sense that you could use it eventually in one form or another for power reactors, one would not spend any money on additional gaseous diffusion plants or production reactors themselves if our goal was commercial power. One would simply take the uranium ore and store it, feeding it later into specially designed power reactors.

(10) I should like to stress a portion of the report which we have made to the NSC; namely, that dealing with the importance of our getting priorities if the dates mentioned in the DOD-AEC study are met. I cannot over-emphasize the fact that the assumption made in this study is that we will get the materials we need when we need them. This is a rather naive assump-

tion if we are not going to face up to assigning to the AEC program every possible expediting facility. If we do not have such an assignment the schedule will not be met and we might as well face up to the fact of a possible year's postponement.

But what is more important to me is the matter of priorities on our *present program*. Such priorities will give us a payoff in the years immediately ahead. We have already slipped badly behind on our present construction schedule at Savannah River and we feel that if we are to get such a payoff, Mr. Wilson must be authorized to give us some kind of a high band priority—in terms of dollars it will take only about $200,000,000—which will enable us to get certain critical items in short supply.

The importance with which we regard this program can be gauged by our willingness to establish the necessary priorities to get it done on time. The impact on various critical materials by AEC alone is not of great consequence when the total availability of materials for this country at large is noted.

1. Both the Dean statement and the following memorandum are now found in official commission files. Both originally were a part of the diary. The underlining and the blanks appear in the original.

2. The three expansion programs were probably the DR waterworks and the K-31 plant, the Savannah River plant, and the program approved by President Truman on October 9, 1950.

≡ MEMORANDUM FOR THE FILES:

Yesterday I went over to the White House as the spokesman for the AEC (that is, myself, Glennan and Smyth, since Murray had objected to the whole approach to the NSC) and attended the meeting of the NSC on the Canadian paper,[1] which was approved, representing our first interchange under the amendment to Section 10 of the Act.

The President then called, as he had advised us in advance he would, for a meeting immediately thereafter of a special committee of the NSC composed of himself; Secretary of Defense Lovett; Secretary of State Acheson; General Vandenberg for the Joint Chiefs of Staff, in Bradley's absence; Lawton of the Bureau of the Budget; Charles Wilson, Defense Mobilization Director; myself and James Lay, Secretary of the NSC.

The President opened the meeting by stating that the issue before us was whether to enter into a major expansion. He said he regarded this as one of the most important matters that had ever come before him and certainly the most important step the AEC had taken at any time. He wanted all the considerations on the table and said that is why he had summoned this group. He asked Secretary Lovett to start out the discussion.

Lovett spoke principally to two points:

First, he sketched the growing interest in the military in tactical weapons, pointing out that if we were only concerned with strategic targets it would be comparatively easy to fix a number, but that in view of the very rapid technical developments in the atomic energy field which would make permissible quantities of tactical weapons, and in view of the much larger tactical targets the whole concept of numbers had changed.

Second, he pointed out how expensive HE [High Explosive] was compared to fissionable material from the standpoint of energy release for dollar expended. As I recall it was something on the order of twenty to one in favor of nuclear detonations, but these figures can be checked. He also pointed out the fact that HE deteriorates whereas the fissionable material does not, and then turning to the President, said that even if this material is not exploded, it can be useful for our peacetime economy. He asked me if I agreed. I then said I would like to clarify somewhat the statement concerning peacetime use and I pointed out that it must be appreciated that while none of the material processed into plutonium or U-235 is wasted, in the sense that you could use it eventually in one form or another for power reactors, one would not spend any money on additional gaseous diffusion plants or production reactors themselves if our goal was commercial power. One would simply take the uranium ore and store it, feeding it later into specially designed power reactors. I ended by saying that we must not kid ourselves into thinking that this program could be justified as a purely peacetime measure. Then the President said, "But isn't the only thing that we really waste the non-nuclear part of the bomb?" I agreed that this was so, but I also insisted that the gaseous diffusion plants and production piles themselves would be wasted if we did not have a tense international situation. I was not sure that Lovett completely understood this at first, but I am confident that he did when I finished.

Lovett went on to point out that the Joint Chiefs of Staff in October had recommended * * * * program and he then turned to General Vandenberg to discuss uses of atomic weapons.

General Vandenberg said the Joint Chiefs had come up with a minimum requirement in recent discussions of _____[2] bombs as being necessary to insure the safety of the United States in an all-out conflagration. He said that this number was not a magic number, but that it took into account such factors as the different interests of the services in different types of bombs. He indicated the interest of the Army in the artillery-fired piece, the interest of the Navy in Elsie, the newly acquired interest of the Air Force in a penetrating Elsie for air-fields, the strategic targets and the necessity for dividing weapons between the three services in order that each might perform its mission.

He also explained that another factor that must be considered was the necessity for dispersal in order that we might be ready where conflagrations broke out to hit the targets of opportunity. This meant a greater number of bombs than one would use if the plans of the enemy were limited to a geographical area and his intentions were clear. He pointed out that in the target studies many targets had been developed for the USSR, some requiring HE and some requiring atomic bombs, but that we had much less information on the available targets in the USSR than we had on Japanese targets in the last war and that our experience in Japan had shown us that roughly twice as many targets developed as had been known before. He thought that in the USSR it was safe to assume that perhaps three times as many targets would develop as are today known. This factor therefore must be considered in fixing a minimum number.

A chart was then produced showing how long it would take to get the number given by General Vandenberg, assuming each * * * * I pointed out that this was hardly a correct assumption * * * * Perhaps in a matter of a year later the minimum number would be accomplished.

The President then turned to Secretary Acheson and asked for his judgment on the proposed expansion. Acheson in a brief statement, paralleling the letter sent to the NSC by the State Department on this question, indicated that there was no guarantee and very little sign that the international tension would ease in the period from 1955 to 1960 any more than it would ease in the period from the present to 1955; that the State Department believed that we must be at our greatest possible strength during these years; that the Russians would certainly be maximizing their program; and that the State Department therefore regarded the program as one which should be undertaken.

The President then asked me to comment and I opened by explaining that the effort on the part of the Commission to get this matter before the NSC and our unwillingness to make a unilateral judgment on the program should not be interpreted as opposition to the program; that we had been in substantial agreement with the Department of Defense, as witness the DOD-AEC study; that we thought it feasible and reasonable, but that we thought the single question upon which the decision hinged was the criticality of the period between 1955, when the first effects of the expansion would be seen, and the succeeding ten years.

(See my memorandum which I used as a basis for my presentation. My only significant departures from that memorandum were that I did not use the chart on strategic manpower.)

The President then turned to Mr. Wilson and asked for his comments. Mr. Wilson said that he had sent a letter to the NSC raising various questions because the size of this thing knocked him out of his chair the first time it was brought to his attention by me, and he thought some of the questions should be explored. He said this is going to have an impact—a terrific impact—and you can't minimize it. He said he supposed we could get it done, even under the schedules Mr. Dean has talked about, but it certainly assumes a few miracles. I interrupted to say that *several* of the assumptions involved miracles and that that should be understood. He said he had received a letter from one of Mr. Dean's associates—not naming names—taking him to task for a statement to the effect that we could reach any production goal with existing facilities, if we simply had the time to produce. I interrupted to say that that had come originally out of the AEC's letter to the NSC and that all we meant was that the whole issue was one of time. You could reach any production goal with existing facilities if you had the time and that the only excuse for an expansion was to shorten that time for reaching the goal. It seemed to be generally understood what we meant. Mr. Wilson seemed to be under the impression that the impact of the expansion program would be minimized somewhat if the big dent came in 1954 and 1955, since 1952 and 1953 are going to be rugged years. I hastened to point out that from our schedule the largest push of the impact would come in 1952 and 1953. We would have to order electric generating equipment soon if we were going to get any deliveries in 1953 and the schedule called for 1953 deliveries. The same went for the impact on each one of the strategic materials, nickel, stainless steel tubing, etc. Mr. Wilson said he had been impressed by the importance of trying to meet the military needs and that he assumed that even though we had a lot of trouble ahead—and nobody should minimize it—we probably ought to go along on the program.

The President turned to Lawton who asked one or two questions which I do not recall, except that he did ask whether if we assumed that our foreign sources of ore were cut off would we go ahead with such an expansion. Lovett and I agreed this depended largely on when the foreign sources were cut off, but that by a great effort following the completion of the expanded facilities, we could, with foreign ore cut off, manage to get something on the order of * * * *

There was a general statement by the President concerning the military needs, a recognition that the program would have a very substantial impact. Then, turning to the group, the President said, "In view of these considerations, does anyone feel that we should not undertake this?" No hands being raised, he turned to Lawton and said Lawton should go ahead and prepare the necessary budget documents to get this before the Congress.

1. The Canadian paper stressed greater atomic cooperation with Canada, a policy Dean had fought for and had kept the Burgess-MacLean defection from destroying.
2. The blank and the underlining appear in the original.

≡ *January 17, 1952*

Off-the-record meeting at the White House this afternoon at 3:45. All the Commissioners went. Stockpile report.[1]

1. The president had approved 1952 uranium and plutonium production goals at this meeting.

GD called James Lay, NSC; Lay asked how GD and his Commissioners were getting along. GD said oh, just fine—all peaches and cream. I thought I would tell you that I go over (to the White House) once a year for the AEC on fissionable material requirements. I have a two-page letter signed by Lovett and myself recommending to the President the accomplishment of fissionable material of both types during the year. We leave the letter, but bring back the chart. The President approves the letter and sends it back. I am trying to get an appointment for today or tomorrow, and after the meeting I would like to raise this question of priorities on the present program. Have you talked to him yet? Lay said he had; went over at 10:30 and gave him a memo that said that at the meeting the Special Committee recommended a program to accomplish so forth and so forth. One way of stating his objectives . . .[1] GD said the objective is . . . Lay said it was "terms that leave the form of the program open." The Special Committee agreed on the approved program designed to expand. At this meeting was Vandenberg, who originated the program of this magnitude. What he has asked me to do is put out a directive for him which asks the Commission, in collaboration with Defense and ODM to develop the program for his consideration; which will give you the responsibility of working out the form and type of directive on this program you had in mind. GD said would this be a second step? Lay said a second step, yet, put in my terms, he has approved the objectives and he is asking you to take the lead on what program would consist of—a proposed directive from him to you— directive on completion dates, priorities, etc. and a chance to work out the question of sites. GD said you would not think of such detail as what site? Lay said oh, no; something on this magnitude. . . . GD said this would give scope and time. Lay said on this question of new sites, that is still a significant question as to implications of dispersal and implications of additional materials which ought to be worked out with the others. GD said I see, to accomplish this objective. I think that sounds alright. I was very much afraid it would be something such as the thermonuclear which gives us a lot of trouble like joint working on rates and scales which got into details. Lay said this charges you with putting in the directive in collaboration with the others. Another point is announcements. The President feels he ought to say something about this. GD said in his message? Lay said not in the message itself, but he is having a press seminar on the budget on Saturday and then will send the budget up to the Congress on Monday. They get the story on Saturday, but are not to publish it until Monday. He gives a briefing to Lawton on things he would announce to the press on Saturday. GD said I have a suggestion. He has an appointment with McMahon at 11:30. I think you ought to suggest he raise this with McMahon and tell him to hold off calling AEC up there to explain until Monday. I am afraid they will want us to come up tomorrow. I have got to send some kind of a report to the JCC. Lay said one thing he asked me was to make sure you are going to let Lawton see what you are going to send up. GD said he thought it was over there. It is a joint study by AEC and DOD and is a letter from Lovett on maximizing the role. You have not seen it? Lay said who has that—you mean it is over at the White House. GD said it may not be; I have asked him for an appointment and I will take along also the letter of requirements and the transmittal letter I propose to send with the report. Lay said the timing is that your letter should go up on Monday at the same time as his announcement to the press. GD said I see; I think he should tell McMahon—Lay said can you do that without it coming out in the press today or tomorrow? His feeling is that he ought to announce that he has approved this program and that your letter to McMahon should hit the hill at the same time that it comes out in the press. Can you hold until then? GD said I will have to; that is all. Here is what I was thinking of saying to McMahon "would you please hold off calling AEC and Defense at least until Monday because I would like to give this program a boost" and if he takes McMahon into his confidence, I think he will hold it. Lay said that's swell; will try to get that across before McMahon goes in. (McMahon later broke the story to the press immediately upon coming out of the President's office.)

1. All ellipses appear in the original.

Joe Short, White House press man, called and said the President told him to call GD and talk about this "damn McMahon thing." (McMahon broke story on approval of expansion program.) GD said I don't know why he did it. It is damned interfering. You apparently cannot even talk about a delicate matter. Short said there was very little talk about it. The President told him to talk to you about it. GD said he had not talked to anyone, including McMahon. Short said McMahon left immediately for the Hill to hear Churchill and the President told him to talk to you about the expansion. GD said I think probably the thing to do [is to make a statement] in view of the way it was broken, and since the President cannot deny it. It seems perfectly proper for him [to make it] on Saturday if not before, better before so as to come on the heels of the McMahon leak, [because] two days wait give more prestige. Short said unless Acheson and Wilson have some ideas on public reaction and foreign reaction to it, or if people will get upset all over about it. GD said I think your idea to hold it—saying "nothing to say about the subject"—perhaps not even confirm it. Short said I can say I do not know what the Senator is talking about. GD said you can do that, but that will not stop the circulation of "can't you get it from the President!" Short said I could say that he has directed the AEC to give him a program for his consideration. GD said he would be happy to get some language about this to you. Short said he would appreciate it; and would like to have it today. GD said hold the phone, I will give you something now; do you have someone to take this down? This would be a possible statement for release by the President on Saturday. "I have directed the AEC to develop, in consultation with the department of Defense and the Office of Defense Mobilization, a program to accomplish an appreciable increase in the production of fissionable material. The cost of which program would be in the range of 5 to 6 billion dollars for additional plant and equipment. While the bulk of this amount would probably be committed in the calendar year 1952, the construction of these facilities would be spread over several years." Short said expenditures would be over several years? GD said this is something I would have to get from Lawton, the commitment in 1952. What the costs are generally and also would not be built in a year. Short asked GD to read the last sentence again. GD said there may be a better word for committed. . . .[1] Short said if "contractual" is what is meant by "committed" alright. GD said that is what I am talking about. Short said shouldn't there be another sentence indicating that only a portion of this would be spent during the new fiscal year? GD said yes, that is true, so far as actual dollars out of the Treasury, but I think the big bulk of expenditure (I do not have the charts before me) would be in 1953. One thing I want to avoid is exact rate and scale of our progress because it would be security information to the Russians, so do not want to indicate four years, but want to leave it fuzzy as to where in 1952, 53, or 54, as to when we get the returns on the investment. Short said do you think that "only a portion spent during 1953" is bad then? GD said I would say "not large bulk will be spent in 1952." While the bulk of this amount would be committed in 1952, although not expended in the calendar year 1952. Short said would that take the place of the last sentence? GD said let's leave years out. Start "The bulk of this amount would be committed although not expended in the calendar year 1952." Short said let's go back to what I want to say now. I was just thinking about the effect of saying "no comment"—it is a confirmation. GD said it always is or practically always, as you know. I think if you say today, if he is pressed and it depends on the pressure—"I have no comment to make on the expansion program and probably will not have for several days." Short said that is a confirmation. GD agreed and said it indicates he will have a comment some time. That is bad for the standpoint of State. Short said he could say "As you know, McMahon came up and saw the President and what impression he got you would have to talk to the Senator about." GD said that is good. Short said o.k. GD said that is good under the circumstances and the other might be used. I am seeing the President this afternoon. Short said "you are really!" I have one for half-an-hour at 3:30 o.k.[2]

1. The ellipses appear in the original.

2. There are other entries in the diary during the winter and spring of 1952 about the expansion directive. They have not been reproduced.

GD called James Lay and said "I guess some of the questions bothering us this morning got taken care of by events!!" Lay said it certainly got into the press in no time. I did get in to see the President before he saw the Senator, and he said he would hold off the pressure on you and would hold off until Monday. He did say a decision had been made. GD said Short said the President said he had better get in touch with me on it. McMahon ran to the Hill, made the statement, and then listened to Churchill. I am disappointed that he did not allow us to get in touch with the State Department on the foreign angle. Lay said he had suggested that he just say that he would have an announcement on it on Monday, not indicate any decision at all but asking that it be held off until Monday at which time he would have an announcement. GD said maybe that is all the President told him. Lay said it may be, and reading between the lines, he may know of our Council meeting and put two and two together. . . .

*Table 3. Atomic Energy Commission Production Plants*

| Production Plants | Start-Up | Shutdown |
|---|---|---|
| Inherited from the Manhattan Engineer District: | | |
| *Oak Ridge* | | |
| K-25 plant | 1945 | 1964 |
| K-27 plant | 1946 | 1964 |
| *Hanford* | | |
| B reactor[†] | 1944 | 1968 |
| F reactor | 1945 | 1965 |
| D reactor | 1944 | 1967 |

*Table 3. Atomic Energy Commission Production Plants (cont.)*

| Production Plants | Start-Up | Shutdown |
|---|---|---|
| Authorized in response to Cold War crises, 1947–49: | | |
| *Oak Ridge* | | |
|   K-29 plant | 1950 | * |
|   K-31 plant | 1951 | * |
| *Hanford* | | |
|   H reactor | 1949 | 1965 |
|   DR reactor | 1950 | 1964 |
| Authorized in June 1950 to produce tritium | | |
| for the hydrogen bomb program: | | |
| *Savannah River* | | |
|   R reactor | 1953 | 1964 |
|   P reactor | 1954 | In Operation |
| Authorized in October 1950: The first Korean War expansion program: | | |
| *Hanford* | | |
|   C reactor | 1952 | 1969 |
| *Savannah River* | | |
|   L reactor | 1954 | 1968 |
|   K reactor | 1954 | In Operation |
|   C reactor | 1955 | In Operation |
| *Paducah* | | |
|   C-31 plant | 1952 | * |
|   C-33 plant | 1953 | * |
| Authorized in January, 1952: The second Korean War expansion program: | | |
| *Oak Ridge* | | |
|   K-33 plant | 1954 | * |
| *Hanford‡* | | |
|   KE reactor | 1955 | 1971 |
|   KW reactor | 1955 | 1970 |
| *Paducah* | | |
|   C-35 plant | 1954 | * |
|   C-37 plant | 1954 | * |
| *Portsmouth* | | |
|   X-26 plant | 1955 | * |
|   X-30 plant | 1954 | * |
|   X-33 plant | 1955 | * |

\* Power to these gaseous diffusion plants was periodically reduced, 1964–1970.

† Shutdown in 1946; restarted in 1948.

‡ One other production reactor went into operation at Hanford in 1963. It was designed to produce both plutonium and electric power and was the last production reactor built by the commission.

# FIVE

## THE NEW SUPER
## AND A NEW PRESIDENT

*March 27, 1952, to January 15, 1953*

The diary excerpts in this chapter cover Gordon Dean's last months in the second Truman administration. The successful thermonuclear detonation in November marked the commission's most significant single accomplishment under Dean's leadership. Although the shot was a scientific experiment and not a weapon, it demonstrated dramatically that Edward Teller had found the key to igniting a fusion explosion. The Republican victory in the 1952 elections a few days later marked the end of Dean's days as an influential policymaking official. Although he served to the end of his term in June 1953, he was not called upon by the Eisenhower administration to help make atomic energy policy. He continued his diary, nevertheless, until virtually his last day on the commission.

After the National Security Council decided to embark upon a second major expansion program, the issue of a second laboratory still remained unresolved. Air Force chief scientist David Griggs, General James A. Doolittle, and General Elwood R. Quesada supported Teller's arguments for a second laboratory. Ernest Lawrence urged Teller to establish the laboratory at Livermore, California, as a branch of Lawrence's radiation laboratory. Lewis Strauss and William Borden pressed for the laboratory, and Borden's position as executive director of the Joint Committee on Atomic Energy enabled him to play a key role. Gradually Teller won Secretary of the Air Force Thomas K. Finletter, Deputy Secretary of Defense William C. Foster, Secretary of Defense Robert Lovett, and, perhaps indirectly, Secretary of State Dean Acheson to his cause.

The diary picks up the second laboratory issue on March 27, 1952, as arrangements were being made for Teller to brief the National Security Council. Dean fought against the laboratory at the council meeting, but with little success. Dean was forced to establish a second weapons research laboratory or watch the Department of Defense do it for him. Thus the University of California Radiation Laboratory was brought into thermonuclear work. Dean was careful to inform Foster of the commission's actions and by September the second laboratory was a reality.

The diary is a key source for the decision to establish a nuclear weapons research laboratory at Livermore, California. It shows Teller's success in gaining support and Dean's opposition to the laboratory. Dean's notes of the April 1, 1952, meeting were later taken from the diary and incorporated into official commission files. As Dean realized, the meeting was the turning point in the battle of the second laboratory.

As spring became summer the hydrogen bomb program neared success. Work on the New Super proceeded apace with a test scheduled as part of the commission's fall two-shot Pacific *Ivy* weapons test series. One shot, *Mike*, would prove the New Super concept and the other, *King*, was a large fission shot. Because *Mike* would be the world's first thermonuclear explosion, Dean had Norris Bradbury brief the Joint Chiefs of Staff and President Truman.

When J. Robert Oppenheimer and Hans Bethe warned that firing *Mike* three days before the election might inject the issue of the hydrogen bomb into the presidential campaign, Dean could hardly ignore their fears. The timing of the *Mike* shot became a major issue for Dean when he returned to Washington in early August after a long vacation in California, and his diary is a major source for the debate within the administration about when to fire the shot. On August 8 Dean and Secretary of Defense Robert Lovett examined the problems raised by postponing the *Mike* shot. Delaying the shot could substantially retard the *Ivy* series, for there were only a few days between October and December that promised appropriate weather conditions for such a large shot. Furthermore, as Lovett pointed out, postponement would cost millions of dollars and damage the morale of scientists and technicians assembled in the Pacific. It was far better, Lovett argued, to proceed as planned.

On September 10, 1952, President Truman approved the firing of the *Mike* shot, still scheduled for early November. Privately the president hoped that technical problems would delay the shot. Dean had no strong feelings about *Mike*'s timing but his fellow commissioners wanted to postpone the test. When it became apparent that technical problems would not delay the shot, Dean sent Commissioner Eugene Zuckert to the Pacific for a personal assessment of the costs of postponing *Mike*. Dean, meanwhile, kept in touch with the president and put in the diary a copy of Truman's itinerary during the last week of the presidential campaign.

On October 27 Dean learned from Zuckert that *Mike* could not be postponed. Dean alerted Lovett, wrote out a message for President Truman in letter form, phoned the news to the president, then placed the message in the diary. On October 31, 1952, Los Alamos scientists touched off the 10.4 megaton thermonuclear explosion. *Mike* was dramatic proof of the New Super, obliterating the test island of Elugelab. Dean estimated it would be at least a year, however, before the commission perfected a deliverable weapon. Dean conveyed the news to President Truman and to Lovett but to few others. *Mike* stayed out of election politics but, as the diary shows, Dean soon learned that news of the hydrogen bomb shot had been leaked to the press.

Two days after Dwight D. Eisenhower was elected president of the United States, Dean briefed President Truman about *Mike*. Trying to provide a smooth transition to the new administration, Dean also told President-elect Eisenhower about the hydrogen bomb shot. His action led to two secret meetings with the president-elect for which the diary is a key source. First Dean wrote a letter (see Appendix) and then selected commission secretary Roy B. Snapp, whom reporters would not recognize, to deliver it. Snapp carried the letter to Augusta, Georgia, where the president-elect was vacationing. He saw Eisenhower on November 11 and spent twenty minutes discussing atomic energy programs. Eisenhower quickly recognized *Mike*'s implications for warfare and declared that the United States should not develop the nuclear power to destroy everything. Before he left, Snapp scheduled a more comprehensive briefing for the president-elect at the Commodore Hotel in New York.

Dean carefully prepared for the Commodore Hotel meeting. He had his staff devise a series of charts describing commission programs, then he drafted introductory remarks and put them in the diary. Dean planned to mention the importance of atomic energy to the Korean War, then to make a few statements about weapons programs before turning to the charts. The heart of the talk was to follow: the stockpile, commission organization and operation, the commission's relationship with the president and the Department of Defense, and a list of current problems. Once preparations were completed all the commissioners traveled to New York for the November 19 meeting. Unfortunately Dean did not enter in the diary an account of what actually transpired with Eisenhower.

After the briefing, Dean did little but routine chores as the second Truman administration drew to a close. In January 1953 he took a two-week vacation to Florida. He returned to Washington to join his fellow commissioners in presenting atomic energy memorabilia to President Truman. At President Eisenhower's request he remained on the commission for five months to give the new administration time to pick its own chairman.

For a list of Teller's supporters on the second laboratory issue, see also Teller, *Legacy of Hiroshima*, pp. 59–61; and York, *The Advisors*, pp. 129–30.

## ≡ *March 27, 1952*

Secretary Foster, Acting Secretary of Defense, called GD (did not hear the call) and asked him about the thermonuclear program; mentioned Teller's briefing and the Rand briefing; GD said the Teller story was not new to him but he was not familiar with the Rand briefing. Meeting was arranged for GD, Acheson and Foster in Foster's office at 3:00 on April 1st to listen to the Teller and Rand briefings.

## ≡ *March 28, 1952*

Mr. Arneson called and asked GD if he had received a communication from Foster (on the thermonuclear briefing on Thursday).[1] GD said he had. Arneson said he was a little disturbed by some of the conferences on how much a certain guy (Fuchs)[2] passed on. You know who I mean? GD said Teller? Arneson said no, Fuchs. In Teller's appraisal of how well the enemy is doing. GD said he didn't know what [the communication] says yet. [It] makes an appraisal of what was passed? . . .[3] Arneson said he thinks Teller is trying to scare the daylights out of the people in DOD needlessly. You remember, there was a whole series of interviews with Fuchs and we learned from that what he claims to have passed. It does seem to me it would be very helpful for you to get your people to review what he did pass, etc. But this does not affect the main problem that is presented by Foster's letter. GD asked what the problem was. Arneson said it was rate and scale of effort. GD said just a general gripe, huh? Teller has end-runned it again. He is taking the occasion to go off on the second lab question again. These poor guys topside (DOD) don't know what it is all about. I live with it every day and I think I do know. They don't get a rounded picture this way. Arneson said it seems we have a job to do on Tuesday. GD said he was going to expose them to a few facts of life. Arneson said he was not going to be in a position to be of much help, but I hope you will do your duty for us. GD said it seems to him that he has an obligation to put out a few warning remarks to him. Arneson said he would be checking around his shop; there is this April 1946 feasibility report from Los Alamos which I don't happen to have. GD said that is when we knew nothing. Arneson said at least you didn't know the kinds of things you know now. This letter from Foster tends to assume we did. GD said fine; he was glad to have this red flag. I will get the documents out. Arneson said o.k. thanks.

1. On March 28, 1952, Foster sent Lovett a memorandum which asked that the National Security Council reevaluate the thermonuclear program. Foster urged that the program be broadened and intensified.

2. Klaus Fuchs was convicted in 1950 of betraying American nuclear secrets to the Soviet Union.
   3. The ellipses appear in the original.

## ≡ *March 31, 1952*

General Fields was in for 1½ hours this morning on thermonuclear situation—in connection with tomorrow's meeting with Teller and Rand boys
at Foster's office.

GD called Walt Whitman (Defense Department Research and Development Board)[1] and asked if he knew about this thermonuclear meeting that
we are having tomorrow. Whitman said he was not familiar with it; didn't
know you were having it. GD said he got a call from Foster; he sent me
some papers which result from a briefing [from] Rand [that] Teller gave to
the Secretaries on this general problem. Whitman said he did talk to Foster
about something else and he mentioned this. He has been at Sandia and
Los Alamos and has also been out to Rand and ~~he got~~ I gather the issue of
whether a separate thermonuclear lab ought to be set up was a major part
of his thinking from this visit. He got the reaction from Los Alamos,
maybe from Teller, that Bradbury was not really too keen to see him down
there in a way and maybe the thermonuclear stuff was not being pushed as
hard as it would by a separate lab. GD said he understood the visit was not
too well handled. Whitman said when Foster mentioned it, he tried to tell
him that there was an awful lot to this problem and not something you just
barge into in a short time with a few contacts. I have a suspicion he may
have a rather strong view on the matter and may think the DOD's responsibilities are to make some strong presentations. GD said that is what he
has done. Whitman said that is about all I can contribute—I did not know
about the meeting tomorrow. GD said he was wondering—what would
you think of having the Committee on Atomic Energy of the Research and
Development Board take a look at it on the military side? What may happen is that you have Finletter and Foster who have been listening to Teller,
might get the meeting a little out of whack. Whitman said he would think
it would be very natural if the DOD is starting to try to give advice to the
AEC in connection with thermonuclear and research and development
problems, that the DOD should call upon the Committee on Atomic Energy of the RDB. GD said it occurred to me over the weekend and it might
be a good thing to do it before it gets set as a requirement. I am afraid we
might come along one of these days with a "requirement" from the Joint
Chiefs. Whitman said Bacher and Oppi are on the Committee. . . .[2] GD

said neither of whom are particularly enthusiastic about the thermonuclear. This argues against their being part of the controlling group for
DOD. Whitman said he told Foster that one of the most serious difficulties
we had in this whole business was the standoffishness between the DOD
and the AEC. He has come to the realization of that himself, but he doesn't
have any ideas for improving it—it might be through personal contacts. . . . GD said he was going to try and do more of that. We had Bendetsen, Floberg and Alexander[3] over on this question of non-nuclears. It
turned out to be a very thoughtful meeting—nothing resolved but everyone was in good frame of mind and I thought on the whole a very useful
meeting. Whitman said he felt it was a personal problem to establish
stronger and more personal relationships. GD said he agreed.

    1. The Research and Development Board helped the secretary of defense plan scientific
research programs of interest to the military.

    2. The ellipses appear in the original.

    3. John F. Floberg was assistant secretary of the Navy for air and Archibald S. Alexander
was under secretary of the Army.

≡ *April 1, 1952*

Meeting this afternoon at 3:00 in Secretary Foster's office with Foster
and Dean Acheson. Briefing by Dr. Teller and Drs. Henderson and Plesset
of Rand on the thermonuclear. (TS memo to files on this meeting.)

≡ ⟨Memorandum for the File⟩                                              April 1, 1952
    In response to the memorandum of March 28, 1952 from William Fos-
ter, Acting Secretary of Defense, enclosing the memorandum from the
three Secretaries,[1] inviting me to attend, along with Dean Acheson, a briefing by some people in the Rand project, I attended a meeting in Mr. Foster's office this afternoon at 3:00 P.M. The three Rand representatives were
Edward Teller, a Dr. Henderson, and a Dr. Plesset.
    Dr. Teller took up about ¾ hour explaining the early thinking on the ther-
monuclear, going back to the late '20s, the very slight effort at Los Alamos
during the last war (approximately 1%). He made reference to the rather
optimistic Los Alamos Scientific Laboratory report of April 1946 which
had indicated the feasibility of a thermonuclear weapon * * * * At the
April 1946 meeting was Klaus Fuchs who left Los Alamos in June 1946.
Teller stated that the project had pretty well been shelved after the LASL

⟨Reproduced in⟩
⟨AEC 425/19⟩

feasibility report and that it was really not revived at all until the Fall of 1949 after the explosion of the first Russian bomb. He stated that there was an objection in ⟨to⟩ the project on moral grounds in the Fall of 1949, but the President resolved the question in January, 1950 and since then Los Alamos had engendered considerable enthusiasm. He paid tribute to Los Alamos generally but said that they needed more assistance in this field, that not sufficient effort was being placed on the project, that while he agreed with the test * * * * as planned for the Fall of 1953 and the development * * * * for test in 1953, he thought much time would be lost if we did not bring into the program other groups to do considerable component testing at Nevada and other places so that we could capitalize quickly in the event of a successful shot of either * * * * ⟨or know more precisely the reasons for a failure if there were one.⟩ He emphasized the competence of the Russians to develop such gadgets and then introduced Dr. Plesset and Dr. Henderson who presented charts showing the thermal, gamma and shock effects from thermonuclear gadgets for a 5 and 25 megaton bang, also charts showing the fairly large $CEP^2$ which might be expected in the delivery of A-bombs and H-bombs in combat conditions on Russian targets, these ranging from 3,000 to 8,000 feet, where the height of burst was 8,000 feet ⟨altitude at drop 45,000.⟩

Plesset's presentation was, I thought, somewhat unduly simplified, at times a little naive, preachy and based on some assumptions that were not particularly sound. The sum and substance of his little message was that the Russians were probably equal with us[3] and what a horrible thing it would be if they were ahead, and that the survival of the country depended on the most urgent pressing of the thermonuclear project.

Teller, in closing, referred briefly to the importance of getting additional people into the project and the establishment of an additional laboratory in this field.

These three gentlemen were excused and Acheson, Foster and myself were closeted alone.[4] Acheson opened by saying, "I suppose the question before us is Mr. Foster's memorandum." I launched in by saying that it was the question, ⟨stated that Foster's memorandum did raise a concrete question⟩ but I hoped it would not be the question when we adjourned the meeting, that I had been living with this problem for a period of two years, that these things were not new to me or to the people in our shop, that I thought that Mr. Foster and Mr. Acheson should not be swayed by Teller because, ⟨permit their thinking to be determined simply on the basis of a Teller briefing that⟩ while ⟨he⟩ representing⟨ed⟩ the very finest in scientific brains, he did not always have a good feel for the administrative headaches which were involved in implementing such a program. I indicated it would be a great mistake for either of them to pass judgment on the problem presented in Foster's letter until what might be termed "the other side of the question" had been heard—certainly they should hear from Norris Bradbury who had the primary responsibility in the field and from others. I said I thought in fact that this did not belong in the NSC at all at this point, that we could not make an intelligent recommendation at this point to the President, and that it would be unfair to ask the President to make a decision on a question which involved numerous technical considerations and numerous personality items. I said that we were now operating under a Directive from the President whereby the Department of Defense and the AEC (not the NSC) were to jointly determine the rate and scale of the thermonuclear effort, that I thought therefore that I would like first to explore this question with scientific men from both the AEC and the DOD, that perhaps if we could not then work out a sensible system for rate and scale there might have to be someday a presentation to the NSC. Foster told me that he had come into the program recently but had made a great effort and had taken great pains to get acquainted with the problem, that he had talked with Ernest Lawrence, Norris Bradbury, Edward Teller, the Rand people and others. He had a feeling, although he hoped it was not justified, that Bradbury rather resented confiding in him on the problem, that Bradbury gave no appearance of having a sense of urgency about the program. I gathered, in short, that a different reception of Foster at Los Alamos on his recent trip might have had quite a different effect on his whole attitude on the question and probably the attitude of the three Secretaries—Whitehair,[5] Alexander and Finletter. Foster said that he never visualized the building of a completely separate lab out from under the jurisdiction of Los Alamos, but rather the building up of a component group or groups in other places around the country such as the Radiation Lab (showing the effect of Ernest Lawrence's visit). I told him we already had several groups working on weapons programs outside of LASL and these included the American Car and Foundry, the Wheeler team at Princeton, the Bureau of Standards work at Boulder, the Cambridge Corporation contract,[6] etc. ⟨and that to draw upon the skills of people outside Los Alamos was not a departure from our policy in any way.⟩ I said I personally felt that we could do more of this and that we should make every effort to bring into the program anyone who could make a real contribution to it, that I would like to explore with people at the Radiation Lab what they might do and perhaps explore with Loper, Withington and Bunker[7] what they thought might be done and talk fully with Bradbury and the other members of the Commission. I said I thought ~~they~~ ⟨these⟩ should ⟨first⟩ be informal explorations which would help us fill in the chunks, that we then might subsequently have a larger meeting at which the joint rate and scale might be discussed and in the meantime I thought it best not to formalize an answer to Foster's letter but to examine some of the particulars involved in bringing other groups into the program. ⟨Specifically I said I wanted to get from Teller more details on component testing—what types and where they could be performed. I pointed out the difficulties with this second lab problem were well illustrated by the fact that DOD could in a matter of two weeks perform a 180° turn in position. I referred to Lovett's letter to McMahon* which had said things were rolling along quite nicely but we should be thinking about a second lab for fission work.⟩

Acheson agreed that this made sense that the NSC should not at this time act on the matter, that it would be unfair to recommend anything to the President at this point. He asked that four of his people, including Arneson, be permitted to see the briefing by the Rand people and said he would be happy at any time to hear from Bradbury on the subject or any of our people in order that he might have a rounded picture of the issue. ⟨*AEC 425/14⟩

Gordon Dean<br>April 1, 1952

1. The secretaries of the Air Force, Army, and Navy sent the secretary of defense a memorandum on March 27, 1952, urging the creation of a second weapons research laboratory.

2. CEP = circular error probable, a method of calculating the number of bombs that would land within a specified radius of their targets.

3. The United States actually held a substantial lead over the Soviets in atomic energy in 1952.

4. The Dean-Foster-Acheson meeting held after the Teller briefing was a meeting of the Special Committee of the National Security Council.

5. Francis P. Whitehair, the under secretary of the Navy.

6. American Car and Foundry built parts for the thermonuclear program. The Wheeler team was called Project Matterhorn. The Bureau of Standards did cryogenics work for the thermonuclear program. (Cryogenics is the science that deals with materials at very low temperatures.) The Cambridge Corporation also performed cryogenics work for the thermonuclear program.

7. Air Force Major General Howard G. Bunker, a member of the Military Liaison Committee. On Februry 28, 1952, Admiral Withington and Generals Bunker and Loper signed a memorandum for LeBaron arguing that a second laboratory should be established.

≡ ⟨Memo to File[1]⟩

On April 7, 1952 I advised Mr. Lay of the conference ⟨held April 1, 1952⟩ between myself, Secretary Acheson and Mr. Foster on the thermonuclear program. At this conference it seemed generally agreed that this was an AEC-DOD problem, certainly one with which State was not directly concerned, and as the matter was left I would keep Mr. Foster fully informed as to any efforts made inside our shop concerning the thermonuclear program.

⟨Reproduced in⟩                                                          GD
⟨AEC 425/19²⟩

1. The April 1 and April 7 memoranda are now found in official commission files but were originally a part of the diary.

2. The Dean memoranda of April 1 and 7, 1952, were placed in staff paper 425/19 and circulated to the commission.

≡ *April 7, 1952*

Jim Lay called GD and said he had a couple of questions he wanted to ask. You went over last week on the briefing that Teller and the Rand folks gave at the DOD. Wanted to check with you as to what you thought should be done concerning it. If there is any validity in the thing, it is something that at some point soon the President should get a similar briefing on. GD said the trouble is that it is all one-sided. It is old stuff to me. I have heard Teller for two years. You have to know some of the history to appreciate what has happened. I have encouraged him time and time again to stay on. He has also acted as consultant with Rand. He originally kicked up this question of the 2nd lab. There is considerable sentiment growing for it. We have analyzed it several times and the consensus of the Commission is that it would be a great mistake at this time to set up a 2nd lab. All of the talent would be concentrated in one spot, etc. This thing hits Foster for the first time and all he gets is one side of it. I don't think it belongs in the NSC at this point anyway. Foster should talk with such folks as Norris Bradbury who has a responsibility for it. We have approximately 3,000 people there at Los Alamos and about 35% of their effort is in this program. Teller has no conception of the administrative problems involved. He has no feel at all of [how] much a primadonna he is. This is a little too one-sided. There are some specific things I think might be done, however. One is to strengthen the group at the Radiation Lab at Berkeley. I think it is impossible to go to the President with this problem which it is impossible for him to have any feel for because it involves an awful lot of technical things and an appraisal of all the people and facilities in the picture. Lay said he talked to LeBaron and told him if there is to be any presentation to the President I thought it ought to be a completely rounded presentation and one that for the purposes of such a presentation I felt it ought not to be a DOD but a Special Committee one where everybody had their say. GD agreed. Lay said he didn't know what they planned to do about this briefing. GD said at the meeting, he had said he didn't think this thing belongs in the NSC at all. There is a Presidential Directive to AEC and DOD. That is where it belongs, it seems to me. Foster should have asked to set up a meeting soon to determine rate and scale. Acheson agreed with me fully. He was of course interested and would like to be kept fully advised but he really felt that it was something AEC and DOD should work out together. Lay said that was fine with him. His only concern was that they have this show "on the road" and where does it go next? GD asked where the next step was. Lay said there seemed to be only one place it can go and my only concern is that when it does go there—to the President—that the whole picture be presented. I don't know what their plan is. . . . GD said there is a very interesting document sent to the JCC about three weeks ago. A letter from Lovett to McMahon in response to his asking what should we be doing on the thermonuclear. Lovett's letter enclosed a memorandum which had been done by Withington, Loper and Bunker. It was a very careful appraisal, said things were going well, etc. Now with Teller on the scene with a few charts, now we get *this* letter. The other suggested as a *possible* step taking some of the fusion work [so] that Los Alamos wouldn't be so crowded. This is all just one man kicking up a fuss with people over there who don't know the background. Lay said what made him sit up was the Soviet side of it. GD said this has always been known; there is nothing new about it. As a matter of fact, there are a lot of assumptions in the presentations which have no basis at all; of course, we always use these assumptions in our planning, but they are only assumptions. Lay said he had been wondering about that; you give quite a bit of credit there. GD said he had questioned the Rand boys on this and they admitted they were only assumptions; as I said *I* assume them to be true too for working purposes. Lay said it made quite a bit of difference with him. GD said he had gotten out the exact wording of the Fuchs stuff—what he did say and what he didn't say. That doesn't help us. We don't get it done any faster by guessing and worrying what they are doing. You come right down to the question of are you going at top speed—is there anything we could be doing. This is a daily problem with us. We have in the program everyone who is a cryogenist— every single one of them. Lay asked what GD planned to do next. GD said it seems to me it should not go to the President at this time because it is a joint responsibility under his Directive to determine rate and scale. This should be done and I don't see that State Dept. comes in at this point at all. Acheson and Foster both agreed with me. I said I would go back and take a look to see if there is any place we could bolster the program and then come back and we will have a little session on joint rate and scale. Lay asked if GD was planning to follow up with them. GD said that is right. It won't be bolstered by memoranda between Foster and myself and I don't think it is fair to submit a question of this type to the President at this time until we have fulfilled his Directive. Lay said that is fine. My only concern is that if there is to be a presentation to the President that it be rounded.

GD said sure. It should not be one sided—it should not be this presentation. This is just one guy who is a consultant who has "ants in his pants." He is always in crying on my shoulder. He is impossible on organization and the [worst] thing in the world would be to disrupt the morale of the Lab when they are breaking their necks to get something done. . . .[1]

1. The ellipses at the end of the conversation mark the deletion of extraneous material; the other appears in the original.

≡ *April 15, 1952*

Dr. Teller came in this morning to meet with GD on the old question of the 2nd lab, etc.

≡ *April 16, 1952*

Dr. John Wheeler called from Los Alamos about a question which he says came up before he left Princeton. Fred Seitz[1] of Illinois came to see me as a member of the scientific advisory board of the Air Force. He had been asked to consider a question of the desirability of conceivably setting up of some sort of center of nuclear physicists by the Air Force. He wanted to know [how] he ought to think about that in connection with Matahorn [Matterhorn]. GD said it had come to him rather suddenly and I am not in a good position to appraise it. I would hope that until we had this thing settled of where the other emphasis will be in the program—where it will be located—that nobody would make any definite plans to link up with anything else. At first blush it doesn't make too much sense. Wheeler said Fred isn't talking about this in connection with his own activities. . . .[2] GD said the Air Force on its own has done this with no collaboration with us and with the obvious fact that it touches on our program so vitally. General Fields is heading west this week and will be talking to Norris Bradbury and the people at the California Lab and will come back through Chicago and I hope he will get some appraisal from the Air Force of what it's all about. Wheeler said he himself was taking on part of this. I am quite content with working at the project at Los Alamos but, on the other hand, we can't be indifferent to what the Air Force is doing. If this separate center is set up—for example, in Chicago—that would take the heat off of us. We could stop our work. If that is going to happen, I would like to know about it and . . . If it is to be set up, as I understand it from Seitz, the Air Force . . . maybe I am talking out of turn . . . Edward Teller is pushing . . . and you know his attitude on this. I have been neutral on this question. My only point is that *if* such a thing is going to be set up, we can't be indifferent and the University (Princeton) cannot be indifferent. I have talked to the folks at Princeton on what their attitude would be on it. I have already talked to Hugh Taylor[3] and Woodrough[4] at Princeton and their feeling is that the University would not want to have any part in it directly but AUI[5] would be a very appropriate agency to do it, if the Commission wanted something done. GD said this is all on the assumption that the Air Force project goes through? Wheeler said this is with the idea that the Air Force and AEC might work out something on the idea of the other center of nuclear physicists. GD said Berkner[6] has had some talks with the Air Force. We are going to have to wrap this up a little bit. The Air Force has talked to Chicago and Brookhaven. I would hope that within a matter of two weeks we could get together and get the views of everyone who is working on this phase of the program. . . . Wheeler said he did not mean to be pushing for this. I just think we should consider it, if it is to be set up. GD said he understood that perfectly. The only point is that at this point the Commission has had no part in it. We have only recently learned of it and we are trying to see if it makes any sense, etc. Wheeler agreed and said he was perfectly neutral. The ~~work~~ reason I am calling is that I learned from Taylor that AUI is having a meeting tomorrow and the next day to consider some other project. If they take that on, it might well have exceeded and excluded this thing. Therefore, if there were any likelihood of this thing developing, it would be something to think about—whether they might better hold off the decision on the other point. GD said he thought Chicago could be induced to hold off a decision. It might be a slightly different project there. I don't know what the details are that they are going to discuss with the Air Force. I think it would be different. Let me see if we can pull this together within the next two weeks. Wheeler said his immediate question is this: Should anybody say anything to AUI before their meeting tomorrow about the considerability of such a thing so that they would likewise hold off? GD said he thought it would be well for someone here to touch base with AUI and they might make this meeting tomorrow only a preliminary discussion. Wheeler said that was his only purpose in calling this morning. GD said he was glad Wheeler had called and will do that.

1. Frederick Seitz was a professor of physics at the University of Illinois.

2. The ellipses appear in the original.

3. Hugh Taylor, professor of chemistry at Princeton University. Taylor had worked for the Manhattan project.

4. I have not been able to determine Woodrough's identity.

5. AUI = Associated Universities Incorporated, the contractor that ran the commission's large research laboratory at Brookhaven, New York.

6. Lloyd V. Berkner, president of the board of trustees and chairman of the Executive Committee, Associated Universities, Incorporated.

≡ *May 5, 1952*

Dr. DeHoffmann from Los Alamos came in this morning at 10:30 for about an hour to discuss thermonuclear, second site, etc.

James Lay called GD and said he had a couple of things to mention. One, you know PSB (personnel security board)?[1] They have someone in Defense that has suggested to them that they make a plan of the type they do have for the Fall tests. GD said he thought that is an excellent idea and most important. Lay said they usually set up a panel including information people [from] various agencies and some experts that know about it in order to keep it factual and correct. PSB did not want to undertake it without clearances and to check with the Special Committee (of the NSC). GD said they will not need very much in the way of clearances. Lay said they can organize it and you would be employed by PSB for this purpose. GD said I would try to hold it down in numbers that they want cleared. One or two would be able to do it. Lay said right; I think I will talk to the President about it; this is a very emotional subject. GD said he had one of our chief scientists (?) in the other day and he feels the same way (probably was Bethe). Everyone will watch with interest and it is an excellent thing to do. Lay said it would be you and Defense and CIA. . . .[2] Lay said in connection with the briefing by Teller et al., GD said he would get in touch with Defense. GD said yes; I am about in a position to do that now; I am dictating our proposals, [we have] a lot of tough problems but I think we have a program that makes sense over here and the GAC has addressed itself to it recently.[3] Lay said he is taking the position that it has not officially come in yet. The Special Committee has no official reference to time in this. They want to get it after Acheson agrees with you, and you and Defense for rate and scale reach an agreement on where we go from here. It need never come into the Special Committee. GD said he had his own very definite ideas and I am trying to reduce them to writing and give to each [commissioner] today and see if they agree with this approach. As soon as there is a Commission position I will get it back to Lovett and refer to the briefing. Lay said he was perfectly will to take it on. . . . GD said Acheson saw my point right away. Lay said Arneson had confirmed Acheson's viewpoint. Waiting for you all to try to work out the problems between the two departments. All I have done was tell him that Defense has raised some questions and that you and Defense are trying to work out something. GD said I have the annual report that I usually bring over; is there any time this week? Lay said this is one you usually do? GD said yes; it will only take five minutes and I would like to see him (the President) about what we have just been talking about; stress not doing anything in this field because they want to send it back to NSC. But I am afraid they may catch him at a time when he would be without the background. Lay said that is what I am trying to guard against. A briefing on it has been given to him, but it is in the minimum. You ought to have your story and I would feel better if you get together and present it to him. GD said there is a lot of emotion in that people are talking about something they do not know anything about. I would urge that he please keep on handling it the way he has been and give assurance that there is no lag over here—never has been. GD said he would call Matt. Lay said he would call Matt if GD wanted him to. GD said he would rather call him. . . .

1. PSB is actually the Psychological Strategy Board, formed in April 1951 to plan and coordinate national "psychological operations."

2. The ellipses following "and CIA." and "call him." mark the deletion of extraneous material; the other appears in the original.

3. At an executive session on May 27, 1952, the commission decided to ask the University of California to perform instrumentation and component testing for the thermonuclear program. The decision was the commission's first official step in establishing a second laboratory.

## ≡ June 5, 1952

GD called James Lay. . . .[1] (missed middle portion of call) GD said . . . did bring MLC up to date at last meeting. Lay said oh, then you did discuss in the MLC the subject Teller raised in the briefing. GD said more specifically the implementation in our own program. I probably should get a round-up letter off to Lovett. Lay said in regard to your views on JCS memo, would like to have discussion on that, but only in principle—try to keep this thing out of it. Your reactions to Teller briefing and argument—I would rather they did not. . . . GD said they are completely unrelated. I think I had better get a letter off to Foster bringing him up to date on the thermonuclear and Teller.[2] Lay said I wish you would. Wherever they go, your viewpoint should be clearly stated. GD said he thought it would work out better; I have had several talks with Lovett and Foster lately, and Gilpatric[3] called me the other day and said they were looking forward to a new regime. I think it is going to be much better. Lay said that is good. I just had that concern that somewhere your viewpoint on the thing. . . . GD said ~~your~~ you have our views on the Joint Chiefs and I will get a letter off to Foster. Lay said I think that would be swell.

1. The first ellipses mark the deletion of extraneous material; the others appear in the original.

2. On June 6, 1952, the commission decided to encourage the University of California to participate aggressively in the thermonuclear program. Dean informed Foster of the

commission's moves to establish a second laboratory three days later.
  3. Roswell L. Gilpatric, the under secretary of the Air Force.

## ≡ *June 20, 1952*

General Fields called and said would it be o.k. to plan the dry-run of the briefing for your office for Monday morning. GD said it would be. GD said he would want to open it; is Bradbury bringing the model?[1] Fields said it is already here, and he has some charts and some slides. GD said Fields might be thinking of what kind of an opening he wants; I should probably say something. Fields said GD should probably say something to start it off and something to conclude it. Bradbury probably will say most of this and I should probably also say something. GD said one of the things that might be done by Smyth would be a little summary of the history of this thing. It is the sort of thing that Bradbury can't quite speak to because some of the events occurred back here—the Princeton meeting, for example, and the original decision by the President—maybe I should make that reference because of the way I stood on the issue. Fields agreed that there were probably some aspects here that probably GD or Smyth should talk to. Maybe some opening remarks from GD to the effect that the danger here is the pendulum swinging too far the other way in the public minds. GD said o.k. he would be thinking about it.

  1. Norris Bradbury used a small model of the *Mike* device to explain the thermonuclear test scheduled for the Pacific to the president and the Joint Chiefs of Staff.

James Lay called. . . . Lay said he really called to check with GD on the meeting with the President. We necessarily have to have regular council meeting on Wednesday and Connelly wanted to know how long it would take for our briefing. He can make ½ hour available on Thursday. GD said this will probably be 1½ hours with the military, but we should cut it down for the President. Lay said yes, but I think it would be better to get another time if it would cut down on getting the picture across. GD said we will have Bradbury here but could bring him back, of course. Let me talk to Fields and see if he would prefer the ½ hour on Thursday or some other date. Lay said there is the possibility I could put more pressure on. GD said this will be ½ hour at what time on Thursday? Lay said at 11:30. GD said he would check with Fields and call Lay back.

GD called Lay back and said the 11:30 Thursday time is o.k. Lay said what he was hoping was that we could get our briefing over with and would leave enough time for a discussion period afterwards. GD said 45 minutes would be a lot better for us than 30 minutes. That is about the minimum we need to get the story told. Lay said that wouldn't leave much time for discussion. GD said I was anxious to get this in while Bradbury is in town. See if you can't squeeze another 15 minutes out of Matt (Connelly). Lay asked who GD would like to have present. GD asked if Acheson will be back. Lay said no; it would have to be Bruce.[1] GD said he would probably lead off the presentation with a bit of history; perhaps Smyth and Bradbury and General Fields. GD said he would get together the names; it would be on the order of 5 or 6 people. Lay said just let me know the people you would like to have. In the case of the DOD I had thought of Bradley, Le-Baron and Lovett or Foster; in the case of State I thought about Arneson. GD said he thought that should be it. Lay said he had had so much experience with these NSC meetings—with these big meetings. I have high hopes for this briefing and if you will let me know who you want to come . . .[2] and in the meantime I will try and squeeze in another 15 minutes. GD said that would be fine. It would be a top of nine people if you have all the Commissioners—five Commissioners and 3 or 4 staff. Will call you back.

1. David K. E. Bruce, the under secretary of state.
2. The ellipses appear in the original.

GD called General Fields and reported to him on Lay's call. Asked what people should we have from AEC for the presentation. Fields said he thought Bradbury, GD and Fields. GD said he thought he better include the Commissioners. Fields agreed that it would be good if he would do that. Fields said the MLC thinks Bedell Smith[1] should be included somewhere— not necessarily in the one with the President. The one Lay gave me had very small attendance with the President. GD said he was going to check the calendars of the other Commissioners.

1. Walter Bedell Smith, who succeeded Admiral Hillenkoetter as director of the Central Intelligence Agency.

≡ *June 23, 1952*

Dry-run on briefings for Joint Chiefs tomorrow and the President next week on the thermonuclear program. Dr. Bradbury in from Los Alamos for it.

≡ *June 24, 1952*

Briefing on the thermonuclear for JCS and Secretaries by Bradbury, etc. at the Pentagon, Room 3-E-912 today at 10:30.

≡ *June 30, 1952*

Briefing of the President on the thermonuclear today, at 11:45. All the Commissioners went and General Fields and Dr. Bradbury.

≡ *July 1, 1952*

Dr. Raymond Allen, Psychological Strategy Board, called and said we have this instruction from the NSC and it appears to set up a panel on the psychological implications of the projected H-bomb tests and suggests that Mr. Arneson serve as chairman of the Panel. We would like a nomination from you of someone to represent the Commission. GD said alright. Allen said do you want to mention the name now? GD said he didn't have one handy at the moment, but let me think it over and I will call you. Allen said we would like to meet on Thursday. If we had the name by tomorrow our man could get in touch with your representatives and make all necessary arrangements for the meeting the next day. GD said alright.

≡ *August 8, 1952*

GD went to see Secretary Lovett today at 2:30. Discussed changing date for IVY.

≡ *August 11, 1952*

Gordon Arneson called. . . . Arneson then mentioned the "problem you and Nitze[1] and I had talked about (postponing IVY); did you talk to Lovett about it? GD said he had and Lovett has some definite ideas on it. He was to call me back today. Is Acheson back? If there is strong feeling in State Dept. I think a call from Acheson to Lovett is in order. Arneson said he would get on that right away. GD said Lovett's reasoning shakes his a little. Arneson said well, of course, the mechanism for finalizing this thing is to get the President's decision authorizing the use of the stuff. GD said yes, but I don't think it is quite fair to put it up to the President. Arneson said this may be just exactly what the President would like to make a decision on—but I will leave that to Acheson. Our interest is primarily in the foreign policy issues, so it might be that the President should express his views from the domestic point of view. GD said let's see if we can't work this out inside the executive branch without the President. We have not had a chance to discuss it again among the Commissioners over here. For myself, I was a little bit shaken after discussing it with Lovett—the cost of postponement and the inevitability of it being known that it was postponed for political reasons. Arneson said well, let me talk to Acheson about it.

1. Paul H. Nitze, director of the policy planning staff at the Department of State.

Secretary Lovett called and said he had a chance to check his instinctive reactions with two other people: Bradley and Foster. They both have the same hunch that I have. The thing to do is go ahead. The change would be far more brutal than to "let nature take its course." You could certainly handle it like your other tests and say "there is to be a *series* of events." And you could put this out in advance. GD said he thinks Acheson has a view on this, but is not sure; have you talked to him? Lovett said he had not. GD said he only gathered this from something Arneson said; I'm not sure. I find that usually on these things we get up a little paper for Presidential signature which is the authorization for expenditure of the fissionable material—which also sets the time and place, etc. That would ordinarily come before yourself, myself and Acheson. That would be the vehicle. I would think we should have that paper up in a matter of a week. Personally, I lean toward your particular reaction. Lovett said it was very interesting; I put it up to them cold, without any slant. Their reaction was instinctive on it—and both from a somewhat different approach, but with the same conclusion. GD said alright. Let me pass this along to our people. Thanks a lot.

## ≡ *August 12, 1952*

Dr. Bradbury called to find out if a decision had been made about postponing IVY. GD said it had not; he had talked with Lovett who had also talked to Bradley and Foster about it. Acheson has not been given a crack at it yet. GD promised to let Bradbury know as fast as possible.[1]

1. On August 13, 1952, the commission formally approved Operation *Ivy*.

## ≡ *August 19, 1952*

GD called James Lay and said there is a matter that has to do with a change. There is a paper to the NSC which said it will occur roughly in a certain period (IVY)—it does not fix a date before which something could not be done—you know what I mean? There is a little difference in attitude but no hard feelings between ourselves here. I personally do not feel strongly about it, but it is unanimous here that it would be unwise to do it before the crucial date. There is a feeling by Defense, and shared by State, that we should go ahead when ready. I hate suggesting the question be answered by the President, but I think in view of the fact that the plan of expenditure of fissionable material has to receive his approval, we cannot help pointing out the two alternatives to him. You see what I mean? Lay said yes. GD said he would like to do it soon because of the pressure from lobbyist people. Any ideas? Lay said he had been talking to LeBaron and [has] circulated your recommendation. He said what they planned to do was get some kind of a statement from the Chiefs, not a recommendation but information on Joint Task Force planning.[1] He reported that they feel strongly. . . . GD said yes . . . to go ahead when ready. . . . Chase said State is ready to go ahead on your recommendation. Lay said he guessed that was their position. GD said there are two points of view. One is the somewhat emotional atmosphere you get prior to such date (election day). It is not quite cricket to put emotional feeling at this time which might have influences. The other is the people. Ready even if weather is uncertain, let-nature-take-its-course idea. Lay said it is the taxpayer's money! GD said he had talked to Lovett, Bradley and Foster. He comes up with this as his considered judgment. Lay said he could not help but ask what I know is a foolish question. These clocks do not start running until thing is in motion. . . . is it necessary to get people out there[?] . . . GD said oh, yes, had to do it some time ago. Lay said the schedule is all set then? GD said there will be a readiness under the plans. That does not mean that weather etc. may not make it impossible. . . . Lay said under the schedule as laid out, it could be before. . . . GD said God permitting, yes. Lay said I do not know anything left to do but to point this up to the President at the time of your recommendation. GD said I think he should know about it. It will be to him in the next few days. If, while I am away, anyone here could present this view. Lay said I would be very happy, if you want a special occasion, to arrange it. I shall also be happy to explain this concern. GD said all the Commissioners have the same feeling; it is not my personal feeling. Lay said then on the other side, find out if he would like to go into it and talk with the other people. GD said the reason I am calling today is that the sooner the better in giving the date to our people. Lay said I gather there is no delay in State; the only thing is Defense getting the statement of Joint Task plans. GD said our action would be "we concur" but pointing out that there is this consideration. The only one that was not specifically raised by our paper. Lay said the matter of the opposition to delay is solely the question of cost and would not be any serious gamble on the weather delaying it indefinitely?

You will not lose by a bad weather cycle? GD said oh, no. Lay said part of this question of what you are going to say . . .[2] has that been decided? GD said in our paper to you the statement roughly would be that there would be a series but without saying when. Lay said LeBaron gave the impression that it would not say much. GD said no one wants to say much. That is all we had in mind. Nothing that mentions number of times. Lay said I will certainly go after it and try to get this decision as quickly as I can; particularly from Defense. If I get to, I will present it to him and say here is this concern; if you want to talk about it the Commission, State and Defense are prepared. GD said just one Commissioner is needed if it is necessary in the next couple of days. Just grab the one that is here. Lay said he hoped he could get the decision for GD soon.

1. Joint Task Force 132, a military/civilian unit created to conduct the *Ivy* tests.
2. All ellipses appear in the original.

## ≡ *August 27, 1952*

GD called Lay. (He was still out of town so talked to Gleason.)[1] GD stated he had sent over a paper which raised the question of date and asked if Gleason was familiar with it. Gleason said "yes" and GD asked has that been resolved. Gleason stated that to his knowledge it had not but he knew that Lay has taken it up with the President. He recalled Lay's coming back and saying that the thing must take place shortly after. Gleason said he would have Lay call that he would possibly be back this afternoon, if not certainly tomorrow. Gleason added that he was pretty sure the decision has been made to postpone it but to have it shortly after, within a few days. He said he would check with Souers and see if he has a recollection of what it was. GD said he would appreciate that and for him to call anytime.

1. S. Everett Gleason, James Lay's deputy.

## ≡ *August 28, 1952*

GD talked to Lay and Lay stated that he understood GD had called concerning the date and that he thought it might be passed on direct. It was not clear that Lay was to communicate it. He had made a double check this morning and he was asked to pass his thought on to GD. He would not want to make it an order but he preferred to see it happen not sooner than the fifth. GD stated I think you can tell him that for operational reasons it may have to be after then. Lay stated that would please him as he thinks it should not happen before or during that time. GD stated he would not consider it an order. Lay stated that if operational reasons do occur that will be very pleasing. I might say also that I mentioned the other side, the cost, and he said he could not see how five days or so could make much difference and would much prefer to see it happen after the event. GD said thanks very much.[1]

1. Lay was giving Dean President Truman's thoughts about postponing the *Mike* shot.

## ≡ *September 9, 1952*

Gleason of NSC called GD and stated he had just returned from the White House and that regarding approval of IVY, in which the Secretary of Defense had concurred, that he apparently was unaware of the President's desire for a delay and therefore the President was reluctant to sign the approval. Gleason stated that he had spoken to Lovett and that Lovett would take it up [with] the President at his regular 12:30 appointment today. Gleason also stated that he knew Lay had taken up with the President the cost in money but did not know if the President is aware of the weather, is that correct? GD stated that at time of the year you do not have too many days—the early part could be better or worse. Gleason stated this is not so critical as to rule out possibility of the day you want. GD said Oh no. I had assumed that Lay had told Lovett. Gleason stated anyway Lovett is now told and that he thought in a day or two can clear the matter up. GD said we are going ahead on the assumption that it is the first date. I think it would be a mistake to issue any orders because of the large number of people involved and that he would tell the President this. Best to issue just before as I would not want to see the President out on a limb on this. Gleason stated he gathered that he did not want to issue a directive on it. GD remarked that it would start a whole train of arguments in the Pentagon. I am sorry Lovett had to write in the date. Gleason stated all he says is that he understands this date has been set and it did raise the question of whether he was clear as [to] the President's wishes on it. GD said if he had just not put in the date. I thought to do it quietly and administratively to carry out the President's wishes and I can do that best by not issuing any orders now. Gleason said he would probably let GD know after 12:30. GD asked that he call him back.

Gleason called this afternoon and stated that Lovett had talked to the President.[1] (Did not listen to call.)

1. President Truman formally approved the *Mike* shot the next day.

≡ *September 23, 1952*

GD called LeBaron and said he had just been talking with McKay Don-kin.[1] I have instructions from the President to keep this thing very much bottled up (psychological aspects of IVY) and not to extend the list in any way. LeBaron said that is right. GD said there is some suggestion that this should go to the Psychological Strategy Board? LeBaron said that is right. The question is what they are going to do. . . .[2] GD said don't they know about it generally now? LeBaron said oh, yes. But by doing this it doesn't get any broader than it is. It is a question of what they are going to do with it. This is something that has developed at General Bedell Smith's request for guidance as to what he should do. GD said it was all decided for Bedell. LeBaron said his understanding was that Bedell didn't want to accept the full load of responsibility for this. GD said he doesn't have full responsi-bility—because he doesn't have custody or control or anything. What I am afraid of is that you are extending this to State Dept. etc. when you give it to PSB. LeBaron said all that was intended here was—Foster and Lovett are the only two people who have any idea what this is all about. They and the Joint Chiefs are the limit on this and Loper. I have been needling Foster and saying something has to be done. When you get it finished you have to have some course of action. It is up to me to make him aware of that course. GD said if you extend it to State Dept. you are really extending it—ex-tending the list considerably. LeBaron said Foster came to me and he had talked with Bedell about it. To be perfectly frank, I did not know that State was on the PSB Board. GD said he was sure they are represented. LeBaron said he would take a check with Foster and make sure there is no extension of the list that you have. We are not. . . . GD said I don't think you need to extend it to give Bedell guidance if that is all he wants. LeBaron said that is my understanding. It is my impression from Foster's remarks. Bedell just asked for guidance. GD said another caution that the President gave me was that there must be no transfer of this matter to any other agencies and the list must not be extended and that there must be no shipments outside until he gives his blessing. Those are the three cautions the President gave me. LeBaron said this is also my understanding and I am sure Foster un-derstands that. GD asked if LeBaron would raise the question with him this morning on the extension because this does involve an extension if you take it to State Dept. LeBaron said my problem is that if we don't have a mechanism that is entirely outside of the military side of our shop, we are a little bit vulnerable. GD said if it is extended to PSB and if we get it into papers—which we never have up until now—then we get into reporting to the Joint Committee and we lose all we have gained on it. Will you tell Fos-ter about those three restrictions the President put upon us? LeBaron said he would give them to Foster again and put the flag on it. I want to assure you that nothing has been extended beyond where it was. GD said o.k. fine; thanks.

1. McKay Donkin was Commissioner Glennan's assistant.
2. The ellipses appear in the original.

## ≡ October 7, 1952

Mr. Williams called. . . . GD said he was a little concerned at Oppenheimer's recently undue interest in postponement of that operation. I can see the plays from where I am sitting and I am not happy about it. Just a minute, let me see if he tried to get me. (Oppy had not called.) Williams said Oppenheimer had said he had tried to get "the persons concerned" and so I assumed it was you. He said Bradbury wanted him to come. GD said check and see if Bradbury had asked him to come on. Williams said in the meantime I will wait until Fields gets back.

## ≡ October 9, 1952

Arneson called and said there is a problem I want to alert you on. . . .[1] You remember some months ago there was a panel formed under the Psychological Strategy Board to work up what we might say about "coming events." GD said yes, Salisbury participated for us? Originally the terms of reference for that panel were quite broad Arneson said and everybody got so unhappy about some of the PSB members on the panel that it was decided that after the report on what might be said was completed that the panel was dissolved. You remember a week ago Lay sent around a letter saying any further follow-up would be done in the Special Committee. Acheson has been troubled by some aspects of this problem and Oppi has talked to him and Nitze and I have talked to him—the whole question of timing. He feels after this 2:45 meeting today if you and Lovett could stay behind and talk about this problem. . . . GD said o.k. fine. Arneson said we will keep the group as small as possible; we have invited Lay to be there. GD said fine.

1. The ellipses appear in the original.

## ≡ October 10, 1952

James Lay called and said he wanted to follow up on the decision to re-do announcements, did not want to postpone action on that. I wondered how you would like to handle it; work on it yourself or have some of your people . . .[1] GD said he would like to take it up with the Commission informally and see if I can get any thinking out of them. Don't you think that would be useful? I do not know the answers right now. Lay said if you have them look over the PSB proposals, then we could get together. I would be leaving after today for two weeks duty. Of course, Gleason is thoroughly familiar with them. GD said I will see if I can get Commission views from our people and then will send it over to Gleason for Defense and State. He will be prepared to go on with it in your absence? Lay said yes; thanks a lot. GD asked if he had been to Los Alamos before. Lay said he had not. I took this as an excuse to do some of these things. I know they are planning in Loper's office on giving me a fill-in on all the up-to-date stuff. GD said fine. Lay said he was sure it would be very helpful.

1. The ellipses appear in the original.

## ≡ October 15, 1952

GD went to see Secretary Lovett today at 3:30 re IVY and letter to Clarkson,[1] etc. See attached memo for the files.

1. Major General Percy W. Clarkson, the commander of Joint Task Force 132.

Secretary Lovett called and said how did you make out? GD said roughly this: He (the President) has given me what amounts to an oral order which I will put in terms of a memorandum to the man there, to be carried by Gene (Zuckert) who is going out early. Lovett said does it adopt the system of authorizing a day? GD said just the one we talked about . . .[1] that day or the one after. Lovett said I will get in touch with Bradley tomorrow morning. GD said I asked him about notifying people. He said he certainly would notify them prior to their departure, but he said he would like to have this thing really held tight. Lovett said I will tell Collins and nobody else. GD said if you can do that I would appreciate it. Lovett said how do I will do that, but of course I can't guarantee that . . . after they change their flight plans, etc. GD said I understand that. Lovett said well, just so that you are protected. . . . It is just the "ready" date as far as you are concerned. GD said right. Lovett said thanks.

1. All ellipses appear in the original.

GD and General Fields also saw the President this afternoon re next above. Appointment at 4:15 P.M.

≡ MEMORANDUM FOR THE FILES:                                    October 15, 1952

In an Executive Session of the Commission this morning, following the return of General Fields from the Eniwetok area, it was reported that the preparations for the first shot were on schedule and that it did not appear at this time that there would be any delay arising from operational reasons. It also became apparent that if there was to be a delay in the shot—which all agreed there should be—this could not be accomplished without a communication of some sort to the Commander of the Joint Task Force. Since this was a joint Task Force, the question then became one of devising a method of getting an AEC-DOD-blessed directive to General Clarkson. It was suggested that Mr. Zuckert, who was going out early, might be the bearer of the order. With this in mind, I dictated the following letter, which I asked Mr. Lovett whether he would be willing to sign with me jointly:

> Dear General Clarkson:
> The bearer of this note is Eugene M. Zuckert, Commissioner, Atomic Energy Commission. He is coming to Eniwetok at the request of both of us to discuss certain test matters which we have reviewed with him.
>                                                    Sincerely,

Mr. Lovett indicated that to sign such a memorandum would make it necessary to advise many people in the DOD and it would have to have Joint Chiefs blessing, etc. While not agreeing completely with him, I had to respect his wishes. He then suggested that I take the matter up with the President and that he would follow, of course, any directive from the President.

Learning that the President was to leave town this evening, I saw him at 4:15 P.M. with General Fields. The President stated during the conversation that it was his opinion that to interject into the campaign, already charged with considerable emotion, news of the Eniwetok first shot—which in itself had great emotional potential—would be a mistake and should be avoided if at all possible. He said he wanted to do nothing which would interfere with a successful test, however, because he felt we had invested a large amount of money in it and he thought it important that we do everything possible to secure a successful test.

After discussing the problem for some time, I suggested to him that since Commissioner Zuckert was going out to the Islands that I might send with him a letter to the Task Force Commander, signed by me, stating that the President, after reviewing the proposed plans for the test at Eniwetok, had concluded that the shot should take place on or after the 5th of November, Eniwetok time. He blessed this procedure.

I also told him that I thought it would be necessary to advise some of the high-ranking VIPs, such as members of the Joint Chiefs, etc., on a very confidential basis of the postponement in order that they would not arrive in the area five days sooner than necessary.

I told the President that I proposed to advise the Secretary of Defense of our conversation and this plan.

Gordon Dean

## ≡ October 16, 1952

General Fields stopped by this morning to let GD know that Darol Froman came down to his office this morning all excited because he had just learned from Murray that MIKE shot was to be postponed until November 5th or after. Fields said several other people in DMA[1] seem to know all about it too. Fields said he thought GD should clamp down on that right away and GD said he certainly would do it—and he went down to Murray's office immediately. This information was supposed to be extremely closely held. The boys in DMA should not know about it at this point.

1. DMA = the Division of Military Application.

## ≡ October 24, 1952

Mr. Salisbury called GD at home about non-concurrence of the Defense Department.[1] GD said he expected it. Salisbury said this is non-concurrence on not saying anything at all—not on the test. GD said this he had understood at the NSC meeting. The way it was left was that the second appendix A would be a statement which would be issued if in the judgment of the AEC it seemed apparent that it would be generally known. It was not to be issued "whether or not." Salisbury said that was his understanding also. Was there anything said about the final statement at the NSC meeting? GD said he had said we would bless that; we thought it was good. Salisbury said o.k. GD said I don't think we should go to the President independently if Gleason is taking it up. But if the President wants a huddle on it, I will come down. Salisbury said he thought it would be a sad mistake not to put anything out at all. It would leave the field open for the wildest speculation and would certainly contrast with the British announcement.[2] Well, we will get in touch with you if there is anything developing.

1. Salisbury was calling about a proposed public announcement of the *Ivy* tests.
2. The British had announced their first atomic test the day before.

≡ *October 27, 1952*

GD called Lovett and said he had been out of the office for a couple of days and wasn't sure he (Lovett) had been brought up to date on what had happened on IVY. Lovett asked if GD had seen the telegram from Clarkson. GD said he hadn't seen that, but [he] did see a letter on it from Zuckert. What was indicated to me is apparently it is not very easy to do (change shot date until after November 4th). Lovett asked if the President knew about that. GD said no; he left it free with me. He said he didn't want anything to interfere with the original objectives of this test. Lovett said then it will come off nearer the original date? GD said yes; I am inclined to take Zuckert's appraisal. Lovett said, in other words, Zuckert has made the point that you asked him to determine, that the delay is not easily possible. Ok, then I guess the best thing to do is to let the boys get out there on the original basis. Alright. GD said he would undertake to reach the President. Do you think it is necessary for me to do it today? Lovett said no; I don't think so. GD said he had told me to just use my own judgment. I felt it was quite a flexible instruction. Lovett said and you have made every effort to comply. GD said yes. Lovett said o.k.

≡ *October 28, 1952*

GD called General Fields and said Lovett called concerning ~~a letter as to~~ whether Clarkson's instructions were clear. Apparently a letter came in to me to Lovett's office dated about the 22nd of October apparently written prior to the time of Zuckert's arrival. It is in the hands of the Colonel in Lovett's office. They couldn't read it to me over the phone. I told him if it said what I thought it probably said this was understandable because Zuckert had not arrived. I did not see any instructions were necessary either from the Army or from us. Fields said I don't know what this could be about. It might be about subsequent operations—and I do mean "operations" not tests. I can't think what it could be about except subsequent operations. GD said could you get it for me? Fields said well, I certainly will—if he will give it to me. GD said I think he will; it is addressed to me; he just couldn't read it over the phone.

≡                                                                    ⟨diary⟩
Mr. President:[1]                                                  ⟨10/29/52⟩
    You will recall my conversation with you concerning Eniwetok and that I sent Gene Zuckert out there to see if there were serious operational rea-

sons in the event we postponed. He now finds that there are. I have advised Secretary Lovett and he understands fully.

Since you had left it to me to do the best I could, and since the operation might be jeopardized by the postponement, we are now planning to go ahead, weather permitting, on the earlier date, Eniwetok time.

I have, however, taken every possible precaution to see that no word of the event is made public until after Tuesday, and I would propose that the party line be, in the event of a speculative story or leak, that we refrain from making any comment, at least until after Tuesday. I sincerely hope and expect that there will be no leak.

I trust that this procedure is agreeable to you.

1. Dean put his record of his call to the president about *Mike* in letter form.

≡ Monday, October 27th: Gary, Indiana—night speech
Tuesday, October 28th: Duluth, Minnesota—late
Wednesday, October 29th: Chicago, after 4:30 P.M.
Thursday, October 30th: Detroit, after 4:00 P.M.
Friday, October 31st: Cincinnati, after 4:00 P.M.
Saturday, November 1st: St. Louis, after 4:00 P.M.
Sunday, November 2nd: To Independence. Will be there until after election day.

Always contact him through White House.

⟨If you wish some info I can have it                    ⟨President's schedule⟩
flashed to you at Independence⟩[1]
⟨On the matter which I discussed with you the other evening this is simply to report that the mission was carried out with highly successful results. I'm doing everything possible to keep this info from becoming public until after Tues.⟩

1. Dean added the notes following the president's schedule by hand. Probably they were very close to the words he used over the phone in informing Truman of the successful *Mike* test.

≡ *October 30, 1952*

James Lay called to say he was wondering if GD had had a talk with the President. GD said he did. Lay said what were the results? GD said he told him about the situation, he said he appreciated the situation and thanks a lot. I did emphasize that we made every effort to keep the information controlled. I did not think it was an appropriate time to raise the question of what is to be said. I think there is every reason to keep to the line that nothing will be said. Lay said well, he said he appreciated your advising him which was in effect a "go-ahead." GD said that is it. Lay said in the absence of having ruled on the other, I guess we should assume that until he does rule nobody should say anything. I just wonder isn't it possible that it would be best that orders be issued, pending his decision, that nothing be said. There seems to be a void here. GD said yes, I think such orders would close that void. It would give us also some flexibility if something did break fast. Lay said where is the danger of that? Out there? GD said no; I think if it happens, it will happen here. I would certainly be in favor of closing that vacuum. Lay said you could do it yourself internally for the AEC. GD said yes, certainly, Lay asked if GD was planning to advise Lovett and Bruce of this new development. GD said I have already told Lovett what I would tell the President. He agreed with me that yesterday was the time to get him. Lay said how about Bruce? GD said I haven't filled them in yet. Lay said he would do that if GD wanted him to. GD said I think that is a good idea if you would do it, as Secretary of the NSC—particularly on the question of talking. Lay said alright, I will suggest that they issue orders that nothing be said; will Lovett just issue a memo? GD said well, practically nobody over there knows about it and if they start issuing memos that would circulate the news more. Lay said that is right. LeBaron is out. I might just call Lovett direct and ask him about this order. GD said you might mention to him that I did talk to the President about it. If something develops . . .[1] Lay said if he doesn't get back until next Wednesday that is sufficient time. And you think that nothing should be said until then. GD said yes; that is my feeling. Lay said fine, I will follow that unless something different comes along. GD said if an emergency comes along, I'll get in touch with you immediately. Lay said fine.

1. The ellipses appear in the original.


≡ *October 31, 1952*

Bill Borden came down about 4:45. GD asked him to come down so that he could brief him on MIKE.


≡ *November 1, 1952*

Secretary Lovett called and said "got any word from MIKE yet?" GD said yes, I did. Lovett said how is he? GD said excellent, far better shape than we had thought. I am simply doing everything possible not to send out reports on his health. Lovett said I think you are right. GD said alright.

GD called James Lay at home and said "you know MIKE, don't you?" Does that [ring] a bell with you? Lay said I'm not sure that it does. GD said you know our major activity of the moment? Lay said oh, yes; I think it does ring a bell now. GD said well, it has transpired and successfully. Lay said wonderful. GD said what do you think I should do about notifying the boss on this? It is a little difficult to do on the phone. Lay said yes, it is. GD said I told him of the time the other evening. There has already been one inquiry from a weekly magazine which has far too much knowledge and we have not commented on it.[1] Lay said so far so good, well . . .[2] GD said I could always talk to him through the White House line. Do you think it is information that he would like to have immediately? Lay said I think it might be worthwhile letting him know it has occurred and the success of it. What about letting Matt Connelly know? GD said where is he? Lay said he is on the train too. GD said the train is due in St. Louis about 4:00 today and I thought I might put in a message to talk to him then. Lay said I think he will understand alright on the phone. GD said well, suppose I try it. Lay said I think he would appreciate it. If anything comes up and it is needed that someone go to him, don't hesitate to let me know.

1. Dean was furious about the leaks and wanted to prosecute those who were guilty of such a serious breach of security.
2. The ellipses appear in the original.

GD wrote note to Dr. Bradbury thanking him and the lab for the work done on the thermonuclear.

## ≡ November 3, 1952

James Lay came over at 3:30 today and was given a briefing on MIKE.

GD called James Lay and said I just wanted to tell you that I reached the President by phone. I sent out Fields to give him a fill-in. Lay said good, I was wondering about that. GD said he seemed to appreciate the fact that we notified him right away. Lay said I'm awfully glad he got the fill-in. Did you see the article in this morning's Post? GD said yes, I saw it (about a tidal wave hitting parts of Alaska)[1] but we can't be blamed for that. GD then offered to give Lay a briefing on MIKE. Lay said he had been ~~wode~~

wondering if he could ask for a fill-in of some sort. GD said come over this afternoon.

    1. I have not been able to locate the tidal wave article.

Admiral Withington called to say "I think it's grand!"

## ≡ *November 4, 1952*

General Eisenhower elected President today.

## ≡ *November 5, 1952*

Curt Nelson[1] called from Savannah River to say that General Eisenhower is going to be in the Augusta-Aiken area for about ten days now. It is already informally known to his local friends that he is most welcome at the site, to take a tour of the site if he is interested. It occurred to Nelson that perhaps GD would like to issue a more formal invitation to the General—or would he like for Nelson to do something.

    1. Curtis A. Nelson, manager of the commission's Savannah River operations office.

## ≡ *November 6, 1952*

GD had an 11:45 A.M. appointment this morning with the President— off the record—to discuss release on latest Eniwetok tests.

≡                                                                  ⟨Diary⟩
                                                              ⟨11/7/52⟩

    In talking over some matters with the President yesterday, there was one item that he suggested that I should advise you of as soon as possible. Unfortunately, I cannot do this over the phone. I have written a message out and it is rather highly classified. It would therefore have to get to you by courier. I wanted to know from you ~~when~~ ⟨whether⟩ you would be willing to receive such a courier and where.
    ⟨Roy Snapp Secy of Commission
    Should not be identified by reporters⟩[1]

1. Dean's note about Snapp is a handwritten addition to his record of his November 7 diary entry which contained his notes of his telephone call to President-elect Eisenhower.

## ≡ November 13, 1952

KING shot[1] delayed until Friday evening.

1. *King*, the second and final shot of the *Ivy* series.

GD called Trapnell and said before getting the Ike thing in final form, I would like to see a draft of the stuff. Trapnell said o.k. What is your availability over the weekend? GD said pretty bad; I will be out of town. Maybe Monday morning. Trapnell said will have a batch of it ready by Monday. GD said we should have a list of the functions of the Commission: (1) complete responsibility of the Commission for acquisition of ore, using CDA; (2) complete responsibility for feed and fissionable materials; (3) manufacture; and (4) running of labs. It would mean a lot to him, don't you think? Trapnell said yes. I have got some old notes that I'm getting out. I think it will be pretty good.

## ≡ November 18, 1952

Bob Corsbie and Howard Brown came in at 2:15 with some charts for the Eisenhower briefing on Wednesday.

To New York tonight on sleeper train.

Ned Trapnell called and left the following message: The very "hot" figures of actual stockpile numbers of gadgets, locations, etc. Major Cooper[1] is getting up, is going to put them on a sheet of paper and come up and show it to you. After you have seen it, he will seal the envelope. LaPlante and Trapnell are also going up on the sleeper train. They will carry this "hot" material and give it to you in the morning.

1. Major Kenneth B. Cooper was in the production and storage branch of the Division of Military Application.

## ≡ November 19, 1952

GD away—in New York. Commission meeting with Eisenhower this morning 9–11 at the Commodore Hotel. See attached notes GD intends to use.

≡                    OPENING WITH EISENHOWER
                      *November 19, 1952*

We dislike bothering you at this time when you may have more immediate problems which require your attention, but we did feel that you should know, *first of all*, about ~~our test series~~ ⟨this high yield development shot⟩ in the Pacific. We also felt that within the next few months you would need some information on the atomic energy program since it relates so directly to such problems as national defense; the ~~possibility to the~~ Korean situation; and the budget.

We have not lined up any formal presentation for you today but we are prepared to answer any questions which you have concerning the program.

We thought it might be helpful to you, as a starter, to tell you what our mission is and what it is not, particularly as far as weapons are concerned. The Commission has never attempted to judge what the weapons requirements should be; ⟨in terms of *numbers* although virtually all weapons development ideas have originated with our labs.⟩ Such requirements have always originated with the Joint Chiefs. They have been, in turn, blessed by the Secretary of Defense and ultimately the President. Our role has been simply that of advising the Secretary of Defense and the President as to the feasibility of meeting requirements and the cost in terms of dollars, men, and critical materials. The Chairman of the Commission is not a member of the National Security Council, however, there have been occasions when the President felt that a particular atomic energy program should be reviewed by the National Security Council. For such situations he established what is called a Special Committee of the National Security Council, composed of the Secretary of State, the Secretary of Defense, and the Chairman of the Commission. The recent three billion dollar expansion program of the Commission was reviewed by this committee and ultimately by the National Security Council.

We thought today that we would first indicate how we operate as a Commission; next the status of our weapons program, including our present stockpile position; what we can do with such a stockpile in the event it is used in war; what our strength will be in the years immediately ahead; where these weapons are presently deployed; something of our budget picture; and, if you desire, something of the prospects for power from atomic energy as to which there will be much discussion and perhaps some legislation in the next session of Congress.

First, as to the weapons picture, our research and development effort has primarily been directed toward five things: (1) getting more and more energy release from smaller amounts of fissionable material; (2) developing weapons which are lighter and smaller and which can be carried by fighter aircraft; (3) developing weapons of very high yields, including both hydro-

gen and fissionable weapons; (4) developing the warhead for guided missiles; and (5) the suitcase weapon. In speaking of weapons we use the
terms non-nuclear and nuclear. Nuclear means that small portion of the
center of the weapon made up of plutonium, U-235, or both. All the rest
of the weapon, including the high explosive, the case, the firing unit, we
call non-nuclear. We have several types of nuclear cores containing small or
large amounts of fissionable material. In most of our weapons we can use
any type of core that we wish. For example, here is a chart of the weapons
now available.

Chart[1]

1. Dean's note that he would speak from a briefing chart for the rest of the presentation.

## ≡ November 20, 1952

Mr. Boyer called and said I understand yesterday was quite successful?
GD said I think so. Boyer said I didn't read anything in this morning's papers. Gd said that makes it even more so. . . .

## ≡ November 24, 1952

GD called President Truman and said there is one matter [about which]
I thought I should touch base with you. You blessed my telling Eisenhower
about the developments in the Pacific? Truman said yes. GD said I did that
right away. He also expressed an interest in having a briefing on what the
program is about, so I did go to New York—nobody knows about this and
I wanted it to be quiet. Truman said I am glad you did because I am trying
to get him as much information as possible in an orderly fashion and I appreciate your telling me about it too. GD said alright. I just wanted to be
sure you knew about it. Truman said that is fine; I appreciate your telling
me.

## ≡ January 12, 1953

GD called Dr. Smyth and stated he thought that the Commission, before
the President pulls out, [should] perhaps go visit him. Smyth stated he
thought the same thing. GD said they had two gifts, the electric light bulb
that was lighted with atomic power and the tests.[1] Smyth stated he had
seen one of them. GD asked how he might be feeling by Thursday or Friday

and Smyth stated he thought he would be alright. GD said he would see Murray and then get President's schedule. . . .

1. One of the gifts the commission gave President Truman was one of the bulbs lighted with electricity produced by Experimental Breeder Reactor I.

GD called Matt Connelly and stated he supposed the President's schedule was something terrific but that the Commission had a couple of mementos which might fittingly go into his museum. One being the first electric light globe lit with atomic power and a couple of other gadgets. Also would like to use the occasion for the Commissioners to come over and say goodbye. Would not take more than five minutes. Connelly said let's see how we're doing. GD suggested Thursday or Friday. Connelly asked (and it was agreed to) how about 11:00 Thursday morning.

≡ *January 15, 1953*

Commissioners went over to White House this morning at 11:00 to give gifts to President Truman.

≡                                        United States
                              ATOMIC ENERGY COMMISSION
                                  Washington 25, D.C.

                                                    January 20, 1953
                                              [written on January 13, 1953]
My dear Mr. President:[1]

I herewith submit my resignation from the office of Chairman of the United States Atomic Energy Commission, to be effective at your pleasure.[2]

While the intent of the atomic energy law is clear that the terms of office of the several Commissioners should be such as to achieve continuity of operation, it likewise appears to me to be clear that the Chairman should hold the office of chairman at the pleasure of the President.

I wish you every success in the application of your great talents to the very heavy responsibilities of your new office and pledge you every possible assistance.

                                                              Respectfully,
The President                                                 Gordon Dean
The White House                                               Chairman

1. Dean's letter of resignation is not a part of the diary. It is found in collections in the Dwight D. Eisenhower Presidential Library, Abilene, Kansas.

2. On January 14, 1953, Eisenhower asked Dean to serve the remainder of his term because the president-elect had not had time to examine the needs of the commission. Therefore, Dean remained chairman until June 30, 1953. Dean had dated his letter January 20, 1953, to make his resignation effective upon Eisenhower's inauguration.

# SIX

## THE EISENHOWER BUDGET

*January 20, 1953, to June 29, 1953*

When the Eisenhower administration took office, Dean was immersed in the routine business of the commission. Two crises, however, erupted before the budget battles began. First former president Truman denied publicly that the Soviets had the atomic bomb. Truman was obviously wrong and Dean had to refute him, giving newsmen a colorful story just after inauguration. Then John Wheeler, a key physicist in the hydrogen bomb program, lost a highly classified document on a train ride to Washington. Wheeler's loss was potentially more damaging than Klaus Fuchs's treason, and Dean had to defend the scientist before an angry President Eisenhower. Because the Wheeler case was so sensitive Dean committed little of it to his diary.

The diary picks up the budget struggle on March 5, 1953, with Dean's opening salvos for a joint review of the Atomic Energy Commission and Department of Defense budgets. Because so many commission programs were based on military requirements Dean argued that the administration could not cut the commission's budget without first establishing priorities among military programs. Dean took his arguments all the way to the National Security Council, and his stand resulted in Lewis Strauss's appointment to review the budgets of both agencies. Dean then moved quickly to brief Strauss on the commission's budget.

By April budget-cutting reached commission reactor programs. Deciding to revise the Atomic Energy Act before launching a civilian power program and believing that private industry could develop power-producing reactors with minimal assistance from the government, the administration eliminated funds for all civilian power programs save for the Shippingport project. Although the Korean War and the hydrogen bomb program had focused reactor programs on the production of plutonium and tritium, the commission wanted to realize peaceful benefits from the atom. But the commission's vision for a strong federal role in power reactor development differed fundamentally from the president's belief that private industry could largely do the job. The philosophical difference between the commission and the president is perhaps no better expressed than in the April 22 opening Dean prepared for the National Security Council.

Meanwhile the *Upshot-Knothole* weapons test series presented Dean with a crisis. The first six shots were fired routinely but the seventh shot sent a fallout cloud across local highways, and the commission's test manager had to halt traffic and wash off contaminated vehicles. The ninth shot, fired on May 19, produced a fallout cloud that not only caused more impromptu car washing but also forced the residents of St. George, Utah, to spend the morning indoors. At the same time reports reached the commission that a relatively large amount of fallout had descended on Troy, New York, and that fallout from the first *Upshot-Knothole* shot might have contributed to the abnormally high number of sheep deaths experienced in local Utah herds that spring.

Complaints from St. George prompted Utah congressman Douglas Stringfellow to seek assurances that the tests were safe. Dean quickly arranged to see Stringfellow, who then flew out to Utah with Kenneth Fields, chief of the Division of Military Application. Fields then reported to Dean about Stringfellow's activities as well as the successful results of the tenth *Upshot-Knothole* shot, the first field test of atomic artillery.

Now Los Alamos scientists wanted to add an eleventh shot to the series. The laboratory had completed some design work for the 1954 Pacific thermonuclear test series ahead of schedule and needed a test shot to confirm laboratory computations. Firing the shot at Nevada would save the expense of a single-shot Pacific test series but the shot would be twice as powerful as the May 19 shot. Commissioner Eugene Zuckert was so concerned about the shot that he demanded a statement describing the weather conditions under which the shot would be fired and recommended that Dean inform Strauss and the president of the safety and public relations aspects of the shot. Despite Zuckert's qualms, Dean obtained presidential approval for the eleventh shot and it was fired without incident on June 4.

The *Upshot-Knothole* fallout produced little concern outside of Nevada and Utah. Most Americans were convinced that the atomic explosions were causing the unusual number of severe tornadoes experienced around the nation that spring. So great became public concern that Dean had to rush a letter to the Joint Committee assuring that atomic explosions could not alter the weather. As a result of worries about the weather, Dean's staff had to answer far more public inquiries about weather than about fallout.

By the time Dean assured the Joint Committee that atomic tests could not change the weather only a few days remained in his term. He dealt with little other than the routine now as Strauss prepared to become chairman.

Dean left on June 30, 1953, a hot, steamy Washington summer day, after four years, one month, and four days on the commission. He received a brief thanks from President Eisenhower for serving until the end of his term.

For data on the Truman statement and the Wheeler case, see also Atomic Energy Commission Press Release no. 469, January 30, 1953, AEC; and the *Washington Post*, December 29, 1975. For additional information on the *Upshot-Knothole* tests, see also Minutes, Commission Meetings 862, 863, and 866, May 13, 18, 22, 1953; and Eugene M. Zuckert, Memo for Mr. Dean, May 20, 1953, all AEC. For Eisenhower's thanks to Dean, see also Dwight D. Eisenhower to Gordon Dean, June 9, 1953, DDE.

## ≡ *January 20, 1953*

General Eisenhower inaugurated President today.

## ≡ *February 9, 1953*

Jim Reston called and talked to GD about his term and new chairman, etc. Gd asked not to be quoted at all.

## ≡ *February 10, 1953*

Jim Reston came in at 12:00—and stayed to lunch.

## ≡ *February 11, 1953*

GD's resignation announced in today's papers—to become effective in June, to give the President time to appoint a new member of the Commission to fill Glennan's vacancy; [the new member] will take over the Chairmanship when GD's term is up.

Lewis Strauss called GD and said I wrote you a very nasty note this morning. I am sorry I mailed it. GD said he understood, and it was a little unfortunate the way it broke. All I said was that I planned to serve out my term until June and then I felt I should get out, that I had been in long enough. Strauss said would you stay if requested? GD said I don't think I can. It is getting to be quite a drain, and I feel I have had it. Strauss said I would like to see you change your mind. GD said well, I want to see it through this Spring. There will be a lot of headaches in Congress. . . .

## ≡ *February 24, 1953*

Cong. Holifield called GD and remarked he did not know how long GD would be here. GD remarked until June 30th. Holifield stated you will be leaving then—do you have any ideas who might come in? GD stated no. Made announcement early so they could get the man and let him get his feet wet. Holifield stated I see. You have probably taken about all the time out of private life you can spare. You have done remarkably well. . . .

## ≡ *March 5, 1953*

Sec. Wilson[1] returned GD's call. GD stated the other day we had a session with MLC on this general question of relating military requirements to budget presentation. Out of that came a recommendation to the Joint Chiefs. They will be getting a recommendation concerning the expansion program to you. We wanted an opportunity to talk with you after you receive it from the Chiefs. I thought better you get the recommendation and then we can discuss it. Wilson stated maybe you can come over for lunch. Does LeBaron know about it? GD remarked he does. Wilson said he could talk to him about it and make sure it does not drag too long. GD stated, we have to go to Dodge[2] and some assumptions are very important. Wilson remarked [the budget] comes out of taxpayers' money—same tax dollar. Alright I will work on it.

1. Charles E. Wilson, Eisenhower's secretary of defense.
2. Joseph M. Dodge, director of the Bureau of the Budget.

## ≡ *March 10, 1953*

Schaub of the Bureau of the Budget called and said I just wanted to report progress. I saw LeBaron and gave him the figure from 3 to 5, to see what the implications of it are and he is going to prepare a paper on the 10 questions we had and talk to Wilson and then we will talk to Bradley who will not be back until Sunday. The feeling I got was that he didn't have a very clear understanding of what the implications would be. He knows in general, but not the specifics. GD said well, he can come to us for specific information as he works out the problem. The more I thought about it and after talking to Boyer today, I think I must see Dodge and ask him to let us talk to the Task Force from the Congressional Committee concerning the items in the amended budget. I think we are going to buy such ill-will on the Hill, that I would like to put the problem to him and see what he says about it. Schaub said yes, why don't you talk to him. GD said I was going to talk to him in the morning anyway; I will see him at the NSC meeting. Schaub said you might tell him about the approach with LeBaron. GD said alright. I will make it a point to bump into him.

## ☰ March 12, 1953

See attached letter to Secretary of Defense Wilson on budget cut.

GD called Schaub of Budget ~~called~~ and said the more I have been thinking of this assignment the more in favor I am of having this over-all look. Had it occurred to you to give DOD those figures and say this has to come out of DOD and AEC. After all, this is the way it has to be racked up eventually. It is battleships vs bombs. Was that considered? Schaub said yes. It is now in separate pieces but it will be brought together in the end. LeBaron was given that. . . .[1] GD said LeBaron is also ~~talkin~~ taking a look at orthodox weapons? Schaub said he is not going to, but he will talk with Wilson about it. The question is whether this will come up jointly with DOD on the 24th or whether it will be taken into account after that. GD said what gives us real concern is LeBaron sitting down with our budget and saying you can save $5 here and $5 there, and then finally coming out with something without facing the fact that this cut will come out of fissionable material. Schaub said that is right. That is one of the [three] basic questions we raised: (1) the level of production; (2) the timing; and (3) the relation to DOD expenditures. GD said when LeBaron is finished, will he coordinate it with Kyes?[2] ~~Schabu~~ Schaub said he is going to prepare it and show it to us. GD said I hope before he prepares any papers that we get a crack at it. Schaub said I do too. I was amazed at his lack of knowledge of the program. Did you have a chance to talk to Dodge yesterday? GD said yes, I spoke to him about both items. He said we could talk to them about the program, if we didn't relate it to dollars. Schaub said right. GD said he saw my point. Schaub said what did he say about the other? GD said LeBaron? He and I agree if you are going to have a cut you have to have a top dollar and then ~~talk~~ take a look at the whole program and see what is the most important. Schaub said o.k.

1. The ellipses appear in the original.
2. Roger M. Kyes, the deputy secretary of defense.

## ☰ My dear Mr. Secretary:[1]                                    ⟨Diary 3/12/53 draft⟩

A matter has arisen which has given the members of the Atomic Energy Commission very grave concern. I refer to the assignment by the Director of the Bureau of the Budget to Mr. LeBaron of the task of indicating, in the event that a cut of $300,000,000 is to be made from our Fiscal Year 1953 funds and a $500,000,000 cut from our Fiscal Year 1954 funds, what portions of the atomic energy program must be eliminated.

We are very much in sympathy with Mr. Dodge's desire to have priorities established for military projects in the Department of Defense and in the Atomic Energy Commission, and we are convinced that there can never be an intelligent review of our security needs without the assignment of priorities. To assume, however, in advance of the setting up of such priorities that a blanket figure of $300,000,000 must be taken from the atomic energy program does violence to the principle to which I am sure Mr. Dodge subscribes.

We know, from the analysis of our budget, that if anything like this sum is to be eliminated from the program, it can only be done by the elimination of facilities for the production of fissionable material, facilities which were blessed by the last session of Congress and which are in our current expansion program.

We are anxious to meet with you and to explain to you our concern in some detail.

Sincerely,
GD

1. The letter was addressed to Secretary of Defense Wilson.

≡ OPENING:[1]

We are delighted to meet with you gentlemen today and give you a brief survey of the atomic energy program. The fact that you have been chosen as a group of consultants to the National Security Council is in itself a significant fact. It is but one of the evidences that the President is determined to make the fullest possible use of the National Security Council, which today in our government is the only mechanism by which the civilian leaders of the government can bring together the over-all policy questions relating to our total national defense. Most of the big policy questions cannot be settled, and should not be settled, unilaterally by a single agency of the government, and we of the Atomic Energy Commission are singularly aware of this. Most of our program today is based upon military requirements originating in the Joint Chiefs and blessed by the Secretary of Defense, and yet, astounding as it may seem, when it is determined by the Bureau of the Budget and the President that there are only a given number of dollars available for national defense, there is no resolution today by any group of the priorities of the various component programs related to the national defense. There is no way today, for example, of determining whether it should be atomic bombs or battleships, aircraft or aircraft reactors, submarines or bazookas. This, then, is one of the policy questions which eventually I think must come to the National Security Council. This is a burning question with us at the moment because we are but ten days away from the submission of our budget to the Appropriations Committee of the House.

There are other policy questions which properly should come before the NSC and arise from the atomic energy program. What shall be the size of our stockpile? Is one year more important than another in our program to produce fissionable materials and weapons? When, if ever, do we level off? In this the Russians have a great advantage over us for they have "Five Year Plans." We in the atomic energy program have attempted to have "Five Year plans" but we run into the very distracting situation that the plan, because of budgets and shortages of dollars, etc., becomes but an annual plan with a resulting lack in long-range planning and the costs which come from cutbacks once momentum has been achieved.

Another problem related to the first one which I have posed is this: What are the assumptions behind the military requirements? Another problem: What shall be the attitude of the Executive Branch of the government toward the whole question of production of economical power from the atom? We have a specific proposal, of which you have copies, and we are anxious to talk this over with you later on in the briefing.

Another problem: How shall we handle the psychological strategy problems which result from our program? How, for example, shall we play the thermonuclear developments? What impression do we want to leave with the Russians, the American people and our allies concerning it? These must be determined at high level. What shall we do in such fields as the exchange of information concerning atomic weapons with other countries?

Let us leave the problems for a moment and have a look at the program, because before one can address himself to these large policy questions he must have some detailed knowledge of the program which gives rise to these policy questions. Our discussion breaks down easily into five divisions:[2]

1. Dean prepared these remarks for the National Security Council meeting of March 18, 1953.
2. The original document ends at this point.

≡ *March 18, 1953*

GD called Strauss and asked if Cutler[1] got a hold of him last night. Strauss stated no, was in Baltimore. GD stated he called from Humphrey's[2] house and was trying to work out system of Defense budget and ours [to see if they could] be determined together relative to priority. Strauss asked isn't that constructive from your point of view? GD stated wonderful and they want you to be the guy and that makes it doubly wonderful. Strauss stated you are the man. GD stated I cannot do it—we have requirements but no priorities and [Strauss's review of AEC and DOD budgets] would be the greatest service you could render. Strauss said but it has to be done by March 25th? GD stated I think you would have two or three weeks. Strauss remarked the presumption is that he will call me and if he calls will say I will discuss it with you. GD remarked that this had come directly from Humphrey. Strauss suggested let's leave it that if I hear from him will call you back. There is another thing I would like and that [is] a memo of present status of these proposals on power reactors from various companies and what proposals are so I can look at [them].[3] Also I am getting a young guy in to read stuff and in order to indoctrinate him, he is not cleared, I would like to get him reading material of semi-annual reports of Commission which are unclassified. I will send over for them on Friday. GD said would have all together when you come in Friday.

1. Robert Cutler, head of the Planning Board of the National Security Council.
2. George M. Humphrey, the secretary of the treasury.
3. The Dow Chemical Company and the Detroit Edison Company led a group of companies in a joint study with the commission of a reactor which would produce electric power. No specific project was undertaken as a result of the study.

Schaub of the Budget called GD and stated things have been in motion apparently—little bit of help. Cutler called you and indicated the essence of it. GD stated he called last night and [said] we would propose going over this. Schaub stated have a draft copy of what the President approved. GD stated he was very anxious to see the criteria of issue that was put to him. Cutler read it to me—Schaub stated will have one over to you. Dodge to have little transmittal note indicating President's approval of this. GD remarked I think this is wonderful. Must convince him that he has to take this job. Schaub stated I think that has been done. GD remarked he thought if Dodge wants to put on the pressure a personal call would be useful. Schaub stated Kyes talked to Strauss. GD stated I do not think letter to Wilson hurt. It was designed to help it along. Schaub stated reference to Joint Chiefs and get answers back and because unclassified they thought you were trying to maneuver them—but this will square it any way.[1]

1. I am not able to clarify this sentence any further.

≡ *March 19, 1953*

GD returned Murray's call. Murray asked if GD had had time to take a shot at the letter to Cutler. GD said time is what stopped me. Do you have any suggestions? Murray stated as I keep reading this it looks as if they were telling us to stretch this out—in telling us not to cut facilities but telling us also to spend less money in '54 and '55. I would like to get an interpretation of that. If so then our whole approach might have to be from a different angle. Point is is it stretch out or cutting out? GD stated what [are we] really talking about in '54 and '55[?] If [we are] really going to save any money [we] have to save it in '53 expansion. Murray remarked maybe they are [doing] a tricky thing in a way we have not caught yet. I am not sure. Just asking stretch out your program—that may be angle. GD stated the criteria of relative importance comes pretty close to what we would like to see. Ratio cut in the two at the same time. Murray stated we must get some answer. Let's say we do not understand this. GD remarked also refer Cutler to letter to Wilson. Murray suggested give copy of Wilson letter and then meet with Strauss. GD stated that appeals to me. Murray suggested thinking it over and GD said let's get to it some time today.

Schuldt of the [Bureau of the] Budget called GD and said would like to ask this question in regard to matter of paper. I think Mr. Dodge is sending over today the official transmittal on it. This question occurred to Schaub and me—would you see any advantage in our discussing what might be anticipated in the way of questions that might be raised in NSC after the Admiral there gets underway?[1] I gather if time permitted is not going to be very great—any advantage in anticipating how he might approach it? GD stated I do not know how he will approach it. I am seeing him tomorrow and will urge a full scale briefing of the program, the speed, and particularly in terms of program's projects. Schuldt remarked also implications of construction program. GD stated oh sure. ANP,[2] submarine reactors, etc. That is only way anyone coming in can get it, otherwise load them down with books on budget. Schuldt remarked I think it is broader subjects. GD stated [we] should do anything we can to let him see what we are spending, on what, and what assumptions. Also going to urge [him to] come in as soon as he can because of time. I think following a briefing he will know how to approach this total thing. Do not know if they have signed him up. Schuldt stated Schaub seemed to think they did but signing up may still be a good question. I just wondered if any advantage in making factual data. GD stated it is hard for me to make any constructive suggestion. I think maybe go around with him first. Schuldt asked did you have a meeting scheduled? GD stated oh no, he is coming down on something else. I am going to suggest meeting with you next week. We have our budget hearings postponed to the 18th of May so that gives us a lot of room. Schuldt stated the other date I mentioned to you yesterday apparently has some magic—this date of the 31st of this month as far as total of this program. As you pointed out yesterday [that] makes [his schedule] awfully crowded. GD stated let me see him first.

1. The admiral in the NSC probably refers to Lewis Strauss, who rose to the rank of rear admiral during World War II and was often referred to by his naval rank.

2. ANP = Aircraft Nuclear Propulsion, a program that futilely attempted to design a nuclear reactor that would power an airplane.

Sec'y Wilson telephoned Mr. Dean in connection with Mr. Dean's letter and proposed that Mr. Dean come to lunch next Wednesday at one o'clock to "talk over where we think we are. In the meantime the Chiefs are trying to take a look at what we might think our military requirements are as the best guide of our needs." Mr. Wilson says, "We have this NSC decision of the other day and Lewis Strauss is getting into it. Apparently the Council has designated him as the man to take a real look at it. We can talk about that Wednesday pretty good and maybe I will have more information out of my organization."

## ≡ *March 23, 1953*

General Cutler called and said he understood that GD was concerned lest something that GD had said or done [had] been taken as a concurrence with a cut for AEC. Cutler said we don't feel that you concurred in any such thing, but that you simply blessed the idea of a review of both budgets. GD said he was concerned a little bit by the language in the letter from Dodge to Lewis Strauss; that he (GD) had expressed his concern, orally and in writing, to Strauss on this point. GD said he was sure we all understood each other now. Cutler agreed. GD said his reason for asking for the letter back was because of the mistake in it—referring to "your telephone call" to the President, when it was Cutler who had called. Cutler then asked if GD would hold himself in readiness after lunch on Tuesday, the 31st. The NSC is going to have a meeting with the consultants on that day and sometime during the afternoon, probably early, they might like to discuss the nuclear power question with you and also this matter that Strauss is working on. GD said fine.

GD called Boyer and said he had just had a call from Strauss and he will be down Thursday and Friday. I think we ought to be prepared for an early briefing on Thursday. He has to have a report in by the 31st. Let's make it [as] easy [a] one for him as we can. He has asked that we be prepared to talk to the NSC memo. Boyer said we better have it reproduced. GD said yes, if it has not been done. It has been; it is information paper 533/26. I do not think we will talk to point #4—but the first three we will have to come up with some answers.[1] Boyer said maybe we should have a meeting on Wednesday afternoon before the Thursday thing. GD said o.k.

1. The four points in paper 533/26 listed the program areas in which Strauss would review the budgets of both the commission and the Department of Defense.

## ≡ *March 25, 1953*

Lunch with Secretary Wilson today at 1:00.

## ≡ *March 26, 1953*

Briefing for Mr. Strauss this morning at 10:30.

Boyer called and said Schuldt has been bothering us on cancellation costs on two Savannah River reactors. I have a great dislike for giving him cancellation costs and having him use them. So, we have been stalling him and he still insists we give them to him—how do you feel about this? Since we have mentioned it to Lewis Strauss I don't suppose there is anything too bad in giving them to Schuldt. GD said does he ask for the last or the dollars? Boyer said the dollars. GD said I don't see any problem on the dollars, but I do the last. I think you have to do that. Boyer said it turned out to be 164 million. So, I will correct that with Strauss when I see him. GD said I see. You lose 2/5 of the production to save 10% of the cost. Boyer said there is a tendency to think we could cut something out—remember when he was talking about the number of test drops and he said there might be some place where you can cut out some fat. Sometime we can point out to him that the appropriation boys take a bit out too. GD said that is why . . .[1] that is the point I want to make: you are bound to get a 10% cut; we have to keep that in mind. . . .

1. The first ellipses appear in the original: I have added the second.

## ≡ *April 1, 1953*

GD called General Cutler and said I was not clear when I left on the consensus of the group on SGR (Sodium Graphite Reactor), on the 3 million point. Cutler said we are trying to write out a memo to cover the matter and will include a statement on this. I hope at the next Council meeting to bring it up for approval. That was not a regular Council meeting. GD said I just got a little feeling that the President and the others were not for it— others against the expenditure. Cutler said my understanding is that there is no more money, 3 million ~~einl~~ included at this time. Going to change the statute first.[1] GD said the statute will not get you your reactors. In view of the President's seeming interest in the thing, was this a definite decision of the Council? Cutler said it is not a definite decision of the Council for the next Council meeting is not until next Tuesday. GD said is there any way to point this thing up. Cutler said it would be helpful if I had a one-page memorandum. Give it to me at lunch tomorrow—I am coming to lunch, am I not? GD said oh, yes. Cutler said well, nothing will happen on this until next Tuesday. GD said o.k. will do that memo then.

1. The statute was the Atomic Energy Act of 1946.

≡ *April 16, 1953*

Price of Westinghouse[1] called about a morale problem they are having at Bettis Field[2] because the men there hear rumors to the effect that the CVR ~~submarine~~ program is to be cancelled; a story to that effect was in the Pittsburgh press last Friday; it was a UP story out of Washington. GD said we have a request to cut our budgets for 1954 and 1955 and this may result in the stretching out of some of our programs on ANP or things like that, but we don't expect any cancellations. No decisions have been made and I would tell the people that until they get the word from the horse's mouth to assume that the program will continue as planned. There will always be rumors. Price said then you don't feel there is much chance of the CVR being knocked out? GD said my best judgment at the moment is that the CVR will not be knocked out . . .[3] it might be stretched out a bit; that is a possibility. Price said thanks very much; I would appreciate knowing when you do have something to tell me. GD said I will try to keep you posted.

1. Gwilym A. Price, president of the Westinghouse Electric Corporation.
2. The commission's Bettis Laboratory was designing a reactor to power an aircraft carrier or CVR.
3. The ellipses appear in the original.

≡ *April 17, 1953*

DMA[1] briefed Strauss this morning on certain questions involved in tests and the budgets for them.

1. DMA = the Division of Military Application.

Lay called and said he wanted to check on the prospects for the atomic energy program that we were looking forward to on Monday. Is that the proposed reduction? Is that pretty well along? GD said the Commission has not ~~bels~~ blessed it but it is coming along pretty fast. Lay said any chance of getting it on Monday morning? GD said sure; I think so. Lay said we would like to give it to the planning board. GD said this is the budget? O.K. We are working on it now; it is in the General Manager's office. Lay said if you could get it to me on Monday morning, we would appreciate it. GD said we will try and get it to you. Lay said o.k. and you will be invited to the meeting on Wednesday. GD said I won't be there, but we will send somebody. Lay said o.k. fine.

## ≡ *April 20, 1953*

General Cutler called and said I guess you can understand the questions I am going to ask. On the last page of the memorandum to the Executive Secretary of April 20th . . .[1] we added the figures for 1954 up to 223; you added them to 224; but we carried your figure of 224 in our reprint which you have probably received by now. GD said I see, you think there is a mathematical error? Cutler said we added it a couple of times. The other thing: The reduction in expansion on account of pilot plant three. . . . GD said as against 16? Cutler said in your letter you spoke about 11 million 4. In the paper it says 3 in one year and 4 in another. I wondered what that discrepancy was. GD said let me check that too. . . . On the SGR? What time is the meeting? Cutler said I think 11:15 is the time; there are a couple other things first, that you have no interest in. GD said alright.

    1. The ellipses appear in the original.

## ≡ ⟨*April 22, 1953*⟩

NSC meeting this morning at 11:15. See attached statement.

Bill Borden called about the NSC meeting this morning. Said the whole proceedings were all over town. Asked if GD had any comment to make on the discussions on power policy. GD said he had nothing; nothing had been decided at the meeting. (Did not hear call).

Boyer called and said Bill Borden had called him and asked the same questions and said that the discussion at the NSC meeting this morning was all over town by now. Borden wanted to know when we would appropriately advise the JCC of the various budget adjustments and estimates, etc. ~~Borye~~ Boyer told him that he would not think we would do it until we got the word officially from the NSC. GD said it is too bad that this is all over the countryside already. I think the people should be cautioned that this is not to get out because it embarrasses the President and the NSC and a lot of these things are so tentative. I don't think we should ever ~~ben~~ be in a position where we can be charged with a leak of an NSC meeting. Somebody is leaking it, you know. I am sure it is not from our shop, however. Boyer said I agree.

≡                                                        ⟨4/22 diary⟩

Sometime ago the Commission furnished to the NSC its statement on power policy. This was turned over by the NSC to the committee of seven consultants. They came back with a revised statement, which appears at page 4 of the paper before the NSC today.

While many of the points in the AEC statement and in the statement here before us are the same, there is nevertheless a fundamental conflict between the two approaches. The thesis of the NSC statement seems to be that power reactors development from now on should be done primarily by private industry. Notice I emphasize the term "development." As opposed to this, the AEC policy statement was that a vigorous power reactor *development* program should be continued by the AEC with help from private industry. This is the fundamental difference between the two policy statements. The Commission is of the opinion that in the developmental period, which will last something on the order of five years, government support is requisite to securing economical power. No assistance from the government will, in our judgment, mean a substantial delay, perhaps several years, in realizing economical power from reactors. Certainly without experimental and prototype reactors, the technology is such that private industry will not invest large sums of money necessary for the construction of power reactors. We believe, if the NSC statement were taken literally and in the next five years the Commission were not permitted to build experimental reactors and industry were not willing to invest the money for such experimental reactors, no such reactors would be built and it is quite possible that the United Kingdom, or Canada, or France, would build a commercial power reactor before the United States.

There are two ways in which this might be handled today. One is to preserve a clash between the Commission point of view and that of the seven consultants. This will be needlessly embarrassing when the Commission appears before Congressional Committees to present its views and to make its prediction for economical power and to urge the legislation necessary to entice private capital into the program.

A way of resolving this clash more comfortably for all concerned would be for the NSC to either (1) adopt the statement of policy prepared by the Commission without the implementing portions of that policy, or (2) reword the consultants' statement, preserving the first sentence of 7a; modifying the second sentence to read as follows: "A program for such early development should be carried forward vigorously with every encouragement to participation by private industry . . ." and strike the four points made in 7b which the Commission thinks are unsound premises; preserve all of 7c which describes the type of legislation which the consultants and the Commission believe is essential if industry is to enter the program.

Either of these two courses would seem better than to have a clash on the policy grounds at this point.

I would also suggest that there is another place where we clash, but that it need not appear in a policy statement. The subject-matter of paragraph (d) is essentially a budget item as distinguished from a policy item and I would suggest that it be stricken from this statement, even though the limitation budgetwise has been placed upon the Commission in the building of the Sodium Graphite Reactor.

I would also suggest that if the two positions are to be harmonized we insert in paragraph (e) the word "eventually" before "participate" for it is clear to the Commission that there will not be industrial participation in the building of either full-scale power reactors or experimental prototypes in the years immediately following the legislative changes.

## ≡ April 23, 1953

GD called Bill Borden and said he had just read in The News the remarks attributed to Congressman Price.[1] How was the Joint Committee "officially advised of serious budget cuts?" Borden said I presume what he had in mind was the testimony of a week ago yesterday. Remember, Cole asked you where you stood on the budget and my recollection is that you said something about you are figuring how to do it up to a certain figure? I assume that is what he had in mind. It is, of course, also obvious that he got wind of yesterday's meeting (NSC). I got that myself from other sources. GD said I wonder how that gets out of an NSC meeting? Who sits around in NSC meeting who goes talking after that? The point is that I get blamed for it. Borden said from where I sit, routinely I got something that alerted me to the fact that the meeting had taken place and something important had happened. So I made a project of calling people and I pieced together the story by rather Machiavellian methods of setting for each piece I did know, etc. and also indicating that I had some knowledge of it, and as a result of seven or eight calls, it appeared to me that essentially the whole story had been laid out. That is the way it came about to me. GD said o.k.

1. Representative Melvin Price of Illinois, a member of the Joint Committee on Atomic Energy.

〈May 7th diary〉

Dr. Smyth called Mr. Strauss in New York and said he had a couple of things to mention. First, we are supposed to go up on budget hearings in about two weeks and this creates a real problem. There are two aspects to this. Have you any idea when the review of the requirements is going to get done? Strauss said he had pressed the DOD on it, and was told that a draft had been completed. Kyes[1] has gone out to the test and is due back on Saturday and maybe Sunday. Strauss said he would talk to Kyes on Monday; doesn't want to send him a telegram about it. Smyth said fine, and the other aspect is perhaps less important but it is the question of whether we could get the Bureau of the Budget to go over with us all of the parts that do not depend on the expansion program. Strauss said he didn't think we had any trouble getting hold of them, or did we? Smyth said we seem to be having a little trouble; he promised to keep in touch with Strauss on this. Smyth said it is a question of whether Budget would be willing to have formal hearings on our budget before this final decision which will alter some actions. Strauss said when AEC is ready, why don't you send a note to Dodge and tell him you would like to set a time, and if you don't hear from him in a day or two, let me know. Smyth then mentioned the formal "requirements" letter.[2] Told him that he had decided that since in the past this has always been an occasion for the whole Commission to call on the President and since in this particular case there is this slight difference that the Secretary of Defense has not signed, he had decided to let this ride until next week when the Commission could go up as a group. Strauss agreed with this. Smyth then mentioned the power policy statement as formally adopted by the NSC—was really quite turned around from the way AEC had put it. In terms of the action yesterday, it is really quite inconsistent with that action, but Smyth said he thought he would let that ride and maybe in a few days we could some way very informally—or maybe it would have to be formal—get their statement of the power policy revised so that it is more consistent with AEC's and the action now envisaged. Smyth then said the last thing he had on his mind is in connection with the course of actions to be taken—there will not be any actual cancellations;

only revisions of scope. Smyth said Murray is completely unwilling to do anything until he has had time to study it etc. etc. Strauss asked how long that would take and Smyth said he hoped it would not be more than a day or two. Smyth said he had Dean's proxy and Zuckert would be back tonight. Strauss asked if Murray always acted like this; and Smyth said he wouldn't say "*all* the time," but he isn't the easiest fellow to deal with. Strauss said he appreciated that. Strauss then asked how the hearing went and Smyth said apparently quite well—in an unusual fashion.[3] We had thought that we were to send a Commissioner and a staff member up simply as observers and that Admiral Fechteler[4] was to testify. But about the first 1½ hours was devoted to testimony from Murray (who went up as the Commissioner) on the improbability of private companies coming in with their private money. Strauss thinks Murray might be quite wrong about this. Smyth said then Fechteler came along and didn't know much about the program and didn't put up any kind of fight for the CVR program. Strauss said that must have puzzled the Committee because Floberg[5] last Friday made quite a case for it. Smyth told him we had a hearing yesterday morning on the cancellation legislation; Boyer and some of the staff went up yesterday morning and met with Phillips[6] and everything apparently went off well. Strauss then asked about tomorrow's test, what did it involve, etc. Smyth told him it was primarily an "effects" test—DOD and Civil Defense; no troops that he knew of. Strauss said he would be in Washington tomorrow afternoon, Monday afternoon and back again on Wednesday.

1. Kyes observed the eighth shot of the 1953 test series at Nevada.

2. The "requirements" letter was a presidential directive specifying the annual amounts of uranium 235 and plutonium the commission would produce.

3. On May 6 the Joint Committee held a hearing on the cancellation of the carrier reactor project.

4. Admiral William M. Fechteler, the chief of Naval Operations.

5. John F. Floberg, the assistant secretary of the Navy for Air.

6. Representative John Phillips of California.

## ≡ *May 15, 1953*

Lewis Strauss called GD to talk about the amount of the cut in the budget and what GD expected to do about [it]. Dean told him he had a meeting with the Budget people this afternoon and that he had several points he wanted to bring up. Strauss asked that GD have McCarthy[1] get in touch with him and alert him to the points GD expected to use. GD said he would try and get them to him today. . . .

1. Francis J. McCarthy, the commission's assistant controller for budgets.

## ≡ May 16, 1953

Dean called Gen. Bradley to congratulate him on his excellent speech of yesterday (Friday)[1] and to also ask a favor. GD stated he understood the Joint Chiefs were considering the military requirements which were set forth a year or so ago and which tie into the expansion program. One issue constantly coming up is this—should Commission consider existing or planned plant facilities[?] Commission feeling is to get all the plutonium they can. As to military requirements, is it based on x number by x date—run ¾ time or shut one down to come out even. Bradley stated we based it on amount of material you would have available and broke it up in various groups. We want high number as soon as possible. If something starts [war, we] may not have it [sufficient weapons]. GD stated when Chiefs get through with evaluation and send it to the Sec. of Defense we expect AEC to get fullest benefit for existing or planned plants. I had to fight for improvement to Hanford piles—this would increase our capacity far beyond dollars. I think some expression from the Joint Chiefs [is necessary]. Bradley stated alright we can put that on. We hope to get it out this week. The Secretary has to have a briefing on this. Dean stated he was afraid the Secretary would not make improvements or make new developments and that this would be a terrible mistake. Bradley said alright, we will sure do that.

1. Speaking to the Women's National Press Club, Bradley warned that the administration should not put economy ahead of security in making budget cuts.

## ≡ May 21, 1953

Dean called Cong. Stringfellow of Utah[1] and stated I am calling because I know of your plan to go to Nevada and I know you are concerned about St. George. I understand and I have a suggestion. Stringfellow stated I will be receptive. GD said I know you are going out with this group and I think it would be to your advantage to have information on the question of radiation damage and if you have the time I would be happy to send a couple of our people—Stringfellow remarked I would be most receptive and I appreciated the books you sent over. I have received a good many calls and I would like to talk to your people. This article that came out in the local press, in the Wash. Post, the guy asked for discontinuation of the blasts. Dean stated I did not see it but I think this will be helpful to you. Stringfellow stated he wanted to calm down the St. George people. Dean stated he thought we had an obligation to explain this and we have spent a good deal of time on it. What time would you prefer, morning or afternoon? Stringfellow said in the morning anytime after 9:00. GD suggested 10:00

and that was agreed upon. Stringfellow stated I appreciate this a great deal.

1. Representative Douglas R. Stringfellow of Utah. The papers reported that Stringfellow had asked the commission to end the 1953 tests quickly because of the fear and anxiety among his constituents around the test site.

## ☰ *May 22, 1953*

GD ill today.

Dr. Smyth talked to GD re: desirability of the formality of getting letter to Pres.[1] and getting it approved. Stated Zuckert very unhappy over it in terms of public relations (re: 11th shot). Dean stated yield is so important we will have to [go] ahead, we just have to take a chance. Obviously will have to be careful on the weather. The alternative would be go to Eniwetok and Smyth stated yes/ Smyth asked, on formality, if it is desirable to get to the President on Saturday what would be the state of your health? Dean stated unless you need me I really do not feel like going. Smyth stated he thought Monday would be alright. Dean stated for planning purposes tell Los Alamos "go ahead."

1. The letter requested presidential approval to add another shot to the spring test series.

## ☰ *May 25, 1953*

Fields called GD from Mercury[1]—message about shot. Everything went off very well. From looks the fallout problem very minor. GD stated fine— news account said there was a lot of dust. Fields stated not much to do with fallout. Particles were much smaller than in other areas, only the finest stuff collected. GD asked if it went near St. George and Fields stated did not go near there. Dean asked if the Utah Congressman flew out with him. Fields said yes and that Stringfellow was going on to Ogden tomorrow. He got what he wanted and I think he will be very helpful to us. The yield looks a little better than what we had predicted. GD said the ticker says 15. Fields stated it is something on that order. Everything is going well. Session with Tyler and Graves[2] went off extremely well. Questions I believe were answered in good shape. I understand the Pres. is the one at the White House. LeBaron has not gotten DOD answer. He rode out with Wilson but did not get answer. Wilson wanted to see this one today and I heard he said it was very effective. Dean said I think the only way to play it is to say may have additional shot later. Fields stated after looking things over here I think we should go ahead with this. He did say something on what it would cost if [we] go to Eniwetok and I hope that does not get into the discussions. Dean stated more essential to make a strong case here. Fields said there is no reason not to do it out here, it would be useful to get information here. Dean stated we may not be able to tell you before your news conference. I would say this concludes our present series. We may have another this spring. Fields stated we might we say we might be in a position to go ahead Saturday or Sunday. To which GD replied with newspapermen you could get into trouble with that. Fields said we could say we are considering another which may be added immediately. Dean stated I would not say that. If you say "almost immediately" you are in trouble. Fields stated would like no official observer, [would like to] do it with almost no schedule—do it on that basis. Dean stated if we get any information we will tell you. Fields stated I will be coming back this afternoon. I think the Congressmen are well taken care of. Dean asked if they were coming back soon and Fields stated this afternoon

    1. Mercury was the Nevada test site.
    2. Alvin C. Graves, the leader of the Los Alamos J division and deputy test director for the *Upshot-Knothole* weapons test series. He reported directly to test manager Carroll L. Tyler.

Strauss telephoned the following message for GD at 4:20 p.m.
    "Assuming that it will not take as long as I was told to set the test up for the picnic grounds[1] and that the maximum delay would be of the order say of a month and a half, would it not be better to accept that rather than run the risk of a situation which might make all future continental tests impossible?"

    1. Picnic grounds was the Pacific proving grounds.

≡ *May 26, 1953*

Strauss called GD and stated did you get message I dictated, to which GD replied yes. Strauss stated I just had the feeling that possibly the ultimate result from this may make—GD stated I think on evaluation you will find this less risky than ones we have shot before because of the energy release. Some of the others have sucked up from the ground—I have talked to Fields on possible delay and will put it into a memo. Strauss stated no that makes it too formal. Dean stated two months would be too late. One reason is radio chemical and also on certain types of aircraft which cannot be flown there. Strauss commented I see what you mean. Dean said they are specially rigged up. Another is the Edgerton, Germeshausen & Grier, Inc. who do our technical work. Strauss asked how far up in the air will you do this? Dean stated it will be over 1000 ft. Strauss asked higher than any you have done? Dean stated it is higher than some. We have shot one considerably higher. Strauss asked you would not want to do this one that way and Dean replied it is a question of where they can get their readings. Strauss said I will get it to him (Pres.) and get an answer if I can. Strauss asked then re: meeting with Joint Committee this afternoon on power. Dean stated there is some difference between us in our estimate as to what will be the effect on permitting industry to come in. NSC thinks industry will [come] in and put up money for prototypes—we think differently. Strauss said the thing for him to do is to ask men for industry to come in. Dean stated this is an executive meeting. Strauss then asked what were you planning to put in the memo? Would you say it would cost a great deal more? Dean replied oh it will double the price if you give it that priority. It would be 50 thousand against 750,000 thousand. Strauss remarked that much. You might write the memo but I will not wait for it (had to go to NY because of death in family). Knowing that it will be coming I will go ahead and try to get an answer before I leave.

## ≡ May 27, 1953

Presidential approval for 11th shot given today.

## ≡ June 4, 1953

The 11th shot at Nevada went off this morning. Report very good.

## ≡ June 8, 1953

Cong. Yates of Illinois[1] called GD and asked if he could get information in your shop (perhaps should be brought out in the record) it seems to me the decision of NSC did not make sense on power plant (CVR) your appropriation is only for civilian use. GD stated build land based prototype then could be put in an airplane. We have to have a line item which should say "design and construction." Yates said when you say "design and construction"—GD stated just construction and Yates asked but not earmarked CVR. GD remarked any way you want. CVR is you say design and development of pressurized light water reactor. Yates asked that is what you requested? GD stated will cover power plant acceptable for civilian use. Yates stated my question is do you, in your shop, have somebody that can give me the language to earmark for land based prototype and arguments for its continuance? GD said sure, would you like someone to come up? I can have someone come up in the morning. Yates said that would be fine. Room 1740—New House Office Building.

1. Representative Sidney R. Yates of Illinois.

GD called Mr. Boyer and stated Yates called independently of Phillips. To which Boyer replied he called McLane[1] first. GD stated he is interested in continuing CVR as it was. Does not think NSC decision makes sense. He wants language for design and construction. I told him I would have someone come up who could accomplish such an objective. Who should go? Boyer stated McCarthy should go. He can give the language. McLane and Rickover are here now. GD said tell him my problem. Boyer said we could tell him what it was originally and GD stated this is not only as it was but language the Committee believes that the CVR should be built. He is in room 1740.

1. I have not been able to trace McLane.

≡ *June 9, 1953*

Cong. Phillips of California called GD and said he wanted to straighten Cole out and that he was under the impression, and have checked back to your statement on p. 375. I was under impression [it was the] civilian power plant but I think I had in mind Hafstad. GD stated it was Hafstad. Phillips stated I have Boyer's letter of May 29th in which he recites major amounts for civilian and industrial use of atomic power at 4.2 billion. GD stated 4.2 billion is operating cost of laboratory at Bettis Field. Most of work is development work; it is neither design nor construction. Phillips asked what about 800,000 for portion of general research and development attributable [to] pressurized reactor. GD stated I cannot identify that. Phillips stated 3,150 million for funds for design of atomic power reactor, not construction. GD stated that is for design of SGR (sodium graphite reactor) and should not be related to light water one. Phillips stated we have in this Bill maximum 5 million, 4.2 million plus 800,000. GD stated that is all development. Phillips stated Cole wants 12 million on 70 million and GD stated we do not need that much. 7 million would adequately do it. Phillips said Cole wants flat top, power for flat top. 10 million plus 70 million would produce power plant applicable to flat top. Would produce necessary experience and design, do you agree? GD stated I do not quite. The original program called for Navy reactor which had gadgetry you would not put on unless you went to sea. That would have cost about 150 million. NSC said no military requirement for such a thing and so we had to re-scope our plans. If Coles' bill original reactor the assumption is that of a Navy need and they have said that they do not have it. Phillips said Cole may have been needled by the Navy. Why doesn't in 4.2 [billion] some of it apply against the 12 [million] or 7 [million].[1] GD stated it is purely re-search and development. Phillips said not 7 for construction? GD stated 7 is design and construction; 4.2 is development. Phillips said with money you have and possible changes evidenced by things coming out in the paper why not get money transferred to that construction work—money appro-priated in the bill—money already appropriated, wouldn't that be satis-factory? GD stated it is satisfactory in getting Congressional blessing but not money. This 7 figure would be quite adequate, could not complain about that; say 5 and could do it. I explained to Cole that 12 was in orig-inal Truman budget. We did not need as much as 12 and I think he under-stands that. Phillips said alright I will talk to Cole.

1. Here Dean is probably explaining portions of the commission's budget request to Phillips.

## ≡ June 11, 1953

Strauss called GD. . . . Strauss asked you were expecting a visit from Dr. Urey,[1] did you get anything from him? GD said Urey came in here biting his fingernails about the Rosenberg case. He's very much upset over their case. I told him that the AEC had to declassify the material in order that they could be tried and that I personally am very anxious to get them to talk. That is the AEC's only interest. . . .

1. Dr. Harold C. Urey, a Nobel Prize-winning chemist who had led research teams studying the gaseous diffusion process during the war.

## ≡ June 12, 1953

Walt Williams called GD and said Corb Allardice[1] has called me and Cole wants to get a letter out to AEC about the weather conditions. They have been getting so much pressure that Cole feels this is necessary. He will state in the letter that he has been assured by AEC that there is no connec-tion between "tests" and weather. Reassurance of people who still have

some doubt in their minds and would like to be reassured again that everything has been done to determine this fact. It seems as though Langer[2] is
about to introduce a resolution. GD remarked the letter will be unclassified. Williams stated he wants to put it out to the press and Dean asked
why don't they wait for our reply? Williams said I think Cole feels that the
pressure is so bad he wants to get it right out. GD said we could have our
reply in four or five hours. We could get Marion Tate to write the reply this
afternoon. Williams said he would suggest that to him. GD said have your
secretary take the letter over the phone and let us see it.

1. Corbin Allardice had succeeded William Borden as executive director of the Joint
Committee staff. Representative W. Sterling Cole of New York was now chairman of the
Joint Committee.
2. Senator William Langer of North Dakota.


≡ *June 15, 1953*

GD called Congressman Phillips of California and thanked him for the
decent treatment he gave them on the budget. Phillips said we are still having trouble with Yates—he wants to mandate you to make a flat top power
plant. GD stated it is really hard to do when there is no military need. Phillips said Yorty[1] became the big man because he got a letter from Wilson
and he now wants to be the savior of the Navy. Yorty is promoting Rickover. We are not going to pay too much attention to it. He talked to the full
Committee for half an hour on Friday and was voted down. What are you
going to do now? Is it true that Strauss—has it been announced? GD said
oh no. Phillips said I am sorry to see you go. When a man retires it is when
he is of value to the organization. Are you up to Cosmos Club. GD stated
yes. Phillips stated I think it is the nicest club I belong to.

1. Representative Samuel W. Yorty of California.


≡ *June 16, 1953*

GD called Congressman W. Sterling Cole and thanked him for his assistance on the budget.


≡ *June 23, 1953*

Spivak[1] called GD about "Meet The Press"—Sunday, June 28th. Spivak
said it has been set and asked who told you. GD said Martha (Roundtree)

did. Said my name came up as possibility and that she was not enthusiastic
as I would not say anything. That Urey would talk about the Rosenbergs,
etc. I said I think you are quite right. Spivak said would like to explore avenues [on] which you can speak freely. Would like biographical material
and few of addresses sent to my New York office. GD said some you have
to be cosey on and others have to say cannot answer. Spivak mentioned remark like 200 bombs is almost as good as thousands. Do not know how
far have gone in peacetime. Dean said usually program, so far as news, has
interest. Usually news story breaks out somehow, maybe in answer to just
one question. Spivak began to list possible topics: Oppy, Russian potentials, American potentials, peacetime use, making weather, security, atomic
reactor submarine, airplane. GD agreed anything in those fields. One current thing is budget. I just appeared before the Senate. Spivak asked how
much are you asking for? GD said slightly over one billion for next fiscal
year beginning July. GD said I think they will give it to us—do not have a
budget problem. We are going to get along alright. I think question of
budget would be in order. Spivak asked how long have you been a member:
GD said on Commission over four years; Commissioner in May of 1949,
Chairman in July 1950. My term expires on June 30th. Spivak asked are
you a Republican-Democrat? GD stated have not been active but nomi-
nally a Democrat. Spivak then asked about new chairman. GD said not announced yet but probably will be before Sunday broadcast. Spivak then
asked do you know what you are going to do and GD said take a vacation.
Spivak then asked do the secrets weigh you down, are you afraid you will
talk in your sleep? GD said oh no. Spivak then asked story on Russian ex-
ploding three bombs. Do you have any assurance they have not exploded
any more. GD said it was virtually certain. Spivak then asked can you tell
size. GD said we can tell reasonably certain—pretty good—we underes-
timate them. I would like to go into that a little bit. I think the next two or
three years are crucial. Question is how to break stalemate of the two
growing stockpiles? I have done some thinking on it. Spivak asked do you
know how? GD said think must find the answer. Spivak asked him to do
some thinking on it in the next few days; unless find answer may blow ourselves out. GD said when you have been in the business of making them you
cannot make them very long without facing up to this. There is one controversial thing, these public hearings on power, two or three people are
charging us [with] giving away things gotten with the taxpayer's money.[2] I
would like to answer it. I am first witness on. We recommend changing the
law to permit it. That could provoke a few questions alright. Spivak then
asked that material be sent to him at his New York address, 570 Lexington
Avenue, New York 22, New York. He then asked about newspapermen.

GD named Al Friendly, Joe Myler of UP, Ernest Lindley, Marquis Childs, Ned Brooks.

1. Jerome Spivak, moderator of "Meet the Press."
2. Representative Chet Holifield had recently charged that the commission's proposed private power policy made too many favorable concessions to industry.

≡ *June 24, 1953*

The New York Times came out today with story about Lewis L. Strauss being appointed by the President to succeed Gordon Dean as Chairman of the Atomic Energy Commission. Announcement had not come out of the White House at that time. Appointment was sent to Senate today.

Dean called Strauss and said I suppose you have seen the New York Times. Strauss said oh, yes. GD said when this thing is made, I wanted to be able to say something officially. I can't do it on a speculation. We are getting calls from Washington newspapers. Suppose I say this: "I have no knowledge of this at all and there has apparently been no announcement by the White House." Strauss that's right. I don't like the story at all, particularly the part about the Pike business.[1] GD said I thought it was a pretty good story except for that. As soon as you know anything officially when the name is sent over, I wish you would call me. Strauss said he would.

1. The *Times* story alleged that in July 1950 Strauss was involved in a dispute with Commissioner Sumner Pike about a 1948 disagreement over whether to discuss the metallurgy of plutonium with the British.

≡ *June 25, 1953*

GD had lunch with Jim Bennett at the Colony Restaurant at 12:30.

At 4:00 this afternoon GD held his final Press Conference in Room 236.

≡ *June 26, 1953*

Senator Anderson called GD re: making a fifteen minute recording for radio station program. GD went to room 9-B at 2:00 this afternoon to make recording.

A group from Detroit-Edison came in this afternoon at 3:00 with Mr. Pickard to talk to GD a few minutes re: their testifying before Joint Committee on industrial power.

Zuckert farewell party this evening at their home for GD.

## ≡ *June 28, 1953*

GD on "Meet The Press" this afternoon at 6:00.

## ≡ *June 29, 1953*

GD had lunch at 1:00 at the Belgian Embassy with Ambassador Silvercruys.

Cong. Condon came in to see GD this afternoon at 3:30.

GD had final clearance from LaPlante in preparation for his leaving tomorrow.

GD dinner in honor of Strauss at The Sheraton Park Hotel this evening.

Finis

# EPILOGUE

Gordon Dean drafted the following paper but did not add it to the diary. Because it is such a fitting conclusion to the diary excerpts, I have chosen to reproduce it here.

|  | G. Dean |
|---|---|
| What's Ahead? | 6/10/52 |

The big question posed by the expansion program studies was: "How much is enough and when do we need it?" In answering this question the Commission had to look to the Armed Services for guidance. It is the responsibility of the Department of Defense to defend the United States against aggression and to be in a position in the event of war to win the war.

In the National Security Council meeting which discussed the expansion program General Vandenberg stated that in the event of an all-out war the minimum number of bombs necessary for the security of the United States was ⟨have⟩ .[1] This was the first time the Joint Chiefs of Staff or the Department of Defense had ever expressed needs of this magnitude. General Vandenberg and Secretary Lovett both stated that this was a *minimum* requirement for the security of the United States in the event of an all-out conflagration. It became apparent that ⟨even⟩ without completion of Paducah and Savannah River and other items in the current expansion programs, such a number could not be manufactured until 1964, even making reasonable allowances for higher power levels at Savannah River and Hanford, some increase in the efficiency of the gaseous diffusion operations, and the introduction of substantial improvements through weapons research. It also became apparent that this number

1. The blanks appear in the original. Dean noted the figures he had and those he needed in pencil as well as making penciled changes to the original. Two of Dean's penciled notes are classified and have been deleted. Dean discussed these thoughts with his fellow commissioners.

*could* be reached *with* the 50/150 expansion by 1960, thus assuring the requirement four years earlier than would be possible without such an expansion.

This new expansion assumed that ~~some of~~ ⟨the first⟩ cells in the new gaseous diffusion plants would be in operation on ⟨ April 1954, and in C-31 in May, 1952,⟩ and that the first plutonium would be coming from the first Savannah River pile on _____, ⟨and from Jumbo on 10/1/54–11/1/55.⟩ It also assumed that the highest priorities would be given to the Commission for the completion of these jobs.

⟨C-31⟩

⟨Need⟩

⟨inc⟩

⟨Portsmouth⟩

Congressman Jackson's speech of June 5, 1952, in which he labeled the new expansion "a half-way program" and urged the expenditure of twice this amount of money in new facilities, or approximately seven billion dollars additional in plant and equipment, raises the question of whether the new expansion program provides enough. In arriving at the answer to this question a few facts stand out:

1. ~~It means that w~~When a steady state of production is reached under this new program, and such steady state ~~is~~ will be arrived at in 1958, the United States ~~is~~ ⟨will be⟩ producing annually more weapons than it has produced in all of the years from 1947 to 1952.

2. ~~It means that t~~⟨The⟩ ~~amount~~ ⟨number of weapons⟩ which the military says is the minimum necessary for the security of the United States in a total war will be reached in 1960.

3. ~~It means that t~~Twice the ~~amount~~ ⟨number the military considers to be⟩ necessary for an all-out war will be reached by 1964 or 1965.

4. ~~It means that t~~The amount of ore required annually to feed virgin material to the piles and gaseous diffusion plants will be 9,150 tons, or approximately four times the total ore available to the United States in 1950.

This raises the question of what should be the course that the U.S. atomic energy program should follow when it has produced the number which the military state to be necessary for a total conflagration? Or to measure it another way, and to ~~play~~ ⟨stay⟩ on the liberal side, what should be the course of the U.S. atomic energy program when it has reached twice the amount which the military state to be necessary for the defense of the United States? Is there any point in producing bombs beyond this point? I think not. By this time the numbers of bombs produced by the United States are such that the deterrent effect

upon an aggressor has been established. No aggressor, regardless of the number of bombs he may have in his stockpile, is
going to provoke a war which will bring upon him in retaliation
⟨have⟩  bombs.

    And would more weapons than this number be of any use to
the United States in waging war in the event it came about?
I think not. The fire power represented in such a stockpile is
_____ times the energy released by all high explosive bombs       ⟨Need⟩
in World War II. If the stockpile were divided evenly among the
three Services it would mean ⟨have⟩ for the Navy, ⟨have⟩ for
the Army and ⟨have⟩ for the Air Force.

    If the U.S. Navy at this point had * * * * carriers and this
were the primary method of Navy delivery (that is, by carrier-
based planes) it would mean that the Navy would have available
for each carrier ⟨have⟩ bombs.

    To make an arbitrary illustration, the Army, having ⟨have⟩
bombs available to them, could assign ⟨have⟩ to the warheads
for rockets and ⟨have⟩ for Army controlled guided missiles and
⟨have⟩ for artillery fired pieces. This would mean that the
Army alone would have available to it for use against opposing
troops in the field one A-bomb for every _____ men (this is       ⟨Need⟩
on the assumption that the Russian army has a composition of
_____ troops.)

    The Air Force would have available to it ⟨have⟩ bombs. If it
assigned one-third of this number to large industrial popula-
tions, it would mean that of the _____ ~~bombs~~ cities of Russia     ⟨Need⟩
with a population of over so-much, it would have available to
drop on each of such industrial complexes ⟨have⟩ bombs. This
would still leave ⟨have⟩ bombs to be distributed among such       ⟨Need
targets as major air fields, bridges, munitions centers, rail yards,   how many
refineries, etc.                                                      to wipe

    When this point has been reached, regardless of all the claims   out city?⟩
that can be made for an infinite number of "targets of opportunity," it simply means by any method of reasoning that we
have more than enough. If this be true, some rather significant
conclusions must be drawn.

    It means to me that even leaving the stockpile intact and using
none of the fissionable material for industrial uses, the amount
of ⟨new⟩ U-235 ⟨production⟩ which would be necessary for a
power program would be relatively small, far less annually than
the present output of K-25-27-29-31 complex at Oak Ridge.

    If this be true it means that the country should close down the
entire operation at Paducah, close down the entire operation at

the new projected site set up in the expansion program and perhaps only use a fraction of the cells at the Oak Ridge plant—all this in 1965.

In the reactor program, since it is unlikely that one would go through the step of manufacturing plutonium as a fuel element for power reactors (and plutonium has no other possible use) the Commission should close down all of its plutonium-producing facilities. * * * * This means the shut-down of all existing piles at Hanford, the shut-down of any new piles projected for Hanford, and it means the shut-down of all of the Savannah River piles which are now being constructed. It means, in short, at most, a period of ten years operation for virtually all of the gaseous diffusion facilities and all of the production piles now operating or projected in the expansion program.

What does this mean in terms of our feed materials operation—the facilities at Mallencrodt, Harshaw, Fernald, the UF-6 plants and any other feed materials processing plants which may be necessary in the expanded program? Here, for the first time, there will seem to be some reason for continued operation, but again on a much reduced scale, for it will be in these facilities that the uranium will be concentrated, refined, and brought to the metal stage for the manufacture of fuel elements for power reactors. One can only guess what the demand for fuel elements will be in 1965, that is, how many power reactors will be in operation in this country. It seems hardly likely, even making allowances for very efficient power reactors, that more than a fraction of the feed materials processing plants would be used for supplying the fuel elements for these power reactors.

What does this mean in the complex of facilities, including those presently built or those planned in the expansion program, which are or will be devoted to the manufacture of weapons components? It would seem that virtually all of this complex would be closed down, except sufficient HE facilities as would be necessary for the manufacture of fresh HE to replace the HE in the stockpile, and except such facilities as would be necessary a̶s̶ ⟨for⟩ replacement of other non-nuclear parts of the weapon, such as electronics gear. Certainly for a replacement program it would seem that less than 50% of this complex of facilities would be in operation.

What does this mean in terms of our ore procurement program? It means to me that we should be extremely wary about large expenditures of money in the procurement of ores over and beyond the amounts of ore necessary to feed existing and proposed facilities; that is, in our stockpiling program—stockpiling beyond the requirements—we should acquire ores only where they are comparatively cheap. It means also to me that we would be extremely careless with public funds were we to make contracts which would commit us to the purchase of ores for any period beyond 1964.

What does this mean to the National Laboratories now supported by the Commission with public funds? What does it mean to Los Alamos, specifically the scientific and technical staff of which this year reaches 3,050 persons? Is it not almost inevitable that the weapons research laboratory would shrink considerably at such a date? Admittedly, it is very difficult to predict how much. Perhaps by this time it has turned its efforts to entirely new types of weapons of warfare, but certainly in the very uncertainties of the situation it would seem that in our planning for the community and particularly in determining whether buildings should be permanent or semi-permanent, we might at this time, when our economy is somewhat shaky, well explore the assumptions upon which permanent construction is undertaken.

What of Argonne? What of Oak Ridge? What of Brookhaven? Perhaps the answer here is easier in view of the fact that the emphasis in these laboratories is more on basic research and on the peacetime applications. Presumably these will have to receive governmental support if they are to operate. The annual operating budgets of these laboratories has reached the figure where they could not be supported by private funds. The annual operating costs of Argonne this year ⟨in FY 1952 was⟩ is _____; and Oak Ridge is _____; and Brookhaven is _____. ⟨Need⟩ But it is worth thinking about. Suppose we were in a position where we could state flatly today to the directors of these laboratories that the United States will have achieved by 1964 such a stockpile of weapons that it is going out of atomic weapons business. What changes would the directors of these laboratories make in their plans for the years ahead? How differently would they organize the laboratory?

I have not talked to date of the effects which one might well predict for such years as 1957, 1960 and 1965 on⟨f⟩ a thermonuclear program, but I think we might assume for 1952 that by 1958 there will be in our stockpile _____ thermonuclear ⟨Need⟩ weapons, which would draw upon the fissionable material in

our stockpile only to the extent of an equivalent of _____
A-bombs, and that we could have by 1960 in our stockpile
_____ thermonuclear weapons, drawing on our stockpile
of fissionable material only to the extent of an equivalent of
⟨Need⟩    _____ A-bombs, and by 1964 we could have in our stockpile
⟨Need⟩    _____ thermonuclear weapons, which would draw on our stock-
pile of fissionable material only to the extent of an equivalent of
⟨Need⟩    _____ A-bombs.

If the assumption for 1964 is a reasonable one, this would
mean that ~~instead of~~ ⟨in addition to⟩ having the energy release
from _____ fission bombs in 1965 of _____ KTs, we would
⟨also⟩ have ~~in addition~~ the energy release of _____ thermonuclear weapons, an energy release of _____ KTs, or virtually a
⟨Need⟩    ____% increase in the total energy release in our stockpile of fission and fusion weapons.

If this be straight thinking, where does it leave us with a proposal such as that introduced by Congressman Jackson, namely,
that instead of expanding by 50/150% we double the amount
and expand by 100/300%. It would mean:

1. that none of the facilities, which is true of the present expansion program, could begin production until 1955.

2. that the steady state of these facilities could not be reached,
as in the present expansion program, until 1958.

3. that in order to feed these facilities with virgin feed we
would have to find annually _____ tons of $U_3O_8$.

4. that the minimum stockpile required by the Department of
Defense would be reached, if in fact it could be done in terms of
critical materials, war, etc., only two years in advance of the
present program.

5. that the facilities thus built, like the facilities which are
now built and which will be built under the expansion program,
will be shut down and simply serve as monuments to the hys-
teria of man in 1952.

G. Dean

Gordon Dean wrote this paper after Congressman Henry Jackson of the
Joint Committee delivered a speech urging that the commission double the
second Korean War expansion program. As Dean's thoughts demonstrate,
there was little justification for a third multibillion-dollar expansion program and nothing ever came of the Jackson proposal. Dean did not place
the paper in his diary but it addresses an issue of more than passing interest

to Dean: What would happen to the commission's production plants and laboratories once the commission built a stockpile which would satisfy the "*minimum* requirement for the security of the United States in the event of an all-out conflagration?"[1] Setting aside the continuing need to make technological improvements to nuclear weapons, as Dean apparently did, the future of the commission's production plant complex, and perhaps its weapons laboratories, was a matter of time and simple arithmetic. By the mid 1960s sufficient weapons would exist to satisfy all the military requirements of 1952.

Of course, Dean could not anticipate all the factors, such as international agreements or technological breakthroughs, which might affect production requirements. For example, the Korean War, which had stimulated production increases, ended when the Eisenhower administration signed an armistice with the Communists on July 27, 1953. The *Castle* weapons test series in the spring of 1954 dramatically concluded the quest for a deliverable hydrogen bomb. But, as Dean had foreseen, the new production plants gradually came into operation and, as production efficiencies increased, the United States was indeed producing "annually more weapons than it ha[d] produced in all of the years from 1947 to 1952." In fact, by 1955, the commission was the single largest consumer of electric power in the United States.[2]

The second weapons laboratory at Livermore, California, that Dean had futilely opposed eventually became a full-scale facility. In what Livermore's former director Herbert F. York called "a great leap forward in nuclear weapons design and deployment," Los Alamos and Livermore created nuclear weapons from multimegaton thermonuclear weapons of large size to bombs weighing less than one hundred pounds and artillery shells of only a few inches in diameter. Indeed, in the early 1960s, Secretary of Defense Robert McNamara reported that there were seven thousand nuclear weapons deployed in Europe alone. By the early 1970s the stockpile consisted of "some tens of thousands" of weapons.[3] Dean laid the foundation for this arsenal.

As Dean anticipated, the commission eventually produced enough weapons to meet the country's defense needs. Acknowledging the sufficiency of the U.S. nuclear arsenal, President Lyndon B. Johnson announced in January 1964 a 25 percent reduction of uranium 235 production and the shutdown of four production reactors. Throughout the rest of the decade the commission gradually closed down all the Hanford production reactors and two Savannah River reactors. Output from the gaseous diffusion plants was reduced to a fraction of its former rate. As the production plants closed, the weapons stockpile declined in numbers, although perhaps not in destructive power.[4] The weapons laboratories, meanwhile, remained vital by creating new weapons designs and by expanding research programs into nonweapons fields.

President Johnson's announcement signaled the end of the unrestricted arms race initiated when President Truman decided to develop the hydrogen bomb. With the limited test ban treaty of 1963 and other arms control agreements of the 1960s and 1970s, the United States and the Soviet Union slowed nuclear arms development. The commission, its scientists, and its engineers, spurred by urgent defense requirements and a perception of aggressive Soviet behavior, had performed the brilliant technological feat of transforming nuclear weapons from a laboratory experiment into the backbone of the nation's defenses. With military stockpile requirements satisfied and a less hostile international environment, America had less need for an independent agency to manage the atom. A casualty of its own success, the energy crisis of the 1970s, and other factors, the Atomic Energy Commission was abolished and its activities split between the Nuclear Regulatory Commission and eventually the Department of Energy.

In the long run it was easier for Dean to anticipate the commission's future than his own. He left the commission for New York and the investment firm of Lehman Brothers, where Lewis Strauss helped him obtain a position. Gradually he established a solid position in the business community, being named to boards of directors of the Norden-Ketay Corporation, the Callahan Zinc-Lead Company, and the Fruehauf Trailer Corporation. Dean organized the Nuclear Science and Engineering Corporation and merged it with the General Dynamics Corporation in 1955, taking the post of senior vice-president.[5]

Business executive Gordon Dean joined the emerging American nuclear power industry. He was named to the board of directors of the Atomic Industrial Forum, an association of business leaders organized by former commissioner T. Keith Glennan to facilitate nuclear power development. He had organized the Nuclear Science and Engineering Corporation to furnish technical advice to companies developing nuclear power plants. He sometimes criticized the Eisenhower administration for its seemingly slow pace of atomic power development and participated in a comprehensive study of the civilian nuclear power industry sponsored by the Joint Committee on Atomic Energy. Despite his hope to speed nuclear power development, Dean was sensitive to safety issues and urged that more effort be devoted to safety education before the United States generated significant amounts of electric power with nuclear power plants.[6]

Dean published his only book a few months after he left the commission. Entitled *Report on the Atom*, it was not an account of his experiences on the commission but rather an effort to give the lay reader a basic understanding of atomic energy programs. Dean's *Report* described, in very general terms, ore mining and refinement, the production of plutonium, uranium 235, and atomic weapons, spies and security, and the peaceful atom. Although not an autobiography, it was drawn from Dean's experiences on the commission and perhaps on his diary.

Dean's career in the business and publishing world was accompanied by changes in his personal life. In September 1953 he divorced Adelaide Williamson, his wife of twenty-three years and in December married Mary Benton Gore, a niece of Senator Albert Gore of Tennessee. Dean became the proud father of a son and a daughter in his second marriage.[7]

As a former chairman of the Atomic Energy Commission Dean was never far from matters of nuclear policy. Although his diary captures his concern about J. Robert Oppenheimer's lack of enthusiasm about the hydrogen bomb, Dean testified for Oppenheimer at his security hearing in the spring of 1954. The commission later removed Oppenheimer's clearance, but Dean had no doubts about his loyalty, character, or devotion to the United States. Later Dean was named to a panel chaired by General Albert C. Wedemeyer to examine the role of atomic energy in continental defense. Meanwhile, he chaired a Council on Foreign Relations panel that explored American foreign policy in the nuclear age. Out of this effort came Henry Kissinger's *Nuclear Weapons and Foreign Policy* with a foreword by Gordon Dean. He was mentioned as a potential candidate for the post of director general when the International Atomic Energy Agency was formed in 1957. He dabbled briefly in the activities of the National Committee for a Sane Nuclear Policy and served on a panel that advised the Joint Committee about commission production programs.[8]

But Dean was never to hold another official atomic post. On the evening of August 15, 1958, he boarded Northeast Airlines flight 258 out of LaGuardia Airport bound for Nantucket. Fog delayed his departure for two hours. Fog later claimed his life when the Northeast flight crashed a mile short of the mist-shrouded Nantucket runway, killing twenty-two of its thirty-three passengers. Gordon Dean was just fifty-two. The Atomic Energy Commission, President Eisenhower, Lewis Strauss, and Senator Albert Gore joined others in paying tribute to Dean. The commission, lamenting the passing of one of its most successful leaders, briefly considered naming an award after Dean. Funeral services were held in Washington and Dean was buried in the capital's Fort Lincoln cemetery.[9] Both the commission and the nation had suffered a grievous loss.

And what will be said of Dean's place in the history of the commission? He was an able, astute, pragmatic, flexible leader. A staunch anti-Communist, he was at home in a Truman administration locked in rigid confrontation with the Soviet Union. Dean brought a businesslike approach to his job as well as the political skills required to lead a federal agency successfully. Although closest to Senator Brien McMahon, he served President Truman loyally and built a relationship based upon mutual respect with the president.

Dean devoted most of his time and energy to the military atom. At the subcabinet level he played a key role in the beginning of the nuclear arms race. His diary never once indicates that he doubted the righteousness of his task. Although his defeat in the second laboratory debate revealed the depth of political support for increasing nuclear armaments in the early 1950s, the absence of concern about the implications of a nuclear arms race in Dean's diary is striking.

Dean's skills at management were his most important contribution to the atomic energy program. He made the commissioners themselves directly responsible for program management, and his successors all followed that practice. More than any other chairman Dean made teamwork among the five commissioners a method of policy formulation. He began the practice of informing the Joint Committee in advance of commission actions, and few chairmen have maintained as good relations with that body. He gave the commission a period of stable, firm management between the tenures of David Lilienthal and Lewis Strauss, who were more controversial figures. As a result twenty-five years after his death Gordon Dean is little known even in the atomic energy community. He believed in the task he performed and he did his job efficiently and ably. For better or worse, his accomplishments are enduring, although we might now wish that his contributions had been to the peaceful, rather than the military, atom.

# APPENDIX

The Appendix contains documents which never were a part of the diary but which illuminate major events in Gordon Dean's chairmanship. President Truman's hydrogen bomb directive of January 31, 1950, and Dean's letter of November 7, 1952, to General Eisenhower mark the beginning and the end of the hydrogen bomb quest for Dean. "The Responsibilities of Atomic World Leadership" speech reveals Dean's views on tactical atomic weapons, communism, and Soviet postwar behavior. Finally President Truman's letter of January 19, 1953, to Dean demonstrates the respect and esteem that Dean had earned from the chief executive.

All the documents printed in the Appendix, except the January 19, 1953, letter, can be found in the official files of the Atomic Energy Commission. President Truman's letter is found in the President's Secretary's files at the Harry S. Truman Presidential Library.

≡

471.6 (10-5-49) Super[1]
THE WHITE HOUSE
WASHINGTON

My dear Mr. Lilienthal:                                    January 31, 1950

After consideration of the report by the Special Committee of the National Security Council consisting of the Secretary of State, the Secretary of Defense, and the Chairman of the Atomic Energy Commission, designated by me to advise me on this problem, I hereby direct the Atomic Energy Commission to proceed to determine the technical feasibility of a thermonuclear weapon, the scale and rate of effort to be determined jointly by the Atomic Energy Commission and the Department of Defense; and that the necessary ordnance developments and carrier program be undertaken concurrently.

I have also decided to indicate publicly the intention of this Government to continue work to determine the feasibility of a thermonuclear weapon, and I hereby direct that no further official information be made public on it without my approval.

I am sending copies of this letter to the Secretary of State and the Secretary of Defense for their information.

Sincerely yours,

This document received                      Harry Truman
from office of Commissioner
*Lilienthal* on *3-29-50* for
file in Commission
records. Reference
material not available
to the Secretariat in
all instances.

       Honorable David Lilienthal
       Chairman
       Atomic Energy Commission
       Washington
Circulated in AEC 262/17
Appendix of paper
       cc: The Secretary of State
           The Secretary of Defense    Received in Office of Chairman
                                Date 1/31. Time 4:08 . .

    1. The 471.6 file designation and the notes about AEC 262/17 were added by hand by the commission secretariat staff.

---

  ☰

UNITED STATES
ATOMIC ENERGY COMMISSION
Washington 25, D.C.

Tel. ST 8000                        FOR RELEASE AT 11:00 A.M. (PST)
Brs. 307, 308                      FRIDAY, OCTOBER 5, 1951

Remarks Prepared by Gordon Dean, Chairman,
United States Atomic Energy Commission
For Delivery Before the University of Southern California,
Founder's Day, Los Angeles, California
Friday, October 5, 1951

*THE RESPONSIBILITIES OF ATOMIC WORLD LEADERSHIP*

It is a real pleasure for me to return to this familiar setting and to renew the many pleasant associations and friendships I enjoyed during my years here as a law student and later as a member of the Law School faculty. This is my first visit to the University since I left in May, 1949, to join the Atomic Energy Commission in Washington. It is good to be back, if only for a day or two, and to see again such good friends as President Fagg, who, incidentally, is a fellow alumnus of my undergraduate alma mater, the University of Redlands; and Dean Elliott, whom I first came to know and respect when he was a classmate of mine in the Law School here from 1927 to 1930.

I am proud of my associations with the University of Southern California, and I consider it a particular privilege to be invited here today to participate in these ceremonies honoring the University's 71st anniversary.

The 71 years that the University of Southern California has been in existence have been dynamic years. They have been dynamic for the University itself, for the region of which it is a part, and for the United States as a whole. In the years since 1880 we have seen the University of Southern California grow from a student body of 53 and a physical plant of one $5,000 building—to the great institution of higher learning that it is today. We have seen the Southern California region grow from a remote and undeveloped outpost to its present position as one of the most populous industrial, cultural and agricultural centers of the North American continent. And, during the same period, we have seen the United States advance from a position of decidedly secondary importance in the world scheme of things to one of political and economic leadership among the free nations of the world.

Certainly the men who founded the University of Southern California and who have set its course and guided its destinies during its distinguished 71 year history are deserving of a great deal of credit for the spectacular progress it has made. But we sometimes tend to forget that these same men—and others like them at other similar institutions—are also deserving of a good share of the credit for the progress this nation, and its various component regions, has made. We in the United States have advanced, not only because of our favorable geographic position, the technological skill of our people, and our abundant natural resources, but also because of the distinctive character of our political institutions and the policies, ideals and practices that collectively have come to be known as the American way of life.

The nature of this way of life was of course initially determined by the men who founded the Republic and who wrote the great documents that declared our independence and established the legal and political principles by which we live. But if you have ever stopped to consider why this way of life has persisted and flourished through the years, to our great advantage, I think you will agree with me that it is at least partly due to the men who have been conscious of our political heritage and who have somehow caught the spirit of our past and interpreted it and communicated it to their contemporaries in each succeeding generation. In this endeavor our universities and colleges—including this great University—have played a leading and highly significant role. They are the beacons that have sent out the light by which we have charted our course. To men who founded these institutions of learning, to the men and women who teach in them, and to the students who have learned from them, must go a large share of the credit for our ability as a nation to build and maintain the kind of society under which we have ascended to our present position of world leadership. Upon these same people and their successors there rests a great responsibility to make sure that, in our hour of world leadership, we hold fast to the principles and ideals that made us great.

It is this question of world leadership that I should like to discuss today. I think it is a subject that is appropriately discussed in an academic setting, and I think it is particularly appropriate that we should discuss it here at the University of Southern California, where there has always been a continuing awareness of the relationship between education and the kind of society in which we live. This has been true ever since the day—exactly 71 years ago almost to the hour—when the first President of this University, the Reverend Marion McKinley Bovard, delivered his inauguration address on the topic: "Education as a Factor in Civilization."

Education was a factor in civilization in 1880, and it is today—and it will remain so for so long as it effectively interprets and reports the lessons of the past in the light of the ever-changing current situation. So let us examine this current situation—this position of world leadership in which we find ourselves today—with the idea of attempting to determine how the lessons of the past can best be utilized in facing up to the problems that now confront us. In this discussion, I shall emphasize particularly the subject of atomic energy, partly because this is a subject with which I am familiar, partly because our accomplishments in atomic energy are one of the main reasons why we occupy a position of leadership in the world today, and partly because the question of how we handle ourselves in atomic energy will inevitably have a direct bearing upon the course that we as a nation must follow in world affairs.

It is generally recognized, I believe, that there are three principal ingredients in world leadership. These I would call economic, political and military. Every great power throughout history has been strong on these three counts, and so, I believe, are we.

But to these three ingredients I would add a fourth—no less important than the others, and perhaps the most important of all—and this I would call morality. Hand in hand with world leadership goes the responsibility to hold fast to the highest possible moral standards. This is often not easy to do. In the course of history many nations have risen to places of leadership, and they have not stayed there, because they were lacking in moral strength. This is one of the important lessons of the past, emphasized once again in the World War that ended as recently as six years ago.

The reason why it is not easy for great nations to hold fast to the highest standards of international morality are not hard to find. In the first place, together with great power, there goes a lessening of the outside pressures and restraints which normally operate to enforce adherence to accepted standards of good international behavior. As a substitute for these lessened outside restraints, the nation that has achieved great power must provide new restraints from within. What I mean by this is a kind of national self-discipline, based on an understanding and awareness of the moral lessons of history.

Another reason why it is difficult for powerful nations to adhere to the highest standards of morality is the fact that there is no simple moral yardstick that can be easily applied when important national policy decisions are being made. In the economic, political and military spheres, self-interest is the handiest yardstick and it is relatively easy to use. But when we are talking about morality in the large sense, we are talking about those things which are in the best interests, not of any single nation, but of all humanity. Here the yardstick is fuzzy, and it is often distorted by self-serving philosophical concepts and sophisticated rationalizations of the muddiest sort. But again I think the firm answers are to be found in the past—in the noble ideals of freedom and human dignity to which mankind has always aspired and which have reached their greatest fruition here in our own country.

During our period of growth and development, the record of the United States in the area of international morality has, in my judgment, been good. We have not been a militaristic nation, we have built no empire; we have made a positive effort to live in peace and prosperity with the rest of the world; and, in the great wars in which we have engaged, we have consistently been found on the side opposing the aggressor. It is a record of which we may well be proud, and it is a tradition that should stand us in good stead in reaching the difficult decisions of the future.

But what of the future? Today the United States stands before the world with the lamp of liberty raised high in one hand and the atomic bomb in the other. To many people—both at home and abroad—this is a spectacle that is more fearsome than comforting. It is not surprising that this is so, for the peoples of the world have seen the power of the atomic bomb demonstrated at Hiroshima and Nagasaki. They have seen the devastation that lay below the towering mushroom clouds and they have no difficulty in imagining the suffering and desolation among innocent civilians that would follow in the wake of an all-out, global atomic war. So vivid is this picture that, even in the face of persistent Communist acquisitiveness and aggression, many sincere, thinking people have asked themselves the question: "Is the United States really pursuing the right course?"

I believe that we are. In essence, we have taken the position as a nation that war is bad, and aggression is bad, and any weapon that serves to prevent war and aggression, or to stop aggression once it has been undertaken, is good. This is not an unreasonable position, particularly when one considers that to take any other position would in all likelihood mean the end, not only of our freedom and our way of life, but of all of the noble ideals to which man has aspired through the ages.

I said that I believe we are following the right course. I would like to qualify this to the extent that I believe we are following the right course insofar as moral considerations influence the actions we take. Up to the present, in our period of atomic world leadership, we have undoubtedly taken the moral factor into account. We have been mindful of the heavy responsibilities that go with our position, and we have handled ourselves accordingly. For evidence of this, I think one needs to look no further than the obvious embarrassment we experienced when, at the conclusion of World War II, we found ourselves to be the only nation in the world with the atomic bomb. I think it will forever redound to our credit that our awareness of the moral ramifications of exclusive possession of such a powerful new weapon resulted in our unprecedented offer to place the facilities for its manufacture under international control—an offer that, as you know, was subsequently turned down by the Communists, who meanwhile were busy developing a bomb of their own. I think it is also pertinent to note that—during the post-war period when we had exclusive possession of the atomic bomb—we never once resorted to its use to settle our international differences, even in the face of great provocation.

Unfortunately, I believe, the Communists have been aware of the important role played by the moral factor in our deliberations and they have counted on it and taken advantage of it in such instances as the Czechoslovakian coup d'etat, the North Korean aggression, the Chinese revolution, the Berlin blockade and their flagrant violations of the Balkan peace treaties. We have quite obviously been reluctant to unleash upon the world the horrors of atomic warfare as the world has visualized it, and the Communists have consequently been granted a freedom of action they otherwise would have been denied. In the meantime, they have also been left free to pursue an atomic weapons program of their own, a program which they may well hope may someday cancel out this weapon as a means of warfare and thus permit them to utilize their great manpower superiority and the advantages of their strategic location in carrying out their master plan to achieve world domination.

But, in the long run, I am convinced our policies will be proved to have been right, for, in pursuing them, we have gained in moral strength, while the Communist leaders are being revealed to the world as the predatory conspirators they really are.

You may ask why I raise these questions today when, in addition to the moral restraints which we have imposed upon ourselves, we now have the further restraint—now that our monopoly is gone—of possible retaliation. I raise them for a reason I believe all Americans, our friends overseas, and our Communist antagonists should know and appreciate. I raise them because, through our atomic energy expansion program and recent technological developments in the atomic weapons field, we are entering an era where our power to wage warfare with atomic devices is so great, even in comparison with the recent past, that our fundamental concepts of what atomic warfare is and what it might mean to us must undergo a revolutionary change.

In the past, most of us have thought of atomic warfare in terms of intercontinental bombers striking at the great cities and industrial hearts of an enemy nation, and we have been appalled by the enormity of the destruction that would be wrought. We have thought of atomic warfare in these terms because that is the way we saw it demonstrated—in capsule form— at Hiroshima and Nagasaki, and because we have considered the atomic bomb to be so rare and expensive and devastating that it could not be used on any but the largest and most profitable strategic targets.

This concept of atomic warfare, while still true, is now no longer the whole truth. It is but one kind of atomic warfare, and there is now a new, quite different kind, much less fearsome as far as non-combatants are concerned, and much more promising as a means of halting aggressors without the risk of destroying large parts of the world in the process. Because of our great technological strides, we are now entering an era when the quantities of atomic weapons available to us will be so great, and the types so varied, that we may utilize them in many different ways heretofore not possible. This means that we are gaining the capacity to meet a given situation with an atomic weapon tailored to meet that situation. It means— in the language of the military man—an era when we can use atomic weapons tactically as well as strategically.

In the past, we in America have been inclined to attach an unusual significance to numbers as far as atomic weapons are concerned. Although the number of bombs we have has been an extremely closely-held secret, and still is, there has been what amounts to a preoccupation on the part of many people to speculate on this number and to attempt to deduce it from the small bits and pieces of information that have been made public. This number, I believe, has held such an unusual significance to these people because they have felt that it is relatively small, and they have attempted to guess whether it is greater or smaller than the number of potential targets atomic bombs might logically be used against. To my knowledge, there has not been nearly the same amount of intense curiosity about the number of artillery shells, TNT bombs or torpedoes that might be in our national stockpile. In the case of such conventional weapons, most people tend to accept the military man's evaluation of what he can do with them, and they do not necessarily wish to know how many he has—partly, at least, because they have the general impression that he has a very large number.

It is this kind of situation into which we are now moving in regard to atomic weapons. It is what our military people feel they can do with them that is important, not the exact number we have, for we have reached the stage where we can begin to meet the tactical needs of the armed services while still retaining our immense capacity for strategic retaliation.

I would like to be able to tell you how far into this new era we have advanced, but I cannot, for to do so would be to give the Communists the kind of information they would dearly like to have as a basis for their evil calculations. I can say, however, that we are definitely in this new era. It is not something that is entirely around the corner. We are in it now—at least far enough to utilize the tactical capabilities [of] the atom in certain kinds of situations that might be termed ideal. And, with each passing day, our design and production progress is steadily adding to the number of situations in which atomic weapons can be tactically employed against military targets.

But where does this leave us in terms of our moral position? I think it leaves us fundamentally where we were before—with a very heavy responsibility to use our new power wisely; to use it only in defense, never for aggression; and to use no more of it than is absolutely necessary to handle any given situation. But I think also it leaves us in a position where we can with complete justification treat the tactical atom—divested of the awesome cloak of destruction which surrounds it in its strategic role—in the same manner as other weapons are treated. In other words, I think that when a situation arises where in our carefully considered judgment the use of any kind of weapon is justified, we are now at the place where we should give serious consideration to the use of an atomic weapon, provided it can be used effectively from the military standpoint and that it is no more destructive than is necessary to meet the particular situation in question.

I think our recent technological advancements constitute a message, not of despair, but of hope—hope to the millions of people throughout the world who have feared that the only two alternatives left to mankind are gradual submission to persistent Communist encroachment on the one hand or atomic obliteration on the other. We now have the third possibility of being able to bring to bear on the aggressor himself—at the place of his aggression—the fruits of our technological capabilities, and to meet the invading force in the field with a firepower that should cancel out any numerical advantage he might enjoy. Not only does this provide hope that we can stop aggression once it has started, but, insofar as those who might be contemplating aggression understand the full import of what I am trying to say, it provides a real hope for peace.

It might well be asked, "But if we did use an atomic weapon in a tactical way against troops in the field, isn't it possible that our adversary, assuming he had the capability, might retaliate with an atomic attack against the United States itself?" I think there would be no more chance of that than there is now, for I think our potential adversary fully appreciates our capability for strategic retaliation. It is this capability that he has feared all along, and it is this capability which, in my judgment, has prevented World War III. If we can prevent all-out war by means of our strategic capability, and stop these endless nibbling aggressions with our tactical capability, we will have done much to bring stability and a sense of security back to an uneasy world.

I said that our potential adversary appreciates our capability for strategic retaliation. I am sure he does, for he has never challenged it directly. An excellent way of lessening the possibility of his challenging it directly is to do all we can to reduce the effect of any blow he might feel he can mount against us. We can do this by two means, one involving the military services, and one involving civilians, including the members of this audience. I refer in the first instance to such military defenses as radar screens, anti-aircraft guns and interceptor aircraft, and in the second instance to civil defense.

I trust that no one will find in anything I have said this morning any assumption that a new war is inevitable. What I mean to imply is quite the opposite. No calamity is inevitable except insofar as we steer our course toward calamity, or seeing calamity, like a hurricane approaching, resign ourselves to destruction. Scores of factors can change the present threat of war into the realization of world peace and toward this, while building our strength, we must work with patience. In Othello we read this passage:

> How poor are they that have not patience
> What wound did ever heal but by degrees.

We must therefore set our goals for peace, but at the same time, level our sights and keep them leveled upon those who would break the peace.

I have so far this morning discussed only one part of the responsibility of atomic world leadership—what we might call the negative part—the part having to do with military application. But this is not, by a very wide margin, the only responsibility we assumed when we got into the atomic energy business in this country. There is, as you know, another side to this picture, no less important than the military side, and, in the long run, perhaps very much more so, and this is what we might call the positive, or peaceful side. When we undertook an atomic energy development program we also acquired the responsibility—not only to ourselves, but to people everywhere—to do all we can, consistent with our defense and security, to realize the peaceful promise of the atom.

This we have tried to do, mainly—because of the world situation in which we find ourselves today—by trying to discharge our defense responsibilities in such a way that we obtain a peacetime dividend. This is not too difficult to accomplish, for most of the things we do in atomic energy have both a military and a peaceful application. The materials we make can be used either for weapons or to fuel atomic power-producing plants and machines. The reactors we are developing can someday be used to propel a submarine or to light a city. The medical information we develop can be used to treat or prevent atomic casualties in time of war, or to diagnose and treat disease in time of peace.

When most of us think of the peaceful promise of atomic energy, I believe we think of power—cheap power to do man's work and to bring light into dark corners of the world. This, of course, is one of our objectives. I would like to be able to tell you today that we have reached a turning point in the road to this objective similar to the one we have reached in the field of weapons, but I cannot. We are still some years away from having the answers to the questions that will have to be answered before we can estimate with any degree of assurance how far we shall be able to advance toward the goal of cheap atomic power, or which is the best road or roads for us to follow. We are now entering a very critical phase of our work in nuclear reactor development which should give us at least some of these answers.

I say we are entering a critical phase in our progress toward power because of the experimental reactors that are now being built and the studies which are now being made. In these machines and in the results of these studies will be the answers to many of the problems that today confront us.

When these answers begin to come in, we will have a much better basis than we do now for plotting our course into the future and for making intelligent estimates as to just how far we can go. As you know, there have been many guesses made, some very pessimistic and some spectacularly hopeful. For myself, I would like to reserve final judgment until we have answers to more questions than we do now. I do know this: We are going to have atomic energy power plants, but just how many we will have and what contribution they will make to our economy hinges largely on the factor of cost. To make atomic power worthwhile, we must get the cost of these plants down to where they can compete with coal, gas, oil and hydro-electric plants. When this will be, and in how many areas it will be true, is something about which today we can only guess. But we *are* going to have atomic power, and we are going to have it first for military use, where developmental costs can be charged to the national security. Later, when we know more, and have gotten this developmental phase out of the way, we can make a better estimate about how far we can go. We are now in that critical period when the answers to our questions are beginning to come in.

When we talk about the golden promise of the atomic age, there is one extremely important factor we must take into account—a factor many of us often tend to forget. This is the factor called basic research. Today we make our estimates and guesses and plot our course on the basis of the things we know, and from this vantage point we can see only so far into the future. What is beyond our present limited horizon no-one can tell. Ten years after Benjamin Franklin sent his now famous kite into the air, how many people were able to predict our modern utilization of electricity? Not many, and this is the position we are in today in atomic energy. What the future holds we do not know, but we can attempt to find out, and this is what we are doing at the great atomic research centers and in the universities and private laboratories located all over the country.

It is unusually fortunate, I believe, that the atomic energy industry itself has produced one of the tools by which the future can be probed, not only in the atomic energy field, but in the whole range of scientific endeavor. This tool is the radioisotope, which has often been called the greatest research discovery since the microscope, and which is already finding many direct applications for the benefit of health and welfare in addition to its inestimable value to research.

We have recently entered a room, the door to which was labeled the atomic age. We are in that room and we have found that it is so large and so dimly lighted that we cannot begin to perceive its size or to recognize what is in it. And we do not know how many doors lead from this room into other rooms, perhaps just as significant in the history of man. But we have crossed the threshold and we cannot turn back. All we can do is go forward as boldly—yet as wisely—as we can. I think one of the great responsibilities we assumed when we gained our position of atomic world leadership was to lead the way into the atomic age. To do it well, we will need all of the guidance we can obtain from those who study the past and interpret it and communicate its lessons to us. I know that during the next 71 years, as it has during the past 71 years, the University of Southern California will be among those institutions of learning which have recognized this obligation, and have accepted the responsibility to discharge it as honestly and as capably as possible.

10351                                    End

≡                                United States
                        ATOMIC ENERGY COMMISSION
                           Washington 25, D.C.

Dear General Eisenhower:                              November 7, 1952

In a consultation with the President yesterday it was his opinion that I should notify you immediately concerning the weapons test program which is being conducted at the present time at Eniwetok.

The significant event to date is that we have detonated the first full-scale thermonuclear device. This took place on October 31st, Washington time. This was an experimental device which demonstrated that a thermonuclear explosion is feasible. It will probably be a year before we will be able to test the first deliverable thermonuclear weapon.

From early and incomplete evaluation of the results, the yield is estimated roughly to have been approximately 10 megatons, that is, ten million tons of TNT equivalent. If the more precise and lengthy methods of measuring yield, which are now in process, confirm the above yield, the detonation exceeds what we had anticipated.

The island of the Atoll which was used for the shot—Elugelab—is missing and where it was there is now an underwater crater of some 1500 yards in diameter.

No significant fall-out of radioactive contamination has occurred. As a precaution against fall-out, Joint Task Force 132 had evacuated the Atoll for the shot. The personnel have now returned to the Atoll.

Present plans call for the conduct of the second and final detonation of this operation not earlier than, but probably on, November 12th, Washington time, depending upon weather. * * * * detonation will be a * * * * * of a high yield * * * * bomb dropped from a B-36 aircraft.

We are attempting to keep the Russians in the dark as to what has been and will be exploded in the test series. In view of the large number of personnel involved in the operation, and in view of the size of the detonation and the fact that the light could be observed at sea for several hundred miles, it is not likely that we can for long keep from the Russians the fact that there has been a thermonuclear explosion; although to date weather has played into our hands in that the winds have held the cloud for a period of seven days over the Pacific making it virtually impossible for the Russians to obtain samples from the cloud and thus determine the nature of the explosion.

Unclassified seismic stations picked up the explosion. They will be able to place the epicenter of what they will probably regard as an underwater earth tremor as being in the neighborhood of the Eniwetok Atoll. We nevertheless do not propose to confirm that the tremor was attributable to our test series.

Since calling you on November 7th a speculative story, originating in Los Angeles, to the effect that we have detonated a hydrogen bomb, has received rather wide dissemination. However, barring some now unforeseeable circumstances, it is our plan to make no announcement concerning the test series until after it is concluded—probably on November 13th. We have always made such concluding announcements in the past. In the announcement we propose to say, as we did at the conclusion of the 1951 tests, that "the test program included experiments contributing to thermonuclear weapons research."

While the information concerning the Eniwetok tests is of immediate significance, there are other problems facing the Commission in the next few months concerning which you may wish to be informed.

We have prepared for you a Top Secret memorandum, running to about fifteen pages, dealing with our current stockpile position, the organization and operation of the Commission, its relationship to the office of the President, the Department of Defense, the Congress, and which sets forth some of the current problems facing the Commission in the next few months. We are prepared to make this available to you at any time you choose. We are also prepared to brief you completely, at any time you designate, on the atomic energy program.

Be assured that the Commission is happy to assist you in every possible way.

|                                      | Sincerely,         |
| ------------------------------------ | ------------------ |
| General Dwight D. Eisenhower          | Gordon Dean        |
| Augusta, Georgia                      | Chairman           |

≡

THE WHITE HOUSE
WASHINGTON

Dear Gordon:                                                        JAN 19 1953

As the end of my term of office approaches, I want to express my appreciation for the manner in which the Atomic Energy Commission's program has been carried forward during the period you have served as chairman.

Under your very capable leadership, the Commission has made truly remarkable progress in the development and production of weapons, and in expanding the productive base of the entire atomic energy program. The work of the Commission has been carried forward with imagination and vigor, and you and your colleagues have made a significantly useful contribution to the efforts of our government to strengthen and maintain the security and stability of the free world.

It is a source of real personal gratification to me that, while this progress in the weapons field has been going forward, the Commission has also found the time and energy and inclination to advance the state of the atomic energy art to the place where substantial realization of some of its peaceful promise may be expected in the relatively near future.

I wish to thank you most sincerely for the close and cordial relationship the Commission has maintained with my office during your chairmanship, and for the confidence and respect the Commission has earned for itself in the minds of the public, the Congress and the governmental agencies with which it has dealt. I have also been deeply impressed and gratified by the spirit of teamwork and cooperation that has prevailed among the Atomic Energy Commissioners, and between the Commission and its staff and its many scientific and industrial contractors, for which I feel you are in large measure responsible.

Thank you for your unselfish and devoted service. You have my best wishes for the future.

Sincerely yours,

HARRY S. TRUMAN

Honorable Gordon Dean,
Chairman,
Atomic Energy Commission,
Washington, D.C.                                                                    jlc

# NOTES

## Preface

1. James R. Newman and Byron S. Miller, *The Control of Atomic Energy: A Study of Its Social, Economic, and Political Implications* (New York, 1948), p. 4.

## Editor's Note

1. Lewis L. Strauss, *Men and Decisions* (New York, 1962), p. 263; David E. Lilienthal, *The Journals of David E. Lilienthal*, vol. 3, *The Venturesome Years* (New York, 1966), pp. 522–23.

2. Gordon Dean, Diary, July 26, September 19, 1951, April 8, May 21, 1952, March 10, 1953. These excerpts are not included in this volume but are available from the History Divison, Department of Energy.

## Introduction

1. Unlike later presidents, President Truman established no system for routinely recording presidential conversations. See Benedict K. Zobrist to the editor of this volume, personal correspondence, November 16, 1981.

2. The history of the commission during the Dean years is told in detail in Richard G. Hewlett and Francis Duncan, *Atomic Shield, 1947–1952*, vol. 2 of *A History of the United States Atomic Energy Commission* (University Park, Pa., 1969). Hewlett and Duncan include an excellent description of the commission's official files in *Atomic Shield* on pp. 595–96.

3. President Truman warmly lauded Dean for his leadership of the commission, and the *New York Times* noted that he had earned the "gratitude of the nation." See Harry S. Truman to Gordon Dean, January 19, 1953, HST; *New York Times*, June 28, 1953. In a conversation with the editor of this volume, historian Richard Hewlett rated Dean as one of the two most effective chairmen of the commission. Examples of respect from his colleagues can be found in Lilienthal, *Venturesome Years*, pp. 248, 266; David E. Lilienthal, *The Journals of David E. Lilienthal*, vol. 4, *The Road to Change* (New York, 1969), p. 256; Arnold Kramish and Eugene M. Zuckert, *Atomic Energy for Your Business: Today's Key to Tomorrow's Profits* (New York, 1956), pp. 117–19.

4. Gordon Dean, *Report on the Atom: What You Should Know about the Atomic Energy Program of the United States* (New York, 1957), pp. 68–69.

5. U.S. Atomic Energy Commission, *Major Activities in Atomic Energy Programs, January–June, 1951* (Washington, D.C., 1951), pp. 5–6; Joint Atomic Energy Commission/Department of Defense Press Release no. 377, June 13, 1951, AEC.

6. Apart from standard details that appear in many sources, specific biographical data about Dean are virtually nonexistent. The most complete biography of Dean appears in Anna Roth, ed., *Current Biography: Who's News and Why, 1950* (New York, 1951), pp. 113–15. Two other good sources are the biographical account of Dean by Richard G. Hewlett in John A. Garraty, ed., *Dictionary of American Biography, Supplement Six, 1956–1960* (New York, 1980), pp. 155–57; and Joint Committee on Atomic Energy, *Confirmation of Gordon E. Dean and Henry DeWolf Smyth as Members of the Atomic Energy Commission* (Washington, D.C., 1949), pp. 23–25. The National Archives preserves some of Dean's office files from his years in the Department of Justice. Many of the details about Dean's experiences in the Justice Department are drawn from these files. The Dean office files are in Record Group 60, General Records of the Department of Justice, Series of Records of the Special Executive Assistant to the Attorney General 1935–1940.

7. Dean begins *Report on the Atom*, his only book, recounting the news of Hiroshima. It is one of the few autobiographical details in the book (p. 3).

8. Robert J. Donovan presents an excellent picture of the new president and the problems he faced in *Conflict and Crisis: The Presidency of Harry S. Truman, 1945–1948* (New York, 1977).

9. Donovan, *Conflict and Crisis*, p. xv.

10. President Truman's view of the Soviets at the end of 1945 is discussed in Daniel Yergin, *Shattered Peace: The Origins of the Cold War and the National Security State* (Boston, 1977), pp. 160–62. The origin of the Cold War involves a number of complex issues and is the subject of an extensive historical literature. Interpretations vary and authors, often using much the same evidence, reach conflicting conclusions about the breakup of the Grand Alliance and Truman's role in the beginning of the Cold War. Among the more helpful books on the Cold War were: Barton J. Bernstein, ed., *Politics and Policies of the Truman Administration* (Chicago, 1970); John Lewis Gaddis, *The United States and the Origins of the Cold War* (New York, 1972); Louis J. Halle, *The Cold War as History* (New York, 1967); Walter Lafeber, *America, Russia, and the Cold War, 1945–1966* (New York, 1967).

11. Yergin, *Shattered Peace*, p. 235; Lafeber, *America, Russia, and the Cold War*, pp. 23, 28–29, 31; Gaddis, *Origins of the Cold War*, pp. 356–57.

12. Richard G. Hewlett and Oscar E. Anderson, Jr., thoroughly describe the political battles fought over the McMahon Act in *The New World, 1939–1946*, vol. 1 of *A History of the United States Atomic Energy Commission* (University Park, Pa., 1962), pp. 482–530.

13. The quote is from Joint Committee on Atomic Energy, *Atomic Energy Legislation through 94th Congress, 1st Session* (Washington, D.C., 1976), p. 353. Hewlett and Anderson introduce the first commission in *The New World*, pp. 620–23.

14. A. R. Luedecke to the Commission, August 16, 1963, AEC 1140, History of Expansion of AEC Production Facilities, p. 2, AEC (hereafter cited as AEC 1140).

Dr. Richard G. Hewlett was the primary author of the paper. Hewlett and Anderson, *The New World*, pp. 2, 723.

15. AEC 1140, pp. 2–3; Hewlett and Duncan, *Atomic Shield*, pp. 39–40.

16. AEC 1140, pp. 3–4; Hewlett and Duncan, *Atomic Shield*, p. 31.

17. AEC 1140, pp. 3–4; David A. Rosenberg, "U.S. Nuclear Stockpile, 1945 to 1950," *Bulletin of the Atomic Scientists* (May 1982): 26. Bacher is quoted in AEC 1140, p. 3.

18. Hewlett and Anderson, *The New World*, pp. 565–74, 577–79, 583–97, 606–19; Donovan, *Conflict and Crisis*, pp. 203–6; Zhores A. Medvedev, *Soviet Science* (New York, 1978), pp. 46–47, 50–52, 93–94; Alonzo L. Hamby, *The Imperial Years: The United States since 1939* (New York, 1976), p. 119; Edward Crankshaw and Strobe Talbott, eds., *Khrushchev Remembers* (London, 1971), p. 541; Lafeber, *America, Russia, and the Cold War*, pp. 35–36; Donald R. McCoy, *The Presidency of Harry S. Truman* (Manhattan, Kansas, 1984), p. 37.

19. Donovan, *Conflict and Crisis*, pp. 266–67; Robert J. Donovan, *Tumultuous Years: The Presidency of Harry S. Truman, 1949–1953* (New York, 1982), pp. 66–73.

20. Yergin, *Shattered Peace*, pp. 294–96; Hamby, *Imperial Years*, p. 124; Lafeber, *America, Russia, and the Cold War*, pp. 44–45. The quote is from *Public Papers of the Presidents of the United States: Harry S. Truman, 1947* (Washington, D.C., 1963), pp. 178–79. See also McCoy, *Presidency of Harry Truman*, pp. 118–22.

21. Athan Theoharis discusses President Truman's federal employee loyalty program in *Spying on Americans: Political Surveillance from Hoover to the Huston Plan* (Philadelphia, 1978), pp. 202–9.

22. Samuel F. Wells, Jr., "Sounding the Tocsin: NSC 68 and the Soviet Threat," *International Security* (Fall 1979): 152–53; Gaddis, *Origins of the Cold War*, p. 356; *Public Papers, Truman, 1946*, p. 15; *Public Papers: Truman, 1947*, p. 11; Yergin, *Shattered Peace*, p. 270.

23. Robert Patterson, James Forrestal, William Leahy, and David Lilienthal to President Truman, April 2, 1947, and Report to the President of the United States from the Atomic Energy Commission, January 1–April 1, 1947, April 3, 1947, both AEC; Hewlett and Duncan, *Atomic Shield*, pp. 47–48; Rosenberg, "Nuclear Stockpile," p. 27. The quote is from Patterson et al.

24. Halle, *Cold War as History*, pp. 112–13, 123–25, 149–51; Hamby, *Imperial Years*, pp. 126–27; Lafeber, *America, Russia, and the Cold War*, pp. 47–53, 60–61; Yergin, *Shattered Peace*, p. 306; McCoy, *Presidency of Harry Truman*, pp. 124–25.

25. AEC 1140, pp. 5–6.

26. Yergin, *Shattered Peace*, p. 351; Halle, *Cold War as History*, pp. 74–75; Lafeber, *America, Russia, and the Cold War*, pp. 63–64. Clay is quoted in Yergin.

27. David Lilienthal to President Truman, May 3, 1949, AEC; Hewlett and Duncan, *Atomic Shield*, p. 178; AEC 1140, pp. 7–9.

28. Hewlett and Duncan, *Atomic Shield*, pp. 167–70; Lafeber, *America, Russia, and the Cold War*, pp. 68–71; Hamby, *Imperial Years*, p. 128; James Forrestal to President Truman, July 21, 1948; David Lilienthal to President Truman, July 21, 1948; and Harry S. Truman to James Forrestal, August 6, 1948, all correspondence in HST.

29. AEC 1140, pp. 7–9; David Lilienthal to President Truman, May 3, 1949, AEC.

30. Donovan, *Tumultuous Years*, pp. 29–33, 163–64, 169–70; Donovan, *Conflict and Crisis*, pp. 422–31; Irwin Ross, *The Loneliest Campaign: The Truman Victory of 1948* (Westport, Conn., 1968), pp. 266–69; Hamby, *Imperial Years*, pp. 155, 158; McCoy, *Presidency of Harry Truman*, p. 165.

31. Donovan, *Tumultuous Years*, p. 365; Hamby, *Imperial Years*, p. 153.

32. Harold P. Green and Alan Rosenthal examine the role of the Joint Committee in *Government of the Atom* (New York, 1963).

33. Donovan, *Tumultuous Years*, pp. 37–39, 114–18, 332–39, 372–81; Hewlett and Duncan, *Atomic Shield*, pp. 8–12, 48–53, 89–95, 468; *New York Times*, March 13, 1951. Examples of the charges of waste, fraud, etc., faced by the commission can be found in Joint Committee on Atomic Energy, Hearing Before the Joint Committee on Atomic Energy, *Wage Payments at Nevada Test Site* (Washington, D.C., 1952), Appendix B.

34. *New York Times*, May 10, 21, 1949.

35. *New York Times*, May 10, 1949; Hewlett and Duncan, *Atomic Shield*, p. 443; "The Atomic Energy Commission," *Time*, January 14, 1952, p. 20; "People of the Week," *U.S. News and World Report*, August 25, 1950, p. 32; William S. White, "Custodian-in-Chief of the Atom," *New York Times Magazine*, January 27, 1952, p. 11; Lilienthal, *Venturesome Years*, p. 295. The quote is from the *Time* article.

36. Gordon Dean, "Horizons for Atomic Energy," speech delivered at New York University, January 11, 1950, AEC; Oliver Townsend, Random News of Interest, November 15, 1951, unpublished portion of Dean's Diary; White, "Custodian," *New York Times Magazine*, p. 35. The first two quotes are from the "Horizons" speech. The Miss America contest quote is from the Oliver Townsend note, and Dean's daughter is quoted in White, "Custodian."

37. Hewlett and Duncan, *Atomic Shield*, pp. 18–20, 675.

38. AEC 1140, pp. 8–12; *FRUS, National Security Affairs, 1949*, pp. 482–85, 501–3. McMahon is quoted on p. 482.

39. Hewlett and Duncan, *Atomic Shield*, pp. 358–61.

40. Donovan, *Tumultuous Years*, pp. 98–104; Hewlett and Duncan, *Atomic Shield*, pp. 363–68; Barton J. Bernstein, "Truman and the H-Bomb," *Bulletin of the Atomic Scientists* (March 1984): 12–18; Gordon Dean, Memorandum to Those Listed Below, September 23, 1949, Dean, Diary; Sidney W. Souers, Memorandum for the President, with enclosure, October 10, 1949, HST; Lewis L. Strauss, Memorandum to the Commission, October 5, 1949, AEC. The quote is from the Strauss memorandum.

41. Hewlett and Duncan, *Atomic Shield*, pp. 373–84; Donovan, *Tumultuous Years*, pp. 149–52; Bernstein, "Truman and the H-Bomb," pp. 13–14; Herbert F. York, *The Advisors: Oppenheimer, Teller, and the Superbomb* (San Francisco, 1976), pp. 153–57. York reprints the committee's report with appendixes on pp. 150–59. York argues persuasively that the committee's advice was technically sound when it rejected a crash program.

42. Gordon Dean, "The Alternatives," n.d. but about November 1, 1949, Dean, Diary; Hewlett and Duncan, *Atomic Shield*, pp. 386–91, 394; Donovan, *Tumul-*

*tuous Years*, pp. 153–54; Richard F. Haynes, *The Awesome Power: Harry S. Truman as Commander in Chief* (Baton Rouge, La., 1973), p. 78.

43. Lilienthal, *Venturesome Years*, pp. 25–26.

44. Donovan, *Tumultuous Years*, pp. 155–56; Hewlett and Duncan, *Atomic Shield*, pp. 394–409. President Truman's order is reprinted in the Appendix. *FRUS, National Security Affairs, 1950*, contains the report of the special National Security Council subcommittee on pp. 513–17.

45. Roy B. Snapp to the Commission, May 8, 1950, Information Memorandum 273/16, AEC; Hewlett and Duncan, *Atomic Shield*, pp. 313–14, 412; *New York Times*, February 4, 1950.

46. David E. Lilienthal, *The Journals of David E. Lilienthal*, vol. 2, *The Atomic Energy Years, 1945–1950* (New York, 1964), pp. 459–61, 471–72, 593; *New York Times*, March 25, 1950; Dean, Diary, February 24, April 3, 1950 (excerpts not published). Dean's conversation with Reston and the quote appear in the diary. See Dean, Diary, March 20, 1950 (conversation not printed). W. Averell Harriman, Charles Luckman, the president of Lever Brothers Company, General Lucius Clay, and former Secretary of War Robert Patterson were just a few of the people mentioned as potential successors to Lilienthal. See *New York Times*, February 8, March 24, 1950.

47. Hewlett and Duncan, *Atomic Shield*, pp. 447–48; Lilienthal, *Venturesome Years*, p. 26. The simultaneous expiration of all the commissioners' terms on the same day was an anomaly born of political compromise in 1948. That year all five original commissioners, who had all been appointed to two-year terms in 1946, came up for renomination. To avoid a bruising political battle over Lilienthal's renomination in an election year, then Joint Committee chairman Bourke B. Hickenlooper suggested that all five commissioners be reappointed to two-year terms, these terms all expiring on June 30, 1950. Hickenlooper's strategy worked, but it led to the unusual situation in which a federal agency faced the loss of all of its leaders at once. See Hewlett and Duncan, *Atomic Shield*, pp. 326–32.

48. Lilienthal, *Venturesome Years*, pp. 248, 266, 295; Dean, Diary, February 24, 1950 (excerpt not printed).

49. I have drawn the discussion of Dean's management style from several sources. Dean's own views on management are reproduced in Chapters 1 and 2 of this volume. Hewlett and Duncan examine the styles of both Lilienthal and Dean in *Atomic Shield*, especially pp. 315–18, 444–45, 467–69, 478–79, 587–89. William S. White has some interesting comments about commission management in "Custodian," as do Kramish and Zuckert in *Atomic Energy for Your Business*, pp. 117–19.

50. These sketches are drawn from Hewlett and Duncan, *Atomic Shield*, pp. 5, 218, 446–47, 468, 588; Kramish and Zuckert, *Atomic Energy for Your Business*, pp. 119–20.

51. Dean's relations with President Truman are drawn from Dean's diary; White, "Custodian"; Gordon Dean to President Truman, March 31, 1952, AEC; President Truman to Gordon Dean, January 19, 1953, HST. (The January 19 letter is reprinted in the Appendix.)

52. Hewlett and Duncan, *Atomic Shield*, pp. 351–54, 450–51, 478–79, 483–84; Green and Rosenthal, *Government of the Atom*, p. 11.

53. My inferences about the relationship between the commission and the Department of Defense are drawn from Dean's diary.

54. In a major speech Dean gave his most complete statement as chairman on relations with the Soviet Union. Calling Soviet leaders "predatory conspirators" with a "master plan to achieve world domination," Dean was able to envision warfare waged with tactical atomic weapons without Soviet retaliation against the United States. President Eisenhower, on the other hand, decided that the threat of atomic warfare made even small steps toward disarmament imperative and declared that of all the problems he faced as president "none transcended in importance that of trying to devise practical and acceptable means to lighten the burden of armaments and to lessen the likelihood of war." See Gordon Dean, "The Responsibilities of Atomic World Leadership," speech delivered at the University of Southern California, October 5, 1951, reprinted in the Appendix; *Public Papers of the Presidents of the United States: Dwight D. Eisenhower, 1953* (Washington, D.C., 1960), pp. 813–22; Dwight D. Eisenhower, *Mandate for Change, 1953–1956* (New York, 1963), pp. 254–55, 507, 509–10; Dwight D. Eisenhower, *Waging the Peace, 1956–1961* (New York, 1965), pp. 466–69, 484. The Eisenhower quote is from *Waging the Peace*, p. 467.

55. Donovan, *Tumultuous Years*, pp. 241–47; Wells, "Sounding the Tocsin," pp. 138–39; Samuel F. Wells, Jr., "The Origins of Massive Retaliation," *Political Science Quarterly* (Spring 1981): 49; Omar N. Bradley and Clay Blair, *A General's Life: An Autobiography by General of the Army Omar N. Bradley and Clay Blair* (New York, 1983), p. 535. The quote is taken from *FRUS, Korea, 1950*, p. 158. When he ordered the commission to develop the hydrogen bomb, President Truman also ordered a reassessment of America's military position. NSC 68 was the product of the reassessment and it laid out a strong improvement of the country's military position. NSC 68 is reprinted in *FRUS, National Security Affairs, 1950*, pp. 234–92.

56. Harry S. Truman, *Memoirs by Harry S. Truman*, vol. 2, *Years of Trial and Hope* (New York, 1956), pp. 345–46; James F. Schnabel, *United States Army in the Korean War: Policy and Direction: The First Year* (Washington, D.C., 1972), pp. 67–68, 178; *New York Times*, July 21, 1950; Gordon Dean to the President, July 10, 1950, and Gordon Dean, Memorandum for the Files, July 31, 1950, both AEC; Hewlett and Duncan, *Atomic Shield*, pp. 521–22, 524–25. The ponderous process of launching an atomic attack is described in Rosenberg, "Nuclear Stockpile," pp. 25–30.

57. Lilienthal's battles for civilian custody are examined in Hewlett and Duncan, *Atomic Shield*, pp. 150–52, 159–61, 166–70, 354–55.

58. Louis Johnson to Gordon Dean, August 4, 1950, AEC; James S. Lay, Memorandum for the President, with enclosures, August 7, 1950, HST; AEC 1140, pp. 15–23; Hewlett and Duncan, *Atomic Shield*, pp. 522–29; James S. Lay, Memorandum for the President, October 2, 1950, HST. President Truman's order to make the production study is reprinted in *FRUS, National Security Affairs, 1950*, p. 570.

59. Hewlett and Duncan, *Atomic Shield*, pp. 140–41; Minutes, Commission Meeting 504, December 12, 1950; and James McCormack to the Commission, December 13, 1950; both AEC.

60. Louis Johnson to Gordon Dean, August 4, 1950; James McCormack to the Commission, December 13, 1950; Phil Farley to the Commission, with enclosures, December 20, 1950, AEC 141/8, all AEC; Dean, Diary, July 27, 31, October 25, November 1, 2, 10, 1950. An excellent brief assessment of the political, economic, and military problems facing Communist Chinese leaders can be found in Allen S. Whiting, *China Crosses the Yalu: The Decision to Enter the Korean War* (New York, 1960), pp. 14–23.

61. Dean, Diary, March 27, 1951.

62. Robert A. Divine describes the fallout controversy in *Blowing on the Wind: The Nuclear Test Ban Debate, 1954–1960* (New York, 1978). For the fallout lawsuits see *USA Today*, January 27, 1983, May 11, 1984; *New York Times*, May 11, 1984. Recently a federal judge awarded $2 million to families of eight residents of communities around the test site. His ruling has been appealed.

63. Hewlett and Duncan, *Atomic Shield*, pp. 529–30, 535–37, 540–41; Hans A. Bethe, "Comments on the History of the H-Bomb," *Los Alamos Science* (Fall 1982): 46–49; York, *The Advisors*, pp. 76–80; Edward Teller with Allan Brown, *The Legacy of Hiroshima* (New York, 1962), pp. 47–51. The quote is from Dean, Diary, February 8, 1951.

64. Roger M. Anders, "The Rosenberg Case Revisited: The Greenglass Testimony and the Protection of Atomic Secrets," *American Historical Review* (April 1978): 392–97; Ronald Radosh and Joyce Milton, *The Rosenberg File: A Search for the Truth* (New York, 1983), p. 145; John A. Waters to the Commission, February 1, 1951, AEC 403, AEC. Radosh and Milton argue convincingly that Julius Rosenberg was a spy, that his wife Ethel was an accessory to his activities, but that both were punished too severely.

65. Anders, "Greenglass Testimony," pp. 398–400; Radosh and Milton, *The Rosenberg File*, pp. 145–51, 182–87; Dean, Diary, March 7, 8, 9, 10, 12, 1951. Radosh and Milton assert that the Rosenberg case was the "hottest issue" Dean faced as chairman (p. 143). This is incorrect as the diary amply shows. Although the Rosenberg case was a difficult problem for Dean, the Korean War and the hydrogen bomb program presented him with problems of far greater and more enduring magnitude.

66. Radosh and Milton, *The Rosenberg File*, pp. 444–45.

67. Dean, Diary, April 5, 1951; Truman, *Memoirs*, pp. 440–45; Schnabel, *Policy and Direction*, p. 253; Omar Bradley, Memorandum for the Secretary of Defense, April 5, 1951, HST. The quotes are from Truman, *Memoirs*, pp. 441, 443.

68. Dean, Diary, March 27, April 6, 1951; Truman, *Memoirs*, pp. 445–47. Making the transfer in such haste led to a two-year debate over the procedures for authorizing the use of the atomic bomb in combat. See Hewlett and Duncan, *Atomic Shield*, pp. 539, 579–80, 585. Other than the excerpts in Chapter 3, I have not reproduced diary excerpts pertaining to the debate.

69. Donovan, *Tumultuous Years*, pp. 353–62; Hamby, *Imperial Years*, p. 137; Bradley and Blair, *A General's Life*, pp. 641–42.

70. York, *The Advisors*, p. 129; Stanley A. Blumberg and Gwinn Owens, *Energy and Conflict: The Life and Times of Edward Teller* (New York, 1976), pp. 281–83.

Philip Farley to the Commission, with enclosures, April 5, 1951, AEC 425; Minutes, Commission Meeting 582, July 26, 1951, both AEC; Dean, Diary, April 4, 1951, March 28, 1952; Gordon Dean, Notes on Meeting with Foster and Acheson, April 1, 1952, Dean, Diary.

71. AEC 1140, pp. 28–39; Hewlett and Duncan, *Atomic Shield*, pp. 547–48, 556–57, 559–60, 562–63, 565–68; Gordon Dean, Memorandum for the Commissioners, October 19, 1951, AEC.

72. *New York Times*, May 13, 1950, February 6, 1951; Dean, Diary, July 12, 1951; Wells,"Sounding the Tocsin," p. 143.

73. Dean, "The Responsibilities of Atomic World Leadership." The speech is reproduced in the Appendix.

74. *New York Times*, October 6, 7, 1951; *Washington Evening Star*, October 6, 7, 1951; Dean, Diary, October 5, 11, 1951; Brien McMahon, "Atomic Weapons and Defense," reprinted in *Bulletin of the Atomic Scientists* (October 1951): 297–301; Lilienthal, *Venturesome Years*, p. 240; Wells, "Origins of Massive Retaliation," pp. 49–51; Lawrence Freedman, *The Evolution of Nuclear Strategy* (New York, 1983), pp. 68–69; Hewlett and Duncan, *Atomic Shield*, p. 549.

75. James S. Lay, Memorandum for the President, January 17, 1952, HST; Gordon Dean, Statement for the NSC re: Expansion Program, January 16, 1952; and Gordon Dean, Memorandum for the Files, January 17, 1952, both in Dean, Diary; AEC 1140, pp. 39–46; Hewlett and Duncan, *Atomic Shield*, pp. 576–78. James Lay took the official minutes of the meeting. Dean's notes capture an ebb and flow of discussions more vividly than do Lay's notes.

76. Teller, *Legacy of Hiroshima*, pp. 59–61; York, *The Advisors*, pp. 129–31; Hewlett and Duncan, *Atomic Shield*, pp. 581–84; Gordon Dean, Notes on Meeting with Foster and Acheson, April 1, 1952, in Dean, Diary; Dean, Diary, April 16, 1952; Gordon Dean, Memorandum for Mr. Snapp, May 29, 1952, AEC.

77. Gordon Dean to Harold Urey, April 17, 1952, AEC.

78. Gordon Dean to President Truman, March 31, 1952, AEC; Hewlett and Duncan, *Atomic Shield*, p. 584.

79. Gordon Dean to General Eisenhower, November 7, 1952, reproduced in the Appendix; Hewlett and Duncan, *Atomic Shield*, pp. 590–93; Hans Bethe to Gordon Dean, September 9, 1952, AEC; Dean, Diary, August 11, 19, 28, 1952. The quote is from the letter to Eisenhower.

80. Gordon Dean to General Eisenhower, November 7, 1952, reproduced in the Appendix; Roy B. Snapp, Memorandum for File, November 11, 1952, AEC; *New York Times*, November 17, 1952; Hewlett and Duncan, *Atomic Shield*, p. 592; Dean, Diary, November 7, 13, 18, 19, 20, 24, 1952.

81. Dean, Diary, January 15, 1953; President Truman to Gordon Dean, January 19, 1953, reproduced in the Appendix. The quote is from the Truman letter.

82. Gordon Dean to President-elect Eisenhower, January 13, 1953, but dated January 20, 1953; and Dwight Eisenhower to Gordon Dean, January 14, 1953, both DDE; *New York Times*, February 11, March 8, June 24, 1953; *Washington Evening Star*, February 11, 1953; *Washington Post*, June 25, 1953; Richard Pfau, *No Sacrifice Too Great: The Life of Lewis L. Strauss* (Charlottesville, Va., 1985), pp. 138–39.

83. Eisenhower administration discussions concerning the use of the atomic bomb in Korea are in *FRUS, Korea, 1952–1954*, pp. 769–71, 825–27, 975–78, 1012–17, 1064–69, 1071. The diplomatic threats are described in Eisenhower, *Mandate for Change*, pp. 178–81, and Barry M. Blechman and Robert Powell, "What in the Name of God Is Strategic Superiority?," *Political Science Quarterly* (Winter 1982–83): 590–97. The administration's actions on the labor panel and the National Security Council can be found in Gordon Dean, Memorandum for the Files, March 11, 1953; Gordon Dean to Robert Cutler, March 24, April 10, 1953, both AEC.

84. Eisenhower, *Mandate for Change*, pp. 127–31; Dean, Diary, March 12, 1953; Draft Letter, Gordon Dean to Charles Wilson, March 12, 1953, and Gordon Dean, Draft Opening, n.d. but about March 18, 1953, both in Dean, Diary; Richard G. Hewlett and Francis Duncan, *Nuclear Navy, 1946–1962* (Chicago, 1974), pp. 198–99; Pfau, *No Sacrifice Too Great*, p. 139.

85. Dean, Diary, April 1, 1953; Hewlett and Duncan, *Nuclear Navy*, pp. 198–99, 227–34; Jack M. Holl and Francis Duncan, *Shippingport: The Nation's First Atomic Power Station* (Washington, D.C., 1983), pp. 5–7.

86. Richard G. Hewlett, "Nuclear Weapon Testing and Studies Related to Health Effects: An Historical Summary," in Interagency Radiation Research Committee, *Consideration of Three Proposals to Conduct Research on Possible Health Effects of Radiation from Nuclear Weapon Testing in Arizona, Nevada, and Utah and Nuclear Weapon Testing and Studies Related to Health Effects: An Historical Summary: Responding to Recommendations by the Panel of Experts on the Archive of PHS Documents* (Washington, D.C., 1980), pp. 52–56; Dean, Diary, May 21, 22, 25, 26, 27, and June 4, 1953; U.S. Atomic Energy Commission, *Major Activities in the Atomic Energy Programs, January–June, 1953* (Washington, D.C., 1953), pp. 48–49, 53–54.

87. Dean, Diary, June 15, 16, 23, 24, 25, 26, 28, 29, 1953; *New York Times*, June 25, 26, 1953; *Washington Post*, June 26, 1953; *Washington Evening Star*, June 26, 1953.

## Epilogue

1. The quote is from the "What's Ahead?" paper.

2. AEC 1140, pp. 48 and 50–51; *New York Times*, February 13, March 31, 1955. The dates that all production plants began operation appears in AEC 1140, p. 48. The quote is from the "What's Ahead?" paper.

3. Herbert York describes the variety of weapons and makes the statement about a "great leap forward" in *The Advisors*, p. 137. Robert MacNamara provides the figures for weapons deployed in Europe in "The Military Role of Nuclear Weapons: Perceptions and Misperceptions," *Foreign Affairs* (Fall 1983): 62. The stockpile size is quoted from Joint Committee on Atomic Energy, *Hearings on the Consideration of Military Applications of Nuclear Technology, Part II* (Washington, D.C., 1973), p. 2.

4. *Public Papers of the Presidents of the United States: Lyndon B. Johnson 1963–1964, Book I* (Washington, D.C., 1965), p. 117. The commission announced the production plant closings in its annual reports to Congress for the 1964–70 period. The stockpile peaked in number of weapons in 1967. See Joint Committee on Atomic Energy, *Military Applications*, p. 2.

5. Biographical details for Dean's post-commission career are even more difficult to come by than for his earlier years. I have relied on Richard G. Hewlett's piece in Garraty, ed., *Dictionary of American Biography*, pp. 155–57, and specific citations from the *New York Times* to trace Dean's later years. For his business career see *New York Times*, February 1, 5, July 29, 1955, August 16, 1958.

6. *New York Times*, May 25, June 25, August 17, 1954, September 18, 24, 1956, May 9, 1957; Joint Committee on Atomic Energy, *Peaceful Uses of Atomic Energy: Background Material for the Report of the Panel on the Impact of the Peaceful Uses of Atomic Energy* (Washington, D.C., 1956), 2:325.

7. *New York Times*, August 20, September 12, 1953, August 16, 17, 1958. See also Hewlett, in Garraty, ed., *Dictionary of American Biography*, pp. 155–57.

8. *New York Times*, June 16, 17, 1954, August 29, September 21, 1957, August 16, 17, 1958; Henry A. Kissinger, *Nuclear Weapons and Foreign Policy* (New York, 1957), pp. viii–x; Divine, *Blowing on the Wind*, pp. 165, 167; Green and Rosenthal, *Government of the Atom*, p. 240. See also Hewlett's account in Garraty, ed., *Dictionary of American Biography*, pp. 155–57. Dean's testimony at the Oppenheimer security hearing is in U.S. Atomic Energy Commission, *In the Matter of J. Robert Oppenheimer* (Washington, D.C., 1954), pp. 300–323.

9. Dean's most complete obituary is in the *New York Times*, August 16, 17, 1958. Details about his funeral and estate appear in the *New York Times*, August 19, 29, 1958. The commission's consideration of a Gordon Dean award is found in Harold Anamosa to Paul Foster, August 25, 1958; and in Minutes, Commission Meeting 1399, August 27, 1958, both in AEC. The commission decided to name the award after Nobel Laureate Ernest O. Lawrence, who had also recently died. See W. B. McCool to Arthur Tackman, September 9, 1958, AEC.

# INDEX